Muslim Spain Reconsidered

The New Edinburgh Islamic Surveys
Series Editor: Carole Hillenbrand

TITLES AVAILABLE OR FORTHCOMING

Contemporary Issues in Islam Asma Asfaruddin
Islamic Astronomy and Astrology Stephen P. Blake
The New Islamic Dynasties Clifford Edmund Bosworth
Media Arabic (2nd Edition) Julia Ashtiany Bray and Nadia Jamil
Introduction to Persian Literature Dominic Parviz Brookshaw
An Introduction to the Hadith John Burton
A History of Islamic Law Noel Coulson
Medieval Islamic Political Thought Patricia Crone
A Short History of the Ismailis Farhad Daftary
Islam: An Historical Introduction (2nd Edition) Gerhard Endress
The Arabic Aristotle Gerhard Endress
A History of Christian–Muslim Relations Hugh Goddard
An Introduction to the Hadith Andreas Gorke
Medieval Islamic Science Robert Hall
Shi'ism (2nd Edition) Heinz Halm
Islamic Science and Engineering Donald Hill
Muslim Spain Reconsidered Richard Hitchcock
Islamic Law: From Historical Foundations to Contemporary Practice Mawil Izzi Dien
Sufism: The Formative Period Ahmet T. Karamustafa
Modern Turkish Literature Celia Kerslake
Islam in Indonesia Carool Kersten
Islamic Aesthetics Oliver Leaman
Persian Historiography Julie Scott Meisami
Pilgrims and Pilgrimage in Islam Josef Meri
The Muslims of Medieval Italy Alex Metcalfe
The Archaeology of the Islamic World Marcus Milwright
Islam in China Laura J. Newby
Twelver Shiism Andrew J. Newman
Muslims in Western Europe (3rd Edition) Jørgen Nielsen
Medieval Islamic Medicine Peter E. Pormann and Emilie Savage-Smith
Islamic Names Annemarie Schimmel
The Genesis of Literature in Islam Gregor Schoeler
Modern Arabic Literature Paul Starkey
Islamic Medicine Manfred Ullman
Islam and Economics Ibrahim Warde
A History of Islamic Spain W. Montgomery Watt and Pierre Cachia
Introduction to the Qur'an W. Montgomery Watt
Islamic Creeds W. Montgomery Watt
Islamic Philosophy and Theology W. Montgomery Watt
Islamic Political Thought W. Montgomery Watt
The Influence of Islam on Medieval Europe W. Montgomery Watt

www.euppublishing.com/series/isur

Muslim Spain Reconsidered

From 711 to 1502

Richard Hitchcock

EDINBURGH
University Press

For Meg

© Richard Hitchcock, 2014

Edinburgh University Press Ltd
The Tun – Holyrood Road
12 (2f) Jackson's Entry
Edinburgh EH8 8PJ
www.euppublishing.com

Typeset in 11/13pt Monotype Baskerville by
Servis Filmsetting Ltd, Stockport, Cheshire,
and printed and bound in Great Britain by
CPI Group (UK) Ltd, Croydon CR4 0YY

A CIP record for this book is available from the British Library
ISBN 978 0 7486 3959 5 (hardback)
ISBN 978 0 7486 3960 1 (paperback)
ISBN 978 0 7486 7829 7 (webready PDF)
ISBN 978 0 7486 7831 0 (epub)

Published with the support of the Edinburgh University
Scholarly Publishing Initiatives Fund.

Contents

List of illustrations   vi
Foreword   viii

Introduction: Iberian background   1

1   The invasion of the Iberian Peninsula – the eighth century   14
2   The establishment of the Umayyad state in al-Andalus – the ninth
    century   40
3   Al-Andalus in the tenth century   66
4   The eleventh century – a time of change   113
5   Al-Andalus under the rule of the Berber dynasties   137
6   The thirteenth and fourteenth centuries   161
7   The fifteenth century – the final phase of Muslim rule in
    al-Andalus   183

Conclusion   194

Bibliography   197
Index   213

Illustrations

Maps

Between pages 6 and 7
1 Europe and the western Mediterranean in the eighth century
2 Al-Andalus in the ninth and tenth centuries, showing the frontier zones
3 Granada, c. 1230–1500

Plates

Between pages 182 and 183
1   The bay at Almuñécar where Abd ar-Rahmān I landed in 755 AD.
      Original photograph by Jorge Zabalza.
2   The interior of the Mosque in Cordoba. Modesto Lafuente
      (continued by Juan Valera), *Historia general de España*, Barcelona:
      Montaner y Simón editores, 1883, vol. I, opposite p. 176.
3a   The ivory pyxis made for al-Mughīra in 968, in the Musée du
      Louvre. José Ferrandis, *Marfiles árabes de occidente*, Madrid: Estanislao
      Maestre, 1935, vol. I, plate XX.
3b   San Miguel de Escalada before restoration. Early twentieth-century
      photograph. M. Gómez-Moreno, *Iglesias mozárabes. Arte español de los
      siglos IX a XI*, Madrid: Centro de Estudios Históricos, 1919, plate
      XXXIX. Photograph attributed to Laurent. The identical image,
      without the figure, was published the previous year. See G. T.
      Rivoira, *Muslim Architecture. Its Origins and Development*, translated from
      the Italian by G. McN. Rushforth, Oxford: Humphrey Milford,
      1918, p. 353, fig. 323.
4   Silk banner captured by Alfonso VIII from the Almohads at the
      Battle of Las Navas de Tolosa. Modesto Lafuente, *Historia general de
      España*, vol. I, opposite p. 374.
5   The Giralda at Seville. © Bernard O'Kane.
6   The Alhambra, Granada, northern façade of the Patio de Comares.
      © Bernard O'Kane.

7a   Nineteenth-century chromolithograph of niche in the Alhambra.
       Modesto Lafuente, *Historia general de España*, vol. II, opposite p. 282.
7b   Collage showing fifteenth-century Nasrid armour. Modesto
       Lafuente, *Historia general de España*, vol. II, opposite p. 302.
8a and 8b   Two Hispano-Moresque vases, probably nineteenth century.
       Private Collection.

Note: The photographs of numbers 2, 3a, 3b, 4, 7a, 7b, 8a and 8b are by John Melville. Full details and images of the artefacts represented in 3, 4 and 7b, together with similar objects, may be found in *Al-Andalus. Las artes islámicas de España*, edited by Jerrilynn D. Dodds, New York: The Metropolitan Museum of Art; Granada: Ediciones El Viso, 1992. This is a magnificently illustrated and informative catalogue of Andalusi art.

Foreword

This book was written not out of any presumptuous intention to 'set the record straight', but out of a deeply held conviction that views and interpretations of events, especially if they happen to be different from those currently in vogue, should be allowed an airing. Obviously, any reinterpretation of any given period in history is a serious undertaking, and every effort has been made to justify what has been written. A narrative of the 800-year period between 711 and 1502 cannot hope to take into account every aspect. Where sources are available, they cannot be allowed to speak for themselves. They will invariably give rise to questions, and these need to be addressed. There is both a necessity and an obligation to select and interpret. Selection is required because a study of this nature is perforce limited, and selection itself involves a measure of subjectivity. This is not to say that an objective approach is undesirable; rather that it is consistently unachievable. Within these parameters, it should be possible to open up perspectives on the past, respecting the facts such as they are or such as they can be established.

At the outset I was faced with a number of problems. The first, a terminological one, arose from the phrase 'Muslim Spain'. These two words could refer to any period when Muslims resided in the Iberian Peninsula, irrespective of whether or not this was within an Islamic state. Consequently, this would apply not only to the Moriscos of the sixteenth century, but also to the *mudéjares*, Muslims who remained as such after the conquests in the first half of the thirteenth century. Yet, my concern was with al-Andalus, that part of the Iberian Peninsula which at any one time was under independent Muslim control. Although some attention has been accorded to the influence of Islam beyond Andalusi borders, the primary focus was on al-Andalus. Furthermore, as will become apparent, I am reluctant to accept the distinction between Muslim Spain and Christian Spain, not least because, as has been said by others, Spain as a country had not yet come into being. I felt that it would be possible to overcome this terminological difficulty through incorporating the word 'reconsidered' in the title. This word may imply a radical rethink, but at face value simply indicates that the subject is going to be looked at or thought about again. The reconsideration led me to make a number of decisions.

First, the scope has been amplified. The book is not a rejigging of familiar material. The aim has been to maintain a discernible historical framework within which events are treated chronologically. However, an attempt has also been made to address issues other than purely political ones: economic, societal, religious and climatic, for example. It seemed appropriate to blend literary and cultural aspects into the narrative, rather than deal with them in separate chapters. It is hoped that, in this way, a fuller, rounder picture of a given period has been achieved.

Second, the decision was made to end the narrative at 1502 when, according to the official law of the state, Muslims ceased to exist in the Iberian Peninsula. Although many of the Moriscos, as they were henceforth known, were crypto-Muslims, they do not fall into the same category as their predecessors and ancestors. Furthermore, recent studies, notably the excellent monograph by L. P. Harvey, have provided ample new perspectives on the Moriscos.[1]

Third, with respect to bibliographical matters, the procedure adopted has been to provide chapter endnotes for specific references, both in English and in other languages. Then, at the end of the book there is a bibliographical list of works consulted and recommended. A point to make here, however, is that I have often used nineteenth-century and pre-1970 works or editions, not necessarily because I made a conscious decision not to look at later ones, where they exist, but for reasons that may perhaps be considered to be ideological. As far as editions are concerned, some later editions may improve on earlier ones in the readings of specific words, and they frequently have very good introductions or helpful notes, but the actual text will have altered only slightly. I have had recourse to translations, often in conjunction with the Arabic or Latin texts. Regarding scholarship, our horizons are being constantly extended, but it is salutary to bear in mind the contributions of scholars in past generations. The quality of their erudition has often been ignored, and whilst erudition does not necessarily equate with trustworthy scholarship, we neglect their work to our own loss.

I do not think that any interpretation has been distorted by not taking into account every conceivable book, article or paper written on the subject. On the other hand, nothing has been deliberately disregarded. Throughout, the priority has been to identify and address issues which are judged to have been significant, thereby, it is hoped, both striking chords and expanding perspectives. It will become apparent that two themes have been given prominence, certainly when dealing with the earlier centuries. These are the importance of maintaining a distinction between urban and rural communities, and the need to recognise that religion played a less dominant role in affairs than has been hitherto thought. The second of these themes is not one arrived at lightly; nor has it been superimposed on any given event or situation. It started initially many years ago from a recognition that the Arabic word *ʿajam* was being consistently rendered as 'Christian', whereas it is a religiously neutral word referring to those who speak Arabic imperfectly, and by extension foreigners. This led, over a period of years, to a realisation that the role of revealed religion had been assigned a higher profile than it warranted, notably in the interpretation of the history of the Iberian Peninsula in the Middle Ages.

Throughout the long journey of writing this book, I have been conscious of an enormous debt to those who have undertaken this or adjacent tasks before me. I shall list the works of many scholars in the bibliography, but my immediate responsibility here is to name those who have made a more personal impact. The late Professor Harold V. Livermore wrote to me on a number of occasions with his views on writing history, and I have taken them to heart. The late Professor M. A. Shaban, who spent the final years of his academic career in Exeter, insisted on the primacy of sources. We were planning to write a history of Muslim Spain together and did carry out some ground work, but the venture never came to fruition. I had the benefit of many conversations about Islamic history with him, but this is not the book that we would have written. Professor Edmund Bosworth has read and provided comments on many chapters, and I am exceedingly grateful to him for his time and attention. He is exonerated from all errors. Dr Jane Whetnall kindly proofread a chapter, removing inconsistencies, identifying and correcting solecisms and asking penetrating questions. Being a Hispano-Arabist in a British university has been a lonely occupation, but for forty years I have been encouraged by Professor L. P. Harvey, who has corresponded with me regularly throughout a busy career and an equally active retirement, during which he has published two books of great value on the later period of Muslim Spain and the Moriscos. He has offered a thoughtful, clear and reasoned opinion on a range of issues and controversies, and I have had the advantage of his immense learning and knowledge, the latter always willingly imparted. I have been privileged in having him as a kind of unofficial mentor during my career, but he is not to be held in any way responsible for the views expressed in what follows. I would finally like to thank Professor Carole Hillenbrand and Edinburgh University Press for entrusting this task to me.

Note

1. L. P. Harvey, *Muslims in Spain, 1500–1614*, Chicago, IL and London: University of Chicago Press, 2005.

Iberian background

Iberia was the name given to the Peninsula by Greek authors, notably by Herodotus in the fifth century BC. The only designation of the Iberian Peninsula by Latin writers had been Hispania, a province of Rome, alongside Gaul and others. It was in current use in the first century BC. It has long been supposed that Hispania may derive from the Phoenician, used by the Carthaginians, and subsequently adopted by the Romans. At the time of the invasion, the Peninsula was a Visigothic state. To use the word 'Spain' (España) at this time is to superimpose a notion of nationhood that simply was not present. There were identifiable regions such as Galicia, but nothing to justify the denomination of Spaniard. Spain did not come into existence until the Early Modern era, as a consequence of the unification of Castilla and Aragón during the reign of Fernando and Isabella. Hence there was never any 'Arab' invasion of 'Spain'. The phrase 'Muslim Spain', whilst being more accurate in the first part, presents the same problem. Al-Andalus was the name given by the Muslims to their territory in Al-Andalus with its shifting borders. From the mid-thirteenth through to the end of the fifteenth century, Al-Andalus was confined to a reduced area in the south-east corner of the Peninsula roughly covering the present-day provinces of Granada and Málaga, with approximately 200 miles of coastline. It would be appropriate to employ this term in a study exclusively devoted to the Muslim-controlled area of the Peninsula. There are many other instances when the meaning of a word is of the utmost importance, and much attention will be paid to this aspect.

As a preliminary reflection, it is worthwhile remembering the physical nature of the Peninsula, isolated from Europe by the Pyrenees, divided at intervals by four dominant rivers and characterised by notably contrasting terrains. What might be called a Mediterranean climate prevails over the lower, southern half of the Peninsula. Within this area, the Guadalquivir valley, with its extensive irrigation, cuts a swathe through the landscape. Here one can discern some similarity with the terrain in North Africa, but the analogy should not be over-stretched. The central plateau is by and large flat and arid, whereas the climates of the more mountainous northern and north-west regions are more European, subjected as they are to the seasonal extremes of temperature that are not present in the south and south-west where a more Mediterranean climate prevails. Much has been made of the Pyrenees as a barrier between the Iberian

Peninsula and the rest of mainland Europe. These forbidding mountains have long been considered impenetrable, but in the western area, the lower passes, such as Roncesvalles, have always been reckoned to be passable. The heights are similarly moderate in the eastern zone. It is in the central Pyrenees where the mountain peaks are at their highest. As a generality one could say that travellers therefore avoided these, and crossed at either end. Not only this, but the habitable areas spanned the present-day borders between France and Spain, the Basques in the west and the Catalonians in the east both dwelling in lands to the north and south of the Pyrenees. The Cantabrian mountain chain inland from the Bay of Biscay is another barrier that tends to get overlooked. Yet it effectively separates the narrow coastal stretch from the body of the Peninsula. Most attention, though, has always settled on the Pillars of Hercules, the so-called Straits of Gibraltar. This waterway, thirty-five miles long and an outlet of the Mediterranean Sea into the Atlantic Ocean, is eight miles across at its narrowest point. The rock is plainly visible from the African mainland. A journey across the Straits, then, is a far less daunting prospect than attempting to negotiate the Pyrenees. The landing places from Tangier would be Tarifa and Algeciras, the former named after a Muslim leader and the latter from *jazīra*, the Arabic for island. These are diagonal crossings making the distance somewhat longer, but even a small boat would not find the prospect unmanageable in a day, weather permitting. The natural harbour of Ceuta was also an embarkation point for the south and south-east of the Peninsula. Allowing for the vagaries of the winds and the currents, intercontinental crossings would have been commonplace from time immemorial.

The earliest inhabitants of the Iberian Peninsula were named Iberians by the Greeks. They are largely regarded as having been of Mediterranean stock, from North Africa, which is understandable in the light of the ready access across the Straits, and which may be regarded as a natural demographic movement. They have taken on the mantle of indigenous stock. The Celts, on the other hand, who arrived in the sixth century BC, were of central European origin. They merged, over time, with those already *in situ*, and, as a consequence, the name Celtiberians came into being. The Phoenicians, Greeks, Carthaginians and others who occupied and traded from Iberian ports, both on the Atlantic, notably Cádiz, and in the Mediterranean, deserve to be mentioned but did not leave great marks on the Peninsula. Their collective contribution is dwarfed by the indelible mark that the Romans left, after the defeat of the Carthaginians by the younger Scipio, in 206–7 BC. The Iberian Peninsula was then divided into two vast provinces, Hispania Ulterior (Further Spain), in the south beyond a notional border inland and parallel to present-day Cartagena, and Hispania Citerior (Nearer Spain), incorporating the northern areas. Despite initial and serious opposition from indigenous tribes to permanent Roman settlement, amongst whom the Celtiberians occupying an area roughly equivalent to

Castilla la Nueva were prominent, a succession of Roman armies brought the Peninsula inexorably to heel. A turning point was the capture and utter destruction, in 133 BC, of Numantia, near Soria, which set the seal on Roman supremacy. The final regions in the Peninsula to be conquered by the Romans were those in the far north and north-west, Cantabria, Asturias and Galicia, eventually subdued by the legions of Augustus around 25 BC. Henceforward, a number of subdivisions were created, including Galicia, Lusitania (comprising not only present-day Portugal, but also a substantial portion of Extremadura) and Baetica (Andalucía). The conquest of the Iberian Peninsula had been, in Leonard Curchin's words, 'a war of attrition', but what was to follow is a remarkable story of absorption, as a consequence of which the majority of the inhabitants of the Peninsula came to be known collectively as Hispano-Romans.[1]

The Romanisation of the Iberian Peninsula occurred over several centuries, although it is thought that the southern regions, Hispania Ulterior, came first. A treaty was made with the people of Gades (Cádiz), about 200 BC, and they were accorded Roman citizenship by Julius Caesar in 49 BC. The Roman theatre became a notorious place for the *puellae gaditanae* (the girls of Cádiz), whose dancing and singing made them popular in Rome. The merits of Hispalis (Seville), lying on the banks of the navigable river Betis, later named Guadalquivir (the *wādī al-kabīr*, the Big River), by the Muslims, were recognised by the Roman governors, and an aqueduct was constructed to carry water into the city. Cordoba and Mérida, however, were provincial capitals, and as such demonstrated thorough signs of Romanisation. Cordoba, founded in the second century BC, the smaller of the two and capital of the province of Baetica, was also strategically placed. The nearby Sierra Morena was a source for mineral wealth, gold, silver and copper all being mined there. The foundations of the substantial Roman bridge across the Betis, still in place, made for ready communication with the north and provided essential access for trade. Olive oil from the surrounding groves was regarded as among the finest exported to Rome, as good as the Italian, according to Martial, and its importance cannot be underestimated. The olive oil industry was established by the first century AD, and helped to bring prosperity to the urban community who controlled much of its cultivation. Inscriptions and surviving amphorae indicate that olive oil from Hispania was exported to all parts of the Mediterranean, and in significant quantities. Additionally, Cordoba was the central distribution point for wool, which was held in high esteem, both for its quality per se, and for its products. It seems probable that among the principal reasons why Cordoba was later chosen as the Muslim capital of al-Andalus in the eighth century was because of its being a thriving economic centre, trading in mineral products and agriculture, at the hub of which was the olive oil business.

Mérida (Emerita Augusta), however, was a city of major importance in the Roman Empire, and evidence of its status can be seen today in the existing bridge across the river Anas called the Guadiana (the *wādī ana*), the aqueduct known as Los Milagros, and the imposing restored theatre. When Augustus, in the first century BC, decided to build a network of roads in the Peninsula, the western route went from Seville, through Mérida to Salamanca, crossing the Tagus by a seven-arched bridge. Later Vespasian (9–79 AD) planned a route across the centre of the Peninsula, linking Mérida, via Talavera and Toledo, to Saragossa, following the Tagus for much of the route. The lower route, linking Mérida with Valencia, passed through the important mining town of Almadén, still in Baetica Province, where the cinnabar mines from which mercury was extracted were its raison d'être. They were closed at the turn of the twentieth century after 2,000 years of continual use. During the Roman period, because of the popularity of cinnabar as a colouring agent and its cosmetic potential, these mines were responsible for virtually the entire supply of the Empire's mercury, and later their products were exported throughout the Muslim world. Chrysocolla, used for a greenish blue paint, was quarried in Asturias.

Saragossa (Caesar Augusta) owed its prominence in part to its strategic position on the banks of the river Ebro. Major roads passed through the city, from Tarragona (Tarraco), the capital of the largest Roman province to Palencia, Asturias and Galicia in the north-west, thus linking the Mediterranean with the Atlantic. It was also where the route from the south connected with a smaller road to Jaca and to the Pyrenees beyond. A Roman bridge was constructed, destroyed in Muslim times. The fact that Galicia in the remote north-west of the Peninsula was made readily accessible to transport in Roman times is principally due to its mineral resources. Gold mines in Galicia and in Asturias had been extensively mined in the pre-Roman era. Their value, notably for trading purposes, was incalculable, and ensured that the whole region was far from being a neglected outpost in the northern fastnesses, as has been the general perception. Silver, lead and iron were also mined in Galicia, as is testified by Pliny. The mineral resources throughout the Peninsula were profitably exploited and exported, certainly as far as gold, silver, lead and copper were concerned, by the Romans to Rome, Italy and further afield.[2] Special mention has to be made of salt, which was used to preserve fish, and for medicinal purposes, notably in the treatment of bruises. There were extensive supplies in Baetica and in the provinces of Tarraconensis and Cartaginensis. Salted fish was prepared in Cádiz and in many of the Mediterranean ports, and was transported to Rome by sea.

As the network of roads was constructed across the length and breadth of the Peninsula, so Latin was introduced along the routes. Latin as a language was a unifying factor among the indigenous peoples and, perhaps as early as the first century AD, was in widespread use, certainly amongst urban communities. Latin was the language of the law that was incumbent on all Roman citizens so, alongside Romanisation, Latinisation reached out over the Peninsula. In Baetica, in particular, the process was very thorough, such that one could talk of this province as being not only the home but also the epitome of 'Roman Spain'. The exception to this was the Basque region, which preserved its civic and linguistic independence from Rome. What kind of Latin was spoken in the early centuries AD is difficult to gauge, but certainly the differences in speech would have been reflected in the classes of society. The fabric of society was Roman, but it is important to bear in mind the distinction between the urban and rural communities. The former, notably in the principal Roman cities, would resemble Roman citizens in other parts of the Empire, with the corresponding degree of culture and sophistication. In rural areas, where the demands of the land were the prime concern, the process of Romanisation would have been less rapid and more haphazard. An important factor in this regard is Christianity, which may have spread to the Peninsula as early as the second century AD. The division of the Church into five ecclesiastical provinces took place in 297; the Church Council at Elvira, Granada, in 300 AD had a total attendance of nineteen bishops, and preceded by four years the significant edict of religious toleration decreed by the emperor Constantine, which allowed 'full freedom to all existing forms of worship, with special reference to the Christian'.[3] The fact that Bishop Hosea of Cordoba presided at the Council of Nicea in present-day Turkey in 325 is an indication of the prestige enjoyed by some members of the clergy in the Peninsula. Monasticism appeared in the Christian Church in the fourth century AD, and later, as a consequence of the widespread propagation of the Rule of St Benedict from the early sixth century onwards, became established in the Iberian Peninsula.

When the Roman Empire crumbled, the Iberian Peninsula became the object of interest for a number of Germanic tribes, possibly in part because they were generally rather than specifically aware of the natural and mineral resources over which the Romans had presided for so long. The Alani had established contact with the Suevi and with the Vandals in central Europe. The turmoil in the Roman Empire in the fifth century was precipitated by the destruction of Rome by the Visigoths under their leader Alaric in 410. During the first half of this century, these tribes all penetrated the Iberian Peninsula, leaving either little or, in the case of the first three mentioned, no trace of their presence. In so far as the Visigoths were concerned, from the time of their invasion of the Peninsula in 456 until defeat by the Muslims in 711, they exercised political control from their capital in Toledo, having transferred their headquarters from Toulouse in Gaul. The general consensus is that the legal codes that were drawn up during the Visigothic period were founded on the Roman code of law that had been observed and applied previously. That is to say, whatever impact this legal system may have had on the rural communities in the Roman period was continued after the collapse of the Empire. Urban government was perpetuated, and taxes were collected by representatives of the cities. That is to say that the division between urban and rural communities which was later to be of such significance during the Islamic period, was already prevalent in the earlier epochs.

The rule of the Visigothic state was through monarchy, with around twenty-five kings for the 250-year period. The seventh century was a particularly volatile one, with sixteen kings occupying the throne, and only one for a reign longer than ten years. The momentous decision to adopt Catholicism in place of Arianism was taken at the Third Council of Toledo in 589 AD under the king-ship of Reccared. The state thereby moved rapidly to one in which Catholic doctrine prevailed. This did not bring about a burgeoning of new churches, or at least not in the smaller towns or the rural areas where the majority of the population lived. What it did provide was the cultural context for the most important writer of the Visigothic period, Isidore of Seville (c. 560–636 AD, canonised in 1598). His *Etymologiae*, dating to the 630s, was a compendium of knowledge, encyclopedic in its range, and a resource for scholars in succeeding centuries. His reputation was that of a defender of the Church, and, as with other bishops, he was party to administrative decision-making. This did not necessarily mean rubber-stamping state policies, as indicated by his questioning of the advisability of anti-Jewish measures such as enforced conversion. He was truly an intellectual giant for his generation, and the influence of his writings in later centuries cannot be underestimated.

The position of the Jewish communities under the Visigoths in the seventh century is determinable, to a certain extent, from the measures enacted in the Councils of Toledo.[4] These measures included injunctions from the monarch, so it is evident that anti-Jewish legislation emanated from the highest authority. Although forcible conversion was never enacted, there is a record of escalat-ing persecution, culminating in the measures of the Seventeenth Council of 694, held in Toledo. The property of Jews should be confiscated, their families broken up and dispersed, their youngest children brought up as Christians; they should have the status of slaves, and be forbidden the practice of their religion. Until this point, Jewish merchants had to operate under increasingly severe restrictions, and prominent Jews had held positions of authority. The reasons for the sanctions against the Jewish presence in the Peninsula may include resentment at their evident power and status, fear of their acting collectively in opposition to the state and, towards the end of the seventh century, an obsessive preoccupation with rumours that they may have been planning to establish a kingdom in the south-east corner of the Peninsula, rallying to the call of a second David. There is some indication from the bishops that some of the sanctions were not wholly enforced, particularly in the south of the Peninsula, but the consequences for the rural communities were indeed dire. Those who had relied on Jewish merchants for trade could no longer do so, and found it difficult to dispose of their produce, agricultural or pastoral. They became, in consequence, disaffected with the Visigothic state, and were later, quite naturally, unwilling to

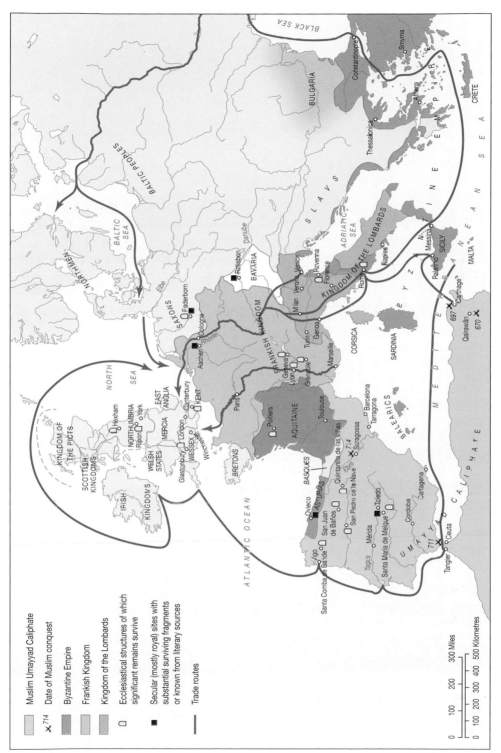

Map 1 Europe and the western Mediterranean in the eighth century.

Muslim Umayyad Caliphate

✕714 Date of Muslim conquest

Byzantine Empire

Frankish Kingdom

Kingdom of the Lombards

⬓ Ecclesiastical structures of which significant remains survive

■ Secular (mostly royal) sites with substantial surviving fragments or known from literary sources

Trade routes

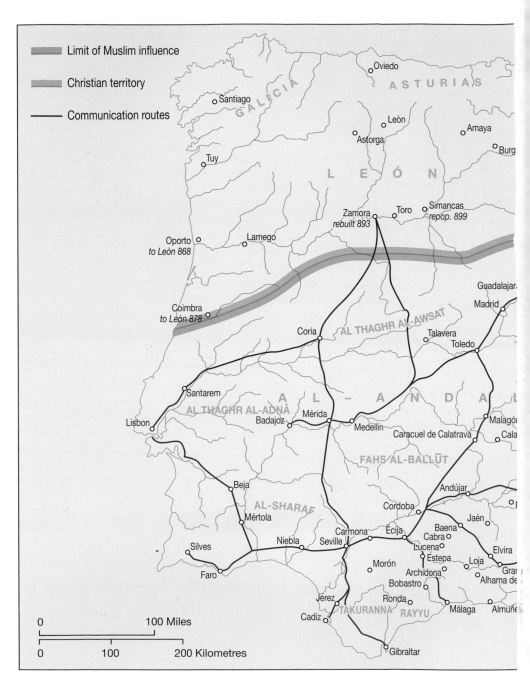

Map 2 Al-Andalus in the ninth and tenth centuries, showing the frontier zones.

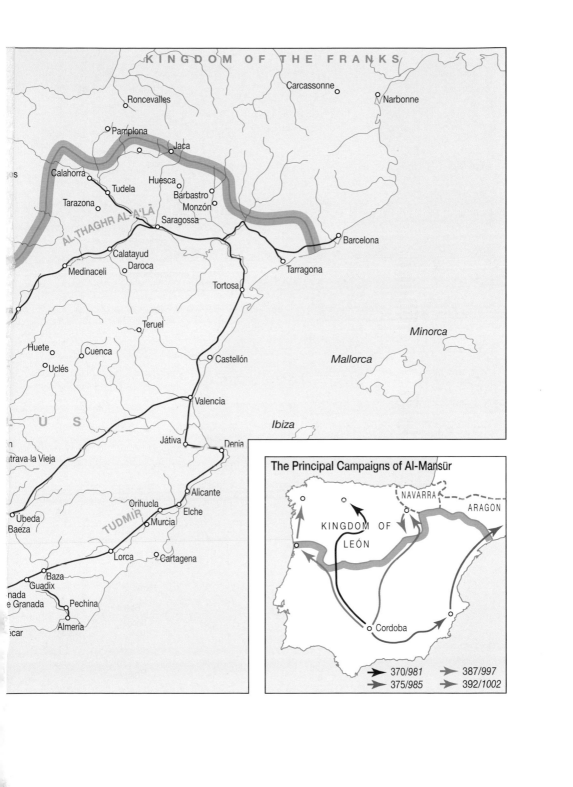

KINGDOM OF THE FRANKS

Carcassonne

Narbonne

Roncevalles

Pamplona

Jaca

Calahorra

Tudela

Huesca

Barbastro

Tarazona

Monzón

AL THAGHR AL-A'LĀ

Saragossa

Barcelona

Calatayud

Daroca

Medinaceli

Tarragona

Tortosa

Teruel

Minorca

Huete

Cuenca

Castellón

Mallorca

Uclés

Valencia

Játiva

Ibiza

Denia

trava la Vieja

Alicante

Orihuela

Elche

Úbeda

Murcia

Baeza

TUDMĪR

Lorca

Cartagena

Baza

Guadix

nada

Pechina

e Granada

car

Almería

The Principal Campaigns of Al-Mansūr

NAVARRA

ARAGON

KINGDOM OF

LEÓN

Cordoba

370/981   387/997

375/985   392/1002

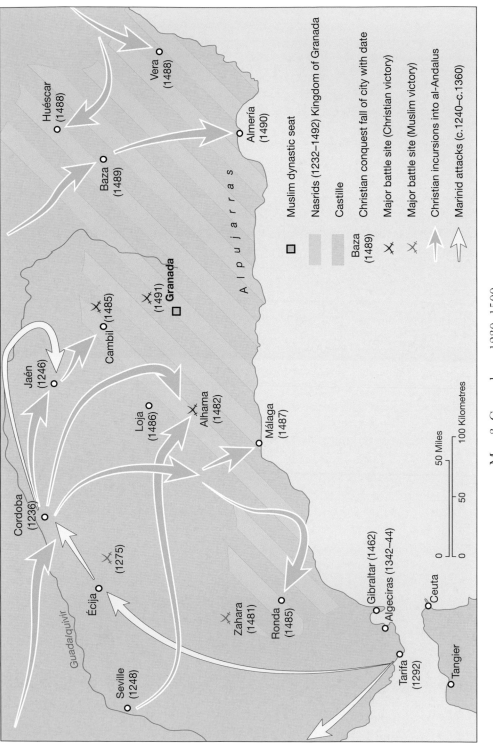

Map 3 Granada, c. 1230–1500.

Legend:

□ Muslim dynastic seat

Nasrids (1232–1492) Kingdom of Granada

Castille

Baza (1489) Christian conquest fall of city with date

✕ Major battle site (Christian victory)

✕ Major battle site (Muslim victory)

⇨ Christian incursions into al-Andalus

⇨ Marinid attacks (c.1240–c.1360)

Vera (1488)
Huéscar (1488)
Almería (1490)
Baza (1489)
Alpujarras
Cambil (1485)
Granada (1491)
Jaén (1246)
Cordoba (1236)
Loja (1486)
Alhama (1482)
Málaga (1487)
Écija (1275)
Zahara (1481)
Ronda (1485)
Gibraltar (1462)
Algeciras (1342–44)
Ceuta
Seville (1248)
Guadalquivir
Tarifa (1292)
Tangier

0   50 Miles
0   50   100 Kilometres

support it against the invaders from North Africa. This may be seen, perhaps, as tacit rebellion on the part of the rural communities, a recognition that, at the level at which they conducted their lives, their livelihood was being adversely affected. As a natural consequence, they would have reacted favourably if not eagerly to any change in regime that would bring their lives back to normal. When the invasion occurred in the spring of 711 AD, the indigenous rural population would learn by rumour that those who had governed them from Toledo were being replaced. They would not know that those who established rule in Cordoba and Seville were Muslims, nor would this fact have meant much to them, had they been aware of it. The Iberian Peninsula is a vast land mass, and few would have come into contact with the invading forces or have witnessed any battles at first hand. The tempo of life in early and mid-summer in the south, where most of the activity took place, would have been slow and have moved at a leisurely pace. One suspects that only those in urban centres would have been aware that regime change was occurring.

Islamic background

The interpretation of the available information concerning the origins of the Muslims in the Iberian Peninsula is fraught with difficulties. It is generally agreed that an invasion occurred in 711 AD, and that the invaders were Muslims. However, the nature of the sources, both Latin and Arabic taken together, makes the construction of a coherent narrative problematic. There is an uneven Latin chronicle of 754 that deals with events at both extremes of the Mediterranean, and this is certainly an early source. Amongst other names, it is known as the Chronicle of 754, this date being that of the final entry. Its author, probably from Toledo, shows a surprisingly detailed knowledge of Arabic dynastic succession, and is evidently an opponent of those in control of al-Andalus. Arabic histories and other writings are some generations in time later than the events or subjects they describe. They do often quote previous writers by name but, taken altogether, are far from providing a coherent account. The circumstances surrounding the invasion of the Iberian Peninsula by Muslims, then, has to be pieced together, constructed like a jigsaw whose pattern is withheld. One can compose a plausible narrative on the basis of a limited number of sources, drawing from both the Latin and Arabic tradition, as Harold Livermore did, in his case using principally the indispensable *Akhbār Majmūʿa* (940 AD) and the Chronicle of 754.[5] Or, one can rely primarily on one account, decrying the merits of others. This was the approach of Roger Collins who gave precedence to the Chronicle mentioned, while maintaining considerable scepticism towards the 'main Arab historical works'.[6] Pedro Chalmeta based his groundbreaking 1994 study of the invasion of Hispania and the Islamicisation of Al-Andalus on both Arabic and Latin sources.[7] Then there is the radical alternative approach adopted by Ignacio Olagüe with his eyecatching title, *Les Arabes n'ont jamais envahi l'Espagne*.[8]

It makes sense, first of all, to enquire into the reasons for invasion from an Islamic perspective, or, more precisely perhaps, from the point of view of the invaders. Since the death of Muhammad in 632 AD, an Islamic empire had come into being, penetrating, soon after the year 700 AD, beyond the eastern borders of present-day Iran into Baluchistan and Afghanistan in the east, and reaching the Atlantic Ocean in the west. This does not necessarily mean that an empire was established over this extent of territory, but it does imply that there was what may be called an Islamic presence. When a city was captured, a garrison was left, and this was not always sufficient to hold the territory after the army had moved on. In the case of the North African seaboard, Qayrawān, in present-day Tunisia, was founded as a military base in 670, and later became the headquarters of the Muslim domains in North Africa.

There is a fundamental distinction that has to be drawn in order to get nearer to an understanding of the seventh- and eighth-century political and social arena. Arabs were inhabitants of the Arabian Peninsula, whereas Muslims denoted followers of Islam. After Muhammad's death, Arabs controlled the empire initially from Damascus which was the seat of the Caliphate until 750 AD, when it moved eastward to Iraq and eventually to Baghdad. Arab tribes-men were recruited into the armies, and received the statutory stipend, making enrolment an attractive proposition. According to al-Kindī, there were 30,000 to 40,000 such tribesmen in Egypt at the turn of the eighth century, thus diminishing the manpower in their lands of origin to a very considerable extent. Around the year 700, almost all Arabs were Muslims, but not all Muslims were Arabs. The further away the Muslim armies were from Damascus, the seat of the Caliphate at that time, the fewer the Arabs amongst their number. By the end of the first century of the Hijra, though, a considerable proportion of troops in Islamic armies were non-Arabs recruited from the subject territories, part of the attraction being the statutory stipend. In order to qualify for this, it was necessary to convert to Islam. This entailed acknowledging the articles of faith incumbent on Muslims and enshrined in the formula 'There is no God but God, and Muhammad is the Prophet of God'. The practical requirements of the convert were the daily prayers, observance of Ramadan, the giving of alms and, if affordable, the *hajj*, or pilgrimage to Mecca. For the rank-and-file soldier, the first of these would have had to be learnt and recited. Apart from prayers which, one imagines, would have been supervised, the others would hardly have had much relevance for a serving soldier. When the Iberian Peninsula was invaded, the Muslim troops consisted almost entirely of recruits from the indigenous pop-ulations of North Africa. A knowledge of Arabic was not a prerequisite, though from one example it is evident that some Arabs were concerned about this. Mūsā b. Nusair, the governor of Ifrīqiyya, when he appointed Tāriq b. Ziyād commander of the Muslim forces in Tangier, sent 'with his army, which was composed almost entirely of Berbers, a teacher to instruct them in the Koran and the essential duties of Islam'.[9] Yet, this does seem to have been a desperate measure. Tāriq commanded about 10,000 troops, and one amongst so many is likely to have had a negligible effect, if any at all, particularly if he only spoke Arabic. The troops stationed in Tangier would have spoken the languages of their own home towns and villages. Arabic is not a language that can be readily acquired. It is simply inconceivable that it could have been understood, let alone mastered, by conscripts. At best, one may suppose that they could have followed basic commands given in Arabic, and that they had a rudimentary grasp of essential military vocabulary. To summarise at this point, the conversion of soldiers, then, even if it occurred on an individual level, would have required them to undertake the basic obligations, such as the declaration of the Muslim credo, which would have been memorised, one assumes, in Arabic. It should be said, though, that certain law schools permitted the recitation of the *fātiha*, the opening *sūra* of the Qur'ān and indeed all the ritual prayers in the convert's own tongue. In the light of this, one might deduce that, for the troops recruited from indigenous populations into the early Muslim armies, conversion was simply a matter of convenience. The impetus for a Berber soldier, for example, to change his lifestyle would have been infinitesimal, reduced perhaps to what was required to avoid any clashes with those who were in authority over him.

The further from the central lands of the Near East the Muslim armies, the greater the percentage of non-Arabs incorporated into their ranks. There had always existed a tension between Arab Muslims, who considered themselves superior in the hierarchy of Islam, despite the unambiguous declaration in the Qur'ān that 'The believers are brothers' (49: 10), and non-Arab Muslims. Muhammad had made it quite clear that it was not lineage that determined pre eminence in Islam: 'The noblest of you in the sight of God is the most god-fearing' (49: 13). Nobility is not therefore conferred through inheritance, wealth or position, but through behaviour, actions and moral responsibility. Yet Arabs sought to maintain their prominence throughout the first centuries of Islam, even though they were far outnumbered by Muslims from other ethnic origins. These were the *mawālī* (converts), sometimes translated rather misleadingly as 'clients', initially because of their attachment to a particular Arab tribe, and thereby entitled to the benefits of being affiliated to that tribe. As the conquests escalated, they were members of the indigenous population of the territories subdued by the Arab and, later, Muslim armies, who converted to Islam. Much of the conflict in early Islam was among Muslims themselves: internecine struggles among Arab factions and religious sects, and revolts by non-Arab Muslims nurtured by deep-rooted resentment that they were considered second-class citizens within Islam. Although the legal status of the *mawālī* has been widely discussed, the precise nature of the conversion is less well attested. For example, as has already been mentioned, there was no obligation to learn Arabic. This is not to deny the primacy of the Arabic language within Islam, especially in the first century of Islam. The language of the Qur'ān and the *hadīth* (traditions of Islam) was Arabic, and it was revered as the language of the Prophet Muhammad and of God Himself. The study of lexicography, and particularly the language of the Arabs of the desert, was a serious pursuit amongst scholars. It was the language of poetry and scientific investigation. In Islamic courts, therefore, Arabic had pride of place, but amongst the converts in urban communities, and notably throughout rural areas in lands subjected to Islamic governance, it could not be expected that Arabic should be spoken or taught.

One of the crucial points for an appreciation of the rapid expansion of Islam in the first century of the Hijra relates to the incentives afforded to those who joined the Muslim armies. Hajjāj, appointed governor of Iraq in 695, paid 300 dirhams a year to recruits to his army, with a putative increase by a hundred soon afterwards, thus setting the precedent of a regular yearly stipend for the troops.[10] These would have been silver coins (dirhams), perhaps minted for the purpose, and there is no reason to suppose that the practice of encouraging recruits with an annual stipend was not also pursued in North Africa. Of course, such payments would have been supplemented by booty, an important fact to recognise in the invasion of the Iberian Peninsula. Hajjāj's pragmatic measure, then, had beneficial repercussions in the farthest reaches of the Empire. A second crucial point in determining the motives for the expansion of Islam is the role of *jihād* (Holy War), that is to say war conducted against unbelievers. Yet, in the first century of Islam, it is not certain that Muslims fought under any injunction of Holy War. This interpretation of the Arabic verbal root *jahada*, which has the underlying meaning of 'strive', seems not to have justification from the Qur'ān. *Sūra* 9, verse 73, which contains the word *jahada*, is translated as follows: 'O prophet, strive against the unbelievers and the hypocrites. Be harsh with them. Their abode is Jahannam [Gehenna] – an evil journey's end'.[11] Similarly, 'Do not obey the unbelievers and strive mightily with it [the Qur'ān] against them' (25: 52). In these instances, the notion is that of striving in defence of one's religion, and there is nothing to indicate that this is to be brought about with weaponry of any kind. Fighting, from the different Arabic root *qatala*, is to be undertaken in defence of the faith rather than in propagation of the faith: 'Fight in the way of God against those who fight you, but do not be the aggressors – God does not love aggressors – And kill them wherever you come upon them, and drive them out of the places from which they drove you out' (2: 190–1). The initial phrase is taken to mean that fighting is permitted when the faith is threatened, a defensive mechanism where a state of war exists. The final sentence has been interpreted as an invitation to fight unbelievers generally, but the context would suggest that that the 'them' are 'those who fight you', a reading accepted by early authorities. From the evidence of the Qur'ān, then, there is no incentive to support the affirmation that *jihād*, in the sense of Holy War, was a motivating factor in the expansion of early Islam.

In the light of this, the idea of religious fervour even as a contributory factor to the rapid expansion of Islam needs to be treated with extreme caution. On the other hand, within the regions of Islam, belief in the efficacy of Muhammad's legacy led to pragmatic policies being introduced. This may be seen in the treatment of subject peoples as Islam spread. Where there was recognition of the supremacy of the Islamic forces, and no armed military resistance, then the terms of surrender were generous, in effect allowing the local scriptural religions to continue to be practised without hindrance, subject only to the payment of a fixed tax, known as the *jizya*. This policy soon brought about the existence of whole non-Muslim communities within Islamic territories. The legal status of these peoples was that of *dhimmīs*, those who lived under a pact or treaty, a *dhimma*, whereby they were protected from specifically Muslim chores, and permitted to go about their business and their religion, always provided that they paid the said *jizya*, and did not offend Muslims in any way in their behaviour.[12] The advantages for the Muslims in having communities of *dhimmīs* in their domains were principally twofold. They benefited from the extra taxation, which in most areas was efficiently collected, and also from allowing the local economy, in the hands of the indigenous population, with their special knowledge of the terrain and of local conditions, to flourish. On the other side of the coin, there were the converts to Islam, the *mawālī*, who enjoyed many of the privileges of being a member of a particular tribal unit; hence they were also called clients. These were integrated in varying degrees within particular tribes, being differentiated principally by the fact that they were not Arabs. Islamic legislation allowed for the presence of many diverse groups within Muslim territories, such as these *mawālī* and the *ahl al-kitāb*; they were assigned specific names, all crucial to an interpretation of the social and political situation in the early centuries of Islam.

There are more cogent explanations to account for the unprecedented expansion of the Islamic Empire. It was military prowess that enabled Arab armies to sweep through the Byzantine and Sassanian empires, bringing much of them under Islamic rule within a few decades after the death of Muhammad. It is a simple and ineluctable truism that successful conquests have changed political maps in what seems to be an inordinately rapid space of time, and this was the case with the Arabs whose militia overwhelmed their opponents. The precise way in which battles were fought, the formation of troops, the tactics of warfare and the organisation required were all paramount. It was an escalating tidal wave of conquest, frequently masterminded by warriors on the field of battle. The rewards for them were booty, and an opportunity to gain preferment in the Caliphal headquarters in Damascus. Although the conquest of Egypt in 640 has been described as 'a classic example of the spontaneous and haphazard manner of the Arab conquests',[13] the strategy adopted by the Arabs when they established their headquarters in Fustāt, Old Cairo, was to allow the existing measures of governance to proceed according to pre-conquest custom, and to allow the mainly agricultural economy to continue to flourish. The land remained the property of the indigenous population, and the arrangements for taxation, so essential in the emergence of Islam because of the statutory amount that had to be sent back to the central coffers, followed very much those when Egypt had been under Byzantine rule. Always providing that the taxes were paid the indigenous population, particularly those who lived away from the urban centres, were able to pursue their lives unaffected by the changeover in political control. This was fundamentally akin to the practice adopted in the Iberian Peninsula some seventy years later.

The subjection of the rest of North Africa was by no means straightforward. There were two principal obstacles to the progress of the Arab armies, the Byzantine coastal strongholds, including Carthage, and the disparate Berber tribes scattered throughout the western regions. In order to thwart the former, the Arabs built up a navy in the Mediterranean, recruited, it should be said, from the indigenous non-Arab populations of Egypt and Syria, which, as the century progressed, turned into a successful facility. It was the eventual construction of a shipyard near Carthage at the turn of the eighth century, where sufficient ships were built to negate the Byzantine threat, that secured Muslim control over the southern Mediterranean shoreline. The initiative to overcome Berber resistance was grasped by the enterprising governor, 'Uqba b. Nāfi', who established his headquarters and military base at Qayrawān, in present-day Tunisia, in 670. From here, he launched his remarkable and spectacular expedition inland with a substantial army, eventually reaching the Atlantic Ocean in present-day Morocco, in 683, before his death and the defeat of his troops by Berbers on the return journey to Qayrawān, which was occupied by Berbers for four years before being retaken by Arabs. Opposition to the Arab/Muslim presence was taken up by the formidable female prophet, Kāhina, whose rebellion eventually ended with her death in 700. At the head of Berber forces, she inflicted a notable and serious defeat on the Arabs, and at one stage controlled the entire province except the stronghold of Qayrawān itself. This period of uncertainty was brought to an end by the appointment, in 705, of Mūsā b. Nusayr as governor of Qayrawān.

Notes

1. Leonard A. Curchin, *Roman Spain. Conquest and Assimilation*, London: Routledge, 1991, p. 54.
2. This aspect is well covered by Louis C. West, *Imperial Roman Spain. The Objects of Trade*, Oxford: Basil Blackwell, 1929.

3. Philip Schaff, *History of the Christian Church*, A P & A (reprint), n.d. (?1970s), 8 vols in 3 vols, vol. I, 3, p. 13. Originally published 1858–90.
4. See, for example, E. A. Thompson, *The Goths in Spain*, Oxford: Clarendon Press, 1969, pp. 246–8.
5. H. V. Livermore, *The Origins of Spain and Portugal*, London: George Allen & Unwin, 1971.
6. Roger Collins, *The Arab Conquest of Spain 710–797*, Oxford: Basil Blackwell, 1989, pp. 1–5 (Introduction) and p. 36.
7. Pedro Chalmeta, *Invasión e Islamización. La sumisión de Hispania y la formación de al-Andalus*, Madrid: Editorial Mapre, 1994.
8. Ignacio Olagüe, *Les Arabes n'ont jamais envahi l'Espagne*, Paris: Flammarion, 1969. See also P. Guichard, 'Les arabes ont bien envahi l'Espagne: les structures sociales de l'Espagne musulmane', *Revue Annales, Économie, Sociétés, Civilisations*, XXIX (1974), 1483–1513.
9. Reuben Levy, *The Social Structure of Islam*, Cambridge: Cambridge University Press, 1962, p. 16, quoting Ibn al-Athīr (d.1233), whose sections on North Africa and Spain, translated by E. Fagnan as *Annales du Maghreb et de l'Espagne*, are an admired and dependable source.
10. M. A. Shaban, *Islamic History A. D. 600–750 (A. H. 132). A New Interpretation*, Cambridge: Cambridge University Press, 1971, p. 105.
11. *The Qur'ān*, translated into English by Alan Jones, Oxford: Gibb Memorial Trust, 2007, p. 188.
12. Joseph Schacht, *An Introduction to Islamic Law*, Oxford: Clarendon Press, 1964 (reprinted 1982). See pp. 130–2 of the 1982 edition.
13. Shaban, *Islamic History*, p. 31.

The invasion of the Iberian Peninsula – the eighth century

Mūsā's impact on the region in the years leading up to the invasion of the Iberian Peninsula is enormous. He may be said to be one of four leading protagonists in the events of 711 and his role therefore deserves careful scrutiny. He figures prominently in Arabic histories and other sources, but they do not all coincide in the information that they provide. It is necessary to make a reasoned assessment. He was born in 640 and died in 714; he was therefore in his sixties when he was appointed to his post in Qayrawān. Before that, he had served with 'Abd al-'Azīz b. Marwān (d. 705), who was governor of Egypt for twenty years in the name of his brother, the Caliph 'Abd al-Malik, and was entrusted with the command of the army and of territory beyond Egypt's borders to the west stretching as far as the Atlantic Ocean. He was experienced as a military leader, as an administrator and, as governor of Africa (*walī* Ifrīqiyya) was handed the responsibility of reclaiming lands that had been appropriated by Berbers. His campaigns were successful and, according to Arab sources, he sent large numbers of captives back to Egypt. On the accession to the Caliphate of Walīd in 705, Mūsā was appointed by him *amīr*, prince of Ifrīqiyya[1] and of the Maghrib ('the Western lands' in Arabic, and the origin of the word Morocco), a promotion which is testimony of the high esteem in which he was held. His remit appears to have been threefold: to secure the terrain already conquered by Muslims, to subdue those Berbers that remained recalcitrant and, to this end, to maintain an army. The conquest and occupation of Tangier before 709 meant that his military objectives were accomplished. The command of Tangier and of the army of Muslims there was given to his client, the Berber convert Tāriq b. Ziyād, whilst he returned to his headquarters at Qairawān. This astute measure ensured that predominantly Berber troops were controlled by a Berber Muslim whose responsibility it was to govern the region and keep it pacified. Mūsā, meanwhile, established the law of Islam in his region. In practice, this entailed collecting taxes from subject peoples, payable by the rural population in kind, and by merchants in coinage. It has to be remembered that the nearby trading port of Carthage was only about 91 nautical miles (105 miles) from Sicily, the narrowest crossing point in the central Mediterranean. Carthage and Tangier were two of the Mediterranean termini of caravan routes that traversed the Sahara from central Africa, notably Timbuktu, bringing merchandise such as slaves and gold. The proximity of the Muslims was not coincidental as it enabled them to control these all-important trade routes.

Whilst Mūsā's was a largely autonomous rule, he benefited from cordial relations with the Caliph Walīd, 'Abd al-Malik's successor, to whom he sent annually what is known as the 'Caliphal fifth', that is to say, a fifth of the revenue received during that period. This tended in reality to be booty from successful military expeditions. With the experience that he had earlier gleaned, he recognised the need for campaigns to fulfil his obligations to the Caliph. Whether he authorised Tāriq to cross the narrow stretch of the Mediterranean that separated North Africa from the Iberian Peninsula may never be determined beyond doubt, but his later response to the success of the initial invasion indicates his interest, if not concern. The fact that he had entrusted the command of the army at Tangier to Tāriq is in line with the practice of the time, and any decision to deploy troops for a particular expedition could legitimately be made by his commander in the field.

Tāriq, the second of the leading protagonists of the events of 711, was evidently a capable commander. By the time that he was in charge of the troops billeted at Tangier, much of the hinterland of present-day Morocco had been effectively subjugated. Several inferences may be drawn from this. The troops had the right to be paid the required stipend, and there was no immediate prospect of booty by leading them south towards present-day Mauretania and Senegal. There existed, then, a pressing need to ensure that the rank and file of the army were paid, in order to avoid potentially damaging unrest; the obvious direction to look was north, to the rock across the water and the land that lay beyond. The extent to which Tāriq was empowered to make his own decisions is by no means certain from the sources, but it could be argued that if Mūsā controlled the overall strategy, then he, Tāriq, took charge of tactics. Amongst the factors that might account for an invasion of the Peninsula at that time, two loom large. The first of these is that the land across the Straits was permanently visible, if not shrouded in mist. Knowing that traders, tribesmen, seamen and others were frequent travellers in that narrow stretch of water, he no doubt received reports, assuredly often garbled, of the land beyond, its fabled prosperity, its people, the nature of the terrain. Whether he took the initial steps to test the veracity of the accounts on his own initiative, having already communicated what he had heard to Mūsā in distant Qairawān, may never be known for certain. What the sources are agreed upon is that, no doubt on Tāriq's instructions, a Berber, probably named Tarīf Abū Zur'a, a *mawlā* of Mūsā (although there is conflicting information concerning his name and status), led a contingent into the Peninsula in the summer of 710. It was well equipped, with 100 horsemen supported by 400 infantry, and landed at a small coastal settlement later to be known as Tarifa, named after Tarīf. He would have deployed his cavalry westward on the flat terrain towards the present-day

Cape of Trafalgar, and perhaps inland to Medina Sidonia. Only foot soldiers could have negotiated the woods and hills that lay to the east and to the coast of the bay of Algeciras. It seems feasible to speculate that he identified this as an appropriate landing place for a larger body of troops. He returned with unspecified spoils and captives which were sent by Tāriq to Mūsā, as an indication of the successful reconnaissance.

This second factor introduces the third of the protagonists, Julian. Under his Arabic name Ilyān, he figures prominently in the Arabic accounts. There is a profusion of information about him, although it is frequently conflicting; the task of compiling a narrative to which all would subscribe is therefore demanding if not unachievable. He is mentioned in sources relating to the year 682, that is to say nearly thirty years before the invasion, as having dealings with the Arab general 'Uqba, when the latter had penetrated the Maghrib as far as Tangier. By the time that Tāriq had occupied Tangier, Julian would have acquired extensive knowledge of the region and its Berber inhabitants; he was most probably governor of nearby Ceuta and was a widely respected and experienced local overlord of considerable standing. He is described as a Christian, may well have belonged to the Visigothic nobility, and have been an appointee of the Visigothic state responsible for trade across the Straits. If this was so, then it is likely that he also had charge of Algeciras, which would explain the fact that he owned boats for the transportation of merchandise. It would have been politically prudent for Tāriq to have approached Julian, and to have agreed a pact with him in return for the payment of an unspecified tribute and for information concerning the situation in the Iberian Peninsula. These pacts or treaties were a feature of early Islam, and often gained concessions for indigenous communities if these accepted Muslim control without armed opposition. Another source states that Julian had recourse directly to Mūsā, Tāriq's superior, offering perhaps even before the reconnaissance incursion of Tarīf in 710, to facilitate the Muslims' advance into the Peninsula. In this case, Tarīf's expedition could have been a 'dry run' for the 'real thing' the following year. The boats that Julian had at his command in Ceuta may well have been a crucial factor in the equation. If Mūsā did indeed authorise the invasion of the Iberian Peninsula, having first consulted his friend and protector the Caliph Walīd, then the availability of appropriate means of the transportation of troops would certainly have been of paramount importance. If, on the other hand, Tāriq had a free hand to make such decisions, which seems a more probable circumstance, then his recognition of Julian's potential as an ally both as a provider of transport for his army and as a guide to affairs in the Peninsula, might well have influenced his policy. Tāriq, then, determined to take the pragmatic step to invade, secure in the knowledge that he had to hand an accomplished and influential elder statesman, effectively exercising the function of mentor.

The reasons why Julian elected to collaborate with the Muslims must be considered. Was he pursuing a vendetta towards the Visigoths and in particular their recently proclaimed king, Roderic? Arabic sources elaborate on personal reasons why Julian should have wanted to exact revenge on Roderic, but these all seem to be the stuff of a later legend. A more prosaic motive might lie in Julian's earlier close ties with the previous Visigothic king, Witiza (sole ruler 700–10), and his feelings of anger and betrayal when the kingdom passed to Roderic who was not of the royal line, rather than to one of Witiza's sons. However, although this seems to be a reasonable surmise, it is chronologically unsound, in that Julian made his treaty or pact with Mūsā in 709, the year prior to Witiza's death. Purely political motivation still remains a possibility, but one has also to take into account Julian's role as a trader and merchant with immense influence over the region of the Straits. Any disruption to trade would pose severe threats to his prosperity and prestige, and the civil war that ensued in the Peninsula after Roderic's accession was clearly not propitious for trade. He would have been impressed by the organisational and administrative skills shown by the Muslims, Mūsā in his governance of the Maghrib, and Tāriq as commander of the army in Tangier. He perhaps shrewdly saw that the Muslims could restore the days of economic affluence that he had enjoyed for around twenty-five years, before the upheavals of 710. Julian's behaviour may therefore be seen as akin to that of an estranged patriot with a desire to restore the Peninsula to its former stability. One may add that he was certainly unworried by any alliance with Muslims and did not see the religion of Islam as a threat to the well-being of his own Christian country.

Roderic, the last Visigothic king, is the fourth of this quartet of protagonists. If Mūsā and Julian were political veterans, then Tāriq and Roderic were of the next generation, the latter perhaps only in his early twenties at the time of accession to the throne in 710. Later historians of Spain have denounced Roderic as a villain for having usurped the throne and reneged on his responsibilities as monarch, and for failing to repel the Muslim invaders. The reality may be otherwise. He was made king by election, one of the legitimate means by which the crown could be conferred among the Visigoths, an act not without precedent among his predecessors, and he had therefore not attained the throne illegally. Nonetheless, there was opposition to his appointment, notably from those who favoured dynastic accession ('he seizes the crown amidst much discord with support of the *seniores*').[2] To have been chosen from amongst the nobility at such a young age demonstrates that Roderic was evidently regarded as someone with exceptional talent. He seems to have been accepted in most of the kingdom, notably in the south-east region which was the domain of Theodemirus. His priority certainly appears to have been securing the hegemony of the Visigothic state, as in 711 he was campaigning against the Basques, besieging Pamplona. He acted with the vigour and perhaps impetuosity of youth ('young and full of adventure').[3] It was well observed by al-Maqqarī in the seventeenth century that when Roderic was alerted by Theodemirus that the territory had been invaded, he, Roderic, 'guessed directly that the blow had come from Ilyān'.[4] This detail would seem to suggest that Roderic was previously aware of Julian as a noble of standing and prestige but now disaffected. Perhaps recognition of Julian's involvement in the invasion led him to realise the gravity of the situation. Indeed, it is not implausible to speculate that Julian could have advised Tāriq to cross the Straits at a time when the young Visigothic king was known to be campaigning in the north with the army, leaving the southern approaches vulnerable to assault.

The invasion of the Iberian Peninsula may have begun in April 711. The consensus from the sources is that around 12,000 troops commanded by Tāriq were transported from Ceuta, in ships owned by Julian that were normally assigned to carrying merchandise, to a landing spot in the Bay of Algeciras. Arabic sources mention that the Rock of Gibraltar is so named because Tāriq landed in its vicinity, *jabal Tāriq* (Tāriq's mountain), but this seems to have been a later designation. Assuming that the number of ships was limited, perhaps to the four that Julian had at his disposal, then the operation could well have been transacted over a period of time, and over a sequence of nights. Two relevant observations here are, first, that the inhabitants of the southern coastline of the Peninsula would not be overly disturbed when Julian's merchant vessels landed, as these would have been seen frequently during the previous twenty years plying their trade across the Straits; second, the disembarkation of troops of bodies of armed men is less likely to have caused consternation at nighttime. The alarm would only have been raised when this large army, encamped *in situ*, was not dispersing and returning with the ships to North Africa. The details in the sources concerning the composition of the troops who crossed into the Iberian Peninsula coincide in specifying Berbers as the chief constituent elements. It cannot therefore be any longer sustained that this was an Arab invasion, as Arabs formed little or no part of the invading force. There may perhaps have been a small handful of Arabs present as representatives of Mūsā. An intriguing detail is the mention, in some sources, of blacks (*sūdān*), varying from a small number to several hundred. These are unlikely to have been slaves, for they would have been named as such, and, furthermore, slaves without any fighting capacity would hinder rather than contribute to the exercise. The *sūdān* are more likely to have been involved in trading enterprises, there perhaps at Julian's instigation as observers, to determine the potential for trade.

The identification of the invading Berbers is a major undertaking in that assumptions have been made about them that should not be taken at face value. The fundamental *point de départ* for what follows is that the word Berber (*barbar*) is an umbrella term, used to describe the inhabitants of North Africa mainly those to the west of Mūsā's headquarters in Qairawān, the Maghrib. These inhabitants were the Latin *barbari*, following a designation given by the Romans to the indigenous population of North Africa who could not speak Latin. The Arabs would have taken over this word in the seventh century but, by this time, the population would have incorporated other peoples, notably the Vandals who had settled there in large numbers in the fifth century. There existed a large number of Berber tribal groups or peoples, who spoke languages that were not mutually intelligible. One such group comprised the largely sedentary *barānis* from the Arabic *barnis* (cloak with hood), and at the time of the invasion, many of them were located in the north of present-day Morocco. A further significant group were the *butr*, some of whose constituent tribes were nomadic, moving their herds from place to place in quest of pasture. The Berbers, then, comprised disparate groups spread over a wide area of western North Africa who, apparently, at the time of the invasion, had the common denominator of being Muslim. It is true that from Ibn Idhārī, an important late-thirteenth-century writer, it is ascertained that the cessation of hostilities came at the cost of accepting Islam. This meant, in effect, that those engaged in the negotiations, leaders of tribes and communities became clients of the Muslims (*mawālī*), adopting Arabic names. The rest, the vast majority, continued their traditional lifestyle regardless of any agreements undertaken by those in authority, and perpetuating their own customs and beliefs. It may be argued that the absorption of perhaps tens of thousands of Vandals in the sixth century provides an important clue for the understanding of what happened in the Iberian Peninsula in the immediate aftermath of the invasion nearly two centuries later, particularly if these Vandals were primarily Latin-speaking.

Descendants of those Vandals who made such an impact in North Africa in the fifth and sixth centuries may well have participated in the Berber army of invasion alongside nomadic herdsmen with their familiarity with horses, warriors from the mountainous zones of North Africa and tribesmen-turned-soldiers who no doubt anticipated plunder on a hitherto unimagined scale. If the crossing of Tāriq's troops occurred in April 711, and if the confrontation with Roderic's forces took place in July that year at a site not too far distant from the landing spot, then one needs to ask why this inactivity on Tāriq's part? There is no consensus as to the site of the decisive battle, although there is a predominance in favour of one adjacent to the river Guadalete, whilst a site near the lagoon of La Janda by the river Barbate is also a possibility. The latter is closer to Tāriq's landing, but may well have been marshy and therefore not an ideal location for a battle. A feasible explanation of the eventual whereabouts of the battle is that Tāriq acted on Julian's advice. It made strategic sense not to stray too far from his landing site and take refuge, if necessary, on the other side of the Straits. Against this is the testimony of Ibn al-Kardabūs, the twelfth-century writer who stated that Tāriq ordered his boats to be burnt to give added incentive to his troops, but this seems unlikely, particularly if the boats belonged to Julian.[5] It also showed sound judgment to proceed westward, away from the sierras that lay to the east, and en route for the famed city of Seville. The Muslims stayed put in a propitious place of their own choosing, awaiting the Visigothic response. If the engagement with Roderic took place in July, then there must have been some frustration amongst the troops over the three months of inaction. On the other hand, Tāriq may have been productively involved in negotiations during this period. It should also be mentioned that, according to another interpretation, the invasion and decisive encounter took place near Cartagena, a couple of hundred miles along the east coast, between Almería and Alicante, but this reading of the source material, though alluring, has not attracted widespread acceptance.[6]

Common to many of the Arab accounts is the role played by treaties. One, in particular, the text of which has not survived, seems to have had great significance. Ibn al-Qūtīya, a fundamental tenth-century source, drawing on reputable informants and oral information, refers to an agreement made between the sons of Witiza and Tāriq. These three sons of Witiza, still youths, may well have considered Roderic to have usurped the throne to which, in their opinion, one of them was rightly entitled. They were therefore aggrieved and, according to Ibn al-Qūtīya, consented to betray Roderic on the night of the battle, in return for the confirmation of their entitlement to 3,000 estates in al-Andalus. There are no specific details as to the actual dates of the meeting, and one may speculate that preliminary negotiations, at least, took place in the summer months prior to Roderic's arrival on the battlefield. At some stage, the sons sought ratification of the agreement both from Mūsā in Qairawān and from the Caliph himself in Damascus. Walīd is said to have provided a document for each of them, corroborating the arrangement with Tāriq. As the journey from the Iberian Peninsula to Damascus is unlikely to have been undertaken in a short period of time, it makes sense to assume that Witiza's sons probably did not go the Middle East until after the decisive battle. Indeed, it has been suggested that if they went at all, then it was among the triumphal cortège of Mūsā on his recall to Damascus.[7] If Ibn al-Qūtīya's testimony is to be relied upon, then it indicates that the Caliph was *au fait* with affairs in al-Andalus and, indeed, that he regarded the affirmation of rights to coalescent members of the deposed regime to be essential in the transfer of power to Islam. It in no way suggests that he authorised the invasion, through the intermediary of his governor Mūsā, nor that the latter instructed Tāriq.

In respect of the battle itself, the Muslim army may have numbered around 12,000, but there is simply no agreement as to the size of Roderic's force. What can be determined is that sections of his battle line, probably the flanks, were composed of troops led by contingents in support of the cause of the sons of Witiza. On his expedition south in the summer of 711, he may have communicated with delegates of his political opponents, persuading them to join him in the common cause of repelling the invaders. If there was a night-time meeting between the sons of Witiza and Tāriq during the course for the battle, that may have spread over seven days, then the former must have thought that that this was a heaven-sent opportunity to rid the country of their rival. It follows that they may well have believed that Tāriq's mission was solely for booty, and that he and his troops would return to North Africa once this was accomplished. When Roderic was deprived of both flanks at a crucial stage of the battle, he was no doubt far outnumbered by his adversaries, and defeat was inevitable. There was plentiful booty to be had by the Muslims after the victory, but it was divided, again according to al-Maqqarī, among 9,000, indicating that a quarter of Tāriq's troops perished. The Visigothic losses are not known, but certain noblemen took refuge, no doubt with their paid troops and retinue, in various cities in the south. When the Muslims started to move up country, reinforced with up to 5,000 new arrivals from across the Straits, it would have become apparent to the Visigoths that the Muslims, far from satisfied with their initial gains, intended conquest and, with it, inevitable settlement. The Visigothic state had fallen, and another era in the history of the Iberian Peninsula had begun.

The eighth century: settlement and adjustment

Whether Tāriq was guided by Julian or whether he employed the use of local guides, he veered north and away from the obvious target of Seville, famed Roman port on the river Guadalquivir. His objective was the town of Écija, perhaps because he had information that some of his enemies, survivors of the initial battle, had fortified themselves there, or perhaps because of its strategic importance, as it lay on the Roman road between Seville and Cordoba, and had a road from it leading north to the centre of the Peninsula. Its fortifications comprised two solidly built ramparts, an inner and an outer one.[8] After a siege and a battle in which the Muslims suffered many dead and wounded, according to the *Akhbār Majmū'a*, in sufficiently notable numbers to be commented upon by a number of sources, the defenders were defeated.[9] Al-Maqqarī appends an anecdote to his brief account, mentioning a secret pact that was made with the governor of the town, whereby if hostilities ceased, the remaining inhabitants would be spared further strife and, subject to the statutory tribute being paid, they could live in peace.[10] Similar terms of submission were common practice as the Muslims made their way into the interior of the Peninsula, but this may be a later embellishment, inserted in order to call attention to the fact that the procedure of surrender on terms was a feature of Muslim practice in their early campaigns. On the other hand, there are a number of texts for the treaty (*'ahd*), made between 'Abd al-'Azīz and Tudmīr in the spring of 713, which may be regarded as a testimony of procedures. There are various extant versions of this treaty, which echo those employed in other regions of the Islamic world. The treaty itself has been extensively studied in part because the terms agreed upon suggest that, at least in one particular area of the Iberian Peninsula, the Muslims intended a permanent presence. Tudmīr is covered by a covenant or pact which Allah guarantees neither he nor any of his companions can set aside. He will not be deposed from his position of authority, nor shall either he or they be killed or reduced to slavery, nor separated from their wives and children. They (the beneficiaries of the pact) should not be forced against their inclinations in the matter of religion. Their temples will not be burnt; neither will objects of value (sacred objects, perhaps crosses) be removed from them (ad-Dabbī has *mulk* (realm), and this would suggest that this specification applied to whatever kind of shrine in whatever location).[11] This treaty relates to seven named cities which are to be ceded to the Muslims. These cities cannot all be identified with certainty but they extend from Alicante to Lorca, themselves about 100 miles from each other, and include Orihuela and Mula. It is also specified that Tudmīr himself is responsible for the continued observation of the terms of the treaty. Furthermore, he will not harbour any refugee or enemy of the Muslims; neither will he harm anyone under their protection. He must not withhold any information that he should hear about their enemies. In return for these conditions, he and his companions must pay the annual *jizya*, comprising one dinar (of gold), four bushels (*amdād*, measures) of wheat, four of barley, four measures of must (grape juice before fermentation), one of honey and one of olive oil. Each farmer, settler or slave should pay half this amount. The reference to slaves (*al-'abīd*) testifies to an existing distinction within society; the category of 'slaves' may have comprised those who did not enjoy the privileges of the Visigothic caste, and therefore include those engaged in agricultural or pastoral pursuits. One is tempted to make the conjecture that there was an urban payment and a rural payment; the gold dinar would form the payment made by city dwellers whereas the other items, which seem more patently associated with the countryside, would constitute the tax burden on the rural communities. There follows a list of Arab names, witnesses to the document.

It may be ascertained from the terms of this treaty which do not coincide in every version that Tudmīr was a man of standing in the Levant of the Peninsula, a former Visigothic nobleman with ascendancy over extensive domain, sufficiently important for 'Abd al-'Azīz, Mūsā's son, to negotiate with in person. The payment of the *jizya* allowed the existing economic structure to continue to function. Taxes had been paid under the previous regime, and for the rural communities these fiscal demands did not represent any change from time immemorial. They had no say in the matter. Indeed, there is a further argument here, in that they had endured restrictive practices that had adversely affected their trade since the middle of the seventh century, and which had come close to throttling it entirely after the Council of the Church in Toledo in 694. Produce of whatever kind needed to be sold at specific times of the year, and sanctions against those who were engaged in this trade, notably the Jewish middlemen, would have had a deleterious knock-on effect. The south-east of the Iberian Peninsula is where they seem to have been particularly active, and it was here that they were reckoned to pose the greatest threat, perhaps going so far as conspiring to form their own state. Even rumours of this would have been sufficient to justify Egica persuading the bishops to confiscate their property, to deprive them of their homes and to reduce them to slavery. These savage measures may not have been enacted upon, at least not in every part of the Peninsula, but their impact would have been felt by many rural communities who had relied on the Jewish intermediaries to dispose of their products. When, under the new administrative regime, sanctions against the Jewish communities were abolished, they would have found themselves free to trade as their ancestors had done and, in the light of this, the new system of taxation to which Tudmīr had subscribed was barely more than an acceptable annual inconvenience.

One may further deduce from the terms of the treaty that it was essentially an urban pact. In return for the pacific transfer of authority of strategic cities, Christians and Jews could go on practising their religions unmolested in their churches and synagogues. Thus, they enjoyed the status of *ahl adh-dhimma*, which afforded them protection within Islam. Theoretically, this also applied to Tudmīr's rural subjects. I say theoretically because there is scant, if any, evidence of the religion that they practised. The sites of very few churches have been located in rural areas in what constituted al-Andalus. One has testimony of Bobastro in the Province of Málaga in the ninth century and of Santa María de Melque in the region of Toledo, but apart from these two, evidence for the existence of others is not, to date, forthcoming.[12] As churches up until the eleventh century were protected for those with *dhimma* status, it seems unlikely that there was any systematic demolition of them. There may be an argument that churches fell into disuse through neglect, 'because of the changing demographic patterns subsequent to the Islamicization of al-Andalus in later centuries', but the more reasonable alternative is that they did not exist in the first place and that, in consequence, Christianity was not firmly implanted in areas away from urban centres.[13] What was in place were local beliefs based on traditional lore, superstitions and age-old cults. This claim is at the heart of the fundamental assumption that the most significant distinction in al-Andalus from the beginning of the eighth century until the tenth century was between town and country, urban and rural. A picture can be built up of the nature of existence in the cities of al-Andalus under Islam, but only an outline may be glimpsed of the circumstances of the majority of the population, those who lived in the rural areas.

In sum, then, this treaty would seem to demonstrate that peaceful submission brought with it immediate entry into the category of *dhimmī* for the indigenous communities both urban and rural. Where a formal religion, Judaism or Christianity, pre-existed, that is to say in urban environments, this was allowed to persist. Elsewhere, the rural economy was encouraged to prosper, without any further interference than the annual visitations by the tax gatherers. In the cities, the signs of Islam would soon become evident, but elsewhere, the indigenous population would have been largely unconscious of the change in regime. They would have been aware of an improvement in their commercial transactions now that the sanctions on the Jewish communities had been removed, but any knowledge of the growth of an Islamic state would have passed them by. For around 200 years, until the emergence of the Umayyad Caliphate in Cordoba in the first half of the tenth century, the majority of the population within the Iberian Peninsula, that is to say those who lived in rural areas, would have been almost wholly unaffected by Islam.

Urban Islam

It is natural to consider first how Islam became established in the cities of al-Andalus, as most of the available documentation, both Arabic and Latin, relates in an unvarnished manner to city dwellers. The principal city in the Visigothic state was Toledo, situated as it was more or less in the centre of the Peninsula, and it is therefore no surprise that Tāriq, after his victory over Roderic, should set his sights on Toledo, prompted to do so perhaps by Julian, and perhaps by tales of the untold wealth that was to be found there. In 712, Tāriq occupied the city, abandoned by its inhabitants according to some Arabic accounts, most likely members of the former Visigothic nobility, whither he was followed by Mūsā who had moved his retinue of around ten thousand Arabs from Qairawān to the Peninsula. This significant act of moving the governorship of his province further west was an indication that a permanent Muslim presence was intended. The Muslims, contrary to what those Visigothic nobles who had collaborated with the venture in the previous year had anticipated, were planning to settle there in anticipation of the establishment of a Muslim state. Envy is mentioned as a motive for Mūsā's entry in a number of Arabic sources: envy of what Tāriq had achieved in such a short period of time, and fear on Mūsā's part that if the Caliph al-Walīd should hear of the success of the conquest, he would be replaced by Tāriq;[14] but stories of untold wealth, described in great detail in the sources, may also have acted as an incentive. It also does well to recognise that the procedure prosecuted by Mūsā echoed a pattern that had held good for the Arabs since the early expansion of the Islamic Empire. His incursion into the Peninsula brought Arabs in conflict with non-Arab Muslims, notably the Berbers, one of many sources of conflict that was to blight al-Andalus.

By the time the two protagonists met, the main inland cities in the south of the Peninsula had been captured by Muslims, and much of the northern sector was in the process of subjugation. If the stories recounted in Arabic histories that Toledo possessed fabulous wealth are well founded, then the riches which

Mūsā took back with him to Damascus in 714 could have originated from here. In any event he met with Tāriq, if not in Toledo itself then en route for that city, perhaps near Talavera, as he had come from Mérida, which he had captured. A number of Arabic sources, independent of one another, relate that Tāriq came to meet Mūsā, as a subordinate officer might greet his commander-in-chief. Some say that Mūsā struck him on the head with a whip,[15] from which one may infer that he was demonstrating to those in his retinue that he was now master of what had turned into the conquest. He would furthermore have asserted, with this gesture, that he, an Arab, was in command, as opposed to Tāriq, a Berber *mawlā*. It is equally plausible that Mūsā should want to appropriate and secure whatever treasure there was in Toledo, before moving on to further conquests. Toledo was a well fortified city, remarkable for the strength and height of its ramparts, situated on the river Tagus with its famous bridge. Writing much later, an Arab geographer commented upon its dominant position vis-à-vis its environs; how it was encircled by gardens, irrigated by water channels and orchards; of ancient foundation, already constructed when the Romans arrived.[16] In short, it was a prestigious city in a central location, an ideal choice, one would have thought, as capital of the newly conquered territory. Yet, Mūsā's interest in Toledo appears to have been singularly mercenary. Once he had taken Tāriq with him to Toledo and had been shown the bejewelled table, probably a legendary embellishment which is nonetheless celebrated in such extravagant terms in the Arabic sources, he appears to have been reconciled with Tāriq, reinstating him; with combined armies, they proceeded to campaign together. Toledo was then plundered, and the property assembled by the Visigoths presumably conveyed by the rearguard of his army further north. There is no mention of the land being devastated, so the economy of the region was unaffected, or at least not adversely affected, suggesting that the city could be considered as a possible location for an Arab settlement once the conquests had been concluded.

Their route from Toledo would have been initially to the north-west to join the main Roman road that traversed the centre of the Peninsula from Mérida to Saragossa, passing through the old Roman town of Sigüenza (Seguntia), before arriving at Saragossa, then still a navigable inland port on the river Ebro. As was the case with the Muslim occupation of Toledo by Tāriq, there appears not to have been any armed resistance on the part of its inhabitants to the inexorable passage of Mūsā and his troops through the Peninsula. Now Saragossa was a larger city than Toledo, laid out on a rectangular grid with four gates in Roman times and had been essential to the maintenance of Roman power in the north.[17] It was situated in the fertile Ebro valley, was at the junction of the Roman road communication network and was evidently a strategic base for future forays north. In his overview of Saragossa, written during the fifteenth century, al-Himyarī was quite clearly impressed by what he had read and what he had heard of the 'White City', named because of the profusion of white marble. The mosque was founded before 718, therefore signifying the city's importance to the recently arrived Muslims.[18] It was about a month's distance from Cordoba, was very much self-sufficient and thrived in circumstances that clearly lent themselves to political independence.

It seems, though, that the destiny of the Arabs in the Peninsula lay with the Caliph in Damascus, as Mūsā was recalled in 714 to give an account of his conquests. By the time of his departure, delayed partly to ensure that the major portion of what had formerly been the Visigothic kingdom was under Muslim control and partly, perhaps, because he was apprehensive about the reception that awaited him on his return, the remnants of the Visigothic nobility would have been aware that the Muslims were intending to consolidate their presence in the Peninsula through settlement. A detail from al-Maqqarī reveals that some of Mūsā's army 'preferred remaining in the towns where they had settled and fixed their domicile' to making the long trek back to Damascus.[19] These urban dwellers would have been Arabs, marking in effect the beginning of a permanent Arab Islamic presence in the Peninsula. Initially, the new governor, 'Abd al-'Azīz, a son of Mūsā, left in charge of al-Andalus by his father, made his residence in Seville. The reasons for this choice of location may be readily deduced. Not only was this populous city located on the navigable river Guadalquivir, near to the sea 'and to that part of the coast where the troops coming from Africa usually landed',[20] but it was prosperous and set within a fertile zone. Seville had been the Roman Hispalis, well known for its trade in olive oil which, even as late as the fifteenth century, was recognised by al-Himyarī for its superior quality. Although there were more churches in Cordoba and Toledo, Seville was the metropolitan city of the Peninsula, with two, perhaps three, churches testified as being in existence at that time.[21] One of these may have been the church dedicated to the saints Justa y Rufina, martyred in 287 AD, next to which 'Abd al-'Azīz is said to have had constructed a small mosque. This point may have added significance when one takes into reckoning the marriage of 'Abd al-'Azīz to Egilona, in the Arabic texts Aïla, the widow of Roderic. There is no unanimity in the sources about the relationship of this person to the last Visigothic king, but what is significant is the intermarriage with a member of the indigenous population. It may be regarded as a political union, one of mutual benefit: for 'Abd al-'Azīz, the tie with the former royal line and the consequent hamstringing of dynastic opposition from the defeated regime; and for Egilona, power and influence, taking on an Arabic name in recognition of her position. The sources reveal that 'Abd al-'Azīz was an able governor who deployed his troops in various parts of the Peninsula, including Galicia, Navarra and Aragón, without actually being present in the field. Whilst dwelling in the city, he improved the infrastructure there by causing to be built 'casas mui buenas et mui ricas'.[22] Furthermore, they make it absolutely apparent that there was opposition to him personally, culminating in his assassination in his mosque in 716 at the hands of an Arab, one of those who chose to remain behind after Mūsā's departure, after he had been in sole charge of the Islamic state in the Iberian Peninsula for about two years. Reasons for this hostility are given, but they are by no means uniform. The obvious one is that under the influence of his wife, he was in the throes of denying Islam and becoming an apostate. This is baldly stated in ar-Rāzī's chronicle: 'se apartaron todos á fablar entre si, et dixeron que se tornara christiano, et obieron consejo que lo matassen'.[23] This presumed apostasy would have been understandably resented by Arabs of standing, but as he was at prayer in the mosque at the time of his killing, this seems an unlikely motive. A different motive is propounded in the *Chronicle of 754* whose author alleged that 'Abd al-'Azīz presumed to throw the Arab yoke off his neck and to hold on to the invaded kingdom of Iberia for himself.[24] This is a cogent alternative but the assumption that the Caliph Sulaymān ordered his death from Damascus because he intended to rebel has to remain uncorroborated. In his brief tenure of the office of governor, 'Abd al-'Azīz had consolidated Islamic presence in the Peninsula, extending the area over which the Muslims held sway. As the majority of Arabs who had entered with Mūsā had also departed with him, this achievement would have had to have been accomplished by non-Arab Muslims, to wit principally more Berbers brought in from North Africa, for the express purpose of pursuing the conquests. I will defer until later a discussion of Cordoba which came to be the capital city of al-Andalus, in order now to consider rural settlement.

Rural settlement

The vexed questions of who settled where and in what numbers during the nascent years of al-Andalus are truly awkward to resolve. It is said that Berbers hived themselves off from the original invading forces and settled in favoured locations en route. As the Berbers were far from being a homogeneous group, these settlers would have prompted differing responses from the indigenous communities. The tenth-century traveller and geographer Ibn Hawqal commented that the Berbers who lived in the Maghrib comprised tribes too numerous to quantify, because of the proliferation of branches and families, and the fact that these were scattered far and wide.[25] For example, with Latin-speaking Berbers, of whom there must have been an unspecified number, there would have been no problems of communication, and the remote possibility exists of shared religious beliefs. As the sources do not recount instances of rural upheaval at the time of these initial settlements, one is entitled to speculate that these Berbers, about whom little in reality is known for certain, were soon integrated into their surrounding communities. There was no question of their having formally adopted Islam, neither was there any compunction upon them to do so. One should mention, in addition, that some of these Berbers would have gone to and fro across the Straits from time to time, as their ancestors had done, maintaining communication with their clans and families in North Africa and returning in varying numbers to their acquired locations in the Peninsula. It is probable that these Berbers depended on agriculture or pasturelands for their animals for their living, and lived in areas remote from the main urban centres.

There were also, on the other hand, those who might be termed the Berber collaborators, who had ties with Arab tribes, and whose prominent members Arabicised, and came in the category of *mawālīs*. These Berbers were politically potent and prominent, and settled in fertile regions in considerable but indeterminate numbers. Their power resided in their numerical superiority over the Arabs, particularly after Mūsā's departure for Damascus, their familiarity with Arab governance and their military acumen. In the sources, reference is made to the *baladiyyūn*, 'the people of the land', those who had settled after the first wave of conquest, jealous of their status. Although some sources differentiate between these *baladiyyūn* and Berbers, it makes sense to speculate that their numbers did include some Berber *mawālīs*, some most probably former clients of Mūsā, since their name testifies to their association with the land. The right to possession of land, particularly in the optimal fertile area in the Guadalquivir valley, for example, was a bone of contention, and fanned the flames of strife between Arab Muslims, who strove to retain their superiority within Islam, and the non-Arab Muslims who formed a vast but heterogeneous majority, but within whose ranks there was also much tension and disagreement. If, as may have happened in certain instances, Arabs sought to deprive *mawālīs* of what they perceived to be their legitimate rights of conquest, and to oust them from their newly possessed villages or estates, then the consequences were explosive.

In a helpful study, making use of toponymic evidence, systematically assembled, Taha was able to locate the settlement of Berber tribes in al-Andalus through their adopted Arabic names, and to demonstrate their links with prominent tribal groupings in North Africa.[26] Yet, it is inevitably difficult to distinguish the truly early settlers from those who came later in the century, and so the extent of any Islamicisation in areas away from the large urban centres is by no means beyond dispute. In addition, the evidence of place names is hard to quantify, as one cannot verify with precision when an area came to be known as *iqlīm al-barbār* (the Berber region or province), for example. One may reiterate that an Islamic fiscal system that did impinge annually upon rural communities was soon in place, in part to satisfy the demands on the governor of the province to maintain payments of the Caliphal fifth. Furthermore, all subjects were subject to civil law of the Muslims, but the imposition of an Islamic state affecting those beyond the confines of a city's walls was two centuries away. It may be deduced, then, that, following the estimates of numbers previously given, approximately three-quarters of the population of al-Andalus at this time, making a generous allowance for some *mawālī* settlers, who may be considered an exception, were unaffected by Islam and unaware of the significance of the changes that were occurring in the cities. In sum, the former Hispano-Roman rural population received an injection of immigrants, whose nature, characteristics and language would not have been unfamiliar to some of them, but who, like them, prospered when times were propitious and suffered when conditions were adverse. What, then, did these communities that lived on and off the land have to contend with?

First, and manifestly, were the vagaries of the climate. The physical geography of the Iberian Peninsula has already been introduced, and one may now add to this the fact that as al-Andalus came to comprise mainly the lower two-thirds, the climate there was generally more akin to that of the eastern Mediterranean seaboard: in the main hot and dry, but not intolerably so. The advantage that the Peninsula enjoyed over the East, though, was the fertility of the land in those areas adjacent to the main rivers, notably the Ebro, Duero, Tagus, Guadiana and Guadalquivir. Ibn Hawqal, who visited al-Andalus in 948, and who shows from his writings his awareness of the importance of water for the welfare of a community, noted that the lands were watered in abundance either as a result of the springtime rains, or through the excellence of the well-maintained irrigation systems.[27] There were inevitable periods of drought when tributary river beds became dry, and when cattle needed to be moved to more favourable pasture-land, for example. Harsh winters in the interior also had serious consequences; the freezing winter that is attested in the northern Mediterranean lands, as well as Britannia and Gaul in 763–4, for instance, was cold for long enough to wither olive and fig trees, and may well have affected areas of the Peninsula and have been the direct cause of the famine in the following year.[28] That al-Andalus was not immune from the vicissitudes of extreme climatic conditions is affirmed by Ibn al-Athīr, who mentions the great famine of 822–3 (which may have been in 812–13, as other sources indicate), which no doubt had its origins in unseasonable and unprecedented cold weather.[29] Later in the ninth century, crops in Gaul, Italy and the Iberian Peninsula were devastated by plagues of locusts in 873, to be followed by a severe winter.[30] As extraordinary weather conditions tend to remain in the corporate memory for at least a generation, one can acquire some notion as to the impact of what amounted to natural disasters. By and large, though, the climate in the Peninsula was a temperate one, conducive to good health, as opposed to an unremittingly hot one.

A person's health in a given area depended on the natural resources available. If there was little demographic movement, then, in cases of ailments recourse would be had to local treatments that had often evolved over centuries and had been found to be effective. Epidemics and diseases that threatened to decimate a community's population would emanate from elsewhere and were perennial hazards. Leprosy became prevalent in Europe from about the seventh century, and flourished in the hotter drier areas; malaria was a perpetual danger in the marshlands of river deltas; the greatest threat came from the bubonic plague, known and feared in Western Europe long before the pandemic of the fourteenth century. Travellers noted the relationship between climate and illnesses, and the effect of the climate on human behaviour; from this one may deduce that an understanding of local conditions enabled communities to recognise potential hazards and to take appropriate measures to counteract natural adversity in whatever form it presented itself.

Rural dwellers did not only depend on the land for their livelihood. Thousands would have been involved in mining or quarrying. Differently coloured marble from quarries that are known to have prospered in the Roman period near Seville and Cordoba, and along the southern slopes of the Pyrenees, were in great demand as the Islamic cities expanded. As has been already mentioned, gold, silver, lead, copper and other minerals had all been essential to the economy of Roman Spain. Although some mines, such as the immense copper and silver deposits at Rio Tinto, in the Province of Huelva do not seem to have been exploited in the Islamic period, precious metals were much in demand, not only for coinage. Yet mining took and takes its toll on human life, many skeletons having been discovered in disused galleries, for example. Whether or not those engaged in the production of metals fell under the category of slaves is difficult to determine. In Islam, 'the principle was established that there was to be no taking of captives from amongst Muslims and no enslavement of Muslim Arabs',[31] so slaves came from the ranks of the indigenous population or later, as is well attested, from abroad, 'unbelievers captured in hostile territory'.[32] As much of the submission of territory in al-Andalus was peaceful, then the number of slaves resulting from conquest seems likely to have been limited. One still has to consider, though, working in mines, whether as slaves or not, to have represented a hazardous occupation for thousands of inhabitants of rural areas throughout the medieval period.

The political situation until 756 AD

After the death of 'Abd al-Azīz, the control of al-Andalus was in theory in the hands of a succession of governors (*wālīs*), for until 756 there were many parts of this vast area which paid not much more than lip service to the authority of the governor. Although some occupants of the post of *wālī* were appointed directly by the Caliph in Damascus, and others came from within the ranks of Arabs in al-Andalus, many were appointed by the governor of Ifrīqiyya, to whom they were subordinate, among whom al-Hurr (716/17–19) took the significant step of bringing with him some 400 'men of elevated rank' (*wujūh*). These may be taken to refer to Arabs, according to ar-Rāzī, quoted in al-Maqqarī, who adds that these came to form the basis of Arab nobility in al-Andalus.[33] He also moved the seat of government from Seville to Cordoba, no doubt partly for strategic reasons, as Muslims in Seville resented the transfer of power and authority to this newcomer. An attempt was made to govern the territory in the same manner as Ifrīqiyya had been from Qairawān prior to the invasion of the Peninsula. *Dhimmī* status was offered to Jews and Christians within lands conquered by Muslims; this would mainly have been applicable in urban centres. The foundations of an Islamic state were established, certainly as far as fiscal and legislative matters were concerned; above all, a strong military presence was maintained. One can, I believe, see a parallel between Tāriq's deployment of troops into the Peninsula in 711, and the campaigns led by Muslims beyond the Pyrenees. Both were motivated by the quest and, indeed, need for booty, so that the very large contingents of non-Arab troops could be paid. If they were to remain idle, then they, as military forces billeted on the outskirts of cities may be reckoned to do, would pose a very real threat to the political status quo. So expeditions under able leaders were planned, one to the fastnesses of the Cantabrian Mountains, and the other to lands beyond the Pyrenees. The former, sent to quell an uprising led by Pelayo, a former Visigothic noble and now a local chieftain, culminated in what has come down in history as the battle of Covadonga, perhaps in the year 722 although the date is not certain, but which may well, in reality, have been not much more than a skirmish. The defenders, well placed in mountainous terrain, outnumbered and defeated a small Muslim force comprising less than 100 men, perhaps no more than fifty. In later Latin chronicles, this victory came to be celebrated as a defining moment in history, one which heralded the defiance of Christianity against Islam. At the time, the confrontation had more to do with the desire to retain territorial possession on the part of both protagonists, the efficacy of guerrilla tactics on the part of Pelayo and his followers winning the day.

Of greater significance were the transpyrenean incursions. 'Anbasa, *wālī* between 721 and 726, a lengthy period for a governor, personally led troops into Gaul, capturing the cities of Carcassonne and Nîmes, and penetrating as far north as Autun. As *wālī*, he was authorised to act on his own initiative, extending the boundaries, keeping his forces deployed, acquiring booty and ensuring that a fifth of everything gained was returned to the Caliph in Damascus. The *Chronicle of 754* is important as it documents events within a generation of its having been written, but it is couched in a particularly complex Latin which makes interpretation of it notoriously problematic. Furthermore, it is often has conflicting or irreconcilable information that renders its reliability as a source suspect. In the two brief paragraphs that relate to 'Anbasa, the *Chronicle* provides an instance of conflictive information. He was exceedingly successful in conquering all parts of the Peninsula (Spanias) whilst in office, annoying the Christians with the burden of double taxation.[34] The increased toll on the non-Muslims was presumably necessary in order to underwrite the cost of the expeditions. Yet this explanation is not entirely satisfactory in the light of what might be called the policy of self-financing these campaigns through the booty acquired. It seems probable that the Christians upon whom the burden of taxation fell were those who were recognisable as such, that is to say those who lived in urban zones. It is inconceivable that sufficient personnel could have been mustered within what must have been a short period of time, to organise the extra levy on the rural communities whose adherence to any of the revealed religions in any case is doubtful. The author of the *Chronicle*, possibly a churchman from Cordoba or Toledo, would simply have had little or no knowledge of life or events beyond the very narrow confines of his daily urban existence.

In the 730s, perhaps between the years 730 and 732, for the sources are by no means uniform on the dates, the then *wālī* Al-Ghāfiqī reactivated the policy of expeditions into Gaul, the country of the Franks. To the Muslims settled in al-Andalus for coming up to fifteen years, warmongering such a long distance from Cordoba and Seville, out of aggressive and not defensive motives, carried certain messages. A successful campaign thousands of miles from one's home base had immense propaganda value, conferring great kudos on the victor, as it had done in the Roman era. Defeat, on the other hand, as occurred when Al-Ghāfiqī was routed by Charles Martel, the grandfather of Charlemagne, at Moussais la Bataille near Poitiers, probably in 732, meant no more than a replacement governor and a change in regime. Al-Ghāfiqī's expedition had been a particularly well-planned and enterprising one, the route chosen being through Bordeaux and the western part of present-day France. The earlier campaigns had all been through Provence and inland following the river Rhône to the west of the Massif Central. By mischance, for the people of al-Andalus, country and town dweller alike, the new governor, an appointee of the Caliph in Damascus, 'Abd al-Malik b. Qatan, does not seem to have revived their fortunes. The author of the *Chronicle of 754*, in a paragraph replete with incidental details but obscurely worded, implies that he (Ibn Qatan), through repressive policies stretching over a period of four years, weakened and isolated al-Andalus. When he arrived, Al-Andalus (*Spania* in the Latin text) was blessed with prosperity after or despite all the dangers (*pericula*) to which it had been exposed, and flourishing, after or despite so much woe (*tantos dolores*). The language is somewhat poetically phrased, but through this, one may detect not only a knowledge of previous political unrest but also a recognition of the inherent fertility of al-Andalus. Furthermore, the author was evidently aware of the distress among the people who would have suffered the brunt of the dangers. Since he was not writing from the standpoint of an Arab nobleman, he may be reflecting the sufferings of non-Muslims, both urban and rural. One might venture the view that the brief sentences analysed above demonstrate that the agricultural economy had continued to flourish after the conquest. Only from other sources is it possible to deduce that the perils were inflicted from within.

Ibn Qatan did indeed in person lead an expedition to the Pyrenees, but this seems to have been done with some reluctance, and the campaign seems to have been futile. The author of the Latin chronicle may be implicitly mocking the Arab governor for leading his troops through narrow passes, where, one assumes, they could not be effectively deployed. He paints a brief picture of them flailing around and suffering huge losses in the process. This kind of enterprise does not seem to square with the carefully planned military operations that had seen such success in the Occident in the previous twenty years. If credence can be given to the admittedly elliptical account of this fiasco, then one has to attribute the blame to the governor. One further detail may be instructive. The author mentions Ibn Qatan's return to his country on byways (*repatriando per devia*), in other words, steering clear of the main roads. If this was the case, then he must have intended to avoid the principal cities between the Pyrenees and Cordoba, where in victorious circumstances, he might have expected to have been received with pomp and honour. As it was, a picture is painted of him skulking back to base with his bedraggled troops across sparsely populated plains, not wishing his failures to be made known. Clearly, such a journey would have been circuitous, and perhaps have lasted twice as long as one on the old Roman roads. Anyone viewing this retreat would not have been impressed, and would certainly not have seen sufficient evidence to attract allegiance to the governor.

It may be an overstatement to say that there was political turmoil at this time, but certainly there is little evidence of any unified acceptance of one Islamic authority. Until the 750s, the emphasis, as far as successive governors were concerned, was on pursuing military conquest, rather than the establishment of a viable, operational Islamic state. Different Arab families were settled in cities far apart from one another, and were virtually autonomous. The rural population remained largely unaware of, and indifferent to, urban power struggles. This situation of unease changed into one of unrest in the 740s, when a revolt initiated by Berbers in North Africa spilled over into al-Andalus. The circumstances are somewhat confusing and confused, but it is possible to construct a certain narrative. The Berbers in the Maghrib, a federation of disparate clans all nominally subject to the Muslim governor in Qayrawān, resented being treated as what amounted to being second-class citizens within Islam. Their leader, Maysara, complained that Berber troops were always placed at the front line of battle, and that they were not allocated their just share of the booty. Further details of abuse that occur in more than one Arab source relate to the slaughtering of amber (honey)-coloured (*'asalī*) ewes in order to secure the skins of the unborn lambs, and to the seizure of young girls, both to be sent to the Caliph. The enigma of the first petition is far from having been solved. Had the Caliph heard of a breed of sheep, the forbears of the Tunisian Barbary, perhaps, whose lambs are reddish at birth, and did he request the hides for the wool? This seems bizarre given the nature of the Damascene climate. Had he been informed that the hide of the unborn lambs of this breed was remarkable in some way? The *Akhbār*

Majmūʿa records that 100 ewes were slaughtered, with not one (satisfactory) hide being found. In pragmatic terms, the Berbers would have resented the loss of a flock of sheep on such an apparently arbitrary whim, but this hardly seems to have been enough to spark off a revolt, even if one adds the unjustifiable abduction of young women. One should also add that the Berbers may have had just cause if their rights as Muslims were being infringed or denied them, but this attributed motive is founded on the by no means secure assumption that they were at least in part Muslims.

The revolt, however, did materialise, and Maysara inflicted a substantial defeat on the Arab army assembled at Tangier. Harsh retribution was exacted, and the surviving Arabs, mainly Syrians under their commander Balj ibn Bishr who had been dispatched by the Caliph to quell the rebellion, along with his uncle who was killed in the engagement, took refuge in Ceuta. The sequence of events is not entirely apparent, but the statement in al-Maqqarī that 'the Berbers of Andalus, having heard of the victories which their brethren in Africa had gained over the Arabs, shook off all allegiance to the Moslems of Andalus, and imitated in every respect the example of their countrymen'[35] aptly summarises events in 740–1. One might ask why Berbers, who had settled peaceably among the indigenous population some thirty years previously, now felt themselves impelled to bury their tribal differences, to collect themselves into a combined force and to converge upon principal cities such as Toledo, with the overt intention to expel the Arab Muslims from the Peninsula? One may reflect at this point that many Berbers who had settled in the Peninsula still retained close ties with their places of origin in North Africa. Any threat to the livelihood of Maghribī Berbers would have soon become known to their counterparts in al-Andalus, and the latter likewise would have been aware of the oppression of the Arab Muslim authorities. Resentment at what were perceived to be unjust measures against them would have spread among Berber communities. If there was a nominal adherence to Islam, then the fact that they were not treated as equal to other (Arab) Muslims would have soon been realised. One might add that they were emulating the previous generation of Berbers who, in the 680s and 690s, had fought tooth and nail to stem the tide of Muslim advance, and were simply reverting to instinct in wanting to slough off the yoke of being beholden to another power. It seems unlikely, though, that this desire to express solidarity with beleaguered kinsfolk was a sufficient catalyst to trigger such a widespread uprising. At a time coinciding with the Berber revolt, Ibn Qatan, who had earlier been deposed, was once again elevated to the governorship of al-Andalus, on this occasion not on the appointment of the Caliph, nor that of the governor in Qairawān, but internally, by Arabs in al-Andalus. He was now elderly, but nonetheless willing, as events show, to make independent decisions. He initially refrained from assisting Balj and his Syrian troops cooped up in Ceuta, no doubt a politically motivated assessment of the crisis, because he was wary of giving succour to a large number of Arabs of uncertain allegiance on the other side of the Straits. One may surmise that he recognised that his defences were being stretched, as what effective militia he had at his disposal in al-Andalus were being deployed to meet the internal menace of the Berbers in revolt. The Berbers in the Peninsula had asserted their control in Galicia and Astorga, and giving a wide berth to Saragossa, where defences were well marshalled, swept through present-day Extremadura in an inexorable tide southwards, reaching as far as the river Tagus, and posing a real threat to the governorship. At this stage, Arab Islamic hold on al-Andalus was tenuous, but further reinforcements sent by the ailing Caliph in the East bolstered the contingent of Balj. It is not clear the extent to which Ibn Qatan benefited from Syrian troops in his quelling of the Berber insurrection, as the sources provide conflictive details and some data cannot be reconciled.[36] The decisive victory, maybe near Algeciras – the venue seems the likeliest because of its proximity to the North African coast – prevented the Berbers of al-Andalus from combining with those of North Africa, but it came at a price. Whatever the nature of the disagreement between Ibn Qatan and Balj, the former was put to death by the latter who presided over the Syrians who had accompanied him on the campaigns.

The level of violence was high, but it was internecine, Arab against Arab, reflecting similar conflict in the East. Attitudes within Islam became polarised in the seventh century, during which it has been maintained that the Yaman group of Arabs essentially argued in favour of an agenda of assimilation of subject peoples with Islam, whereas the Qays, mainly though not exclusively Syrian clans, forcibly opposed this stance.[37] These are imprecise geographic terms, not coinciding with the confines of the modern states. If this political division is valid, and there are contrary views, then the policies of Yaman served the Empire well at the height of its expansion, as large numbers of non-Arab Muslims, and indeed non-Muslims, performed invaluable services on behalf of the state. Concessions needed to be made, but the benefits of integrating non-Arabs into Islam and thereby securing their collaboration at an early period outweighed the disadvantages. The Qays, on the other hand, sought to deny privileges to non-Arabs, adopting what might be termed an exploitative in preference to an integrationist policy. This became an ideological feud which disrupted the regime of the Umayyad Caliphate in the East, and was to have grave repercussions in al-Andalus. When the Caliphate was overthrown in 750, it was revived and perpetuated in al-Andalus after 756. One should emphasise that this was not a Sunna–Sh'ia conflict, but a fundamental schism within those who accepted the *sunna*. In al-Andalus, what is known and what may be discerned from the settlement patterns would suggest that differences paralleling those of the East were present from an early stage, and exacerbated after the Berber rebellion, when many of Balj's followers remained in the Peninsula. These latter, mainly Syrian Arabs (*shāmiyyūn*) and possibly amounting to between 8,000 and 10,000 in number, acted as a form of superstructure above a kaleidoscopic demographic landscape. In the aftermath of the conquest, clans from Yaman had settled in or around a number of prominent cities including Saragossa, Seville, Toledo and Murcia. Subsequent to the influx in the 740s, Syrian *junds* (large bodies of soldiers) were settled in Seville, possibly in substantial numbers, in Niebla and in areas beyond the sierras, in locations such as Elvira, later Granada, and Jaén. These *junds* were later identified as administrative districts, within which those who had been located there had both privileges and obligations. If one adds to this that there still remained substantial Berber clusters, then the cauldron may be said to have been permanently smouldering.

In the confusion that followed in the wake of Balj's death, there was a period of near political anarchy in al-Andalus. The Syrian faction in Cordoba elected their own successor to Balj, evidently not accepted by the earliest Arab settlers; alliances were made between Arab and non-Arab Muslims; Berber prisoners were herded together for mass execution in Cordoba. The arrival of a new appointee as governor, the last from the East, heralded a calmer period, when attempts were made to appease the warring factions through patient diplomacy rather than drastic measures. Nevertheless, after two years, a new governor took over, and the simmering hostility between the Yaman and the Syrians erupted into a civil war. Rivalry was tribal, and revenge exacted in a brutal manner, what came to be customary in inter-tribal conflict. It is a particularly complex task to compile a narrative that assimilates the bewildering details of some of the Arab sources relating to the events leading up to the advent of the Umayyad Prince 'Abd ar-Rahmān into al-Andalus in 756. The governor between 747 and 756 was Yūsuf al-Fihrī, a descendant of a distinguished Qays family that had entered the Peninsula with Mūsā, though brought up in Ifrīqiyya. The *Akhbār Majmū'a* states that the people of al-Andalus agreed on him as their ruler, perhaps in part because of his age – he was at that time in his fifties. At the same time, this very account implies that he was a puppet in the hands of as-Sumayl, his so-called right-hand man, and one of those who had been sent with the army to quell the Berber rebellion. Nonetheless, al-Fihrī sent as-Sumayl to the Upper March to overcome the Yaman faction of long standing in Saragossa. Whether this was done in order to keep as-Sumayl away from the seat of government in Cordoba may only be surmised, but he seems to have been a reluctant ally, and they were later reconciled in Cordoba. They may have joined forces in order to meet the crisis posed by the presence on the north coast of Africa of 'Abd ar-Rahmān b. Mu'āwiya.

In more than one source, reference is made to famines in al-Andalus during the governorship of al-Fihrī. The details are worth recording: for the year 132 (August 749 to August 750), according to the *Akhbār Majmū'a*, 'God inflicted famine and drought on them, and al-Andalus starved'; 'in 133, the year was auspicious'. These adjacent phrases could reflect the view that, in the author's eyes, famine was a justified punishment inflicted by God in retribution for sins committed, remitted in the year following owing to good (better) behaviour, but there has to be a speculation.

> In 136 [July 753 to June 754], famine overcame them, and the Muslims were also dislodged from Astorga and other places; the people withdrew down other mountain passes to Coria and to Mérida, and the famine became more intense, such that the people of al-Andalus went to Tangiers, Asīla and the Berber Rif. They called these years the years of Barbate; the human habitations [sakān] of al-Andalus were fewer, and the enemy would have defeated them had not hunger also afflicted them as well.

From this, although not all the information is consequential, one may deduce that this was a drought throughout the lower two-thirds of the Peninsula, affecting all areas of al-Andalus as well as Astorga just on the edge of the sierras to the west of León, and causing many aspects of life both rural and urban to languish as a result. Some of the people crossing to present-day Morocco were probably Berbers who had settled and whose ancestors had crossed the Straits from time immemorial. Whether they had cattle to take with them may have depended on the distance that they had to travel in al-Andalus. If the distances were large, then one may assume that cattle had died, crops had failed and that this was their last resort. This hypothesis would seem to be supported by the reference to what may be regarded as the abandonment of their dwellings on the part of the rural population. One of the reasons why the Muslims were obliged to flee from Astorga was that Alfonso I (739–57), who had taken advantage of the political chaos caused by the Berber uprisings, had made substantial incursions into what had been loosely held Muslim territory, taking control of large tracts of land down as far as and even beyond the river Duero. The Arabic source quoted above may be conflating two historical realities: the depredations of Alfonso and the natural calamities owing to adverse climatic conditions. Perhaps, indeed, the author is seeking to blame the humiliating withdrawal of the Muslims from the north of the Peninsula in the 750s on the weather. The description of Muslims going southwards through 'other mountain passes' would seem to suggest a retreat in the face of a physical enemy, rather than evasion of natural disasters. One may also pick up on the detail relating to the river Barbate, presumably mentioned because the exodus to North Africa was made by boats from the river mouth. Yet, the Barbate is one of the lesser rivers that run into the Atlantic in the present-day province of Cádiz, and the distance of the crossing between there and Tangier is twice that of the Tarifa–Tangier route. This would lead one to suppose that the gathering of refugees there was so momentous as to warrant special mention for posterity. When one reflects that it lies almost due south of an imaginary line from Astorga through Coria, Mérida and Seville to the Atlantic coast whence to embark to North Africa, the inevitable conclusion is that the majority of the fugitives were from the western reaches of al-Andalus. For half a decade, then, it was not only civil war that wrought havoc on the Arabs in al-Andalus. If the urban life of the Muslims was rocked to its foundation, the rural communities fared no better, as they had to bear the inexorable brunt of drought and famine.

Notes

1. Pedro Chalmeta, *Invasión e Islamización. La sumisión de Hispania y la formación de al-Andalus*, Madrid: Editorial Mapre, 1994, p. 95.
2. H. V. Livermore, *The Origins of Spain and Portugal*, London: George Allen & Unwin, 1971, p. 261.
3. Ahmed ibn Mohammed al-Makkari, *The History of the Mohammedan Dynasties in Spain*, translated by Pascual de Gayangos, 2 vols, London: RoutledgeCurzon, 2002, vol. I, p. 262. The currently accepted form of his name is al-Maqqarī, which will be used henceforth throughout the endnotes. The Arabic text used is *Analectes sur l'Histoire et la Littérature des Arabes d'Espagne par al-Makkari*, edited by R. Dozy et al., 2 vols, Amsterdam: Oriental Press, 1967, a facsimile of the Leiden edition of 1855–61.
4. Al-Maqqarī, *History of the Mohammedan Dynasties*, vol. I, p. 268.
5. Ibn al-Kardabūs, *Historia de al-Andalus (Kitāb al-Iktifā')*, translated with notes by Felipe Maíllo Salgado, Madrid: Akal, 1986, p. 60.
6. Joaquín Vallvé, *Nuevas ideas sobre la conquista de España. Topinimia y Onomástica*, Madrid: Real Academia de la Historia, 1989, particularly pp. 103–18.
7. Pedro Chalmeta, *Invasión e Islamización*, pp. 198–201.
8. E. Lévi-Provençal, *La Péninsule Ibérique au moyen-âge d'après le Kitāb ar-Rawd al-miʿtār fī habār al-aktār d'Ibn ʿAbd al-Munʿim al-Himyarī*, Leiden: E. J. Brill, 1938, p. 20; Arabic text pp. 13–14.
9. Emilio Lafuente y Alcántara, *Ajbar Machmuâ (Colección de tradiciones) Crónica anónima del siglo XI, dada á luz por primera vez*, Madrid: Ediciones Atlas, 1984, p. 23; Arabic text, p. 9. Facsimile of the 1867 edition.
10. Al-Maqqarī, *History of the Mohammedan Dynasties*, vol. I, p. 275.
11. Ad-Dabbī, *Bughyat al-multamis fī tārīkh rijāl ahl-al-Andalus*, edited by Francisco Codera, Leiden: Brill, 1889 (Biblioteca Arabico-Hispana, vol. III), p. 259; English translation by Olivia Remie Constable in *Medieval Iberia. Readings from Christian, Muslim, and Jewish Sources*, Philadelphia, PA: University of Pennsylvania Press, 1997, pp. 37–8. Details of further texts in Arabic and Spanish together with an analysis is to be found in this author's *Mozarabs in Medieval and early Modern Spain. Identities and Influences*, Aldershot: Ashgate, 2008, pp. 15–16. See also Alfred M. Howell, 'Some notes on early treaties between Muslims and the Visigothic rulers of al-Andalus', in *Actas del I Congreso de Historia de Andalucía*, Cordoba: Monte de Piedad y Caja de Ahorros, vol. I, 1978, pp. 3–14.
12. Jacques Fontaine, *L'Art Mozarabe. L'Art Préroman Hispanique II*, Paris: Zodiaque, 1977, Collection 'La nuit des temps', vol. 47, pp. 61–80.
13. See Richard Hitchcock, *Mozarabs in Medieval and Early Modern Spain. Identities and Influences*, Aldershot: Ashgate, 2008, xiv.
14. Ibn al-Kardabūs, *Historia de al-Andalus*, p. 65.
15. For example, *Ibn al-Kardabūs, p. 67.*
16. Lévi-Provençal, *La Péninsule Ibérique au moyen-âge*, pp. 157–62; Arabic text, pp. 130–4.
17. Leonard A. Curchin, *Roman Spain. Conquest and Assimilation*, London: Routledge, 1991, p. 117.

18. Lévi-Provençal, *La Péninsule Ibérique au moyen-âge*, pp. 118–20.
19. Al-Maqqarī, *History of the Mohammedan Dynasties*, vol. I, p. 292.
20. Ibid., p. 292.
21. Archdale A. King, *Liturgies of the Primatial Sees*, London: Longmans, Green, 1957, p. 466; Rafael Puertas Tricas, *Iglesias hispánicas (siglos IV al VIII). Testimonios literarios*, Madrid: Patronato Nacional de Museos, 1975, pp. 55–6.
22. Don Pascual de Gayangos, *Memoria sobre la autenticidad de la Crónica denominada del Moro Rasis*, Madrid: La Real Academia de la Historia, 1850, p. 80. This is a translation of Ahmad ar-Rāzī (887–?961), *Tarīkh mulūk al-Andalus*, an important source.
23. Ibid., p. 82.
24. Latin text in Ioannes Gil, *Corpus Scriptorum Muzarabicorum*, 2 vols, Madrid: Consejo Superior de Investigaciones Científicas, 1973, vol. I, pp. 15–54; *Conquerors and Chroniclers of Early Medieval Spain*, translated with notes and introduction by Kenneth Baxter Wolf, Liverpool: Liverpool University Press, 1990, pp. 111–77, at p. 135.
25. Ibn Hawqal, *Configuración del mundo*, translated with notes by María José Romani Suay, Valencia: Anúbar, 1971, p. 53. Textos Medievales, 26.
26. A. D. Taha, *The Muslim Conquest and Settlement of North Africa and Spain*, London: Routledge, 1989.
27. Ibn Hawqal, *Configuración del mundo*, p. 69.
28. Chronicle of Moissac, as quoted in Michael McCormick et al., 'Volcanoes and the Climate Forcing of Carolingian Europe, A.D. 750–950', *Speculum* 82 (2007), 865–95, at 879–80.
29. Ibid., 883.
30. Ibid., 886.
31. Reuben Levy, *The Social Structure of Islam*, Cambridge: Cambridge University Press, 1962, p. 75.
32. Ibid., p. 75.
33. Al-Maqqarī, *History of the Mohammedan Dynasties*, vol II, p. 32.
34. Gil, *Corpus Scriptorum*, vol. I, p. 39.
35. Al-Maqqarī, *History of the Mohammedan Dynasties*, vol. II, p. 41.
36. For example, the *Akhbār Majmū'a*, the *Nafh at-tīb* of al-Maqqarī and the *Chronicle of 754*.
37. M. A. Shaban, *Islamic History A. D. 600–750 (A. H. 132). A New Interpretation*, Cambridge: Cambridge University Press, 1971, pp. 120–4.

CHAPTER 2

The establishment of the Umayyad state in al-Andalus – the ninth century

One of the reasons for the tension in al-Andalus between al-Fihrī and as-Sumayl, and within Arab factions, in the early 750s was the knowledge of the proximity of 'Abd ar-Rahmān b. Mu'āwiya across the other side of the Straits. He was an Umayyad prince who had escaped the slaughter when the 'Abbāsids had overthrown the Umayyad state in 750. Calling on support from Umayyads and their clients as he traversed North Africa, he first tried to establish a foothold in Ifrīqiyya, but when this became impossible, he looked further west, towards al-Andalus, as there was no possibility of turning back eastwards. After months of negotiation with the different factions in al-Andalus, in what became vain attempts to gain support, as well as making treaties with Berbers, 'Abd ar-Rahmān and his retinue landed at Almuñécar in 755. Some sources deal with these events in intricate and often dramatic detail, but several observations may be made. One ship was sufficient, which would indicate that the prince, known as *ad-dākhil* (the incomer or entrant), had few accompanying him and was counting on attracting recruits from allies within al-Andalus. Furthermore, Almuñécar, an isolated coastal village east of the city of Málaga, was selected as a disembarkation point enabling him to meet with conspirators at the nearby village of Torrox, prior to making his way, via Elvira, to Cordoba, gathering support en route. At this stage, the importance of the weather conditions becomes apparent from the sources. Al-Maqqarī relates that there had been famine in the previous six years and 'the people were greatly debilitated from want of food'; the soldiers had to subsist on 'herbs and plants that they found on the road, officers and rich men faring not much better'.[1] These graphic details may mask a more prosaic reality – the *Akhbār Majmū'a* specifically states that the soldiery subsisted on green beans – but clearly there was hardship among the entire population, caused by lack of food. The writer then goes to mention that the Guadalquivir was in spate and overflowing its banks in certain areas. From this one may infer that there was loss of crops and ravaged pasture lands. Once the waters receded, though, there would be normal harvests the following year and the promise of more favourable conditions. Crises caused by an adverse climate cannot be underestimated. The sources record, with some differences, the great deprivation that the people of al-Andalus underwent at that time. This was compounded by a state of what seemed to be incessant conflict. Furthermore, if there was not enough food to go round, then what there was would be for the sustenance of the troops. The situation was dire.

Al-Fihrī, the governor, was in Toledo when he was made aware of the threat to his position. With as-Sumayl, he took up a position outside Cordoba, prepared to confront 'Abd ar-Rahmān, who had now mustered support from within al-Andalus. A snippet of information in the *Akhbār Majmūʿa* is here instructive. Al-Fihrī ordered sheep and cows to be brought out and slaughtered in anticipation of a feast in which both armies (*ʿaskarain*) could participate 'because they did not doubt that peace could be achieved'. One may presume that he brought the cattle with him from the central and northern parts of the Peninsula, where the effects of the drought had not been so severe. Perhaps he reasoned that the enticement of a reconciliatory meal would be an attractive proposition for famished troops. Whatever his intentions, which showed an awareness of the physical hardship being endured by communities in the south of al-Andalus and by the opposing troops, his entreaties fell on deaf ears. The battle took place the next day; after being defeated, he and his companions were forced to flee and regroup. As a codicil, it may be mentioned that the victorious forces of 'Abd ar-Rahmān, after they had overcome al-Fihrī, partook of the meal that he had prepared for their joint consumption. Opposition from the two Andalusi leaders continued sporadically, mainly from the eastern area of the Peninsula and from Toledo, but on their death, 'Abd ar-Rahmān was able to start on the lengthy process of fashioning al-Andalus into an Umayyad state.

He was known as *amīr* (prince), not only distinguishing him from his predecessors who were simply *wālīs* (governors), but also *ipso facto* putting out a marker that he was founding a dynasty. His state was an Umayyad state, and therefore founded on traditional Islamic principles, and fundamentally opposed to that of the 'Abbāsids in the East. Henceforward, the values that had served the Umayyads were to be echoed and perpetuated in the Islamic west. Nonetheless, 'Abd ar-Rahmān's priorities had to be to ensure the security of his state, and one source, the *Akhbār Majmūʿa*, itemises a succession of ten rebellions, some more serious than others, in various parts of the Peninsula, all of which he was obliged to quell. One may look for the causes of these risings in the different Arab and Berber factions endeavouring to prevent their authority from being eroded by this Saker Falcon of the Quraysh, the soubriquet by which he was known among the 'Abbāsids, used to describe someone who was a swift and devastating hunter. It is hardly to be wondered at that one of the most significant threats was the 'Abbāsid attempt to oust him from power. This was to be achieved by the governor of Ifrīqiyya who drew on disaffected factions in al-Andalus, but who was ultimately outwitted and defeated by 'Abd ar-Rahmān in 768. One of the most intriguing episodes recorded by both Latin and Arabic sources concerns the interventions of Charlemagne (?742–814) into Peninsular affairs. In the early summer of 778, he led an army to Saragossa, which may be considered to have been the principal city of the Upper March (*thaghr al-a'lā*), although Pamplona and Tudela were also significant, and besieged the city. These *thughūr* were frontier zones between al-Andalus and the northern kingdoms. The main cities of the Middle March (*thaghr al-awsat*), which stretched approximately across the upper centre of the Peninsula, were Toledo and Medinaceli, whilst Mérida directed operations towards the north-west on the Lower March (*thaghr al-aqsā*, literally 'remote'; possibly it opened access to the most distant places). The importance of Saragossa on the Upper March was that that it was strategically located on the river Ebro and was a convenient starting-off point for expeditions beyond the Pyrenees by both the western and eastern routes.

Charlemagne was eager to pursue his ambition for territorial gain beyond the Pyrenees, and may have been encouraged by a mission from the 'Abbāsid Caliph al-Mahdī, ever anxious to secure the overthrow of the Umayyad 'Abd ar-Rahmān. It is not known how this delegation travelled; perhaps they went across the Mediterranean by sea, landing at a spot in the present-day Côte d'Azur, in order to avoid the well-trodden route through the hostile Iberian Peninsula. Nor, indeed, is it known how they communicated; they perhaps had an interpreter in their retinue, but embassies between great powers were often a prelude to deals or treaties in their mutual interest. Charlemagne had no reason to believe that his campaign beyond the Pyrenees would be anything other than a cakewalk. He had not anticipated opposition within the city and was either unable or unwilling to raise the siege. Indeed, there is some suggestion that he had expected or had been led to believe that the Arab commander of Saragossa would welcome him and hand over the city to him, making common cause against the Umayyad *amīr*. When he realised that, with the armaments he had at his disposal, he would not be able to breach the defences of the walled city, or perhaps because he had received information concerning a crisis within his own Frankish territory, he withdrew. He encountered opposition from Arab factions, and also from the Basques, at the hands of whom he suffered a resounding defeat on his retreat. This event was celebrated in the twelfth-century epic poem, *La Chanson de Roland*, much embellished by legend. If Charlemagne destroyed the walls of the city of Pamplona en route, in retaliation against the Basques who had allied themselves with his Arab opponents, then this would have provided ample motivation for the Basques to exact their revenge. It may be seen that there was no religious ingredient in this episode. Two powerful states, one Muslim, one Christian, made a political compact to their mutual advantage, irrespective of religion.

In 781, 'Abd ar-Rahmān led an expedition to Saragossa in order to secure the last of the major regions within his territory, the final major campaign of his amirate. After a siege, he negotiated with the governor of the city, and took his son as hostage. According to another source, he ordered the execution of the rebel leaders. He then took his army westward along the banks of the Ebro, proceeding via Calahorra to Viguera in la Rioja, and then wheeling north to Pamplona and beyond to the Basque country, destroying fortresses en route. What is interesting is that this strategy seems to have been undertaken to establish the frontier zone (*thaghr*) against the Frankish kingdom and its satellites in the Pyrenean region. Furthermore, 'Abd ar-Rahmān was not reluctant to enter mountainous areas, evidence that he was not wholly reliant on cavalry which would have been ineffective among rocky hills and passes. As a postscript, an Arabic source mentions a subsequent letter, perhaps written in 781, from Charlemagne in Aquitaine to 'Abd ar-Rahmān in Cordoba – although he may have sent a delegation – proposing a matrimonial alliance, a standard prelude to the cessation of hostilities. If there had been such an overture on Charlemagne's part, then it would indicate both a recognition of 'Abd a-Rahmān's autonomy and control of the frontier region as well as a rejection of 'Abbāsid claims to al-Andalus.

It is clear that all of 'Abd ar-Rahmān's military activity points to his determination not only to maintain power but also to shape an Umayyad state in al-Andalus. The Arabic sources tend to concentrate on this aspect, together with the politics of the period, at times bewilderingly complex. However, there are references to other features of the period of 'Abd ar-Rahmān's reign (756–88), from which a picture of sorts emerges. A passage in al-Maqqarī quoting an earlier historian, Ibn Sa'īd of the thirteenth century, describes how the *amīr* built the palace of Rusāfa in the north of the city of Cordoba at the beginning of his reign. The striking feature of the palace was to be its garden, the water for which he is said to have provided via an aqueduct from the nearby sierra. Thereby trees, plants and fruit such as the pomegranate were propagated and established. The whole precinct was to echo the Umayyad palace in the East, an indication that what was to take root in al-Andalus was not simply an Islamic prototype but an Umayyad Islamic prototype. This precinct we only know of through written accounts, as it has not survived; all that has survived from his era is the earliest part of the Great Mosque. This is a further instance of the centre of the Umayyad state in Damascus being reflected in the Occident, and a reminder that 'Abd ar-Rahmān was determined to leave this imprint in al-Andalus. He ordered this mosque to be constructed on the site of the sixth-century basilica of San Vicente, previously perhaps a Roman temple, which some sources reveal was purchased for the purpose. Whether the church was then demolished allowing for the construction of the mosque is not known for certain, but it seems reasonable to suppose that the architects would have allowed the formidable outer walls of the basilica to remain intact. One may imagine that these walls were left standing, as their extraordinary breadth of perhaps six feet would have been recognised for their practical function as defensive potential. Large walled areas which could house the majority of the population in times of hostile assaults were an essential aspect of a city's defences, and the site of the mosque, just a stone's throw from the Roman bridge, was ideally suited to this objective. 'Abd ar-Rahmān's original mosque, constructed within this outer courtyard, was later enlarged and embellished by succeeding *amīr*s and caliphs, but if the project was started in 785 or 786, it is unlikely – though not impossible – that it would have been completed by the time of his death in 788. It comprised eleven aisles made up of ten rows of columns which supported horseshoe arches and, above these, a further tier of semicircular arches to provide height. The columns were made of marble of various colours used in edifices in Roman times, brought to Cordoba from a number of venues from within the Peninsula and from other Mediterranean lands. The capitals employed at this time were also pre-existing, and some seem not quite to rest exactly on the columns on which they stand. The abiding and defining feature of the original mosque, and one carried forward in subsequent extensions, is the alternate terracotta and cream-coloured brickwork of the horseshoe arches. It should be noted that there is an alternation of lighter and darker colours, though nothing like as pronounced, in the aqueduct at Mérida which may have been familiar to architects and builders. As for the horseshoe arch itself, it may be discerned in a primitive form in some of the Visigothic churches in the north of the Peninsula, but the strikingly distinctive nature of the form of the arch in the mosque at Cordoba suggests a familiarity with an altogether more sophisticated model. As there are no exact parallels in the Umayyad East, no ready solution to the much-debated subject of the origin of this form of the arch in its Cordoban expression suggests itself. It may have been the case that 'Abd ar-Rahmān imported skilled architects and artisans from among his former Umayyad acquaintances; when in al-Andalus, they would have absorbed and developed local knowledge and techniques. One may endorse the measured conclusion of Henri Terrasse that 'the first Umayyad building [in al-Andalus] provided a happy synthesis of Syrian forms and Hispanic traditions, above all affirming a powerful originality'.[2] In sum, then, 'Abd ar-Rahmān gave the initial impetus to what was to become one of the most remarkable monuments of Islam. His initiative provided an area that was set aside only for Muslims; it could be used for devotional practices, for the purposes of which one wall indicated the *qibla* (direction), where prayer could be directed toward the Ka'aba in Mecca. The elaborate *mihrāb*, or prayer niche, was later placed in this wall. There was no minaret at this time and therefore no public announcement of the hour of prayer, which would suggest that what was of immediate concern to 'Abd ar-Rahmān was the cohesion of the Muslims within the city, rather than the proclamation of Islam to all its inhabitants. Above all, he created a monument, an object of pride, decorative and distinctive as well as functional, something that his successors both revered and sought to enrich, as a lasting emblem of the Umayyad dynasty.

Regarding 'Abd ar-Rahmān's importance in the creation of the Islamic state of al-Andalus, it is possible to piece together fragments from various sources.

One has to look beyond the unadorned statements by the respected historian ar-Rāzī that 'he performed many good acts that were advantageous for the country ... good things that would be a wonder to relate'; and that when he died, there was 'deep grief among old and young, great and small throughout Spain'.[3] The institutions that he set in place were the Umayyad ones to which he and his followers had been used in the East. The most significant position concerning the governance of the state was that of *qāḍī*, or judge, a post created specifically by the Umayyads for the administration of justice within Islam, and in place in Cordoba prior to 'Abd ar-Rahmān's arrival. It was natural, therefore, that the *qāḍī* should be at the centre of the legislative framework in al-Andalus. His remit covered only Muslims and not those of other creeds; his was an urban appointment, and he could be transferred from any town or city to Cordoba. He listened to petitions, gave judgments and imposed penalties in the Great Mosque after the Friday hour of prayer. There exists an excellent anecdotal source for the judges in Cordoba by the tenth-century writer al-Khushanī, from which valuable information relating to the early judges in the city may be drawn. 'Abd ar-Rahmān appointed three *qāḍī*s during his reign, and one can glean glimpses of society and politics from the written account of their periods of tenure. The first of these, Mu'āwiya b. Sālih, was from a prominent Syrian family which had settled in Seville before the *amīr*'s arrival, and was renowned as a religious scholar, that is to say as someone who had a knowledge of Islam and its traditions, *hadīth*. Indeed, it is said that Mālik b. Anas (who was in his eighties when he died in 796), whose legislative system – known as the Māliki law school – was officially adopted in al-Andalus by 'Abd ar-Rahmān's successors, and therefore fundamental to an appreciation of law there, consulted him when he was in the East, on one of the two occasions that he performed the pilgrimage to Mecca. It is evident that having Mu'āwiya as *qāḍī* not only conferred prestige on the Umayyad regime in Cordoba in the eyes of scholars in the east, but also sent a clear message to them that al-Andalus was to be administered according to the highest standards of Islamic law. Judges could be brought in to Cordoba from elsewhere, but wherever they dwelt they needed to possess a reputation of being upright, virtuous and just; when in post, their judgments were made independently of the *amīr*, but the latter could call on them to explain their decisions. For example, one of 'Abd ar-Rahmān's appointees, who came from Mérida, when summoned to explain why he had adjudicated against a particular claimant, called upon a higher authority, Muhammad the Prophet, to the admiration of the *amīr*. Among the lawsuits mentioned in this period, those relating to the possession of land seem to have been frequent, an indication that the acquisition of property outside the city was a facet of an urban Arab's activity and livelihood.

In the economic sphere also, Umayyad al-Andalus reflected that of the Umayyad era in the east. After a ten-year period in which no coinage was minted, during the fraught and disturbed period of revolt, 'Abd ar-Rahmān reactivated the mint. The earliest known coin from his reign dates to 763/4, and was discovered in Anatolia, Turkey in 1937, a remarkable instance of the use of coinage in trading, perhaps. A number of silver dirhams with the rubric al-Andalus have been studied from this period which, according to numismatists, represents Cordoba. No gold coins were struck in al-Andalus for 200 years after 726, that is to say until the time of the Caliphate, perhaps, as has been suggested, because gold coins could only be issued under Caliphal authority, the Umayyads being aware and respectful of the 'Abbāsid adoption of that title.[4] What needs to be borne in mind is that these details reflect light on only a narrow sector of society, what might be called its upper echelons, Arab, urban and Muslim; information concerning the majority rural population at this time is scant.

One *cause célèbre* which took place in the Iberian Peninsula in the 780s and 790s impinged upon the Muslims in al-Andalus hardly at all, yet its denouement did have significant consequences for their subject urban inhabitants. This is what has come to be known as the Adoptionist heresy, the sources for which are entirely in Latin.[5] In outline, Archbishop Elipandus (born in 717), the metropolitan of Toledo, and therefore at that time the senior churchman in the Peninsula, and, significantly, from 785 considered to have been Primate of all Spain, was accused of heresy by two clerics in the Cantabrian mountains, one of whom was Beatus of Liébana, the author of a commentary on the Apocalypse of St John, a charge which he, Elipandus, vigorously refuted. However, this accusation was taken up by churchmen across the Pyrenees, and he was condemned at various Councils of the Church including that of Frankfurt in 794, at which Charlemagne and as many as 300 bishops were present, and in Rome in 798 when Pope Leo III (Pope 795–816) presided. Throughout, Elipandus claimed that he was reiterating doctrine as handed down to him through the Visigothic Church. He never recanted and died, possibly of a great age, certainly over eighty, some time after 800, maybe as late as 808. This summary masks a dramatic sequence of events resembling even the tableau of a melodrama which, it could be argued, had significant political repercussions for Occidental Christendom, and in particular the Iberian Peninsula.

According to the heresy of adoptionism, a variant of the widely dispersed fifth-century eastern heresy of Nestorianism, Christ had two natures: he was both the true, eternal Son of God, and also his adoptive Son in human form. In other words, Christ was adopted by God when on earth, and it was this word 'adoptio' and its derivatives on which the controversy hinged. One aspect of this which is relevant to us here is that the doctrines may have resulted from contact with Islam, although it is difficult to comprehend how the contents of the Qur'ān relating to the Son of God could have come to the knowledge of the Archbishop of Toledo at that time.[6] It is conceivable, but most unlikely, that someone in his retinue might have been able to read Arabic, even supposing that a text of the Qur'ān was accessible. The crux of the matter seems to have been that the offending terms occurred in the liturgical rite used by Elipandus, and which Christians in the city of Toledo had been using for over a century. The route by which the Carolingians came to know of the correspondence between two churchmen in the Iberian Peninsula is not known, but when Charlemagne became aware of the polemic, he certainly exploited it to his own political advantage. He remained anxious to extend his empire into the Peninsula, despite his rebuff at Saragossa ten years earlier, and he took advantage of the opportunity afforded by the internal dissensions of the Christian Church within al-Andalus to further his own political ambitions. To this end, he enrolled the services of Alcuin (c. 735–804), the Yorkshire-born theologian and foremost intellectual of his court. Felix, the bishop of the not inconsiderable County of Urgel, in present-day Catalonia, and a scholar in his own right, composed a treatise maintaining the orthodoxy of his archbishop which was refuted in letters 'contra Felicem' by Alcuin, a formidable adversary. The argument at this point would be that Charlemagne could not possibly tolerate the fact that a bishop within his territory, as he had recently acquired control of that region of the Pyrenees, should swear allegiance to a Christian authority outside his domain. He may have presided at Frankfurt in 794 with the authority of Pope Hadrian I and, although the protagonists were absent, no doubt urged all his intellectual advisers to secure the condemnation of the Adoptionist heresy. Not content with this, Charlemagne may well have been the driving force behind the Council of the Church at Rome in 798 when the new Pope Leo III condemned the heterodox teaching of the Iberian churchmen. The following year, 799, at the Council of Aix, Felix was present and having debated the theological issues with Alcuin agreed to refrain from using the word 'adoptio' because of its echo with Nestorianism. It should be noted that, subsequent to this perceived defeat of Adoptionism, Charlemagne was crowned Roman emperor by the new Pope, Leo III, marking the foundation of the Holy Roman Empire. Elipandus did not leave his archdiocese, which is not surprising given his great age, and continued with the liturgy as he had received it. It is improbable that the Muslims were aware of the controversy, although it has been argued that the substance of his teaching relating to Jesus was acceptable to Muslim theologians since it could be reconciled with the Qur'ānic view. When Elipandus died, the heresy faded away, but Charlemagne had achieved his object of driving a wedge within the Hispanic Church. Henceforward, the Archbishop of Toledo did not enjoy jurisdiction outside al-Andalus, as he had previously. Not only the Pyrenean region but also the entire northern swathe from Asturias through to Galicia ceased to acknowledge the supremacy of the Church in Toledo. What might be considered an anomaly whereby dioceses in nominally Christian lands were accountable to a higher authority in Muslim-held territory was eradicated within 100 years of the Islamic invasion of Iberia. Finally, it should be emphasised that this sea change occurred without affecting the majority of the population of the Peninsula.

'Abd ar-Rahmān died in 788 and was succeeded by his younger son Hishām (r. 788–96). His short reign saw no let-up in the aggressive policies that had characterised much of his father's time in control. The targets were the Frankish territories to the north-east and the Asturian kingdom to the north, which were invaded on at least five occasions. His troops penetrated the Pyrenean region twice, recapturing Gerona and Narbonne, as well as destroying crops. This latter was a severe tactic, also employed on campaigns to Álava and the Basque area, one of which he himself led, and designed no doubt to discourage resettlement on the part of the enemy. It was as if the *amīr* felt that he needed to create a parched, depopulated frontier zone as an annual show of force. This would have had the joint effect of inspiring awe amongst the urban communities, particularly in Cordoba, and fear together with loathing, perhaps, in those regions devastated by his armies. He must have been cognisant of the legacy of his father who, tracking a bold and sometimes perilous course, had succeeded in transplanting the Umayyad state in al-Andalus. He had to be ruthless, notably when dealing with recalcitrant family members, in his case his elder brother who eventually settled in North Africa; he needed to be practical and so he continued to oversee the construction of the Great Mosque; he also restored the much-admired Roman bridge across the Guadalquivir, to the benefit of both citizens and traders. Furthermore, he introduced night-watchmen, the forerunners perhaps of the Spanish *sereno* who used to keep vigil in city streets at night after houses were shut up and locked. He even adopted the democratic measure of instituting a survey of administrators and public officers in al-Andalus. To do this, he is said to have solicited the opinion of his subjects as to their satisfaction in the way they were being governed. He would remove from post those found to be corrupt, and require them to make amends for their actions. In short, he was acting in the tradition of distinguished Arab chieftains: securing his domain, crushing opposition, maintaining prestige and ensuring that Muslims under his protection were treated justly.

It was during his reign or that of his successor, his son Al-Hakam (r. 796–822), that the law school of Mālik b. Anas became what one might call officially adopted in al-Andalus, largely as a consequence of visits made by prominent Andalusis to Madina where he resided.[7] This was a significant step in ensuring that the legal foundation of the Umayyad state both favoured and upheld the status quo. Hitherto, the opinions of the Syrian al-Awzā'ī regarding legal judgments had prevailed. The *fuqahā'* were the religious lawyers who interpreted the law, whereas the *qādīs* were those who administered it. Under the Māliki system, these two bodies controlled the theory and practice of the law, and thus a closed and powerful elite emerged which, in regard to the law, embraced existing Islamic practices and was opposed to innovation. The *amīr*, though, was the last port of call in making a judgment, and Muslims could and did appeal to him against the ruling of a judge. Significantly, under Māliki precepts, the non-Arab client was not a second-class citizen within Islam, and was therefore entitled to the same treatment as Arabs. It follows, then, that one need not look so much to *mawālī*, especially Berbers complaining about exploitation from their Arab *coreligionnaires* as a source of disaffection this time, as to Arab Muslims nurturing resentment for any number of cogent reasons. Overall, then, it was a stable, orthodox system, strict and uncompromising in its enactment of justice.

The ninth century

Much of al-Hakam's reign mirrored that of his father. He had to combat internal dissension, from Arabs, family members among others, who inflamed revolt. He took drastic measures in combating an attempted coup within Cordoba in which family members and prominent citizens were implicated. The ringleaders were all executed in public. Some years later, towards the end of his reign, during the month of Ramadan in March–April 817, a widespread rebellion within Cordoba itself is said to have shaken the city to its foundations. The whole suburb (Arabic *ar-rabad*; Spanish *arrabal*) to the south of the city rose en masse and stormed the castle in which he dwelt in an attempt to oust him, but then wilted when confronted by the *amīr*'s troops, who engaged in whole-scale slaughter. This episode is recorded at length in a number of Arab sources and, according to Ibn al-Qūṭīya, some 15,000 were deported in reprisal, and then settled in various locations in North Africa.[8] A motive for the uprising is suggested by this author, namely that there had been resentment on the part of many inhabitants at the harsh manner in which the earlier attempted coup had been put down. Al-Hakam, however, was following Umayyad precedent in his ruthless treatment of opposition, and his lavish rewards to those loyal to him. For example, the elderly *faqīh* Tālūt, who had visited Mālik b. Anas in the east and was a renowned and revered scholar, was one of those caught up in the *arrabal* insurrection. He went into hiding in Cordoba for a year, taking sanctuary in the house of one of the members of the Jewish community. The story as recounted in more than one source is that he wished to be reconciled with the *amīr* and gave himself up to a *wazīr* (minister), who then promptly denounced him as a traitor. This denunciation was considered by al-Hakam to have been an act of betrayal on behalf of the minister whom he removed from his post. Tālūt was restored to favour and reinstated. This anecdote not only reveals the punctilious sense of justice of the *amīr*, but also something of the interaction between Muslim and Jew within Cordoba. Jews together with Christians (*nasārā*) were *ahl al-kitāb*, and thereby allowed to live as second-class citizens within Islam, subject to certain constraints, mainly additional taxation and abstention from cursing Islam and Muhammad in public. A quarter for the Jewish community in Cordoba is known to have existed in the ninth century, but whether Tālūt took refuge there cannot be ascertained. Perhaps he knew of a fellow scholar, like-minded in learning; one presumes that they would have communicated in Arabic.

Of long-lasting consequence were the depredations occurring on the frontiers, which began to signal a change in the relationship between north and south. It was in al-Hakam's reign that Barcelona was overpowered by the Franks and passed definitively out of Muslim control. This occurred in 801, and virtually put paid to any further military adventures on the part of the Muslims beyond the Pyrenees, although isolated pockets remained until the tenth century on or near the coastline, as is reflected in the name Côte des Maures, and in the range of mountains, the Massif des Maures, in the south of present-day Provence. It is noteworthy that, apart from the eleventh-century historian Ibn Hayyān, the surviving portions of whose history are an indispensable and detailed source, few Arab writers appear to lend much attention to Barcelona during the ninety years or so when it was in Muslim hands. On the other hand, that area of present-day Catalonia, both fertile and prosperous, was clearly of great strategic importance to the Franks who also made three attempts before 810 to take possession of Tortosa, the former Roman town that stood just inland of the mouth of the river Ebro. These efforts were thwarted, as it remained under Muslim authority, although its rulers did not always acknowledge allegiance to Cordoba, until the twelfth century. The attention that al-Hakam paid to ensuring that Saragossa remained under his control is evident from the measures that he took to prevent it from falling into either Frankish possession or rebel Muslim hands. Saragossa, at the head of the Upper March, was more centrally situated than Barcelona; it was accessible by a Roman road, and from it troops could branch north-west towards Pamplona and the Basque regions, or north-east toward Huesca and Lérida. Above all, however, it was admirably located on the banks of the Ebro, economically self-sufficient largely because of the abundance of fruit orchards noted by Arab geographers. By the end of al-Hakam's reign the limits of the Upper March had become more or less established, such that from 820 onwards, Latin chronicles referred to the *Marca Hispanica*. One may note that al-Hakam was equally proactive in responding to the rebellion in Mérida, the capital of the Lower March, which simmered on for seven years until he replaced the recalcitrant governor with his own appointee.

In what may be considered as a further indication of the *amīr*'s intention to keep the borders of al-Andalus intact, a Muslim force was dispatched beyond the Duero to confront the Asturians who, under Alfonso II (r. 791–842), at a time before and after the beginning of the ninth century, had encouraged settlements in swathes of sparsely populated territory. In so doing, he may possibly have ousted resident outposts of Muslims, although this is by no means certain. An anecdote recorded by al-Maqqarī would suggest that al-Hakam was motivated by revenge in one expedition to the Middle March beyond Toledo. Some mounted soldiers had apparently captured or killed the male relatives of a woman near Guadalajara. In reprisal, the *amīr*, in the graphic translation of Gayangos, 'laid waste the land, took many fortresses, destroyed the fields, burnt the houses of the inhabitants, and committed all kinds of ravages, inflicting death on a great number of infidels'.[9] This may be considered, in its context, as an example of al-Hakam relieving the grief of his oppressed subjects, but in retrospect, it epitomises the brutality of the age.

An insight into the conditions of life is afforded by a reference in Ibn Hayyān's history to a grave famine affecting the entire extent of al-Andalus in the year 197 AH, beginning in September 812, as a consequence of which it is said that the majority of the population perished, and others fled to North Africa. This is almost certainly an exaggeration, but al-Maqqarī mentions the same catastrophe, with the added detail that 'the lower classes of people died by the thousands'.[10] This natural disaster may be accounted for by late summer rains destroying harvests, as reference is made elsewhere to rivers bursting their banks. This would have to have been followed by an extensive period of drought, perhaps covering several years. Even so, this is not wholly satisfactory as an explanation, as it does not allow for regional variations of climate. Arid mesetas would become more parched, and a total lack of rainfall in the southeast, traditionally the driest zone in the Peninsula, could enable us to understand a sizeable temporary depopulation. In a situation where neither crops nor cattle could survive, then a large exodus of those who lived in the worst-hit rural areas is comprehensible. For those who dwelt in the most affected regions, translocation to North Africa would have been an inconvenience but no great hardship, as movement across the Straits in either direction in adverse circumstances had been a feature of life over centuries. The assumption is that Berber settlers would have coped with the vicissitudes of nature as their forebears had done, and simply moved en bloc. As for those who had Peninsular ancestry, that is to say those who fell in the imperfectly defined category of Hispano-Roman country dwellers, with no age-old custom of migratory movement to fall back on, their plight would have been more terrible. Perhaps they were unable or unwilling to uproot themselves, and therefore starved *in situ*. One may surmise, from lack of mention in the texts, that the urban areas were less affected, as they would not have been restricted to one source of supply. Moreover, the sources make no mention of any campaign to provide succour for those stricken. The Muslims in the cities were preoccupied with their own political and social concerns; the welfare of those living in remote regions and who had no allegiance to Islam would have been low on any list of priority. If they did not pay their taxes when required to do so, then they would have been punished. If they were not there to settle their dues, then *tant pis*. There is a third interpretation: rural populations are notoriously resilient and resourceful; when faced with nature's reverses, they resort to strategies designed to make the best of often dire situations. The accounts are couched in a disinterested tone and reveal a scarcity of any detailed knowledge of the predicament of the majority of the population of al-Andalus.

Al-Hakam is said to have withdrawn from public view in the last five or so years of his reign. Whether he became remorseful and prone to piety, as is suggested by Ibn al-Qūtīya, may never be ascertained with any certainty, but some features of the final years of his reign may be mentioned. First, and self-evidently, Islam was acquiring permanence in the cities. The system whereby the *qādīs* administered the law enjoyed the confidence of citizens. Amongst the *qādīs*, Muhammad b. Bashīr (d. 813/14), originally from Beja, a scholar who had made the pilgrimage to Mecca and was therefore entitled to be called *hajjī*, was described by al-Khushanī as one of the best judges of al-Andalus. From the many accounts of his practice, his impartiality, rectitude and sound sense are apparent. Two points emerge. He was independent of the *amīr* and communicated with al-Hakam by letter. The presence of what amounts to an unfettered Islamic judiciary meant that the substructure of society could function in the *amīr*'s absence. Regarding the second aspect above, it is said that the use of paper spread from China, where it had been known for centuries, to the Islamic world in the eighth century. The vehicle for the correspondence would have been paper recently introduced into al-Andalus, papyrus from the East. Ibn Bashīr was a trained *kātib* (secretary, although more in the sense of the modern 'secretary of state' than 'typist') – a well-rewarded position in its own right – in that he was responsible for drafting administrative documents as well as writing them out. In this example, he was employing the skills that he had been taught and that placed him, in this transaction, on an equal footing with the *amīr*.

Significant in the development of Islam in al-Andalus, Cordoba itself was generating prestige. There was political turbulence in the Abbāsid east in the first two decades of the ninth century, and mainly on account of this, a number of renowned exiles made their way probably overland, although the trans-Mediterranean route to ports in the Iberian Levant, such as Denia or Cartagena, was also used. The sea journey was swifter though more perilous than the overland route. It was not, however, until the tenth century that Muslim ships became dominant in the Mediterranean.

It was during al-Hakam's reign that Arabic learning and arts in a range of different fields became known in Cordoba. One person to take advantage of this was 'Abbās b. Firnās (d. 887) – whose father's name means 'chieftain' and is also one of a number of words meaning lion – an eccentric polymath of Berber origin and a client of the Umayyads, who was brought up in the region of Ronda. Ibn Hayyān, quoting various sources, and al-Maqqarī provide substantial information about his life and achievements. He was the first person in al-Andalus who was able to understand and explain the notoriously complex Khalīlian system of Arabic prosody. Al-Khalīl b. Ahmād, a Sunni scholar from Basra, had devised this in the eighth century, and it became the standard adopted subsequently by

Arab poets. Ibn Firnās was not only a poet, but a scientist who conceived and constructed a clepsydra, or water clock. Such instruments for measuring time had been in existence for many hundreds of years, but they were of numerous different kinds, and it is not known how sophisticated his was, nor whether it was driven by waterwheels. Gayangos, however, was of the view that what was meant was something akin to the modern metronome, 'by means of which time was marked in music without having recourse to notes or figures'.[11] Other inventions attributed to Ibn Firnās include a form of armillary sphere erected in his own house. Here also, the details are not precise, and it may have been more akin to a planetarium, in which were representations of 'stars, clouds, thunder and lightning', which people came to see.[12] The study of the firmament was certainly practised by Muslim astronomers, and Ibn Firnās is described as such, but there was always a fine line between astronomy, a scientific pursuit; astrology, which is concerned with the influence of the celestial on the terrestrial sphere; and magic with spells. Such activities invariably tended to attract suspicion, and Ibn Firnās was arraigned before the *qāḍī*, although not condemned. The detail that he was responsible for the dissemination of the art of glass-making in al-Andalus is not accompanied with sufficient particulars, but there is one final spectacular contraption which has secured his fame, his flying apparatus. This, apparently, was a sort of frame in the form of wings, within which he fitted himself, having coated his outer garment with feathers. He is said to have flown a considerable distance as a bird before landing uncomfortably, because he had not provided himself with what might be regarded as the compulsory accessory of tail feathers.

A notable contemporary, whose life similarly spanned the reign of more than one *amīr*, was al-Ghazāl, a poet and statesman originally from Jaén, who is said to have lived to the age of ninety-four (he died in 864); this is not necessarily an exaggeration, as there are other examples of exceptional longevity in the ninth and tenth centuries. His name, meaning gazelle, reflected his youthful grace, which was the object of admiration during his ambassadorial visit on behalf of al-Hakam's successor, his son 'Abd ar-Rahmān II, to the Byzantine Emperor in Constantinople. He was highly regarded as a poet and is said to have composed a long poem on the invasion of al-Andalus by the Muslims, which was instructive, useful and popular;[13] this, in itself, provides an indication of how significant their heritage was to the literati. Ibn Hayyān quoted his poetry extensively, and it clearly made an impact among both his contemporaries and succeeding generations. Being a poet denoted learning, a thorough knowledge of the Arabic language and style, and brought with it status, a position at the court and frequently a large salary. A condition of retaining favour with the *amīr* was the facility for spontaneous and witty verse characterised by praise and flattery; a tendency for satire, sometimes of the most direct and crudest type, could lead to instant dismissal. Although Al-Ghazāl achieved the desired patronage of

al-Hakam, he later famously courted the disfavour of the *faqīh*s for a poetic disquisition on the nature of the soul, verging on mysticism, for which he narrowly
escaped censorship. Poets often had other strings to their bow, and al-Ghazāl
enjoyed the reputation of being an accomplished philosopher, astronomer
and theologian. Verses written by *amīr*s themselves are also recorded by some
historians.

One of the accomplishments of Ibn Firnās is said to have been his knowledge
of musicology, but the one person who is habitually cited as the forerunner of
music in al-Andalus is 'Alī b. Nāfi', known as Ziryāb (789–857), a name for a
bird of dark plumage, reflecting his complexion. Much has been said about him,
and he figures prominently in Arabic sources which in itself is an indication of
the mark that he made, and indeed, the esteem in which he was held.

If it is possible to glean an impression of his character from these, then he
appears to have been colourful in his habits, multi-talented and opinionated.
After being obliged to leave Abbāsid court life in Baghdad because of the envy
of another poet, he made his way to North Africa, and wrote to al-Hakam who
invited him to the Umayyad court in Cordoba. The *amīr* had died before he
arrived there, and his successor, 'Abd ar-Rahmān II (r. 822–52) granted him
what almost amounted to a royal welcome, organising receptions for him in
the cities through which he passed and assigning him special apartments in
Cordoba, together with an outstandingly generous salary for him and his four
sons. An interesting detail emerges from al-Maqqarī's account of their early
social meetings (*majālis*), namely that these were accompanied by date wine
(*nabīdh*) and song (*ghinā'*). Intoxicating liquor, specifically *khamr*, which was wine
made from grapes, was prohibited in the Qur'ān (2: 219; 5: 90, 91). It appears
that the Qur'ānic injunction did not extend to wine made from fermented
dates. Thus according to some legal scholars, Muslims could drink *nabīdh* but
not *khamr*. It is further thought that wine from grapes was consumed at certain
times and in certain places, though it was called *nabīdh* to make it permissible.
Whether this was the case in the example given is not known; both dates and
grapes were abundant.[14]

The description of Ziryāb's skills in singing his own songs is hyberbolic, but
from the musicological standpoint the innovation to the lute for which he is
credited is of lasting significance. This refinement, which he may have already
introduced to the instrument in the east, was the addition of a fifth string to
create a more harmonious sound. Furthermore, in place of the wooden plec-
trum, he used an eagle's claw, which put less strain on the strings and therefore
ensured their longer life. He founded a school for musicians in Cordoba which
was continued by his sons after his death, and which may be said to have transformed the musical scene in al-Andalus. He introduced refinements such as a
hairstyle for men whereby the parting was in the middle and the hair did not
cover the forehead, and, in fashion, the wearing of different-coloured clothing

according to the season of the year. He was a noted chef, and dishes that he made popular were incorporated into Andalusi cuisine; he also introduced asparagus, and brought a new sophistication to cooking. As evidence of the impact that he made in this discipline, his recipe for spiced mutton and cauliflower is found in a Hispano-Arabic cookery manual of the thirteenth century.[15] It is relevant to mention in this respect that he encouraged the use of glasses as drinking receptacles rather than metal goblets, albeit whether in silver or gold. He may also have been responsible for instructing his fellow courtiers in the game of chess, which had already assumed a superior status in the upper echelons of society. Furthermore, most arcanely, he used a deodorant for the armpit. In short, he became an arbiter of elegance and taste and, if the sources are to be given serious consideration, he metamorphosed Cordoban society, setting standards that were to persist long after his death. In effect, however, Ziryāb's achievement, and the reason for posterity to take such notice of him, was to bring the refinements already present in the Abbāsid east to the Umayyad state in al-Andalus. The new style of living, the musical novelties, an ethos of culture which he introduced to Cordoba did not emerge from within the Iberian Peninsula, but were superimposed upon society from elsewhere, and they left an indelible stamp. In the first half of the ninth century, then, urban life, at its most refined, mirrored that of the Abbāsid courts of the east.

Among the courtiers in what might be called 'Abd ar-Rahmān's inner circle was one Ibn ash-Shamir, who achieved notoriety as an astrologer. In Medieval Islam the attitude towards astrology was not unambiguous. Ibn Khaldūn was scathing: 'How can anyone learn a subject [such as astrology] that is discarded by the religious law, banned as forbidden and illegal?' In the same treatise, he acknowledges:

> It should be known that one of the qualities of the human soul is the desire to learn the outcome of affairs that concern (human beings) and to know what is going to befall them, whether it be life or death, good or evil.[16]

The examples of Ibn ash-Shamir's expertise given in the sources, Ibn Hayyān for instance, do not correspond with the modern-day notion of astrology. One, in which he apparently foretells which of many doors the *amīr* will use to leave his chamber, smacks of the chicanery of a magician. Nonetheless, the *amīr* was delighted and showered his resident astrologer with gifts. The practice of astrology which had been absorbed into Islam from the Ptolemy was, however, employed by those commanding troops who habitually consulted their astrologers for a propitious augury prior to embarking on an expedition. On a specific campaign, 'Abd ar-Rahmān left Cordoba, having been predicted a safe outcome, and fell headlong off his horse immediately after departure. The astrologer in question was called to give an account of himself and reiterated his original opinion, guided, as he said, by the soundness of his knowledge and the truth of his interpretation. In the event, the *amīr* returned to Cordoba unscathed after having accomplished his mission successfully.

It has been noted that it was the practice of the Umayyad *amīrs* in al-Andalus to enlarge the mosque at Cordoba in order to add lustre and prestige to their reigns. The extensions made to the prayer hall testified not only to the prosperity that 'Abd ar-Rahmān had brought to Cordoba, but also to the more prosaic fact that the population had increased, and that, in consequence, more space was required. As it became apparent to neighbouring states, such as the Christian kingdoms in the north of the Peninsula and the Frankish Empire, that al-Andalus was prospering during the reign of 'Abd ar-Rahmān, so we have notice of diplomatic missions to Cordoba. He may have been approached by a Count of Toulouse in the wrangling following the death of the emperor Louis in 840; after Charles the Bald's establishment in the western region of the Carolingian Empire, there were negotiations between him and the *amīr* that resulted in two ambassadors being dispatched from Cordoba to Rheims to seal a treaty. An ulterior motive on 'Abd ar-Rahmān's part, reflected in two thwarted and ultimately unsuccessful sorties to the eastern Pyrenean region and beyond into Frankish territory, in 840 and 850, was the restoration of Barcelona into the state of al-Andalus. In 839, the Byzantine emperor Theophilos sent a diplomatic mission headed by Curtius, an Arabic speaker, petitioning for friendship, and a reciprocation of embassies. There may have been a twofold purpose, an alliance with the political enemies of the Abbāsids with whom they were in active conflict, and a desire to open up potentially lucrative trade between the two states. There was a positive outcome, in that 'Abd ar-Rahmān sent an embassy back to Byzantium, with the statutory diplomatic gifts, and relations were thus established.

The deepest thorn in 'Abd ar-Rahman's side, though, was the ever-present threat of the Vikings from Scandinavia, including Denmark. The attack on Lindisfarne on the east coast of Scotland in 792 was the prelude for raids and the eventual settlement in Britain of these feared and fearsome Norsemen, or 'Northmen' (*al-Urdumāniyyūn*). Known in the Arabic sources as *majūs* (fire worshippers or 'fire men'), they wrought havoc on the coastlines of Europe and the Mediterranean for over a century. The traditional explanations for their venturing so far afield include intense political rivalry impelling the departure of large numbers of men, a relatively uninhabitable homeland and the enticement of fertile pastures and plentiful plunder. They have been called pirates in that they did demand ransoms for the more prominent of their captives, but this designation cannot apply to what might be termed the second phase of their activity, from the mid-ninth century onwards, when they settled, in eastern England for example. Their strength lay in their boats, shallow-bottomed longships with a sail and oars, capable of great speed and manoeuvrability, each carrying about fifty men. Their preferred mode of attack was upstream from a

river mouth, where they would often encounter the resident population unpre-
pared. They would take what they required in the way of victuals, and devastate
the land, setting fire to buildings and slaughtering the inhabitants. Having
traversed the Bay of Biscay in 844, they rounded the promontory at Cintra,
and having moored in the mouth of the river Tagus engaged the defenders in
battle over a period of days. Whether they were defeated, or had their sights
on more substantial gain, they sailed up the river Guadalquivir, and brought
unanticipated destruction to the city of Seville, catching the residents unawares,
looting, setting fire to the buildings, demolishing the city's defences. It seems
as though the governor of Lisbon had alerted 'Abd ar-Rahmān concerning
the threat of the *majūs*, and he sought support from allies and enemies alike,
urging them to confront the common foe. As a consequence, the combined
Andalusi forces overcame and overran the enemy, retrieving pillaged treasure,
wrecking thirty boats and putting prisoners to death. Ibn Hayyān records that
those of the *majūs* who escaped down the Guadalquivir negotiated the release
of captives in return for provisions, presumably to enable them to make the
hazardous return journey to Scandinavia, or perhaps to facilitate raids on the
North African coastline. 'Abd ar-Rahmān set about the restoration of the city of
Seville, having the mosque and walls rebuilt and the defences fortified. He also
reinforced his maritime defences. Whether he had a small flotilla permanently
engaged near Cádiz and around the mouth of the Guadalquivir is not known
for certain, but he did order the construction of lookout posts at intervals along
the Atlantic coastline, anticipating the policy of his descendant 'Abd ar-Rahmān
III who, in the tenth century, had *atalaya*s (Arabic *tāli'a*, watchtowers), some of
which still survive, erected along the eastern seaboard of al-Andalus, largely to
combat the potential threat of the Fātimids. As a postscript, it may be added that
'Abd ar-Rahmān responded promptly to the crisis in Seville despite a history of
political tension between the two cities.[17]

The martyrs of Cordoba

The *cause célèbre* in al-Andalus in the middle years of the ninth century was one
in which, between the years 850 and 859, fifty Christians, both male and female,
called by tradition the martyrs of Cordoba, were executed. It started, and created
the most stir, whilst 'Abd ar-Rahmān was still *amīr*, then continued in the reign
of Muhammad I, who succeeded him in 852. This episode has attracted extensive attention from theologians and historians over the centuries, and interest in
it has shown no sign of waning. What must be said at the outset, however, is that
the principal sources for it, the writings of two men, are entirely in Latin; they
are the *Memoriale Sanctorum* of Eulogius and the *Indiculus luminosus* of Paul Alvar.
The deaths of these Christians, including eight priests, eighteen monks and
three nuns, on the orders of the Muslim judiciary are not recorded *per se* in the

Arabic sources, although it is possible to identify the judges involved in particular cases with named *qudāt* (judges) known to have presided in Cordoba during this period. Those who contravened Islamic law were examined and punished alongside others who had transgressed, and therefore merited no special mention. The Latin texts relating to this episode are both vivid and informative; they have been analysed and interpreted by scholars, partly because they are in Latin and therefore more accessible to Western historians, and partly because they are held to cast a light on the political and social situation in Cordoba in the ninth century. A problem arises, though, when claims are made, as they have been, concerning Christian-Muslim relations, largely on the basis of these texts. Eulogius was personally involved with a number of the martyrs, and certainly did not write an unbiased account, nor can he be expected to have done so. Yet his prejudice, which may be natural to understand in the circumstances, is conveniently ignored, and his text regarded as one from which one can make reasoned judgments about the attitudes of Christians to Muslims and vice versa in the ninth century. If one recognises that Eulogius was *parti pris*, then the reality of the circumstances of the deaths of these Christians may be nothing like as sensational as they have often been portrayed.[18]

It is helpful, when endeavouring to evaluate these happenings, to review the situation of Christianity in Cordoba at the time. In this and other cities of al-Andalus, there existed practising Christians, known as *nasārā*. When this specific word was employed, it designated those who were demonstrably Christian, those who professed their religion in an outward and evident way, monks and priests for example, but not exclusively these. They had rights within Islam, as *ahl al-kitāb*, according to which they could worship in their churches, a number of which are known by name in Cordoba and environs, and go about their everyday business unmolested, provided they paid the additional tax imposed upon non-Muslim subjects. The protection that this status granted was, however, rendered null and void, if they blasphemed against Muhammad the Prophet in public. If they breached this condition, then they came under the jurisdiction of Islamic law, and could be judged and sentenced accordingly. These *nasārā* were in the minority among the non-Muslim population, and were mainly confined to cities. We can be reasonably assured of this, because the Muslims had other words to use when referring to non-Muslims within the community. These were religiously neutral words and included *muʿāhid* (those protected by a pact); similarly *dhimmī* (protected people); and *ʿajamī* (non-Arab speakers, or those persons who could not speak Arabic properly).[19] This latter word is frequently found in the Arabic accounts where it is used to describe members of the indigenous population of al-Andalus. The following regional names, amongst others, are also found in Arabic texts: *rūmī* (Greeks or Byzantines); *ifranj* (Franks or Catalans); and *jillīqiyyūn* (essentially Galicians, but also used to refer to Leonese and later to Castilians). One word that is unrecorded in the Arabic sources relating to al-

Andalus is *musta'rib*, that is to say Arabicised, or having adopted Arabic customs. As with those three words mentioned above, it is religiously neutral, in other words an essentially cultural term from which the word Mozarab is derived, and was employed at different times and in different places in the Islamic world. It must have been known orally in the Islamic west, as it occurs in a Latinised form in a Latin document in the kingdom of León from the eleventh century, where it refers to a small cluster of people who came from al-Andalus. Nonetheless, the fact that it is not registered in documentation relating to al-Andalus invalidates its use in that context. This, in turn, means that the Christians who died in Cordoba at that time may not properly be termed Mozarabs. Eulogius was not Arabicised; indeed it would have been anathema to him to adopt the customs and character of another religion.

One would not expect to find many *nasārā* away from the cities. In Cordoba, more *nasārā* were in evidence, but there, the indigenous people who had not adopted Islam were in the preponderance. Some of these had a knowledge of Arabic often for the sake of convenience or, as was particularly to be the case in the following tenth century, for self-advancement. The vast majority who made up the non-Muslim population would have been non-committed Christians in the modern sense, or would have belonged to the Jewish community. One may speculate that they may have paid lip service to the formal religion when occasion demanded, but they were, by and large, happy to go about their daily chores, accepting the status quo and paying the annual tax as the price for not attending to the religious observances of the state. In Cordoba itself, non-Muslims could attain high office, certainly in the ninth and tenth centuries, but the writings of San Eulogius provide evidence of tension between them and those who asserted their Christianity through insults to Islam.

On the evidence of San Eulogius, it would appear that the act of abusing the privilege of living as a Christian in an Islamic city escalated after it had been initially triggered by an isolated case. The narrative account of the martyrs betrays his personal involvement with their cause, yet his professed revulsion for the Muslim authorities is expressed with such subjectivity that it is hard to give credence to his impassioned asseverations. He holds the *amīr* personally responsible for the martyrdoms, yet it seems unlikely that the latter would have interfered in the judicial proceedings. Just prior to his death in 852, the *amīr* is said to have ordered the convening of a Council of churchmen specifically to condemn future martyrdoms, but the chapter in which this information is found was considered by the sixteenth-century scholar Ambrosio de Morales to be somewhat obscure, and plagued with errors, so too much reliance should not be placed on it.[20] There is no evidence to support the claim that the actions of this very small number of Christians over a ten-year period constituted a threat to Muslim authority. Had that been the case, one would expect to have found inordinate coverage of it in Islamic sources, but none to my knowledge exists. As a codicil to this episode, and without entering into the psychology of the 'martyr complex', it may be noted that, some fifty years later, a judge of Cordoba, noted for his acute judgment, had to give sentence on 'a man from among the Christians', who was prepared to put his own life at risk possessing, one is led to assume, a similar mindset to that of his predecessors fifty years earlier. In this instance, the judge, after an exchange of repartee recorded by the author al-Khushnī, ordered him to be stripped and whipped in his presence, so that he would come to his senses and realise the futility of his aspiration.[21]

It is somewhat difficult to summarise the rule of 'Abd ar-Rahmān II as the sources provide what appears to be gratuitous and often contradictory informa-tion, but in broad terms he may be said to have brought stability and prestige to the amirate. Whether he used a veil to cover himself when in public in oprder to create an aura, as al-Maqqarī claims, is open to question, as according to al-Khushanī, he interacted with the people of Cordoba on many occasions, and engaged in dialogue with them, something awkward to achieve if the face were swathed in cloth. He is alleged to have ordered the building of mosques in the cities of al-Andalus, which would imply, if they were additional to those already present, that they were necessary to cope with demand, as the numbers of Muslims increased. Yet Arabic was not imposed as a language, and the *amīr* was not above paying heed to what was said in the vernacular, as is exemplified in a brief passage in al-Khushanī. An elderly and respected old man who spoke no Arabic, famous amongst the people for his beneficence and for being learned in the orthodox practice of the law (*fiqh*), was asked by ministers to give his opinion on a judge. In his response, he stated that they, the people, used a pejorative phrase in the vernacular to describe him. As a consequence of this veteran's tes-timony, the *amīr* dismissed the judge. What is implicit in this story, in which what amounts to a Romance nickname was responsible for the downfall of a man in the highest office, is that people, even the majority, spoke Romance, and that it was understood and common parlance among Islamic officials. The upholding of the tenets of the Māliki legal system was what counted in al-Andalus in 'Abd ar-Rahmān's time, not the imposition of Arabic.

There is much anecdotal tittle-tattle in the sources relating to the reign of the *amīr* Muhammad I (852–86). There is, however, a consensus that he had to deal with rebellions of three fronts. The first of these to occur was the conflict with the inhabitants of Toledo who had taken advantage of the death of his predeces-sor to proclaim open revolt. Toledo was to be a running sore in the side of the *amīr* for much of his reign, and he personally led troops there in the 850s and 870s. On the first occasion the Toledans were aided by Ordoño I (r. 850–66), who brought with him detachments from his kingdom of Asturias, but they were jointly defeated in a savage encounter in 854. The relationship of Toledo with its mixed population of *dhimmī*s and *muwallad*s to the Umayyad amirate in Cordoba had always been uneasy. As with the frontier town of Mérida to the west, the inhabitants resented authority being imposed from elsewhere – the governor of the city was an appointee of the *amīr* – and took every opportunity to assert their right to govern themselves. Political expediency regulated their strategy at this time, rather than any religious motivation. They sought allies from outside the boundaries of al-Andalus, irrespective of the fact that these were Christians. Such alliances marked the pattern of conflict between al-Andalus and the Christian states in the north of the Peninsula, until, that is, the time of the Crusades in the eleventh century. Clashes occurred when one side felt powerful enough to dispossess the other of territory. In the ninth century, the Christian states extended their domains southwards at a time when the amirate in Cordoba was in some disarray. The most notable example of this may be seen in the reign of Alfonso III (866–910), who was able to claim much of the frontier lands to the north of the river Duero, repopulating them with communities from all over the Peninsula, as is demonstrated by the toponymy of the region, indicating the places of origin of the settlers. Whether the 'expansion created an egalitarian peasant society, organized for war and governed by relatively democratic assemblies', as Lomax wrote, is open to question, but it certainly altered the demography of the region permanently.[22] In the tenth century the situation was to be reversed. Even though a contemporary Christian chronicle may interpret these gains as Christian victories at the expense of Islam, the truth of the matter may have been radically different. Indeed, Wolf notes, with, it appears, a tone of some incredulity, when discussing the Chronicle of Alfonso III, that 'the lack of references to the religious component of the Muslim threat seems curious at first glance'.[23] There was never any practical reality to the notion of Reconquest, encapsulating the restoration of Iberia to descendants of the Visigoths as represented in the nascent Christian kingdoms of the north, in the sense that the proponents of one religion, Christianity, were intent on restoring it throughout the Peninsula. There are echoes of this sentiment in the Chronicle of Albelda (c. 883), but the monks whose writings have survived seemed more concerned with explaining why the Muslim armies had been sent as a scourge for the shortcomings and failures of the Church.[24]

The fourteenth-century historian Nuwayrī when he treats of this period in al-Andalus, mentions major campaigns by Muhammad I in the frontier areas, in Pamplona, Castile and the Basque country, and in Barcelona, indicative of the *amīr*'s intentions not only to curb dissidents, but also to secure distant territories. The expeditions were largely successful, although the attempt to recover Barcelona in 861–2 was in vain, and many of the engagements with the enemies resulted in enormous loss of life, recorded dispassionately. Given the lack of acknowledgement of the supremacy of the amirate in Cordoba on so many fronts, one may qualify this period as one of *fitna*, when civil discord was rife. The pervasive climate of revolt, though, is most powerfully demonstrated by the rebellion led by 'Umar b. Hafsūn which began in Muhammad's reign in the south-east of al-Andalus encompassing the district of Rayya (present-day Málaga), and was to continue for a further forty years. This is related in a number of Arabic accounts, with a variety of emphases, and with a large number of also varying interpretations.[25] There is some consensus that 'Umar's lineage may be traced back to the Visigoths, and that, along the line, an ancestor, maybe his grandfather, adopted Islam, which classifies him as a *muwallad*. It is now generally but not universally agreed that his base was the fortress of Bobastro, in the mountainous hinterland of Málaga; remains of a church on this site may date to the period of 'Umar b. Hafsūn's revolt. It has been argued that he converted to Christianity later in his life. At the outset he declared himself opposed to the *amīr*, and defeated the troops of the governor of the region, thereby attracting more followers. This pattern continued in the reign of Muhammad's successor, al-Mundhir (r. 886–8), who having been outwitted by 'Umar in consequence took forces from Cordoba to Bobastro, but died of an illness during the siege, to be succeeded as *amīr* by his brother 'Abd Allāh (r. 888–912). Following this, 'Umar's star was in the ascendant. Whether he headed a militia or untrained men from the country regions, resentful of the imposition of taxes, he reached the outskirts of Cordoba in 891, and threatened to overthrow the amirate. Just when this prize was within his grasp, he hesitated, and later that year 'Abd Allāh was able to inflict a heavy defeat on him and his forces. Those of his recruits that were captured were executed, thus discouraging a further wave of support for 'Umar's depleted contingent. In the year 899, Ibn 'Idhārī mentions that he became a Christian – in other words, that he apostatised. He had limited success after 900, and was thwarted in his attempts to attract overseas support for his campaigns; he died in 917, after nearly four decades of defiance. In considering his life and achievements, it would be understandable to explain his actions as being on the same level as the other anti-Arab outbreaks of independence that plagued the amirate in the second half of the ninth century. However, there was no cohesion in these movements, although 'Umar did make overtures to the leader of Seville, the capable and ambitious Ibn Hajjāj, a notable instance of his political expediency, as Seville was an Arab city and therefore not a natural ally. Ibn Hajjāj was later to reach a truce with 'Abd Allāh whereby he could govern the city independently, in return for non-aggression and the payment of taxes. One may look at local grievances, such as hostility towards the annual imposition of taxes, but there had always been taxation, and there is no indication that they were particularly burdensome at the commencement of the revolt. In the early days, the 880s, when 'Umar b. Hafsūn was acquiring prestige as a brigand, operating with impunity in the sierras of the south-east, his escapades would have attracted like-minded individuals or gangs, with no other motive than that of improving their circumstances at the expense of the distant authority.

The effects of adverse climatic conditions can never be underestimated. There are records of drought and famine in 874, and for the first few months of 888, there was no rain, causing a great drought, according to Ibn ʿIdhārī, but one is too early, and the other seemingly too late to have driven the rural communities to take desperate measures. Interestingly, al-Maqqarī records an earthquake in Cordoba in the second half of the year 881, in which houses, towers and minarets were destroyed, and the citizens fled the city in panic taking refuge in the surrounding countryside. The account seems exaggerated when it refers to mountains being 'rent asunder' and 'castles and palaces' 'levelled with the dust'.[26] Yet a fault line does run through Andalucía, and just over 1,000 years later, on 25 December 1884, a huge tremor shook the region of Granada and Málaga, causing around 750 deaths and wounding nearly 1,500. The Arab source, then, was not inventing a natural catastrophe out of ulterior motives, but rather was probably reflecting the devastation wrought by a seismic wave that would have registered highly on the Richter scale. The city of Cordoba would have been known to be suffering the after-effects, thus reducing its aura of supremacy and increasing its vulnerability in the eyes of the people. One needs, further, to consider the reasons for and the impact made by ʿUmar's putative conversion to Christianity, if such it was, as the sources are not uniform on this detail. It could be interpreted as political expediency, in that another body of people, Christians, would see in him one of their own, someone to challenge the authority of the amirate. There does not appear to be any cogent evidence in support of this theory, even though the remains of church at Bobastro have been identified and excavated. There may have been scattered communities of Christians in the smaller towns, but none who would have wished to put their livelihood at risk by falling in with a rebel, even one with the pedigree of Ibn Hafsūn. In addition, one might point to the fact that if the intention of the conversion was to attract new recruits to join his depleted forces, then it backfired as many of his former allies, the *muwalladūn*, were disenchanted by his *volte face* and faded away when it was perceived that he was reneging on Islam. There is no suggestion, however, that this was a religiously motivated rebellion. Ibn ʿIdhārī is clearly hostile and describes Ibn Hafsūn slightingly in pejorative language, commenting that when he publicly professed Christianity he had been clandestinely Christian, in order, one supposes, to further blacken his name. If he was 'a man with a mission' and intended to bring down the amirate, as his fruitless overtures to North African dynasties and even to the Abbāsids would appear to signify, then it was the madcap, headstrong mentality of the charismatic rebel leader, in the mould of Robert the Bruce, that that brought him such success and ultimate failure.

During the long reign of ʿAbd Allāh, the power and effectiveness of the amirate diminished. More than one account states that the revenues were reduced, no doubt because the principal cities of the Marches, Badajoz, Toledo and Saragossa, had severed their allegiance and were therefore not paying taxes. Despite a state of virtual political disintegration in al-Andalus, ʿAbd Allāh seems to have achieved a tranquil atmosphere within Cordoba itself, in part by making himself available regularly to the citizens and listening personally to their complaints, acquiring thereby a reputation for probity as well as piety. His reign is also distinguished for the burgeoning talent of Ibn 'Abd ar-Rabbih (860–940), a poet who celebrated the achievements of his patron, the *amīr*s, in the style of Eastern panegyrics. This in itself would not be remarkable, but he broke the mould in his versifying, writing stanzaic poetry which was an innovation in Arabic literature, alongside the traditional ode (*qasīda*).

Notes

1. Ahmed ibn Mohammed al-Makkari, *The History of the Mohammedan Dynasties in Spain*, translated by Pascual de Gayangos, 2 vols, London: RoutledgeCurzon, 2002, vol. II, p. 69.
2. Henri Terrasse, *Islam d'Espagne. Une rencontre de l'Orient et de l'Occident*, Paris: Librairie Plon, 1958, p. 46.
3. Don Pascual de Gayangos, *Memoria sobre la autenticidad de la Crónica denominada del Moro Rasis*, Madrid: La Real Academia de la Historia, 1850, p. 95. Translation in this and the above quotation mine.
4. For matters relating to the coinage of the Umayyads, see George C. Miles, *The Coinage of the Umayyads of Spain*, New York: The American Numismatic Society, 2 parts, 1950, part I, pp. 88–9.
5. There is an extensive literature concerning this controversy. For the theological aspect, see Archdale A. King, *Liturgies of the Primatial Sees*, London: Longmans, Green, 1957, pp. 465–98; the monograph by John C. Cavadini, *The Last Christology of the West. Adoptionism in Spain and Gaul, 785–820*, Philadelphia, PA: University of Pennsylvania Press, 1993; for the historical context, Ramón de Abadal y de Vinyals, *La batalla del adopcionismo en la desintegración de la Iglesia visigótica*, Barcelona: Real Academia de Buenas Letras, 1949; H. V. Livermore, *The Origins of Spain and Portugal*, London: George Allen & Unwin, 1971, pp. 346–66; Roger Collins, *The Arab Conquest of Spain, 710–797*, Oxford: Basil Blackwell, 1989, pp. 221–30.
6. Juan Francisco de Rivera specifically states that Elipandus proposed his own interpretation of the divine sonship of Jesus having absorbed the literary treasures of the invaders, *Elipando de Toledo. Nueva aportación a los estudios mozárabes*, Toledo: Editorial Católica Toledana, 1940, p. 35. See also *The Holy Qur'ān*, 17: 26.
7. For further details, see Ibn Hayyān, *Al Muqtabis*, II, 1, translated as *Crónicas de los emires Alhakam, y 'Abdarrahmān entre los años 796 y 847*, by Mahmūd 'Alī Makkī and Federico Corriente, Saragossa: La Aljafería, 2001, pp. 104–5.
8. David James, *Early Islamic Spain. The History of Ibn al-Qūṭīya*, with translation, notes and comments, London: Routledge, 2009, p. 89.
9. Al-Maqqarī, *History of the Mohammedan Dynasties*, vol. II, p. 106.
10. Ibid., vol. II, p. 105.
11. Ibid., vol. I, pp. 148 and 426.
12. Ibn Hayyān, *Al Muqtabis*, f. 131, Spanish text p. 139.
13. Al-Maqqarī, *History of the Mohammedan Dynasties*, vol. II, p. 57.
14. See, for a thorough treatment, Manuela Marín, 'En los márgenes de la ley: el consumo de alcohol en al-Ándalus', in Cristina de la Puente, ed., *Identidades marginales*, Madrid: Consejo Superior de Investigaciones Científicas, 2003, pp. 271–328.
15. 'Hechura de verdura a lo Ziryāb', in Ambrosio Huici Miranda, *Traducción española de un*

manuscrito anónimo del siglo XIII sobre la cocina hispano-magribí, Madrid: Editorial Maestre, 1960, pp. 179–80.

16. Ibn Khaldūn, *The Muqaddimah. An Introduction to History*, translated from the Arabic by Franz Rosenthal; abridged and edited by N. J. Dawood, London: Routledge and Kegan Paul, 1978 [first edition in this form 1967], pp. 409 and 259.

17. The episode is aptly and judiciously summarised by Jacinto Bosch Vilá, *La Sevilla Islámica 712–1248*, Seville: Universidad, 1984, pp. 44–51.

18. A case in point is the dramatic narrative of Fray Justo Pérez de Urbel, *A Saint under Muslim Rule*, Milwaukee, WI: The Bruce Publishing Company, 1937.

19. See the useful study of Eva Lapiedra Gutiérrez, *Cómo los musulmanes llamaban a los cristianos hispánicos*, Valencia: Instituto de Cultura 'Juan Gil-Albert', 1997.

20. In *Obras completas de San Eulogio*, translated by R. P. Agustín S. Ruiz, Córdoba: Real Academia de Córdoba, 1959, p. 221. See also, amongst other works, Jessica A. Coope, *The Martyrs of Córdoba. Community and Family Conflict in an Age of Mass Conversion*, Lincoln, NE and London: University of Nebraska Press, 1995, who takes a different view from the one expressed here.

21. Julián Ribera, *Historia de los jueces de Córdoba por Aljoxaní*, Madrid: E. Maestre, 1914, pp. 186–7 (Arabic text); pp. 231–3 (translation).

22. Derek W. Lomax, *The Reconquest of Spain*, London: Longman, 1978, p. 38.

23. Kenneth Baxter Wolf, *Conquerors and Chroniclers of Early Medieval Spain*, Liverpool: Liverpool University Press, 1990, p. 59.

24. These and similar aspects are thoughtfully considered by Norman Daniel, *The Arabs in Mediaeval Europe*, London: Longman, Librairie du Liban, 1975, 2nd edition 1979; John V. Tolan, *Saracens. Islam in the Medieval European Imagination*, New York: Columbia University Press, 2002.

25. These are discussed and assessed by Manuel Acién Almansa, *Entre el feudalismo y el Islam. 'Umar b. Hafsūn en los historiadores, en las fuentes y en la historia*, Jaén: Universidad, Colección Martínez de Mazas, 1994.

26. Al-Maqqarī, *History of the Mohammedan Dynasties*, vol. II, p. 128.

CHAPTER 3

Al-Andalus in the tenth century

The first half of the tenth century in al-Andalus was dominated by the figure of 'Abd ar-Rahmān III (r. 912–61), the grandson of his predecessor. It was thanks to him that al-Andalus became politically unified, with all the outlying cities acknowledging the sovereignty of Cordoba, which attained an unrivalled eminence in the Western world during his time. According to the *Akhbār Majmūʿa*, he conquered Spain (al-Andalus) city by city, 'defeating those who defended them (rebels), bringing them low, demolishing their fortresses, imposing heavy taxes on those who were left alive and inflicting a harsh regime on them, until total submission was secured'.[1] It was also an epoch of Islamicisation, when many people from among what may be regarded as the hitherto uncommitted indigenous population flocked to Cordoba, adopted Islam and so participated in and prospered from the opportunities to be encountered there. After a lengthy period of years in which the rebellion of 'Umar b. Hafsūn and his sons was finally terminated, and in which insurrection in the Marches was eventually but definitively quashed, Cordoba emerged as a flourishing, populous and prosperous Islamic city. Fortunately, the works of the Andalusi chroniclers 'Arīb b. Saʿīd (died c. 980) and Ibn Hayyān (987–1075), amongst other historical sources, cast light on multiple aspects of 'Abd ar-Rahmān's reign. Furthermore, the so-called Anonymous Chronicle that relates to the years up to 930 shows how the power and authority in al-Andalus was vested in one man, the *amīr*, who went about this task in a single-minded way.[2] The first priority was securing oaths of allegiance, followed by systematic campaigning to bring distant and dissident rulers into line. The means whereby the former was achieved was through the dispatch of a *faqīh* in the company of officers to the governors of the regions with letters containing instructions for the return of a signed affidavit of loyalty. On perhaps the first occasion, an oath was revoked, and troops had to be sent from Cordoba to quell the rebellion. It was in reality the leader of the distinguished and powerful Dhū Nūnid family in Toledo who had committed perjury, and whose head after his defeat was displayed in public in Cordoba. This example testifies first to the importance that the *amīr* attached to written pledges of fealty, and second to an awareness that the Cordoban populace needed to know full well what was the fate of rebels. Furthermore, the parade in public of the head of a defeated enemy sent a clear message to the populace of the *amīr*'s authority in other areas of al-Andalus. Such a practice was designed as a measure to enhance the *amīr*'s reputation, and demonstrates his recognition that, first and foremost, the people of Cordoba had to have visual proof of the power that he wielded in al-Andalus. The above episode occurred in the first year of his amirate. It is indicative of the significance of 'Umar b. Hafsūn's insurrection that 'Abd ar-Rahmān himself should go to Bobastro many years later, in 929, and order that the corpse of 'Umar be disinterred and hung on a post between the rotting cadavers of his two sons in Cordoba. Here they stayed until washed away by the waters when the Guadalquivir flooded in 942.

The reign of 'Abd ar-Rahmān III may effectively be divided into two unequal halves, that is to say before and after the year 929. In the year 928, he took the decision that from then on he should be called *amīr al-mu'minīn* (Commander of the Faithful), which was the title that Caliphs inherited, and, in addition, *an-nāsir ad-dīn Allāh*. In other words, he was bestowing upon himself Caliphal authority. He took this step because he needed to establish his independence from the 'Abbāsids and from the Fātimids who were asserting their claims to Islamic territory in the Maghrib and beyond. He needed to dissociate himself totally from a state whose authority had been seriously compromised. Thenceforward, the Umayyad state in al-Andalus was governed by a Caliph who demanded allegiance from all Muslims within this jurisdiction. Hitherto, in theory, their head of state had been the Abbāsid Caliph in the East who was their nominal leader. 'Abd ar-Rahmān was, from 929, the first Umayyad Caliph of al-Andalus, with the *laqab* (surname) *an-nāsir li-dīn allāh* (Victor in (or Protector of) the Religion of God).[3] As a permanent attestation of the *amīr*'s new exalted status, coins minted in Cordoba bore the Caliphal lemma. These were gold dinars (from the Latin *denarius*), and silver dirhams (from the Greek *drachma*). Their value as instruments of communication would have been incalculable as whenever and wherever the 'reformed national coinage' was handled, the news of 'Abd ar-Rahmān's assumption of the title of Caliph would be transmitted.[4] In concert with the circulation of the new currency, the *amīr* reconstituted the mint (*dār as-sikka*), with the installation of a new director charged with overhauling the entire system, including the regulation of the weights.[5] It should also be noted that no coins appear to have been minted in his reign prior to 929, a fact also noted in Arabic sources, perhaps an indication of the prime necessity of bringing order to al-Andalus before embarking on the management of a new state. Not only were 'Abd ar-Rahmān's initial concerns with unity within al-Andalus, but they were also rigorously focused on the frontiers, thus bringing him into direct confrontation with the nascent Christian kingdoms in the north of the Peninsula. The texts of Ibn Hayyān and of 'Arīb, mentioned earlier, are chock-a-block with accounts of frontier campaigns.

The frontiers

As he became more confident of his power base with al-Andalus, so one may reasonably suppose that 'Abd ar-Rahmān felt encouraged to claim disputed areas and to secure fortresses that would deter the Christian enemy from making incursions into al-Andalus. By the turn of the ninth century, the territory in the Peninsula beyond al-Andalus was divided into a number of states. Through the achievements of Alfonso III, *el magno* (r. 866–910), who took advantage of the internecine struggles within al-Andalus, the territory of the kingdom of Asturias extended southward to the river Duero. His son Ordoño II, in 914, established the capital in the former Roman city of León, more in range with the lands to the south. Thenceforward, the kingdom of León, as it came to be called, together with its neighbours Castile and Navarre, provided the opposition to al-Andalus in the north and west of the peninsula. There have been major disputes among Western historians about the nature of the frontier zones. For the Muslims these were the *thughūr* (Marches) north of Mérida, Toledo and Saragossa respectively. Territorially they ebbed and flowed, with the river Duero in the west and north, and the river Ebro in the east forming very approximate geographical boundaries. The issue which has preoccupied the historians is whether these zones were populated or not up until the tenth century. For Sánchez-Albornoz, and others writing independently of him, the valley of the Duero was entirely unpopulated from the reign of Alfonso I (739–57) until the end of the ninth century, that is to say until the reign of Alfonso III, who put into effect a policy of active repopulation.[6] The sources uphold the latter point, but can be interpreted in different ways in respect of the earlier period. Menéndez Pidal, on the other hand, denied that there was total depopulation, a view sustained, though with a different emphasis, by Thomas Glick, in his scintillating reanalysis of medieval Spain.[7] His statement that 'It is probable that the drought more than the king was responsible for the depopulation of the Duero Valley, where in any case at least scattered nuclei of herding folk must have remained' highlights two significant factors.[8] The first relates to the enormous impact of climatic conditions which could drastically transform the demography of a region. Villages could certainly be abandoned and left deserted in times of drought and other natural disasters, but would be repossessed when circumstances improved. Second, the reference to 'herding folk' draws attention to the uses of the land. The immense plateau extending from Zamora to León in the north and from Valladolid in the east to Burgos in the north is said to have constituted a kind of no-man's-land until its repopulation in the time of Alfonso III, yet it is irrigated by two rivers, the Esla and the Pisuerga, both more than 200 miles long, whose numerous tributaries extend like tentacles criss-crossing the region. Even allowing for the dramatic seasonal changes of the weather, extreme heat in the summer months and corresponding cold in the winter, it seems improbable that it should not have been exploited for its pasturelands and crops potential. This whole zone was a far cry from the arid deserts of the Maghrib. It is more likely that there were scattered pockets of inhabitants, villagers or peasants, a threat neither to Muslims passing through nor to the designs of Alfonso and his successors, perhaps 'a vast, if incomplete depopulation' in the judicious words of Derek W. Lomax.[9]

It was Alfonso III who exploited the political disarray in al-Andalus by offering land tenure to new settlers, thereby attracting migrants from throughout the Peninsula. From the evidence of the place names, although the dates in which the settlements were established are not invariably verifiable, it may be learnt that the immigrants came not only from the south but also from the Basque region. Cordoveses and Toldanos (from Toledo) provide unmistakable evidence of place of origin and require an explanation. These would be clusters of citizens connected to the two cities mentioned who were uncomfortable or dissatisfied with their lot and sought a more stable existence elsewhere. The 890s and the first decade of the tenth century gave little promise of a secure future *in situ*. As to religion, they may have been *ahl al-kitāb*, but they were not *a priori* Christians. Given that they were protected in law, persecution is unlikely to have motivated their exodus from al-Andalus. Once it came to be known that land was available to those who settled on it, the lure would have been, in an uncertain social and political environment, well nigh irresistible.

The city of Zamora on the northern banks of the Duero constitutes a pertinent example. It had been a Roman city on the direct road between Mérida and Astorga, and was targeted by the kingdom of Asturias and by the Muslims for its strategic value in the frontier zone. In 893, according to Arabic sources, it was occupied, heavily fortified and restored at the instigation of Alfonso III partly by his own people and partly by *'ajam* from Toledo, that is to say those belonging to the indigenous population who did not speak Arabic. The text has been taken to mean Christians of Toledo but the word *'ajam* does not carry with it any necessary religious affiliation, and therefore does not warrant this interpretation. Much later on in his reign, 'Abd ar-Rahmān III failed in his attempt to recapture Zamora in 939 when he and his army, an amalgam of his own troops and allies of dubious loyalty, were decisively defeated near Simancas, at the battle of Alhándega (*al-khandaq*, ditch or trench), by Ramiro II in alliance with the forces of Castile and Navarre. Given the location, the occupancy of Zamora was crucial. If it was sufficiently reinforced to withstand forays from the south, then the region northward to León was protected; if the Muslims could hold it, then they had a secure command of that area of the frontier. After his victory, for example, Ramiro was able to extend the kingdom as far south as the river Tormes, occupying towns such as Salamanca, thus pushing the notional frontier well beyond the Duero. The provenance of the new inhabitants of this area is not explicit, but it would be difficult to sustain that incomers from al-Andalus as testified by toponymic evidence outnumbered those from other parts of the Peninsula.[10] The abundance of place names of patently Arabic origin may reasonably be ascribed to settlements by immigrants. Where there is no conspicuous sign of a religious foundation, then these settlers fall into the above-mentioned category of migrants seeking to improve their lot in life. Again, to quote the words of Lomax: 'We do not yet know enough about the Duero resettlement to feel certain of its aims'.[11]

Yet there is evidence culled from Latin documents relating to Christian monasteries and to sundry inscriptions for the fabrication of churches, and the creation of monastic communities that generated their own economy. An inscription on the consecration stone, now lost but copied in the eighteenth century and considered authentic, refers to the abbot Alfonso who, in 913, came from Cordoba with his colleagues (sociis) with the express purpose of constructing the church of San Miguel de Escalada on the site of ruins on the plains irrigated by the river Esla to the south-east of the city of León. This task, so the inscription reads, was accomplished in twelve months, significantly without coercing the local populace to help. This detail not only indicates that the Abbot found people already in situ when he arrived, but also, by inference, that he brought his own architects and craftsmen with him. One need not assume that Alfonso was a Christian fleeing from oppression to explain this situation; he may indeed only have had the title conferred upon him on arrival, or conceivably after the undertaking was successfully completed. A further point is that, whereas a number of abbots in Christian monasteries have Arabic names, evidence of their Arabicisation, his is unchanged. Yet even this does not ipso facto demonstrate his adherence to Christianity or his aversion to the Arabs and Islam. What is remarkable about the edifice that Alfonso created is that all its interior arches and those in the cloister are of a horseshoe shape, a characteristic feature of what has come to be termed Mozarabic architecture.[12] As such, it mirrors the interior of the mosque at Cordoba. One might add the detail that after its likely destruction by a marauding Muslim army which ravaged the region in 988, it was rebuilt at the instigation of Alfonso V with the same architectural features. Alfonso III's building had all the outward appearance of a Muslim building, indeed not any Muslim building, but the one that epitomised Islam in al-Andalus in that epoch, the Great Mosque, the jewel in Cordoba's crown. Yet, when the abbot Alfonso, his designers and workmen created in Christian territory something so emblematically Islamic, it was not regarded as at all untoward, nor was any opprobrium directed at him on this account. The horseshoe arch then, so redolent of the interior of the Cordoban mosque, yet now characterising a Christian temple, was perfectly acceptable in a kingdom so militarily opposed to the Umayyad state of al-Andalus. The conclusion is inescapable: the icons of one religion were not anathema to the other. Hostilities were not fuelled by religiously antagonistic sentiments, but by the urge, at times inordinate, to possess and retain land as a prerequisite to enjoying the prestige of power.

Something unprecedented was occurring in the frontier zones in both urban and rural communities. What was distinctive about the nascent Leonese kingdom was its saturation by Islamic and Arabic features, of which the widespread use of the Islamic style of architecture was but one. This phenomenon, known as Mozarabism, flourished only in Christian-held territories yet is a striking instance of the influence and impact of al-Andalus beyond its own boundaries. The Latin cartularies reveal not only a plethora of Arabic names of monks and settlers transliterated unevenly and sometimes unrecognisably into Latin, but also several hundred words of Arabic origin. This trend started in the ninth century and continued throughout the tenth, and is a testimony of the influence of al-Andalus on neighbouring states. One of the rich sources for these names is the monastery of Sahagún, in the so-called frontier zone. It was founded in 904, perhaps by the same abbot Alfonso as was involved in Escalada, who, according to an inscription, 'with his colleagues had come from Spania' – the word is used in the documentation to apply to al-Andalus – 'to live in this region in order to build a monastery in this place'.[13] The monastery at Sahagún grew rapidly, and documents of the tenth century contain Arabic words pertaining to a variety of features. Most conspicuous are references to fine fabrics and articles of clothing, such as *alphaneke* (*al-fanak*, a small North African fox or marten, much prized for its fur), but the pick of the fine materials and textiles that circulated in the monasteries in this area was *tirāz* (embroidered silk material), often a robe much prized for its quality. The embroidered element could take the form of an inscription woven in golden thread. A hundred years later, in the eleventh century, three *tiraceros* at the service of the king of León are recorded in a document of 1026, an indication of the vogue for this luxury product in the highest echelons of society. *Tirāz* had been introduced into al-Andalus from the east, probably in the first half of the ninth century, perhaps as part of the revolution in clothing propagated by Ziryāb. By the time of 'Abd ar-Rahmān III's reign, its manufacture was established throughout the realm, with Seville, Almería where at a later time there is said to have been 800 looms for the weaving *tirāzī* garments, Baeza and Málaga being noted centres of its production.[14] *Tirāz* was even exported to other regions of the Islamic world as, according to the tenth-century geographer Ibn Hawqal, 'in al-Andalus there is more than one *tirāz* factory, the products of which go to Misr [Egypt] and some sometimes to the utmost limits of Khurasān and elsewhere'.[15] Evidently, *tirāz* was merchandise exported also to the Christian states in the north of the Peninsula. Such exports were fundamental to the economy of al-Andalus, and it is no surprise that a special official should have been put in charge of *tirāz* in 923. As political stability was brought to the Islamic west, so trade became more buoyant, helping to create in Cordoba a thriving state that became renowned as a centre for precious items which, in turn, formed part of the lucrative trade with the northern kingdoms. This trade, notably in luxury items, is reflected in the Latin documentation and is evidence of the permeation of Islam in the frontier zones and elsewhere.

Yet the above is a story only half told. The emigrants, who cannot be called refugees if they were not fleeing from persecution, were responsible for the transmission of so many aspects of Andalusi life as to cause what amounted to a remodelling of society in the Christian states of the north. Words were introduced that described a way of life or a particular practice common in al-Andalus, hitherto not testified in society there. They could, for example, refer to institutions implanted in the kingdom of León such as the *azogue* (from the Arabic *as-sūq*, Spanish *zoco* the urban market, or rather its permanent location, to differentiate it, as pointed out by Glick, from the Latin *mercatus* which was a weekly market).[16] The *azogue* came to be an institution throughout the Peninsula, and has left its mark as a street name in many places, from Seville to Santander, including the small township of Villanubla on the road north-east from Valladolid to León, and therefore right in the frontier zone. The *aceña* (from the Arabic *as-sāniyya* water-wheel) was known in Sahagún in the tenth century; also first recorded in Latin in the tenth century were *zafariche* (from Arabic *sihrīj* well), and the ubiquitous *aceifa* (Arabic *as-sā'ifa* a military expedition taking place in the summer). These *aceifa*s were to become almost a yearly feature in the second half of the century. The offices of *alcalde* (mayor, from the Arabic *al-qādī* judge), *alcaide* (Arabic *al-qā'id* governor of a castle), *alguacil* (Arabic *al-wazīr* minister, then regional or city governor), *almojarife* (Arabic *al-mushrif* supervisor, then customs officer) and *alferez* (Arabic *al-fāris* horseman, knight, standard-bearer in battle), all came to designate functions in the Christian kingdoms, either occupying voids or replacing former Latin terms. An echo of this can be seen in the thirteenth-century epic *Poema de Fernán González*: 'Todos los castellanos en uno se juntaron, dos hombres de grand guisa por alcaldes alzaron'.[17] Coins of Arabic origin circulated in the realms; these included the *mescal* (Arabic *mithqāl* weight) and the *maravedí* (of uncertain Arabic derivation), coins that could be of silver or gold. Sánchez-Albornoz assembled a number of texts as evidence of the use of coinage of Andalusi origin in trading transactions in the frontier zones in these centuries.[18] The revival of the mints after 'Abd ar-Rahmān III assumed Caliphal status is reflected in the dissemination of his coins among the new settlers. A final point to make concerning the frontier zone in the north and west of the Peninsula is that it was subject to the vicissitudes of an unceasing power struggle. It had little to do with the now outmoded concept of Reconquest whereby a religious motivation is ascribed to the military conquests of the Christian kingdoms of the north from the eighth century onwards. The idea that northern states were fighting Muslims in order to restore the land to their rightful possessors, the Christians, 'as if recovering property stolen from their ancestors',[19] is articulated in a ninth-century Latin chronicle, but there is an overwhelming lack of evidence elsewhere to apply this to the whole raft of military engagements between Christians and Muslims, certainly until the thirteenth century. It was not until the eleventh century and the era of the Crusades that a religious element entered into the equation, when the armed forces on both sides were conscious that they were fighting to uphold a particular set of beliefs. Before that time, such an ingredient did not form part of encounters between north and south in the Iberian Peninsula.

The Caliphate in Cordoba: the early period

After consolidating the Umayyad Caliphate in al-Andalus, 'Abd ar-Rahmān launched into an extensive building programme. Notable among the projects for which he was responsible was the Madīna az-Zahrā', begun in 936/7 and named according to al-Maqqarī, after a palace favourite, which came to be the outward and visible sign of its prestige and power. As the word *madīna* indicates, this was not just a palace but an entire town, characterised by its *zahra* (splendour), which term was borne out by its whole mien when complete.

Ibn Hayyān wrote that he had heard that the Caliph was so preoccupied with this enterprise that it allowed him to forget the outside world, and in particular the stunning defeat that he had suffered at Alhándega, after which he never led his troops personally into battle.[20] It was situated about four miles from Cordoba itself, on the gentle lower slopes of the sierra, a location ideal for irrigation from the mountains behind and lofty enough to enjoy extraordinary views over the plain in front. It is reckoned that building on the mosque commenced in 941, five years after the new city had been laid out, and that its external fabric and interior were completed in forty-eight days by 1,000 workmen, a testimony to the intensity of the effort expended on this particular part of the whole. The complex was not completed until the reign of his successor, and was not to survive the *fitna* of 1010 when it was destroyed by Berbers and evacuated in 1013. Excavation of the site began in 1910, and the great hall together with the mosque is in the process of restoration using materials in the main excavated from the site. The city, as originally conceived, constructed over an area the extent of a medium-sized airport, was walled and fortified with rectangular towers. It was organised on three levels, the upper one containing the palatial apartments, the central terrace containing gardens, including fountains, and the lower one for the townsfolk and their dwellings. That it was an exceedingly ambitious undertaking is borne out by the thirteenth-century biographer Ibn Khallikān who, quoting earlier sources, mentions that a third of the enormous revenue of the Caliphate went on its construction yearly.

Furthermore, intricate details are forthcoming from Ibn Hayyān; these relate to the number of labourers employed; the number of pack animals, including camels, used for conveying building materials, which included stones used both for sculpting and for paving; the thousands of columns, together with details concerning their place of origin (some being brought from as far afield as Narbonne and Byzantium), their colour and cost; and even the number of doors covered with polished brass. The fact that contemporary historians should go into such lavish detail about Madīna az-Zahrā' is revealing in a number of ways. It tells us that one intention was to glorify the Caliphate in Cordoba, and to heap credit onto 'Abd ar-Rahmān and his successor. One may also infer that this new city was 'Abd ar-Rahmān's consolation; if he could not sweep all before him militarily, then at least he could create something that no other kingdom could match in grandeur. It also in passing begs the question as to who the labourers and workmen were. Some, those more skilled, would have been amongst those who had worked on the Great Mosque in Cordoba and were adept at particular crafts; some would have been drafted in from the peasantry, as forced labour; others perhaps came from North Africa. Clearly, to the historians, they were merely instruments through which the great project was brought to fruition, and of no account or perceived worth as individuals. Historians of art and architecture, such as Henri Terrasse and Gonzalo Borrás, have noted Romano-Byzantine traditions as well as 'Abbāsid ornamentation which, taken together, point to a hybrid structure, encapsulating the best of both worlds.[21]

Ibn Hayyān records in detail an eclipse of the sun in 939, and the occurrence of two natural phenomena in the 940s. The first of these was the sighting in the western sky above Cordoba of a comet (but not Halley's comet as the two years of its appearance on earth in the tenth century were 912 and 989), visible at night for over a week in October 941. The second, in April 942, seems in all probability to have been a typically magnificent display of the aurora borealis, whose glow has not been unknown in different parts of Spain. The accounts of all of these spectacles, and other similar ones in Ibn Hayyān's chronicle, are precise and unadorned, as if they had been recorded by an astronomer or someone used to describing scientific data. The effect on those in the terrestrial sphere is not mentioned, so there was no astrological dimension. The chronicler does, however, register the impact of fires and drought in Cordoba. In 918, there was a large fire in the market, which burnt the stalls of the makers of combs and lathes. In July of 936, there was a much more serious conflagration in the same market, in which the wool warehouse was consumed together with the silk, drapery and perfume stalls. A mosque was also destroyed but 'Abd ar-Rahmān ordered that it be rebuilt straight away with better materials, and that the market be provided with a tiled roof. In the reign of his successor, part of the market was set aside particularly for silks, the *alcaicería*. These disasters occurred within the confines of the city, their impact primarily falling on merchants and artisans. The drought which started in 936, the equivalent to the worst in living memory, caused no hardship to the rural communities. Prices did not rise because precautionary measures had been taken, the necessary provisions being carried great distances, preventing poverty. The ruler is given credit for this forethought, whereby the worst effects of a natural disaster were diverted. In the above instance, the chronicler is doing what chroniclers have been doing over the ages, casting his patron or in this case the patron's ancestor in a favourable light, albeit not in an exaggerated manner. This intervention on the part of the caliph in the affairs of a rural community struck with calamity may be seen as one of the factors that may have encouraged those who lived away from the main cities to be well disposed towards Islam. The prestige and prosperity that Cordoba enjoyed during 'Abd ar-Rahmān's Caliphate and the political stability that had taken two centuries to achieve were all part of the allure of the capital of al-Andalus. When its enormous population increase took place in the tenth century, those who came to Cordoba in their thousands from the country adopted Islam in order to take full advantage of the opportunities on offer. This would indicate that the steepest conversion curve occurred in the tenth century and not in the previous century, as demonstrated by Richard Bulliet in his masterly pioneering work on conversion to Islam, albeit from a limited statistical base which he himself acknowledged.[22]

One of the embellishments in Madīna az-Zahrā', to which a number of sources allude, was a fountain brought from Constantinople, and through this we learn of relations between the Byzantine emperor, Constantine VII Porphyrogenitus (r. 913–59), and Cordoba, a recognition on the part of the former of the prestige acquired by the Andalusi court. Missions may have started in 947, and they took place on a regular basis into the 960s. In 949, Constantine sent two notable gifts: the *De Materia Medica* of Dioscorides in Greek and Orosius's *History of the Romans* in Latin. The former, according to Ibn Abī Usaybi'a (a thirteenth-century physician and author of *Lives of the Physicians*), was a lavishly illustrated pharmacopocia with drawings of plants. According to Ibn Juljul, an eminent physician who worked in Cordoba and who wrote a commentary on the work of Dioscorides in 982, there was no one in Cordoba with a knowledge of Greek sufficient to translate it into Arabic. As a consequence, at the Caliph's express request, Constantine sent the monk Nicholas who arrived in Cordoba in 951 and who, accordingly, made the work accessible to a number of scholars eager to tap into the medicinal knowledge that it contained. One may presume that he translated the *De Materia Medica* into Latin, and that from this language it was rendered by local scholars into Arabic. One of the participants in this enterprise was the Jewish polymath, diplomat and physician Hasdai b. Shaprūt, who was educated according to the Jewish tradition and also in Arabic letters. In the following ten years before his death, Nicholas translated the names of plants hitherto unknown in Cordoba, identifying herbs and explaining their properties to a small group of collaborators.[23] Hasdai became acquainted 'with all the obscure passages in the books by Dioscorides',[24] and made practical use of this knowledge. He was thus representative of those cultured intellectuals who practised *adab*, broadly speaking *belles-lettres*, but inclusive of a range of learning not exclusively in the humanities. As the Caliphate progressed, there was a growing corpus comprising both 'home-produced' scholars and those from abroad.

One of Ibn Juljul's works, *Book of the Generations of Physicians and Wise Men*, contained biographies of Andalusi physicians, and these provide an insight into the practice of early medicine in Cordoba. As I have previously written:

> some of the early practitioners were Christians, as their names testify: Jawād at-Tabīb an-Nasrānī (Jawād the Christian Doctor), Yazīd ar-Rūmān an-Nasrānī, renowned in the excellence of his medicine and Ibn Malūka an-Nasrānī, a surgeon who practised blood-letting (and who kept thirty chairs for patients in the equivalent of his waiting-room).[25]

These physicians who were integrated into the urban community in Cordoba were evidently Arabicised, yet they belonged to the indigenous population, upon whom there was no constraint to adopt Islam. It is relevant here to mention, in addition, the surgeon Ishāq, probably Yahyā b. Ishāq, who wrote a treatise on pleurisy in five books, now lost, following the system of the Greeks, whose knowledge would have been transmitted into Arabic in the east, and communicated to scholars in al-Andalus by those who came to reside in the court at Cordoba. This Ishāq was of sufficient standing in the court circles of Cordoba to be called upon by the Caliph 'Abd ar-Rahmān III, to treat his otitis (inflammation of the ear), a cure which he executed through the application of a folk remedy. The cure may have been eardrops in the form of a distillation of saffron and wine. One source indicates that the remedy was acquired from a monk, which would suggest that Ishāq knew the vernacular language. If this was the case, then a bilingual doctor distinguished enough to be in the Caliph's circle was versed in Arabic pharmacology drawn from Greek sources and also knowledgeable in popular medicine. Clearly, in the examples given, there was no hostility towards these frontline medical practitioners on the grounds of their religious beliefs.

'Arīb b. Sa'īd (918–c. 980) was an Andalusi physician and scholar who may have worked with the monk Nicholas in Cordoba, and was certainly familiar with the *De Materia Medica* of Dioscorides to whom he refers in his treatise on the generation of the foetus.[26] In this remarkable work, the only one of its kind to have been composed in al-Andalus, 'Arīb shows a knowledge of Aristotle and of the fundamental texts of Hippocrates and Galen in his account of the progress of a human being from conception to maturity. He demonstrates an understanding of his topic that derives from the Classical tradition, as well as from local lore, and prescribes cures for particular conditions as a result of personal observation and experience. As a scholar he repeats and often evaluates the respective opinions of previous students of the subject. He also ranges broadly, from apparent deaths when a person has stopped breathing only to come alive again when about to be interred, to the diet of the wet nurse and remedies for epilepsy and smallpox. He also draws examples from named predecessors, both from al-Andalus and from the Islamic east, in most cases to demonstrate the efficacy of a particular treatment, such as the paste made from a mixture of myrrh, aloes, saffron and juice from wolfberries (*lycium afrum*) which is applied to the shaven head of an infant with a swollen stomach. Additionally, he sometimes evaluates these remedies. One gets the impression that 'Arīb's concern is for the health and well-being of his community which he communicates through setting down all the received knowledge on a given topic related to obstetrics and paediatrics. Under 'Abd ar-Rahmān, a state was emerging in which men, having absorbed Greek learning through Arabic, took the lead in an assortment of different spheres, of which medicine was one.

'Arīb's near namesake, Rabī' b. Zayd al-Usquf, that is to say 'the Bishop', provides a window in both his life and works onto a broad spectrum of activities. The two are linked through an almanac-cum-liturgical calendar in Arabic with whose authorship both have been associated. It was first made known when a Latin translation was published by Guglielmo Libri in the 1830s, and has since become known as the Calendar of Cordoba.[27] It was assigned the date 961 from internal evidence by Reinaud in 1848, but is undated, and has come to be related to al-Andalus through its content.[28] In essence, it falls into the category of a *kitāb al-anwā'*, a meteorological work describing a system whereby groups of stars (*anwā'*), influenced natural phenomena such as rain, wind, storms and, conversely, drought and heat. The text provides a great deal of information on a wide sphere of activities which would otherwise have been unknown. Amongst the areas on which light is shed is astronomy; the position of the relevant constellations for each month is invariably mentioned, often accompanied by a crude illustration. Included under this heading are monthly references to the hours of daylight and darkness, to the strength of the midday sun and to the length of shadows measured with respect to the well at Mecca, thus suggesting that the template of the calendar was eastern in origin. At the beginning of each month, the author briefly states to what temperament the weather will be most suited or unsuited; for example July is unsuited to everyone, and June suited to those of cold temperaments and of an advanced age. The paragraph at the end of each month specifies the medicinal plants that are to be gathered, and on occasions for what purpose they are to be used; ailments of the eye get particular mention, and certain specific days are also noted as those on which particular remedies are applied. For the sake of one's health, baths must not be taken in December, and this injunction is emphasised.

A wealth of precise detail is provided regarding the accepted days for planting such and such a crop, for gathering harvest in coastal areas (figs in June) and for pruning trees, and the months when certain fruit ripen (peaches, pomegranates and quinces ready to pick in September, saffron flowers in November). As

far as pasture is concerned, the places and periods of cattle grazing are carefully specified. There is a wealth of references to saints' days observed by the
Christian Church, and to places where named saints were revered, an indication perhaps of the contribution of Rabī'. Of particular interest is the reference,
on 27 November, to the feast day of San Facundo 'whose burial ground is in the
territory of León'.[29] It would seem that this actual entry was made by 'Arīb as
he refers to those who live in the area as *'ajam* (non-Arab speakers) here and in
other parts of the text. One would have supposed that a Christian writing this
in Arabic would have used the Arabic word that specifically meant Christian
(*nasārā*). The name Facundus is the origin of Sahagún, the Leonese monastery
founded in the ninth century, and one that was to acquire great prestige in a
short period of time. As to toponymy, material abounds relating to Cordoba, its
suburbs, outlying villages and monasteries in the nearby sierra, allowing one to
deduce that monastic communities such as the one at Peña Mellaria, which is
mentioned on several occasions, continued until the tenth century. The ornitho-
logical coverage is surprisingly detailed. There is information about Valencian
falcons, the vultures of Niebla and the nesting habits of ostriches (25 September),
as well as the migratory movements of cranes, storks and swallows. A small
number of entries might have had their foundation in popular beliefs. These
include the warning to sailors to keep off the sea for seven weeks (7 March) and
the observation on 24 June to the effect that cereals harvested on this day will
have immunity from worms. It is curious to note that in a calendar attributed to
Ibn al-Bannā' at least 300 years afterwards, the same detail is provided for the
same day.[30] Finally, one may draw attention to the telling entry at the end of
May which states that during this month, letters are sent out to provincial agents
relating to the requisition of kermes for its red dye, silk (*harīr*) and fuller's earth
used in the fabrication of *tirāz*, originally the word for decorative embroideries
on a garment, but here applied to the luxury robes with this characteristic. In
August, the letters ask for blue dye for the *tirāz*. Clearly, the urban market for
fine garments has to be catered for. The value put on horses is indicated by the
fact that the letters sent out in March prescribe their purchase for the government; in June, stags' horns have to be acquired for bows, as part of the necessary
preparatory work for the Caliphal summer campaigns against the kingdoms of
the north. A further aspect of this forward planning is alluded to in February,
when provincial governors are required to look for conscripts specifically for
these campaigns. The letters, which cease after September and January, testify
to the regular contact between the capital and provincial centres, and also demonstrate that the latter are relied upon to supply specified goods as and when
required. The country was at the service of the town.

The supposedly Christian co-compiler of the Calendar of Cordoba has been
identified as a prominent member of the indigenous community known as
Recemundus, whose biography one can piece together from Arabic and Latin

sources. If, as has been suggested, he was known in Arabic circles as Rabīʿ b. Zayd, as above, then he was evidently a bilingual member of the indigenous population, and one who was ambitious and seeking advancement. It would appear that he first came to the notice of the highest authorities when there was a diplomatic crisis in the 950s. Otto I of Germany (r. 938–73, Holy Roman Emperor from 962) objected strongly to the activities of certain Muslims in the region around present-day La Garde-Freinet, in the Massif des Maures, known in the Latin source as *Fraxinetum* (ash forest), where from their fortress base they harassed travellers, interrupted trade and pillaged monasteries over a vast area. Otto, it seems, assumed that because they were Muslims, ʿAbd ar-Rahmān III had jurisdiction over them and indeed sanctioned their predatory activities. This seems not to have been the case, in that these Muslims from the frontiers of al-Andalus were acting independently of the Umayyads in Cordoba, and indulging in what amounted to freelance brigandage. Relations between the two most powerful rulers in Western Europe became strained, and consequently ʿAbd ar-Rahmān sent an envoy to Otto's court in Frankfurt to resolve the difficulties. The sequence of events seems to have been that this envoy died of natural causes in Otto's court without having had the opportunity to formally deliver the letters from the Caliph. Otto then, in 953, sent a mission of his own to Cordoba, headed by the redoubtable abbot John of Gorze (c. 900–74). The Latin account details the overland itinerary of John's delegation, through France and across the Gulf of Lion to Barcelona thence to Tortosa, where they awaited a safe-conduct pass; they were welcomed in all the cities in al-Andalus through which they passed by specific order of the Caliph, and lavish apartments were made available to John and his retinue in Cordoba. It soon became apparent that a major diplomatic incident was imminent, particularly if the handing over of the letters from Otto, believed to be offensive to the Caliph and Islam, was to take place amid the splendid protocol of a state occasion in the Madīna az-Zahrā'. ʿAbd ar-Rahmān sought to defuse the crisis by persuading John to destroy the letters and release the gifts that he had also brought from Otto. He employed as his intermediary Hasdai b. Shaprūt, the noted scholar, physician and confi-dant at court, no doubt because of his linguistic aptitude. His plea for extreme caution fell on deaf ears. As a last resort, a bishop, about whom little is known except his name, John, went to reason with the Abbot. Bishop John's argument was that any major incident would seriously jeopardise the circumstances of Christians in al-Andalus whose very existence depended on compromise. The Abbot had no truck with any conciliatory attitude, and berated the Bishop for his weakness in adversity. He insisted that he could never concede that divine precepts be broken out of love, fear or favour of men, and asserted that as a foreigner he was not subject to the constraints under which the Bishop laboured. In short, he refused to withdraw the letters, even if it meant that he would suffer death on account of his obduracy. ʿAbd ar-Rahmān's response was to threaten the entire Christian community unless the Abbot complied with his request, but again the latter remained firm in his convictions.

This Latin account, particularly of the dialogue between the two churchmen, seems to coincide with the reality of the situation relating to what we know about Christianity in al-Andalus at that time.[31] Those perceived to be living under a yoke by an outside observer recognised the necessity of not 'rocking the boat'. After many months of negotiation, it was agreed by both parties that a delegation should be sent to Otto, appealing to him to send further instructions to the Abbot in Cordoba, thus defusing a potential diplomatic crisis. Muslim officials were reluctant to volunteer for what was acknowledged to be a hazardous mission. The person who finally came forward was a prominent layman called Recemundus, described in the source, perhaps somewhat misleadingly, as *adprime catholicus* (an excellent Catholic). Recemendus asked the Muslim authorities what reward he would receive upon the successful outcome of the enterprise, and was promised the bishopric of Elvira, that is to say Granada. In short, he accomplished all that was required of him; he went to Otto's court in 955, whereupon the Emperor agreed to rescind the instructions to the Abbot who was now at liberty to present his credentials to 'Abd ar-Rahmān. This Abbot John did three years after having arrived in Cordoba, but remaining true to his austere lifestyle, he wore his black monk's habit, a concession which was granted him, when all the courtiers were arrayed in the magnificent attire that protocol demanded at an official ceremony in the Madīna az-Zahrā'. In a bizarre detail, the account concludes by noting that 'Abd ar-Rahmān and Abbot John became acquainted, the former not put off by the prospect of friendship with a Christian, and the latter happy to engage in lengthy good-natured conversations concerning the respective merits of their two worlds. As a codicil, it might be mentioned that the Muslims of Fraxinetum were forced back by the Emperor's forces, leading to their total defeat in 975.

The role of Recemundus was evidently crucial to the resolution of the impasse between Abbot and Caliph. He may be categorised as a politically astute representative of an increasing number of non-committed non-Muslims who were attracted by the lure of material advancement that association with the Umayyad administration could offer. He was bilingual, giving him an evident advantage over rivals. The fact that he was known in the Arabic form of his name as Al-Usquf confirms that the Caliph was true to his word. Yet, are we led to understand that the conferment of a bishopric was in the Caliph's gift? It seems more likely that the title was an honorific one. There is no indication that Recemundus ever went to Elvira, let alone that he practised as a bishop there or elsewhere. He seems to have enjoyed a wholly secular career, as his skills as a diplomat were again called upon when he was sent to Constantinople, and assigned to other missions in the eastern Mediterranean. Here was an individual, not Muslim, undertaking sensitive and responsible tasks for the Umayyads, being valued, as it were, for his indispensable abilities rather than for his religion or race. In this particular administration, during what may be termed the heyday of the Caliphate, Jews in the person of Hasdai, and non-Muslims in the person of Recemundus – there not being sufficient secure evidence to assign him to the group of Christians in the city – were integrated into the higher echelons of the Islamic state.

There is, however, a sure indication that some Christians, at least, were Arabophone under the Caliphate. The Gospels were translated into Arabic by Ishāq b. Velashq (Velasco) al-Qurtubī in 946. Although nothing is known of this person, his translation has survived in three manuscripts, one a copy done in Fez in 1145, an indication that it did have a certain circulation. The copy made in 1335 was later used among Moriscos in the sixteenth century, and certified as orthodox by the Christian authorities in the person of Francisco López Tamarid in 1565. The version of the Gospels is somewhat literal and the frequent insertion of the *bismillah* shows that the translator was well versed in the Qur'ānic tradition.[32] It has been maintained that the Psalter had been rendered into Arabic by Hafs al-Qūṭī at the behest of a Bishop Valentius in 889, though the alternative date of 989 has also been put forward.[33] Irrespective of the dating, Arabic versions of the Gospels and the Psalms were produced and, it may be assumed, propagated amongst those in the Christian community who were not able to understand them in Latin. Increasing Arabicisation in Cordoba under the Caliphate amongst all sectors was a corollary of the burgeoning prestige that it enjoyed.

In all, it is for the creation of an Islamic state with a distinctive Islamic ethos that ʿAbd ar-Raḥmān III should be remembered. In structure and in outward appearances, it was essentially an Umayyad enterprise, in that the observance of Islam was founded on acceptance of the *sunna*, but the constituent parts were diverse. It has been claimed by Simonet, amongst others, although he certainly overstated the case, that 'Spanish Islam' achieved its distinctiveness through the fact that so many of the Muslims were of indigenous stock.[34] A controversial case in point is in the discipline of poetry. The traditional Arabic verse-form was the ode *qasīda*, a continuous poem linked through a common end-assonantal rhyme. The practice of dividing a poem into separate verses or stanzas originated in al-Andalus. These strophic poems were known as *muwashshahāt*, like a *wishāh*, a belt or sash with ornaments with a regular patterning of pearls, which was imitated in the arrangement of the rhymes. A feature of this type of poetry was the concluding couplet, known as the *kharja* (exit verse), which contained words in the Arabic vernacular, and in Romance transliterated into Arabic. Although the interpretation of these couplets makes it difficult to justify the claim that the Romance words, when taken together, represented early Romance lyric, nonetheless the presence of even one word in Romance would suggest some contact, however minimal, with indigenous culture. This may be explained by the fact that the *muwashshahāt*, which were principally panegyrics or had amorous themes, would have been recited in salon-type gatherings. The poets sought to outdo each other in originality, and the more adventurous they were in their verse, the greater the plaudits they received. In such a context, the incorporation of a Romance word, especially one that could come across as an interlingual homonym, that is to say, a word pronounced the same or written with the same combination of letters, but with one meaning in Arabic and another in Romance, could have caused a sensation. An example might be the word *matara*, which in Arabic means to bestow favours upon, and in Romance as *mat[a]re*, 'madre', means mother. A poet who could achieve such dexterity, also apparent in other genres of poetry, would be one who excelled, and thus would attract welcome attention and, often, advancement. The poet might have come into contact with Romance speakers in the capital, in any number of situations. It is quite another matter to affirm that the prosody or rhythmic patterning of the *muwashshahāt* was formulated under the influence of Romance poetry. The currently accepted opinion is that it was a variation of a Classical Arabic poetic form, but one needs to be aware that those who maintain that the indigenous culture made an impact on Andalusi civilisation as it developed in the tenth century still refer to poetry as an example.[35]

One also has to say that the prestige that Cordoba enjoyed under 'Abd ar-Rahmān III arose through cultural contacts with the 'Abbāsid east. This is to say that Andalusi Islam at its apogee had Eastern currents flowing through it. Yet politically, the Umayyad and 'Abbāsid regimes were poles apart, the former conservative and Sunni, the latter to some extent sympathetic to the Shī'a. 'Abd ar-Rahmān was sensitive to the necessity of maintaining the legitimacy of the status of the Umayyad state in al-Andalus, hence the reliance on contemporary historians such as Ahmad ar-Rāzī (888–955), and his son 'Īsā. The former wrote a history of the rulers of al-Andalus, as well as a description of al-Andalus; neither has survived, although sections of the former were included by Ibn Hayyān and al-Maqqarī in their narratives. He is also said to have written a description of the city of Cordoba, and of 'its principal streets and suburbs, together with its public buildings, and the palaces of the nobles'.[36] His work may be considered, therefore, to have been a chronicle of the times in which he lived, and thus a window on concurrent events. Whether he was a chronicler who wrote at the ruler's bidding, and whose accounts are therefore to be treated with as much caution as the official chronicles of European monarchs in the Middle Ages, may never be determined unless a text of his is discovered in its entirety. One could argue, though, that 'Abd ar-Rahmān was in no need of a propaganda machine in the person of someone to blazon his achievements, as news of the 'new' Cordoba particularly after 950, and during the reign of his successor, spread throughout the length and breadth of the Mediterranean.

Throughout his reign, and particularly after assuming the title of Caliph,

'Abd ar-Rahmān was conscious of the need to quell the Fātimid threat in North Africa. The Fātimids, a *shī'a* branch of Islam, had established their state at Mahdiyya in 921 on a promontory in present-day Tunisia. The Fātimid leader had declared himself Caliph and *amīr al-mu'minīn* in 910, and it has been maintained, with some legitimacy, that one of the motives that impelled 'Abd ar-Rahmān into adopting the title of Caliph in 929 was to counteract the claims of the Fātimids over the Muslims of al-Andalus. In the 920s and until the end of the 930s, he was successful at keeping the Fātimids from encroaching on the Maghribī coastline, but his influence declined when he had to deploy much of his fighting force on the frontiers of al-Andalus, culminating in the defeat at Simancas. By 959, he was left with only the cities of Ceuta and Tangier. One event, though, had far-reaching consequences. In 954, an Andalusi merchant ship captured a smaller Fātimid vessel off the North African coast. In reprisal, the Fātimids dispatched a large force from Sicily against the relatively new coastal town of Almería in 955, setting alight all the ships in the harbour, looting the city and taking numerous captives. This incursion onto Andalusi soil prompted 'Abd ar-Rahmān not only to build and equip a fleet – this mainly took place in the shipyards of Seville and Tortosa – but also to order the construction, along the vulnerable Mediterranean coastline, of a chain of watchtowers (as mentioned in Chapter 2). These brick-built towers, with something like the function of lighthouses on land, bring to mind the Elizabethan defensive bonfires on the headlands overlooking the Channel. An official with the rank equivalent to that of admiral was appointed and charged with overseeing and coordinating naval defences.

Since the military demands of the state increased as the Caliphate progressed, it was apparent that manpower was stretched to the limit. One owes to the evidence of the Calendar of Cordoba the fact that governors recruited regularly for conscripts for the armies, but patently in numbers insufficient to meet the need. The solution was found in the recruitment of the light-complexioned men with fair or reddish hair known as *saqāliba* (Slavs), but they were not restricted to the Slavic area of Europe, coming as they did from central and eastern European lands. The sources do not provide us with unequivocal information about these people. A proportion of them would have been incorporated into the armies of the Caliph, occupying thereby a similar role to those *saqāliba* who formed an important constituent part of the Fātimid army of North Africa. They arrived in al-Andalus as *fityān* (young men), and some were used as slaves. Many, though, learned Arabic, acquired *mawlā* status and secured prominent positions in the Caliphal court; after the dissolution of the Caliphate, some established their own independent states. An Arabic source, quoted by al-Maqqārī, states that the Franks made eunuchs of them, in order to trade them to the Muslim East and to al-Andalus but, although many historians have repeated this, there does not seem to be any corroborative evidence that carries weight. If, as such, they came to Cordoba, then it would have to have been in minute numbers. It has been argued by Shaban that the fact that some of these *saqāliba* achieved high positions, both in the governmental administration and in the army, flies in the face of the claim that they had suffered the gross indignity of castration. The confusion arose through disputed definitions of Arabic terms.[37] However, this argument may not be said to apply to the situation under the Ottoman dynasty in the East from the fourteenth century onwards. The increasing authority enjoyed by the *saqāliba* in al-Andalus alienated other *mawlā* and Arabic sectors, and was to blossom into independent power for some of their descendants in the eleventh century.

One has, finally, to consider 'Abd ar-Rahmān III's legacy. Politically, he succeeded in securing the allegiance of all Muslims in al-Andalus, an achievement due both to his adoption of the Caliphal title and to the support of a militia fit for purpose. Economically, he saw Cordoba grow in prosperity, through a buoyant trade and an efficient tax-gathering system.[38] Many commentators have pointed to the enormous wealth accrued during his Caliphate, and the consequent opulence in the city and environs. The number of city dwellers increased to somewhere in the region of 100,000, according to Torres Balbás, which made it as one might suppose, the city with the highest population of any in al-Andalus.[39] Socially, the Caliph managed to forge an integrated society wherein there were roles for the indigenous inhabitants. He did, however, in his recruitment of *saqāliba* and of Berbers from North Africa sow the seeds of discord for later generations when these groupings sought to wield power themselves. Culturally, in his encouragement of learning, he sought to rival the 'Abbāsid court of the East, thereby laying the foundation for the emergence of a distinctively Andalusi culture under his successors. Finally, on what might be called the diplomatic front, he presided over a state whose reputation and splendour were the envy of Western Christendom. The kingdoms in the north of the Peninsula and further afield sent embassies with lavish gifts to Cordoba in order to keep on the right side of the Caliph, perceived in the last twenty years of his reign to be the most powerful ruler in the western Mediterranean. 'Abd ar-Rahmān was a despot who governed in the manner of his Arab ancestors, acutely conscious of his position as leader, fiercely protective of his people, ruthless in his dealings with opponents and aggressive in his attitude towards neighbouring states, whether Islamic or Christian, all the while ensuring that the tenets of orthodox Sunni Islam were upheld. He died in October 961, after a year short of a half-century in power.

The caliphate in Cordoba: the later period

The fifteen-year reign of al-Hakam II (961–76) who was forty-five when he succeeded his father, is well known as a stable period in which the prestige of the

Umayyad Caliphate was enhanced. He adopted the honorific title *al-mustansir billāh* (the one who asks God's help). The political supremacy that had been achieved under the energetic supervision of his predecessor was maintained. An early crisis in his reign occurred in 965, when it became known in Cordoba that the feared Norsemen had made a foray onto Peninsular shores, near Lisbon, presumably on the river Tagus. He visited the ravaged districts in person, ordering the strengthening of naval defences, and the invaders were soon repelled. He had at his disposal an able general in the person of Ghālib who dealt efficiently with Christian incursions on the frontiers. Not only did al-Hakam follow in his father's footsteps in cultivating a personal aura, with a liking for elaborate and grandiose ceremonials, but he was also what might be called in today's terms a proactive patron of learning. The eleventh-century *qāḍī* of Toledo, Ibn Sā'id of Toledo, also known as Sā'id al-Andalusī (d. 1070), in his *Tabaqāt al-umam* ('Categories of Nations'), describes the impetus given to learning by al-Hakam. The following is a paean of praise in Gayangos' lively if antiquated translation:

> The Sultan Al-hakem, . . . having ascended the throne, the cultivation of letters received a new impulse, and by his encouragement of all sorts of studies, by his unwonted liberality towards the learned, whom he invited to his capital from Baghdad, Cairo, and other distant countries, and, above all, by his exquisite taste for literature, which he had cultivated with success during his father's lifetime, the torch of science shone brighter than ever. Indeed, this illustrious monarch spared neither trouble nor expense to propagate learning in his states by all the means in his power. He caused all sorts of rare and curious books to be purchased by his agents in Cairo, Baghdad, Damascus, Alexandria, and other great cities of the East; and no work on ancient or modern science was discovered that was not procured at any cost and sent to him. By these means he collected a richer and more extensive library than the Khalifs of the 'Abbaside dynasty ever did during the whole period of their reign, and the learned of Andalus devoted their attention to the study of the sciences contained in the books of the ancients, and, encouraged by the example of the monarch, made rapid progress in the most abstruse and exquisite learning.[40]

This account has not gone unnoticed, nor to my knowledge has it been seriously discussed. The hyperbolic, uncritical tone does tend to suggest that the writer was casting a backward glance through rose-tinted spectacles, yet one can give credence to some of the details. Al-Hakam did attract scholars from Baghdad to Cordoba with the promise of generous salaries; it is in keeping with what is known of him that he should have spared no expense in acquiring books for his library; and Cordoba did become a haven for scholars, scientists and those skilled in *belles-lettres*.

If one focuses on the subject matter of the books that were the object of al-Hakam's bibliographic hunt, then it becomes apparent that there was a preponderance of scientific works and of books relating to *al-'ulūm al-qadīma'* (ancient sciences). According to al-Maqqarī, in Gayangos' felicitous phrasing, 'Andalusians left luminous tracks in every department of science, with an ardour and success unparalleled among other nations'. There were two exceptions, natural sciences and astrology. Gayangos refers to the former by the old term 'natural philosophy', and says of the two together that they, 'though secretly cultivated by the higher classes, were never taught in public, owing to the prejudices of the multitude against them'.[41] The practitioners of these two sciences were liable to be accused of *zandaqa* (heresy). To be called a *zindīq* (heretic or, in current usage, atheist) could have dangerous consequences. More precisely, M. I. Fierro has described the *zindīq* as being characterised by 'his hypocrisy and his concealment of his true beliefs'. This cannot be said to be true *ipso facto* of the study of natural sciences or philosophy, only when such work is perceived by outsiders to be contrary to the tenets of Islam. Furthermore, in the rulings of the later works of the Mālikī law school, the one prevailing in al-Andalus under the Caliphate, the word was 'applied to every Muslim considered to have become apostate whilst failing to admit his new belief or lack of belief'.[42] What could not be understood had to be discredited. A scholar suspected of heresy ran the risk of having his library and even his house burnt. One may be led to suppose, though, that al-Hakam's known penchant for all manner of learning prevented any drastic anti-intellectual measures from being introduced during his reign. The pursuit of philosophy and astrology was to come to an abrupt halt after his death, as the new ruler, al-Mansūr, uncertain of his position, sought to court the approval of the Mālikī jurists with what amounted to a purge.

Abū 'Alī al-Qālī (901–68?) was one of the notable luminaries of the East whose presence and impact provided a platform for the study of the Arabic language in al-Andalus. He was a philologist and grammarian of exceptional repute who had come to Cordoba in 942, the author of *Kitāb al-amālī* ('Book of Dictations', so called because they were dictated to a disciple), and was included in the circle of scholars that tutored the heir to the Caliphate, al-Hakam. His presence in Cordoba indicates that the Umayyads set great store by the correct usage of the Arabic language, recognising, as did scholars in the East, that this was a prerequisite to the pursuit of knowledge. One might add that poets received extra kudos for their incorporation of arcane vocabulary, the language of the *badū* (nomads) of Arabia being prized as a particularly rich source.

In the field of mathematical sciences, the outstanding representative was the Andalusi Maslama b. Ahmad al-Majrītī (d. 1007?), from Madrid, so called because he was born in the small town of Madrid, as it then was. He moved to Cordoba where he presided over a school of scientists covering a range of spheres, and many of his disciples achieved renown in their own right. He was familiar with Greek texts in their Arabic translations, and he is associated with a now lost version of Ptolemy's *Planisphaerium* (planisphere or chart) which, with his added commentaries, was translated into Latin in the twelfth century. He was much involved in astronomy, and was the author of a treatise on the astrolabe. It has been claimed that although he was familiar with the astronomical tables elaborated in the East, he converted them to the meridian of Cordoba, taking into account 'his own actual observations'.[43] One of al-Majrīṭī's interests, mirroring the preoccupations of his time, was alchemy, the science of transmuting base metals into gold. In essence, this was a form of chemistry, in which experiments were performed on a variety of metals and minerals, to determine their basic qualities and their differences from each other. As such, it came under the umbrella of natural sciences, which rendered experimentation legitimate. If, therefore, Maslama did practise alchemy, and indeed, compose a treatise on the subject entitled 'The Sage's Step' (rutba al-hakīm, literally the quality or rank of the wise man), then he was not at that time transgressing.[44] Later, the pursuit of the elixir, or philosopher's stone, the vital substance that would enable a metal to be transformed, was a breeding ground for 'deceit and trickery', and as such denounced.[45]

Reports of the splendour of Cordoba under the new Caliph must have reached the Christian kingdoms of the north of the Peninsula as quickly as rumours travel. The fact that kings of León and Navarre should make the arduous journey to Cordoba to solicit the Caliph's intervention on their behalf in their own dynastic feuding is a tacit indication of their recognition of his supremacy in Peninsular affairs at that time. There had been delegations in the 950s petitioning 'Abd ar-Rahmān's support, including the redoubtable Queen Toda of Navarre, who had taken part in the battle of Simancas, the Queen Regent, in Lévi-Provençal's phrase.[46] There is the memorable occasion of her visit to Cordoba in 958 to secure the Caliph's recognition of her grandson Sancho's rights to the throne of León, and to seek a cure for his obesity. She was successful on both counts, although at a price: Hasdai b. Shaprūt treated Sancho such that he was no longer deserving of the nickname 'The Fat'. She did receive Caliphal support for his restoration to the throne – he reigned from 958 to 966 – but at the price of yielding ten key fortresses to the Umayyads. In 962, Ordoño IV, who had been ousted by Sancho, in his turn made overtures to the Caliph. The account of the escort he received on his entry into Cordoba, and of the elaborate protocol accompanying his audience with al-Hakam II, and how he was dazzled by the magnificence of the ceremony in the Madīna az-Zahrā', begs the question as to why such trouble was taken. Clearly, the Arabic historian Al-Maqqarī, incorporating the earlier narration of Ibn Hayyān,[47] is demonstrating the subservience of Ordoño to al-Hakam, not because the former was a Christian and the latter the supreme representative of Islam in the West, but rather to magnify the Caliph's immense military, political and economic superiority over his potential rivals in the Peninsula. The Caliph needed also to impress on his own subjects his capacity for munificence – he showered Ordoño with gifts and saw to it that he was housed in circumstances of the utmost luxury.

According to al-Maqqarī: 'For a long time after, the people of Cordoba talked of nothing else than the rejoicings of that day, and the glorious manifestation of Islam', the latter phrase being *de rigueur* in such descriptions. 'The orators and poets, who were present at the ceremony, failed not, as was the custom on such occasions, to deliver extempore speeches or poems allusive to the scene they had witnessed'.[48] As such, the reception of Ordoño was directed as much to the rank-and-file Muslim as to the courtiers; it may therefore be considered to have been a triumphant public relations exercise.

Two further missions to Cordoba which were, I believe, to have enormous repercussions in the formation of European culture occurred in 971 and 974. Although they have not gone unnoticed, they deserve to be considered in some detail.[49] The court of Count Ramón Borrell in Barcelona was another of the Christian states of the north to pay homage to the Caliph in Cordoba, and 'Isā b. Ahmad ar-Rāzī, in Ibn Hayyān's text, relates the journeys to Cordoba and the reception of the delegations in some detail.[50] In July 971, the Count (*qūmis*) Mirón Bonfill on behalf of Borell headed an embassy to al-Hakam's court. He brought with him the statutory sweetener of thirty prisoners of war (*asārā*), together with twenty men of standing. Once in Madīna az-Zahrā', they were received by ministers of al-Hakam, in the company of some notable Christians (here *nasārā*) in their capacity as translators. The text does not specify how long the delegation remained in Cordoba, perhaps until October 971, as there was a farewell audience with the Caliph, in which Bonfill was handed gifts of garments and saddles for Borell. A second embassy was granted audience of the Caliph in 974, this time led by Guitart, who was the bearer of a letter from Borell confirming the existing treaty and eager to renew it. This was not as grand a mission as the earlier one as he was accompanied by a reduced retinue, and perhaps was focused principally on a political objective. It is interesting to note that he was also acting as an escort to the ambassador of Otto I who had similar intentions of securing a peace treaty. One is entitled to address the matter of the discrepancy between the two embassies from Barcelona. Numbers were pared for the second one, as relations had already been established, but if the political aims could be achieved with what was obviously a modest complement of accompanying diplomatic officials, then what was the purpose of the twenty 'men of standing' in the retinue of the mission three years earlier? It seems unlikely that they were present simply to impress the Caliph. It seems likewise improbable that they would have acquiesced in clicking their heels for the duration of the delegation. Their names are not supplied, but it would seem reasonable to suppose that amongst their number were scholars, including perhaps some monks working in Catalonian monasteries who were aware of the advances in scientific knowledge currently being made in Cordoba. These learned men would no doubt have communicated their specific interests to their Christian hosts so that treatises could be located and copied in their original Arabic, or less probably translations made *in situ*. If this supposition is acceptable, then the original mission acquires added significance. Catalonian scholars could thereby remain abreast of current developments in scholarship in Islam.[51]

If one were now to reveal that one of the scholars who formed part of the 971 delegation to Cordoba was Gerbert of Aurillac (945–1003), then the scenario ceases to have just curiosity interest and instead acquires far-reaching significance. When Borell visited the monastery of Aurillac in the Auvergne in 966, he was so impressed by the talent and potential of the young Gerbert that he took him back to Catalonia and entrusted him to Hatto, Bishop of Vich. He in turn sent him to study in the thriving scriptorium at Santa María de Ripoll, where he is believed to have spent three years, from 967 to 970. Whether there existed in Ripoll Latin translations of Arabic mathematical and astronomical works is not known, but a contemporary chronicler comments that, with Hatto, Gerbert studied '*mathesi plurimum et efficacitur*'. What more natural that he should seek, with the approval of Borell, to augment his knowledge in Cordoba, and therefore participate personally in the momentous 971 mission? He later went to Rome where he impressed Pope John XIII (Pope 965–72), who began his advancement. After continuing his researches in the cathedral school at Rheims, he was appointed archbishop of that city, then later of Ravenna, and finally, in 999, he was elected Pope, taking the name of Sylvester II. He died of the Roman fever in 1003. When Gerbert was in Rheims in 984, he wrote a letter in Latin to Lupitus (Llobet), an archdeacon of Barcelona whom he had presumably come to know when studying at Ripoll, and perhaps a fellow scholar who had been in the delegation that went to Cordoba, requesting 'the book *De astrologia* translated by you'. This is one of the first works known to have been translated from Arabic to Latin, especially in the field of science.[52] In the same year he wrote to Mirón Bonfill, Bishop of Gerona, asking to be sent a book on the multiplication and division of numbers. If this contained the data incorporated in the treatise of the Eastern mathematician al-Khwārizmī (who gave his name to algorithms), and if it was indeed sent to Rheims, then it may mark the occasion in which the abacus came to be reintroduced in Western Europe. This had apparently 'disappeared with Roman decline in the West'.[53] It cannot be ascertained whether this was the means whereby Arabic numerals came to be known in Europe; there exists a reference to the presence of nine Hindu-Arabic numerals in a manuscript from the scriptorium of the Castilian monastery of Albelda, c. 976. By the middle of the succeeding century, the northern Europeans were familiar with the abacus and it was adopted in the circle of William the Conqueror and William Rufus. The phrasing that Gerbert uses in this second letter suggests that he was not personally acquainted with the addressee but knew of him by repute. If he was the same Mirón Bonfill who led the mission to Cordoba in 971, then Gerbert would perhaps have employed a different mode of language, putting into doubt the possibility that they knew each other, as they surely would have done if the hypothesis outlined above is valid. Nonetheless, Gerbert was certainly a pioneering scholar, mathematician and astronomer, endowed with a questing and questioning nature, with a later reputation of having being in al-Andalus which would serve to stigmatise him. He is credited not only with introducing the astrolabe into Western Europe, via the translation of an Arabic work, but also with the assembling of a sundial at Magdeburg, which is feasible as he was acquainted with the Holy Roman Emperor Otto II.[54] The astrolabe was a brass instrument used by scientists for measuring the altitude of stars, for determining latitude and for a multitude of other purposes mainly relating to astronomy and astrology.

Richer, a disciple of Gerbert, described how his teacher organised his curriculum, beginning with mathematics and music, and progressing to an explanation of the workings of instruments such as the astrolabe, armillary sphere and abacus. Richer uses the words '*fervebat studiis*', which may be interpreted as 'he was passionately fond of learning'. These comments are reminiscent of the attitude towards scholarship of al-Hakam II. If Gerbert went to Cordoba, as has been suggested above, then not only did he enlighten others as he had been enlightened, but he was also responsible for the transmission of Arabic science to at least one centre of learning in Western Europe. One could say that Rheims, when he was there in the 980s, achieved the same cachet as Cordoba during the reign of al-Hakam II. A comparison may be drawn between the two men. Both acted as catalysts for learning: al-Hakam attracted to Cordoba scholars from throughout the Islamic world, whereas Gerbert's intellectual catchment area extended beyond the Alps to the Adriatic, and ranged widely through northern Europe. There is a further, somewhat unexpected, connection. Both attracted posthumous derision for their patronage of learning. Al-Hakam was disparaged amongst the people for having added an extra hole to the *albogón*, an early form of flute, whereas the addition for which he truly deserved recognition was to the Great Mosque, a byword for magnificence and splendour.[55] The memory of Gerbert amongst historians and chroniclers of the papacy, on the other hand, was irredeemably tarnished by his supposed association with and presumed contamination by Islam. He did not receive his due as a pioneer of scientific and astronomical investigation; rather he was reputed to have been a dabbler in the black arts, *optimus nigromanticus* – the best of necromancers, in the phrase of the translator and scholar, Michael Scot (1175–1235?). Now, in the Middle Ages, to designate somebody as a necromancer, someone who makes predictions though communing with the dead, was to condemn him irrevocably, although Michael Scot does append the comment that he later reformed. It seems, though, that Michael himself was not convinced as he went on to say that Gerbert 'borrowed the astrolabe, conjured the demons and made them explain it fully to him', and that he also 'made the demons teach him all astronomy'.[56] This is not even damning with faint praise, and the slurs continued right up until the twentieth century. In essence, Gerbert as a Christian father and Pope was deemed to have been unsound and his name tainted because he was believed without a shred of evidence to have dishonoured the Church.

One might observe, to conclude this episode, that the cultural prestige of al-Hakam's court was not confined to the Islamic world. Scholarly endeavour had no boundaries and was not obstructed by any opprobrium on the part of Christians towards Muslims. Indeed, it is credible to argue quite the reverse: Western European scholars, in the above example those from Catalonia, positively sought to acquire the scientific knowledge that was available and came to be accessible in Cordoba during the first decade of al-Hakam's reign. Then Gerbert chanced upon the scene and paved the way for a Europe-wide tide of scientific discovery based at Rheims but originating in the Islamic state of al-Andalus. The sting in the tail was that some sciences turned out to be dangerous: the bid of Sylvester II ('The Demon Pope' in Richard Garnett's *Twilight of the Gods*) for a place in the forefront of medieval scholarship was sabotaged because his pursuit of knowledge from whatever source was to provoke *post mortem* first suspicion, then outright condemnation, from unenlightened quarters.

Perhaps the most talked about aspect of al-Hakam's period of power is his library. This is not surprising given that in al-Maqqarī's history one finds that the number of books it contained amounted to 400,000[57] with the catalogue running to forty-four volumes. The first figure at least has to be regarded as one that exceeds all bounds of reality, despite the details given by al-Maqqarī that al-Hakam had agents in all parts of the Islamic world seeking out volumes, and that a period of six months was required to remove them from the palace to another location. An interesting appraisal has been provided by Wasserstein who, whilst questioning the size of the library, does call it a 'great collection', although he was later criticised for his scepticism 'regarding the number of books'.[58] One surviving manuscript from the library, a legal work, has been identified, and Wasserstein, after a careful and systematic assessment, claimed to be able to name 'not much more than around fifty works in the library of al-Hakam II'.[59] How one moves from this realistic figure to one of 400,000 is unfathomable. To take this further, al-Maqqarī records that one of his named sources, 'to give an idea of al Hakem's immense erudition', asserted as a fact

> that not one book was to be found in [his] library . . . which the Khalif had not perused, writing on the fly-leaf, the name, surname, and patronymic of the author; that of the tribe or family to which he belonged; the year of his birth and death; after which followed such interesting anecdotes about the author or his work as through his immense reading he had derived from other writers.[60]

Yet this is an impossibility: over a period of thirty years, al-Hakam would have to have read 365 books every day. Even to catalogue this number in the manner described is neither credible nor conceivable. The staggering figure of 400,000 could be reduced by 99 per cent to nearly 4,000, which would still far exceed that for a library at that time. One doubts whether there was even a fraction of that number of books written by this period of human existence. Indeed, 0.1 per cent, that is to say 400 books, would seem to be a more plausible sum. Even allowing for the possibility that the Arabic historians thought in terms of chapters instead of books, an unbound cluster of unnumbered pages, there is not the remote chance that any figure larger than, say, 600 is conceivable. Collections of manuscripts are a not uncommon feature of monastic libraries in the Peninsula, but small numbers were involved, maybe not in excess of 100. The inventory of Alfonso II's books in the monastery of San Salvador of Oviedo in 882 runs to around eighty.[61] Because of the prestige that the Caliphate in Cordoba enjoyed, one would expect the Caliphal library, and perhaps some of the libraries assembled by private individuals that are also mentioned in the sources, to eclipse that number, by several hundred volumes, say, hardly by appreciably more.

If one tries to interpret the information concerning al-Hakam's library, the first and obvious comment to make is that its reputedly enormous size and the other details that are supplied serve to enhance the Caliph's reputation as a scholar and bibliophile. Wasserstein has interestingly identified a political aspect, namely that al-Hakam was challenging the supremacy of the ʻAbbāsid Caliphate in Baghdad which he classifies as being 'too weak to be of any real significance as a challenge to Cordoba'.[62] This seems to be a reasonable assumption, but in reality, we are simply being made aware of the pro-Umayyad prejudice of the historian. It was sophisticated propaganda, designed to enhance the renown of the Caliph of the West.

Ar-Rāzī's account of four years of al-Hakam's reign, narrated by Ibn Hayyān, is instructive on a number of fronts. Apart from the military activity, including letters to and from his general Ghālib on campaign in present-day Morocco, and foreign embassies already mentioned, one is afforded an insight into what might be considered peripheral aspects. If in general it reads like a court circular, snippets of information are frequently provided in such graphic detail as to suggest that they were experienced or observed by the writer. There are upwards of a dozen meteorological notices. For example, the rain was so heavy on 23 October 971 that planting of seeds could begin in all the neighbouring districts. Not only is the extreme weather recorded, but also its effects on the population. The weather conditions from mid-March onwards veered from heavy rain to drought, such that the equivalent of two 'ministers for rain' were appointed. Black frost which lasted for three days in mid-April scorched vines, fig trees and other crops in the surrounds of Cordoba. Rain arrived just in time for the harvests to be saved. In April 974, severe gales and rainstorms blew down olive trees and others; the effect of this on the local economy is not recorded, but it is a reminder of the destructive power of the forces of nature. When the chronicler mentions that in September of the same year, first clouds were seen to gather and then rain arrived, enabling work to start on the land, it is as if he was not only aware of drought conditions, but was also familiar with seasonal agricultural concerns. Of administrative interest only are the names of the officials sent by al-Hakam into the provinces to requisition horses for the summer campaigns against the northern kingdoms. It seems that the horses had to be made ready in the spring, indicating not only the usefulness of these animals to the military capability of the Caliphate, but also of the onus on the country dwellers to serve the Caliph on demand, as it were. As to the personnel for these campaigns, one brief section refers to volunteers from within the city of Cordoba itself. The text suggests that these recruits were motivated by religious zeal, but this seems *prima facie* unlikely, and may be a case of the chronicler adding this to pay lip service to Islamic piety. Indeed, there are strikingly few references to any religious antagonism towards Christians. The most frequent source of conflict came from dissident groups or individuals within al-Andalus; the material that relates to combating the northern states in the Peninsula is devoid of any inkling of sectarian rivalry. Expeditions, punitive or as a regular show of force, had military or propagandistic objectives; there is not the slightest hint that they were conducted with the imposition or furtherance of Islam in mind.

A number of carved ivories which have fortuitously survived from the time of al-Hakam's Caliphate allow us to get a glimpse of the luxury lifestyle enjoyed by the upper echelons of society. They afford a remarkable link with al-Andalus in the tenth century and are invaluable for the evidence that they provide on several levels. As to the availability of the ivory, al-Maqqarī, quoting Ibn Hayyān, refers to an embassy from North Africa to Cordoba in 991, bearing extravagant gifts including 'eight thousand pounds weight of the purest ivory'.[63] One presumes that this would have amounted to a substantial quantity of elephants' tusks. Although this largesse came thirty years after the earliest dated carved ivory from al-Andalus, one may speculate that this commodity had the same North African provenance. Amongst the exotic animals donated in 991 one finds elephants mentioned, which would suggest that they arrived intact, and that the ivory had been obtained from other less fortunate members of the species *in situ*. There is some indication that the workshops were situated in the city of Cordoba and Madīna az-Zahrā', and that the ivories were commissioned as, in some examples, the name of the recipient is given. Some ten of these remarkable objects, now in various European venues, may be assigned to al-Hakam's reign, and are characterised by the quality of their craftsmanship. Some are small rectangular caskets, whilst others take the form of a cylindrical box, now known as a pyxis (from the Greek for box).[64] They have fitted lids – some missing or incomplete – and many were probably used to contain perfumes and scents. That some were also luxury objects in themselves may be demonstrated by the fact that, externally, the ivory has been pierced, no doubt to provide settings for small jewels, such as pearls or diamonds perhaps. The larger caskets may have contained official documents or emblems of office.[65] Their external decoration has attracted much attention as, in addition to intricate vegetal patterns, they depict scenes of courtly life, both inside with attendant musicians and outside with hawks and their prey.

An outstanding example, a pyxis that once belonged to Juan Riaño, now in the Louvre, dates to 968 and has an inscription around the lid that indicates that it was made for al-Mughīra, al-Hakam's younger brother.[66] Lions are prominent in the decoration, both on the lid and on the sides; in one graphic cameo, two lions, symmetrically positioned, have each secured a horned animal, perhaps a bull, with their claws, and are tearing at its haunches with their teeth. Amongst the creatures depicted are two ibexes with their characteristic curved horns, confronting each other; peacocks, partridges, parrots and eagles, with two pairs sitting on eggs in their nests, are also in evidence. The wildlife representations of the diverse species are so striking as to suggest that they were the result of observation, rather than copied from Byzantine or other sources. Did there exist a Caliphal menagerie with lions? Notwithstanding, the main focus is on human activity. Two men are seen to be wrestling; two others gathering eggs from nests, and two more, on horseback, picking dates from a palm tree. In what might be described as the central tableau, two figures in pleated robes with embroidered armbands, looking out at the audience, as it were, with a musician between them strumming a lute, are seated on what looks like a form of dais, itself supported by the outstretched necks of two lions with interlocking tails. According to the recent intriguing interpretation of Prado-Vilar, these two men in dignified pose are two princes, sons of al-Hakam, one the heir holding a branch and bottle 'the symbolic attributes of the Caliph', the other, his younger brother, 'holding a ceremonial flabellum' (a fan for driving away flies). The court scene in this pyxis is 'a permanent reminder to al-Mughīra (the uncle of the two princes) of the stability of the dynasty'.[67] If this alluring interpretation is accepted, then the craftsmen responsible for carving the ivory tusk were acting under strict instruction. Moreover, if the images on this pyxis were not haphazard, then it certainly seems plausible to speculate that they were authorised 'from on high', perhaps by the Caliph himself, who is known to have ordered that others be made. This one and other similar ivories, some celebrating specific occasions, constitute, as it were, a pictorial chronicle of the 960s. One might also remark that there was clearly no embargo on the representation of living humans or animals in artistic settings at this time. Although some ivories were more severe in conception, with elaborate foliate design, others, including later ones carved in the eleventh century, are not shy of animals and birds, although some of these may have been imitations of earlier examples. In the Qur'ān, depiction of living beings is not unequivocally condemned; after Muhammad's death, some traditions (*hadīth*) disapproved of the practice, which influenced a doctrine of non-animate art. Even in Sunni Islam, however, what one might call this convention was by no means held to be sacrosanct, such that in al-Andalus during the Caliphate no laws were being violated. Finally, it may be observed that those responsible for the carving may have been from the indigenous population operating within a workshop, and sufficiently proud of their work that in certain instances they engraved their individual names in inconspicuous places. Alternatively, these master carvers may have been among those skilled craftsmen who made their way to Cordoba once the Caliphate was established. In either case, the end product affords a glimpse today of a glittering era, and is a testimony of an affluent and pleasure-loving society.

The era of al-Mansūr, 976–1002

Al-Hakam died in October 976, after a fifteen-year reign which was a period of political stability in al-Andalus, arguably the last such period in its history. His cultural legacy ensured that Cordoba should continue enjoying a reputation as a centre of learning. Yet a concatenation of circumstances led to the unravelling of the imperial structure which his father had built up and he had perpetuated. Before his death, he had named his son as his successor, as was the Umayyad custom, a decision considered to have been an error by historians such as Makki who has pointed out there was 'no lack of outstanding princes at that time' more suitable to carry the Caliphal mantle.[68] His son Hishām was maybe twelve years old, and was destined never to succeed to his father's position. He was largely ignored in the power struggle that erupted in al-Hakam's wake, and which led inexorably and inevitably to the dissolution of the Caliphate less than sixty years later, although there was what might be called an Indian summer within that time span. After some initial jockeying for position amongst those who sought to fill the vacuum, Ibn Abī 'Āmir, known as al-Mansūr, a general and *hājib* (translated as chamberlain, an officer of high rank, probably with responsibility for overseeing the Caliph's inner circle, but in actuality chief minister) under al-Hakam, assumed the reins of power, and headed an autocratic state which was to persist until his death in 1002.[69]

Much has been said about his period of control of al-Andalus, and likewise much has been made of his 'usurpation' of power, but as he did not assume the title of Caliph for himself, this is not truly accurate. He did, however, diminish the status of the Caliphate by keeping Hishām II in seclusion, and this policy attracted ongoing resentment on the part of the Umayyad sympathisers. Al-Mansūr reacted to their opposition by reducing to 'obscurity the men who had been prominent during the Caliphate of al-Hakam' and, indeed, by eliminating his rivals.[70] In retrospect, it may be seen as an astute measure on his part to procure the reduction of the influence of prominent and powerful tribes by reorganising the format of his standing army. Instead of the system whereby the military units were made up exclusively of members of the same tribe, he imposed one in which each unit should be composed of mixed elements. This policy may be said to have had a twofold intention, the first being to decrease the chance of any one tribe rising in unison against him. The second, more subtle and farsighted, was to forestall intertribal rivalries which could threaten the stability of the army. However, it was less prescient to bring in, as he did, substantial numbers of Berber warriors to reinforce his militia. They refused to leave their own tribal units, and were billeted in special encampments outside the city of Cordoba whose population feared them and the menace that they potentially represented. The foreboding of the well-to-do Cordoban citizenry was to become a reality within less than forty years when Berbers, having ransacked and destroyed the city in 1013, became the dominant force in Andalusi politics. Al-Mansūr, then, through dismantling Arab tribal units and permitting the Berbers to retain theirs, was defusing one possible powder keg only to replace it with a much more dangerous one, an act that was to have far-reaching consequences for al-Andalus.

Al-Mansūr is most celebrated for his expeditions against the Christian kingdoms of the north, and as there were some fifty-two of these, sometimes two or even three a year, they need to be considered in their context and interpreted accordingly. It was a fact of life in the Iberian Peninsula that when a leader of long-standing departed the scene, his neighbours would seek to take advantage of the vacuum. Thus, on al-Hakam's death, Ramiro III of León, in league with some Castilian counts, attacked the Muslims on their frontiers and even, according to Ibn Hayyān, quoted by al-Maqqarī, extended 'their incursions till within sight of Cordoba', although this is not verified elsewhere.[71] Once this threat was successfully dealt with, al-Mansūr inaugurated a sequence of yearly campaigns which he led and which are quite extraordinary given their frequency and the time they occupied. If one is reminded that there was a tense political situation in Cordoba in the first half of the 980s in which al-Mansūr's supremacy was by no means assured, then it is remarkable that he should have led no fewer than twenty expeditions north between 980 and 986. In that time, during which he conducted incursions into places as far afield as Barcelona (978, 984 and 985), he was away from Cordoba for nearly 700 days (224 whilst engaged on the Barcelona expeditions alone), which amounts to 100 days in each year. Much attention has been accorded to the devastation he wrought on cities in the frontier zones, to the capital city of León (988, 995) and to the Christian sanctuary of Santiago de Compostela (997), but one does not need to resort to *jihād* in looking for an explanation. He was not pursuing 'Holy War'; far from it, he was making a show of his military might to neighbours whom he sought to intimidate. He was not extending the territory of al-Andalus, nor was he securing converts to Islam; the positioning of the frontiers was not altered as a consequence of any of his raids. He was, however, returning at regular intervals each and every year to Cordoba, with the overt spoils of victory, thereby demonstrating to them his prowess, and at the same time keeping at bay his critics and those eager, at least in the early years, to pounce on any sign of political or military weakness. It does not seem to me, though, that this is a fully satisfactory explanation. Certainly, al-Mansūr was alert to the importance of keeping those in his capital contented, yet it was more vital still to demonstrate to his subjects throughout al-Andalus who was in charge, who held the whip hand in Cordoba. Therefore each year, with a splendid retinue of distinguished men, even in the fields of poetry and learning, he would lead his army through different parts of al-Andalus thus reassuring the people not only that he retained command, but that he presided over a glittering assembly of scholars with invincible troops to boot. In other words, these annual and sometimes biannual outings were all window dressing, designed as propaganda for the areas of al-Andalus through which he passed. The success of the expeditions encouraged him to continue with them, and indeed to become more adventurous, but their purpose did not alter; they gave notice to Andalusis wherever they were that he remained in charge in Cordoba.

'Abd Allāh b. Buluggīn provides an insight into the impact of al-Mansūr's warmongering on the indigenous population. He indicates that some of the 'peasantry' were reluctant to be conscripted on account of 'their inability to fight and of the fact that expeditions would prevent them from cultivating their land'. The *quid pro quo* was that they had levies imposed on them and 'assessments of all their property entered into the registers'.[72] It seems that these taxes were in addition to the alms tax (*zakāt*), which was incumbent upon all Muslims and which was to be distributed among the poor and needy in the community (Qur'ān 9: 60). In this instance, it was a property tax, payable in cash or in kind, the sole purpose being the welfare of the Muslim community. From this, it may be adduced that householders and farmers, at least those within the purlieu of the conscripting agents, were Muslims and that those non-Muslim communities that were remaining in the late tenth century were unaffected. As has been mentioned earlier, the incidence of Islamicisation increased by leaps and bounds in al-Andalus during this tenth century prompted in no small measure by the political hegemony of the Umayyad Caliphate. Furthermore, the ruler was sensitive to the needs of the population, not only in Cordoba, but in the country at large, an additional testimony to his preoccupation with his status as *hājib* whilst the rightful Caliph was being deprived of all power and authority.

Allied to the above was al-Mansūr's desire for the approval of the proponents of the Mālikī law school (*fuqahā'*), who had been notably instrumental in his rise to power from his initial office as master of the mint (*sikka*). His action in purging al-Hakam's library of material deemed to be suspect by the Mālikī jurists is seen as his recompense to them. Political expediency required him to make a show of quelling any signs of heterodoxy, and he would not have hesitated in condemning to the flames or the rubbish dumps works that had brought such renown to his predecessor. The works specifically mentioned are those of philosophy, astronomy and 'other similar subjects' which would have included astrology, but excluded arithmetic and medicine. Scholars and teachers in the disciplines that were proscribed ran the danger of being condemned as heretics if they were found to be purveying such knowledge in public. Al-Mansūr also emulated his two illustrious predecessors by enlarging the Great Mosque, ostensibly to cater for the inordinate influx of people into Cordoba, but no doubt in part to allay the doubts of the jurists and to keep in with their affections. He could not match the magnificent prayer niche (*mihrāb*), with its golden mosaics, installed by al-Hakam II, and perhaps as has been suggested he was shrewd enough not to try to compete with the additions of the two Caliphs, bearing in mind that he was not a caliph himself.[73] He added nineteen aisles, which required the purchase of houses in the vicinity in order to provide sufficient floor space, and is said to have been responsible for having wax as well as oil being burnt in the chandeliers 'thus combining the effect of both lights'.[74]

In 997, al-Mansūr led an expedition to Santiago de Compostela in Galicia, a city that had been constructed on the spot where the tomb of the apostle James was allegedly discovered in the previous century. It was suggested by Lévi-Provençal that he was inflicting a resounding insult on all Christianity in the Iberian Peninsula by destroying its most revered site, already by that time a centre of pilgrimage.[75] It runs counter to all his previous campaigns, however, to maintain that this particular one had any other objective than that of bolstering up his own image. There may have been a punitive element, but invading armies were in the habit of destroying crops and wreaking havoc on towns and cities, and he was simply following precedent. The inhabitants of Santiago had evacuated the city before his arrival, so al-Mansūr resorted to destroying its buildings, stopping short of desecrating the tomb of St James. Among the very considerable loot with which he returned to Cordoba were bells from the cathedral, apparently borne by Galician captives. These were later turned upside down and suspended in the Mosque to be used as makeshift lamps.[76] This action in itself may not have had any religious connotation; it was rather a public demonstration of the humiliation of a neighbouring state, a not infrequent occurrence. In the year 1000, al-Mansūr defeated a Castilian count at the battle of Calatañazor (*qalʿat an-nusūr*, the citadel or castle of eagles or vultures), in the present-day province of Soria strategically situated in what was the Middle March just north of the river Duero. Whether al-Mansūr died as a consequence of wounds received in this battle, or whether he died in 1002 at nearby Medinaceli, to the south of the river Duero, and his launching-off place for expeditions into Castile and Navarre, as is generally accepted, is not known for certain. Rodrigo Jiménez de Rada, in his thirteenth-century history, recognised al-Mansūr's military prowess in the phrase 'semper invictus fuerat' ('he was always undefeated'); the English historian Derek W. Lomax is less pithy but hits the nail on the head: he had 'a brilliant career devoted to the interminable and fruitless demonstration of Christian military inferiority'.[77] A fitting but not strictly accurate testimony is supplied by the haiku-like traditional Spanish poem: 'En Calatañazor, perdió Almanzor el atambor' (literally '. . . Al-Mansūr lost his drum'), shorthand for 'was defeated', but in effect alluding to his death. From the writings of later Arabic historians, it may be inferred that he was held in high regard as a Muslim, it even being suggested that he died on the anniversary of the very night in which the revelation of the Qur'ān began, but in reality his strength was as a commander of troops, and his weakness was his assumption of power whilst the rightful heir to the Caliphate still lived.

Period of *fitna*, 1002–31

From 1002 until 1008, al-Andalus was governed by 'Abd al-Malik al-Muzaffar ('the victorious'), who succeeded to the office of *hājib* on the death of his father al-Mansūr. He continued the practice of campaigning annually and led seven expeditions against his northern neighbours, meeting his death during the final one. From Ibn 'Idhārī's account, which includes full details of some expeditions, and which in parts reads as a kind of cobbled together court circular with conspiracies being uncovered, and with the comings and goings of sundry officials at court being recorded in detail, one learns that al-Muzaffar pursued the same style of governance as his father.[78] At the time of his accession, he is said to have been under the influence of *nabīdh*, a wine made from fermented dates, and distinct from *khamr* which was made from grapes. Now *khamr* was, in a later revelation to Muhammad, specifically prohibited in the Qur'ān (5: 92), mainly because of the consequences of overt drunkenness, whereas drinking *nabīdh* was permissible, as there was a tradition that the Prophet himself used to drink it. Although there were possible added ingredients to *nabīdh*, it was generally reckoned that it was less intoxicating than *khamr*. In certain circles and at certain times it is possible that wine from *khamr* was imbibed, but it was called *nabīdh*, thus effectively bypassing the prohibition. This may well have been the case here, as al-Muzaffar would not have wanted to transgress Islamic law and thus incur the wrath of the *fuqahā'*. Alternatively, later writers may have wished to put a more favourable gloss on his drinking habits, and thus, by having him drink *nabīdh*, give the impression that he was behaving within the law. An episode given brief mention is that of the wild boar which ran amok in the streets of Cordoba, not causing alarm among the people of the city but rather unease, as it was interpreted by them as a sign of bad things to come. Again, this may be an instance of a subsequent chronicler crediting the populace with having premonitions about the forthcoming disasters. This is linked to the foreboding of the expeditionary force on witnessing unusual meteorological phenomena in the autumn of 1006; they are said to have been terrified by peals of thunder and continuous lightning flashes that accompanied heavy rain and unseasonal cold, fearing the onset of calamity, which on this occasion did not overcome them. In the following year, a particular conjunction of the planets was interpreted as presaging the overthrow of the state and unprecedented famine. These and similar references may be regarded as credulous reactions by a superstitious population, but the fact that historians looking back on events in Cordoba should record them scrupulously and indeed interpret them in this manner is indicative of a prevailing attitude that prosperity relied on a temperate and clement climate as much as on the rational and beneficent conduct of those in power.

After al-Muzaffar's death in 1008, the first act of his successor 'Abd ar-Rahmān, known as Sanchūl (the pejorative diminutive Sanchuelo, so called because his maternal grandfather was Sancho Garcés II, King of Navarre 970–94), was to be confirmed in the office of *hājib* by Hishām II. The latter was still the titular holder of the Caliphal office, and continued to be deprived of the power to govern which was his by right. Sanchuelo's second act was to have far-reaching and devastating consequences for the entire state of al-Andalus. Within a month and a half he further persuaded the Caliph to decree that he be appointed heir apparent, thus in effect usurping the Caliphate by the transferral of the Caliphal line to that of his own family. He is described as living a dissolute life thenceforward, but this may simply be an instance of a later chronicler, quoted by by Ibn 'Idhārī, discrediting a figure held by many to be responsible for the ensuing debacle.

To describe the succeeding twenty years as a period of *fitna* (civil strife) is warranted by a reading of the sources, but, in effect, what those uninvolved in the political melee witnessed was the dismantling of a whole proud state. Different factions, notably Arab and Berber, sought to assert their authority in Cordoba, some seeking to empower the existing Caliph, Hishām II, occupying his office for three years until his probable death in 1013. A most unsettling set of circumstances for the citizens of Cordoba occurred in 1009 when one of the aspirants for power reined in the support of Sancho García, Count of Castile (r. 995–1017), whose Christians entered the city, achieved their military objective and proceeded to kill some 30,000 inhabitants of the city in a day, according to Ibn Idhārī. This massacre, if such it was, is unlikely to have been religiously motivated, as Sancho and his troops were mercenaries, and allies of Muslims. On the other hand, the scale of the slaughter is difficult to explain. It may have had to do with revenge, in that their leader Sulaymān, known as al-Mustaʿīn bi-llāh ('the one who seeks the support of Allāh'), also commanded Berbers many of whose fellows had been killed by the populace at the orders of the incumbent in Cordoba. A further involvement of Christians in Andalusi affairs took place in the summer of 1010. On this occasion, a different body of Christians, this time northern mercenaries from present-day Catalonia, were recruited by the opponents of Sulaymān, or rather hired at a crippling cost to effect the latter's overthrow. They assembled at Medinaceli, then the capital of the central frontier zone (*thaghr al-awsat*, the Middle March), and, following one source, Ibn Idhārī, announced their unmistakable Christian presence by having bells rung from the minaret of the main mosque, and destroying the *qibla*, indicating the direction of Mecca. These Christians were clearly sufficiently numerous to be able to dictate terms regarding their pay and their share of plunder in any forthcoming engagements. All their demands were met. They then went on the rampage in Saragossa, before moving south to aid their paymaster in ousting Sulaymān from Cordoba. In this enterprise they were not successful, as they were repulsed by Berbers who defeated them and killed their leader, a Catalonian count, Armengol. The remaining Christian militia, numbering some 9,000, remained, but in a later engagement with Berbers were defeated for a second time within a month, on this occasion suffering losses of about a third. The Christians had roamed freely in Cordoba in the period between the two battles, uttering profanities towards Islam and Muhammad, but no one said anything. Even when a pious Muslim sought to intervene, he was told by fellow Muslims not to meddle. In the battlefield, after their defeat, the Berbers found their purses and belts stuffed with dinars and dirhams in incalculable quantities. From the above, it may be determined that the people of Cordoba were cowed by the presence of Christian troops in their midst, and that, furthermore, there existed a consciousness of religion on both sides. Clearly the legal authorities were ineffectual at this time of crisis, when a state of near anarchy prevailed. It seems as though observance of the two religions of Christianity and Islam was subordinate to other interests such as personal security, ethnic hatred and, as far as the leaders and aspirants were concerned, the lust for power. Nonetheless, the populace of Cordoba were not toothless; stemming from the time when they had thousands of feared Berber soldiers billeted in the outskirts of the city, they waited until the majority were away from the city and ransacked Madīna az-Zahrā', obliterating all traces of Berber habitation.

By the end of 1010, then, with signs of disorder in all parts, a number of distinct groupings may be identified: supporters of the legitimate Caliph, Hishām II, resentful of the attempts of al-Mansūr's descendants to wrest the Caliphate from him; Berbers, becoming increasingly involved in the power struggle, buoyed by their numbers and their military strength; Slavs who had flourished in the administration during the final quarter of the tenth century; and the *ʿāmma*, the populace or the (urban) mob, which on occasion could show its muscle. The internecine conflict among these factions was bitter. This was also the first time that Christian mercenaries, in substantial numbers, had cast in their lot with Muslims with decisive effect, an astonishing detail when one recognises that barely a generation earlier the Christian states had been subservient to the authorities in Cordoba, even kowtowing to them. The Christian rulers, too, were becoming bolder. In 1011, Sancho García sent emissaries to Cordoba demanding that certain (unspecified) fortresses be handed over to Castile, in return for his cessation of hostilities on the frontier. These terms were granted and ratified by lawyers (*fuqahā*) and the judge (*qāḍī*), and a document drawn up to that effect. The superiority of the Christian states over al-Andalus in the eleventh century may be said to have been presaged by acts such as these.

It was becoming apparent to the people of Cordoba that the Berbers were increasingly pulling the strings of power; with their backing, Sulaymān regained power in 1013, during which year the long-lived Caliph, Hishām II, died, although the circumstances of his death are unverified. Many inhabitants of the city made a hurried departure, living behind their homes and their goods which were appropriated by Berbers, who rifled and burnt property. Significantly, those Slavs who had been so instrumental in shoring up the Caliphal administration fled to the east of al-Andalus, to cities such as Valencia, Denia and Játiva, where they assumed control, and later in the century established states independent of Cordoba.

Two of the abiding icons of the Caliphate in Cordoba were destroyed in the period of *fitna*. The Madīna az-Zahīra, constructed at the orders of al-Mansūr to the east of the city and about whose architecture virtually nothing is known, had a short life, being destroyed in its entirety in 1009 because it was the emblem of the family of 'Āmir who had occupied it during the first decade of the eleventh century. Much more is known of the similarly named Madīna az-Zahrā', the city of the Caliphs founded by 'Abd ar-Rahmān III, and the epitome of opulence and splendour. As the Berbers had annexed it during the *fitna*, it was the visible focus of hatred for the people of Cordoba. After it had been plundered in 1010, it was subject to further depredations in 1012 when inhabitants of the city set the mosque alight, together with its doors, lanterns, pulpit and rugs. Although Sulaymān and his Berbers repossessed it in 1013, it was later abandoned, fell prey to all and sundry and was reduced to rubble; it is mentioned as an abandoned city in 1058. There are nonetheless many unanswered questions. Excavation began on the site at the beginning of the twentieth century, and many rooms have now been recreated, using myriad fragments of masonry, each one meticulously accorded its position. Destruction on the scale suggested by the small size of the surviving pieces must have been caused by battering rams or equivalent to knock down the walls, and sledgehammers to fracture the decorated stonework. This is likely to have occurred over a period of years, an impression confirmed by a visit to the site where reconstruction is ongoing.

Civil strife persisted until the Caliphate was dissolved by the then incumbent in 1031, but some light is thrown on attitudes and life during the previous twenty years by the writings of Abū Muhammad 'Alī Ibn Hazm (994–1064), a polymath, theologian, philosopher, grammarian and one of the greatest intellects of his time. It has been the case in history that the period when a state is in decline or crisis such as, for example, seventeenth-century Spain, is often one which generates masters of literature and culture. Ibn Hazm's father had been a minister (*wazīr*) in the court of al-Mansūr, although his sympathies lay with the rightful Caliph Hishām II. Following a traditional education from Māliki jurists, Ibn Hazm junior soon became embroiled in the political maelstrom and was forced to leave Cordoba because of his pro-Umayyad sympathies after the family house was burnt in 1013 when Sulaymān and the Berbers regained control. After a spell in Almería, then under the command of the Slav leader Khayrān, he was exiled, but continued to play an active role in the politics of the day: he was captured by Berber troops in 1019, given a government appointment in the six-week reign of Caliph 'Abd ar-Rahmān V in 1023/4, and subsequently imprisoned. On his release, he seems to have taken the decision to wash his hands of political life in order to devote himself, from 1027 onwards, to matters of the intellect and to an ascetic existence. However, it was during the earlier hectic part of his career that he wrote, around the year 1022, the work of his which has achieved most attention in the Western world, the *Tawq al-hamāma* (Ring of the Dove). The subtitle used by Arberry in his translation, 'A Treatise of the Art and Practice of Arab Love', alludes to its content, and the *Tawq* has also been rendered into French, Spanish, Italian, German and Russian, acquiring thereby inordinate fame and attention.[79] It is important to note that this work was not well known in the Middle Ages, surviving in one manuscript only, dating to the fourteenth century, whereas his works on weightier subjects secured his reputation as a serious scholar and have been studied with great assiduity by Arnaldez, Asín and others.[80] In the modern epoch, however, Western Europe has shown interest above all in the *Tawq* because of its subject matter.

The disquisition has many anecdotes taken from contemporary Cordoban life, converting the book into a valuable compendium of information on the upper echelons of society in the city, many based on personal acquaintance and hearsay. Ibn Hazm draws also on material from Eastern Islam, demonstrating that his knowledge was not confined to local issues. The two innate qualities that Ibn Hazm seems to have prized more highly than others in relation to the theme of love were loyalty and sincerity of feeling. Regarding the former, he cites the example of a once close friend of his who knew all his secrets and, after the break-up of the relationship, divulged them to all and sundry. When this friend realised that Ibn Hazm was aware of what he had done, he was afraid that Ibn Hazm would correspond in kind. The latter's response, however, and this is the testimony of his loyalty, was to write a soothing letter to his former friend assuring him that he would not reciprocate in kind. He is an acute observer and commentator, as is testified by his story, scrupulously verified by named sources, of a poet who was smitten by the sight of a girl among a group of women whom he followed through the streets of Cordoba, past the mosque, over the bridge and past the cemetery of the quarter (*maqbūrat al-rabad*), eventually being confronted and outwitted by her. This brief anecdote reveals that women gathered together in public places, did not wear veils to cover their faces and were free to walk around the city on their own; furthermore, although she was a slave girl, she was not permitted to name her master. Ibn Hazm relates a similar story of the infatuation of a distinguished Cordoban citizen, during the reign of al-Muzaffar (1002–8), for a pageboy whom he had seen in a mosque and who, infuriated by the attention, struck his admirer. The latter is said to have been delighted by this, but Ibn Hazm, whilst recounting the protagonist's distinguished achievements in the city, such as the construction of mosques and public fountains, nonetheless describes his behaviour as shameful. There are many similar tales as well as glimpses into the upper strata of society, adding to and confirming knowledge gleaned from other sources. He mentions the father of three brothers, one of whom was put to death on the orders of al-Mansūr in 979, still alive when Ibn Hazm was writing, the best preacher of his time, the most learned and most devout of men, with a scurrilous and amusing wit.[81]

Much attention has been directed to the concluding chapter of the book which extols chastity, echoing the theories of Ibn Dāwūd al-Isfahānī, a ninth-century Persian poet whose ideal of love was expressed in abnegation rather than in possession. This essentially Platonic standpoint was linked by Ibn Dāwūd to the legendary pre-Islamic tribe, the Banū 'Udhra, celebrated among the poets for their practice of unrequited love. Ibn Hazm starts the chapter by stating that one of the best things that a man can do is to maintain chastity in his loves; he sustains his argument with texts from the Qur'ān and provides some, at times, quite poignant examples. We see here, then, a Muslim theologian showing respect for and knowledge of the Qur'ān, and, elsewhere, for the *hadīth*, which he had studied in an earlier phase in his life, and one also totally *au fait* with the amorous practices and escapades of his time.

After he withdrew from politics in 1027, he concerned himself diligently with the application of principles of the Zāhirī school of law, the essence of these being in Watt's words 'that the statements of the Qur'ān and the traditions are to be taken in their literal sense' (*zāhir*, plain or literal meaning).[82] It is not without relevance that the founder of the Zāhirīs was Dāwūd b. Khalaf, the father of the poet whose views are echoed in the final chapter of the *Tawq*. From the Zāhirī standpoint, Ibn Hazm criticised theologians and lawyers defying Christians, Jews and Muslims in public debate. He was particularly critical of the Māliki school of law, the one whose views prevailed in al-Andalus, and he attracted harsh criticism when he accused his rivals of heresy. Central to his ideology was his attitude to the Arabic language, the language of the Qur'ān and of divine revelation. One should aim for 'perfect speech' in accord with *zāhir* and should abjure from the search for hidden meanings. To an extent, his insistence on reverting to the Qur'ānic text and the *hadīth*, which invites comparison with present-day evangelical thinking, is a reaction to the turbulence of the times in which he was writing. In his life, after his retirement, he lived entirely in accordance with his own beliefs.

A contemporary of Ibn Hazm, Abū 'Āmir Ahmad b. Shuhayd (992–1035) was born into a privileged family whose ancestors had settled in al-Andalus at the time of 'Abd ar-Rahmān I in the eighth century and whose prerogative it had become to fill an important position of state. It seemed as though his social status and his advancement were assured, but although he did occupy the post of *wazīr* for a short while, the diminishing influence of the descendants of al-Mansūr meant that his political career was aborted almost before it had begun. One might suppose that the uncertainty of life in Cordoba in the first two decades of the eleventh century would not be conducive to a life of ease and indolence, but Ibn Shuhayd seems to have pursued his pleasures regardless. He has left a legacy of poetry and other writings which, as is the case with his friend Ibn Hazm's literary output, has afforded us a glimpse of life in a time of *fitna*. He moved among both Christians and Jews, and gives an account of his attendance at a nocturnal service in one of the city's churches, mentioning the peal of the bells, the splendour of the lamps, the appearance of the begirt priest and the aroma of the wine. There are different versions of an encounter of a Muslim with the Christian religion as practised; one, in verse, suggests that, presumably on another occasion, Ibn Shuhayd engaged in drinking bouts in a monastery. One may understand from these examples that there were churches still functioning in the city of Cordoba at the beginning of the eleventh century, even during a period of political chaos. As there is no inference that Ibn Shuhayd went to the Mass, if such it was, in disguise or under false pretences, then one may presume that the attendance of Muslims, identifiable from their dress perhaps, was not unwelcome. Furthermore, as Ibn Shuhayd was so enthused by what he experienced, one may gather that at this church, at least, there was life in the congregation, as it were, and that urban Christianity, far from being intimidated, was buoyant. The Muslims were continuing to observe their obligations towards the *dhimmī* communities, even to the extent of permitting bells to be rung.

Leaning on his experience in prison which occurred in 1017 as a consequence of being denounced as a libertine by three detractors, he wrote his *Risālat at-tawābi' wa az-zawābi'*, the epistle on spirits and demons.[83] This relates a literary journey in which Ibn Shuhayd encounters acknowledged genii of Arabic literature in the East, matching their poems with his and securing their approval after the recitation of his own verses. This is not an unknown genre in Arabic, and it has been considered by the distinguished Spanish scholar Miguel Asín Palacios to have been important evidence in the argument in favour of Islamic influence on Dante's *Divine Comedy*.[84] It is not surprising that Ibn Shuhayd, in his poetry, should seek to turn the direction of Arabic poetry in al-Andalus away from Eastern Arabic moulds, championing poetry itself as the product of inspiration, based on his belief that eloquence is imparted from God, not via the written word nor from the preaching of scholars. If, however, al-Andalus was to be in a position to challenge the Islamic East, then its language, or rather the linguistic foundations of Arabic, would have to be stronger. It would have to be transformed from its current state of 'non-Arabic babble'.[85] Accepting that Cordoban grammarians were at fault, and that grammatical adequacy, let alone perfection, was unachievable in al-Andalus, he stressed the importance of temperament and natural talent. In some of his poems, though, he seems to be conforming to the poetic tenets of his age, with elaborate and profuse use of imagery, but in others, and this marks him out from his contemporaries, one is able to detect an incontestable streak of personal emotion. During the final seven months of his life, Ibn Shuhayd was stricken by paralysis; he deteriorated physically to the extent that he was only able to see his friends from a litter. His consciousness of his own approaching death is expressed in poetry of a startling clarity: 'Farewell from one whom Death has bitten, / now become a target for the arrows of his eyes: / for the hand of death is drawing out his soul / and the love inside it makes it easier to die.' One might also quote the deeply moving lines from his poem to his friend Ibn Hazm: 'Seeing that life has turned away his face from me/ and that death is going to catch me without doubt, / I only wish I were living in a high mountain cave/ with the wind blowing about the summit.'[86] The fact that much of his poetry is not a slavish imitation of the poetic practices of the East but rather an expression of his state of mind enables Ibn Shuhayd to be classified as an Andalusi poet, not an as Arabic poet of al-Andalus. At a time of extreme political upheaval, then, a major poet emerged with distinctively Andalusi traits, someone who took poetry to a level that was not be surpassed in al-Andalus.

Internecine conflict continued unabated throughout the second and third decades of the eleventh century during which time Cordoba ceased to enjoy its position of supremacy over the rest of al-Andalus. Arabs, Berber and Slavs were establishing their own seats of power in other cities, exercising their own authority irrespective of the former centre of the Caliphate. When Abū al-Hazm b. Jahwar took control of Cordoba in 1031, he considered his status to be transitional, in that when a person emerged who had a legitimate right to the Caliphate and who had the approval of the people, he would step aside. What one may understand here is that the inhabitants of Cordoba who had viewed the calamitous collapse of what had so recently been such a powerful and prestigious state, now had a say in their future. In essence, they represented the *'umma* (community of Islam) and, as such, had the authority to approve the appointment of a fit and suitable Caliph. The Umayyads had fallen into disrepute and candidates from that family would not be considered. Indeed, according to Ibn 'Idhārī, there was a proclamation in the markets and districts of Cordoba to the effect that no Umayyad should remain in the city. It may be inferred that Ibn Jahwar and indeed the populace expected that a person with the appropriate credentials would be forthcoming and, when that time came, would be acceptable. The Caliphate, therefore, should not be considered to have been dissolved, but rather to have been in abeyance. This date of 1031, then, marks not only the expiry of the Caliphate in al-Andalus, but also the *de facto* end of Cordoba's unrivalled position of supremacy.

What happened may be likened to a large smouldering bonfire whose flickering embers were cast to the wind. Where they eventually came to rest, some soon died out, but some were fanned to life and burnt brightly for a few further decades. The period between 1031 and 1085 in al-Andalus is known as the period of the *mulūk at-tawā'if* – literally, the kings of the parties or factions, rather unsatisfactorily rendered as the party kings, and preferably referred to as the Taifa kings or rulers. Gabrieli appropriately described their states as 'individual local kingdoms'.[87] The fifty or so years occupying the central portion of the eleventh century in many respects represent a remarkable phenomenon within al-Andalus. Some thirty-two city states functioned independently, some with shorter lives than others, some boasting courts that echoed the brilliance of Cordoba in its heyday.[88] As Cordoba's fortunes waned, so those of Seville waxed. If one stands back to observe the overall picture of al-Andalus over eight centuries, the principal city for the first three centuries was Cordoba; for the final three, it was Granada. For the eleventh and much of the twelfth, and sandwiched, as it were, between the other two, it was Seville, the westernmost of these three durable and immediately recognisable symbols of Islamic presence in the Iberian Peninsula, which most closely emulated the splendour of Cordoba in the previous century.

Notes

1. Emilio Lafuente Alcántara, *Ajbar Machmuâ (Colección de tradiciones) Crónica anónima del siglo XI, dada á luz por primera vez*, Madrid: Ediciones Atlas, 1984, Arabic text, p.154; translation pp. 133-4, my adaptation.

2. *Una crónica anónima de 'Abd al-Rahmān al-Nāsir*, translation with introduction and notes by E. Lévi-Provençal and Emilio García Gómez, Madrid, Granada: Editorial Maestre, 1950.

3. See Ibn Khaldūn, *The Muqaddimah. An Introduction to History*, translated from the Arabic by Franz Rosenthal; abridged and edited by N. J. Dawood, London: Routledge and Kegan Paul, 1978 [first edition in this form 1967], pp. 180–1; the quotation is from p. 181.

4. George C. Miles, *The Coinage of the Umayyads of Spain*, 2 parts, New York: The American Numismatic Society, 1950, part I, p. 41, from where the quotation is taken, and part II, pp. 235–98, especially pp. 235–8. (Parts I and II are consecutively paginated.)

5. Juan Castilla Brazales, *La Crónica de 'Arīb sobre al-Andalus*, Granada: Impredisur, 1992, p. 204.

6. Claudio Sánchez-Albornoz, *Despoblación y repoblación del valle del Duero*, Buenos Aires: Instituto de Historia de España, 1966.

7. Ramón Menéndez Pidal, 'Repoblación y tradición en la cuenca del Duero', in *Enciclopedia Lingüística Hispánica*, vol. I, Madrid, 1960, pp. xxix-lvii; Thomas F. Glick, *Islamic and Christian Spain in the Early Middle Ages*, Princeton, NJ: Princeton University Press, 1979. See

also the important work of Eduardo Manzano Moreno, *La frontera de al-Andalus en época de los Omayas*, Madrid: Consejo Superior de Investigaciones Científicas, 1991.

8. Glick, *Islamic and Christian Spain*, p. 45.
9. Derek W. Lomax, *The Reconquest of Spain*, London: Longman, 1978, p. 27.
10. A range of these names is discussed by Ramón Menéndez Pidal, *Orígenes del español. Estado lingüístico de la península ibérica hasta el siglo XI*, Madrid: Espasa-Calpe, 5th edition, 1964, pp. 441–5.
11. Lomax, *Reconquest of Spain*, p. 39.
12. The pioneers in this field were G. T. Rivoira, *Muslim Architecture. Its Origins and Development*, translated from the Italian by G. McN. Rushforth, Oxford: Humphrey Milford, 1918 (first published in 1914), with an important section on Spain, pp. 240–371, and Manuel Gómez-Moreno, *Iglesias mozárabes*, 2 vols, Madrid: Centro de Estudios Históricos, 1919, reprinted in 1 vol., Granada: Universidad, 1975. A very thorough later study is Jacques Fontaine, *L'Art Mozarabe. L'Art Préroman Hispanique II*, Paris: Zodiaque, 1977, Collection 'La nuit des temps', vol. 47.
13. The similarity in phrasing to the Escalada inscription has not gone unnoticed, and it has been suggested that the same group was involved in both enterprises.
14. See Ahmed ibn Mohammed al-Makkari, *The History of the Mohammedan Dynasties in Spain*, translated by Pascual de Gayangos, 2 vols, London: RoutledgeCurzon, 2002, vol. I, p. 51.
15. See R. B. Serjeant, *Islamic Textiles. Material for a History up to the Mongol Conquest*, Beirut: Librairie du Liban, 1972, particularly chapter XVII. The quotation is from p. 165.
16. Glick, *Islamic and Christian Spain*, pp. 119–20.
17. 'All the Castilians came together; two men of great standing rose as mayors' (author's version).
18. Claudio Sánchez-Albornoz, *Una ciudad de la España cristiana hace mil años*, Madrid: Ediciones Rialp, 1966, 5th edition, p. 50. The first edition of this fascinating recreation of life in tenth-century León, the result of the author's trawl through collections of documents, then for the most part inedited, was published in 1926.
19. Lomax, *Reconquest of Spain*, p. 40.
20. Ibn Hayyān de Córdoba, *Crónica del califa 'Abdarrahmān III, an-Nāsir entre los años 912 y 942 (al-Muqtabis V)*, translation with notes by Ma. Jesús Viguera y Federico Corriente, Saragossa: Anúbar, 1981, p. 328.
21. Henri Terrasse, *Islam d'Espagne. Une rencontre de l'Orient et de l'Occident*, Paris: Librairie Plon, 1958, p. 75; Gonzalo M. Borrás Gualis, *El Islam de Córdoba al Mudéjar*, Madrid: Silex, 1997, pp. 66–8. See, for the mosque, the scholarly study of Basilio Pavón Maldonado, *Memoria de la excavación de la mezquita de Medinat al-Zahra*, Madrid: Ministerio de Educación Nacional, 1966.
22. Richard W. Bulliet, *Conversion to Islam in the Medieval Period. An Essay in Quantitative History*, Cambridge, MA: Harvard University Press, 1979, p. 117.
23. Max Meyerhof, 'Esquisse d'histoire de la pharmacologie et botanique chez les Musulmans d'Espagne', *Al-Andalus*, III (1935), 1–41, at 8–13.
24. Al-Maqqarī, *History of the Mohammedan Dynasties*, vol. I, appendix p. xxvi.
25. Richard Hitchcock, 'Arabic medicine: The Andalusí context', in *The Human Embryo: Aristotle and the Arabic and European Traditions*, edited by G. R. Dunstan, Exeter: Exeter University Press, 1990, pp. 70–8, at p. 74.
26. Antonio Arjona Castro, *'El libro de la generación del feto, el tratamiento de las mujeres embarazadas y de los recien nacidos' de 'Arīb Ibn Sa'īd (Tratado de Obstetricia y Pediatría hispano árabe del siglo X)*, Córdoba: Diputación Provincial, 1983, for example p. 143. For the cure for otitis mentioned above, see p. 132.

27. *Histoire des sciences mathématiques en Italie*, 4 vols, Paris: Renouard, 1838–41, vol. I, pp. 393–464. A later edition with the title *Le Calendrier de Cordoue*, published by R. Dozy in 1873, was re-edited by Charles Pellat (Leiden: E. J. Brill, 1961), with an annotated French translation. The text of the Latin translation, in the Bibliothèque Nationale, Paris, shows some variants to the printed edition, notably in the positioning of the constellations. For the genre of *anwā'*, see Miquel Forcada, 'Books of *anwā'* in al-Andalus', in *The Formation of Al-Andalus, Part 2: Language, Religion, Culture and the Sciences*, edited by Maribel Fierro and Julio Samsó, Aldershot: Ashgate, 1998, pp. 305–28. Forcada's study was first published in Spanish in 1992.

28. [Joseph-Toussaint Reinaud,] *Géographie d'Aboulféda*, translated from the Arabic by 'M. Reinaud', Paris: n.p., 1848, vol. I, p. xc.

29. *Le Calendrier de Cordoue*, edited by Pellat, p. 170; my translation from the Arabic.

30. H. P. J. Renaud, *Le Calendrier d'Ibn al-Bannā' de Marrakech (1256– 1321 J. C.)*, Paris: Larose, 1948, p. 43.

31. A. Paz y Meliá, 'Embajada del Emperador de Alemania al Califa de Córdoba, Abderrahman III', *Boletín de la Academia de Ciencias, Bellas Letras y Nobles Artes de Córdoba* (1931), 255–82. First published in 1872.

32. The manuscript that I have consulted, Archives of the Cathedral of León, MS 35, has many curious features in the translation which could suggest that the Arabic version was accessible and acceptable to Muslims.

33. The pioneering study in the field was by Catherine Alder, 'Arabic versions of the Psalter in use in Muslim Spain', unpublished PhD dissertation, University of St Andrews, 1953. Her findings were upheld by D. M. Dunlop, 'Hafs b. Albar – the last of the Goths?', *Journal of the Royal Asiatic Society* (1953), 137–51, challenged by García Gómez in *Al-Andalus*, XIX (1954), 481–2, and reaffirmed by Dunlop in *Al-Andalus*, XX (1955), 211–13. Later studies include: M.-T. Urvoy, *Le Psautier de Hafs le Goth*, Toulouse: Presses Universitaires du Mirail, 1994; Hanna Kassis, 'The Mozarabs', in *The Literature of Al-Andalus*, edited by María Rosa Menocal et al., Cambridge: Cambridge University Press, 2000, pp. 420–34, including bibliography (omitting C Alder, above). This contribution suffers from adopting the outmoded definition of 'Mozarab'. See especially pp. 424–5.

34. Francisco Javier Simonet, *Historia de los mozárabes de España deducida de los mejores y más auténticos testimonios de los autores christianos [sic] y árabes*, Amsterdam: Oriental Press, 1967. This 976-page work was completed in 1867 but not published until 1903, and was as remarkable an achievement in its day as was Gayangos' translation of al-Maqqarī in the 1840s. His life and work have been studied from differing standpoints by James T. Monroe, *Islam and the Arabs in Spanish Scholarship (Sixteenth Century to the Present)*, Leiden: E. J. Brill, 1970, pp. 85–100; and Manuela Manzanares de Cirre, *Arabistas españoles del siglo XIX*, Madrid: Instituto Hispano-Árabe de Cultura, 1972, pp. 131–62.

35. There is an extraordinarily ample bibliography in this field. An interesting and varied collection of articles has been assembled in *The Literature of Al-Andalus*, edited by Menocal et al. Tova Rosen in her chapter entitled 'The Muwahshshah' (pp. 165–89) explains the genre and gives an account of the controversies. For recent studies on specific topics, see J. A. Abu-Haidar, *Hispano-Arabic Literature and the Early Provençal Lyrics*, Richmond: Curzon Press, 2001; also Otto Zwartjes, *Love-Songs from al-Andalus. History, Structure & Meaning of the Kharja*, Leiden: E. J. Brill, 1997.

36. Al-Maqqarī, *History of the Mohammedan Dynasties*, vol. I, p. 186.

37. M. A. Shaban, *Islamic History A. D. 600–750 (A. H. 132). A New Interpretation*, Cambridge: Cambridge University Press, 1971, pp. 158–9.

38. Regarding trade, S. M. Imamuddin, *Some Aspects of the Socio-Economic and Cultural History of*

Muslim Spain 711–1492, A. D., Leiden: E. J. Brill, 1965, provides details of imports and exports, pp. 127–31. Although references are given, the lack of any chronology reduces the information to interest value.

39. Leopoldo Torres Balbás, *Ciudades hispanomusulmanas*, 2 vols, [Madrid]: Instituto Hispano-Árabe de Cultura, no date [1972], vol. I, p. 104.

40. Al-Maqqarī, *History of the Mohammedan Dynasties*, vol. I, appendix p. xl.

41. Ibid., vol. I, p. 141.

42. María Isabel Fierro, 'Heresy in al-Andalus', in *The Legacy of Muslim Spain*, edited by Salma Khadra Jayyusi, Leiden: E. J. Brill, 1992, pp. 895–908, at p. 899. See also, by the same author, *La heterodoxia en al-Andalus durante el período Omeya*, Madrid: Instituto Hispano-Árabe de Cultura, 1987.

43. Juan Vernet and María Asunción Catalá, 'The mathematical works of Maslama of Madrid', in *The Formation of al-Andalus*, edited by Fierro and Samsó, part 2, pp. 359–79, at p. 360. The article was first published in Spanish in 1965.

44. The problems of the attribution of the authorship of this work to Maslama are discussed by E. J. Holmyard, the undisputed authority on alchemy, in *Alchemy*, Harmondsworth: Penguin Books, 1968 [1957], pp. 100–1.

45. Reuben Levy, *The Social Structure of Islam*, Cambridge: Cambridge University Press, 1962, pp. 500–1.

46. É. Lévi-Provençal, *Histoire de l'Espagne Musulmane. Tome premier: De la conquête à la chute du Califat de Cordoue (710–1031 J. C.)*, Cairo: L'Institut Français de l'Archéologie Orientale, 1944, p. 314.

47. Al-Maqqarī, *History of the Mohammedan Dynasties*, vol. II, pp. 160–5.

48. Ibid., vol. II, p. 165.

49. See, for example, Abdurrahman Ali El-Hajji, *Andalusian Diplomatic Relations with Western Europe during the Umayyad Period (A.H. 138–366/A.D. 755–976)*, Beirut: Dar al-Irshad, 1970, pp. 83–5, 93.

50. Arabic text, edited by Abd ar-Rahmān 'Alī Hajjī, Beirut, 1965, pp. 20–2; *Anales palatinos del califa Al-Hakam II, por 'Īsā b. Ahmad al-Rāzī (360–364 H. = 971--975 J. C.)*, translated by Emilio García Gómez, Madrid: Sociedad de Estudios y Publicaciones, 1967, pp. 44–7.

51. Similar ideas were put forward by J. M. Millás Vallicrosa, *Estudios sobre la historia de la ciencia española*, Barcelona: Consejo Superior de Investigaciones Científicas, Instituto 'Luis Vives' de Filosofía, 1949, pp. 55–6.

52. Harriet Pratt Lattin, *The Letters of Gerbert with his Papal Privileges as Sylvester II*, New York: Columbia University Press, pp. 69–70.

53. Charles Singer, *A Short History of Scientific Ideas to 1900*, Oxford: Clarendon Press, 1959, p. 140.

54. Juan Vernet, *La cultura hispanoárabe en Oriente y Occidente*, Barcelona: Editorial Ariel, 1978, p. 108.

55. A most engaging account of this story is provided by the fourteenth-century nobleman Don Juan Manuel in his *El Conde Lucanor*; see Daniel Devoto, *Introducción al estudio de don Juan Manuel y en particular El Conde Lucanor*, Madrid: Editorial Castalia, 1972, pp. 439–40.

56. Lynn Thorndike, *Michael Scot*, London: Thomas Nelson & Sons, 1965, pp. 93–4. See, for a most readable overarching account, D. M. Dunlop, *Arabic Science in the West*, Karachi: Pakistan Historical Society, n.d. [1958].

57. Al-Maqqarī, *History of the Mohammedan Dynasties*, vol. I, p. 139 and vol. II, p. 169.

58. David Wasserstein, 'The library of al-Hakam II al-Mustansir and the culture of Islamic Spain', *Manuscripts of the Middle East*, 5 (1990–1), 99–105; *The Formation of al-Andalus*, edited by Fierro and Samsó, part 2, p. xxvii.

59. Wasserstein, 'The library of al-Hakam II al-Mustansir', 100.
60. Al-Maqqarī, *History of the Mohammedan Dynasties*, vol. II, p. 170.
61. J. Tailhan, 'Les bibliothèques espagnoles du nord-ouest', in Charles Cahier, ed., *Nouveaux Mélanges d'Archéologie, d'histoire et de littérature sur le Moyen Âge*, Paris: Firmin Didot, vol. IV, 1877, pp. 297–346, at pp. 300–4.
62. Wasserstein, 'The library of al-Hakam II al-Mustansir', 102.
63. Al-Maqqarī, *History of the Mohammedan Dynasties*, vol. II, p. 191.
64. A recent publication which contains a wealth of information on many aspects of these objects is 'The ivories of Muslim Spain', in *The Journal of the David Collection*, vols 2.1 and 2.2, edited by Kjeld von Folsach and Joachim Meyer, Copenhagen, 2005. These two lavishly illustrated volumes comprise thirteen essays by leading experts. See also the important works of José Ferrandis, *Marfiles árabes de Occidente*, 2 vols, Madrid: Estanislao Maestre, 1935, 1940, and John Beckwith, *Caskets from Cordoba*, London: HMSO, 1960. This attractive and instructive guide began as a study of the ivory boxes in the Victoria & Albert Museum (some of which may be seen on display), but also includes those in other locations.
65. Sheila S. Blair, 'What the inscriptions tell us: Text and message on the ivories from al-Andalus', in *The Journal of the David Collection*, edited by von Folsach and Meyer, vol. 2, part I, pp. 75–95, at p. 91.
66. Juan Riaño, the son-in-law of Pascual de Gayangos, was a distinguished scholar and author of *The Industrial Arts of Spain*, London: Chapman and Hall, 1879, which includes a section on ivories (pp. 126–42). Many of the items he describes belonged to the Museum of South Kensington (now the Victoria & Albert Museum), whose objects he had catalogued in 1872.
67. Francisco Prado-Vilar, 'Enclosed in ivory: The miseducation of al-Mughira', in *The Journal of the David Collection*, edited by von Folsach and Meyer, vol. 2, part I, pp. 139–63, at p. 141.
68. Mahmoud Makki, 'The political history of al-Andalus (92/711–897/1492)', in *The Legacy of Muslim Spain*, edited by Jayyusi, pp. 3–87, at p. 40.
69. The title of *ḥājib* was, according to Miles, 'the supreme dignity of the Umayyad governmental hierarchy', Miles, *Coinage of the Umayyads*, part I, p. 61.
70. *The Tibyān. Memoirs of ʿAbd Allāh b. Buluggīn Last Zīrid Ruler of Granada*, translated by Amin T. Tibi, Leiden: E. J. Brill, 1986, p. 43.
71. Al-Maqqarī, *History of the Mohammedan Dynasties*, vol. II, p. 188.
72. *Memoirs of ʿAbd Allāh b. Buluggīn*, translated by Tibi, pp. 44–5.
73. Marianne Barrucand and Achim Bednorz, *Moorish Architecture in al-Andalus*, Cologne: Rolf Taschen, 1992, p. 86.
74. Al-Maqqarī, *History of the Mohammedan Dynasties*, vol. I, p. 228.
75. Lévi-Provençal, *Histoire de l'Espagne Musulmane*, p. 441.
76. Rodrigo Jiménez de Rada (Archbishop of Toledo, 1209–47), *De rebus Hispaniae*, Lib. V, Cap. XV: 'Nihilominus tamen campanas minores in signum victoriae secum tulit, et in Mezquita Cordubensi pro lampadibus collocavit, quae longo tempore ibi fuerunt'.
77. Lomax, *Reconquest of Spain*, p. 47.
78. Ibn Idhārī al-Marrākushī (d. post 1313), author of *Al-bayān al-Mughrib*, is an important source for a number of periods. Selections covering the years 1002–68 were translated by Felipe Maíllo Salgado, *La caída del Califato de Córdoba y los Reyes de Taifas*, Salamanca: Universidad, 1993.
79. London: Luzac & Co., 1953. Spanish translation by Emilio García Gómez with the title *El collar de la paloma. Tratado sobre el amor y los amantes de Ibn Hazm de Córdoba*, Madrid: Sociedad de Estudios y Publicaciones, 2nd edition, 1967. The first edition of this version was published in 1952.

80. Roger Arnaldez, *Grammaire et théologie chez Ibn Hazm de Cordoue. Essai sur la structure et les conditions de la pensée musulmane*, Paris: Librairie Philosophique J. Vrin, 1956; Miguel Asín Palacios, *Abenhazam de Córdoba y su crítica de las ideas religiosas*, 5 vols, Madrid: Revista de Archivos, Bibliotecas y Museos, 1927–32; reissued Madrid: Ediciones Turner, 1984, the first volume being a biography.

81. Gómez, *El collar de la paloma*, pp. 122–3, 155–7.

82. W. Montgomery Watt, *Islamic Philosophy and Theology*, Edinburgh: Edinburgh University Press, 1962, p. 134.

83. *Risāla at-tawābi' wa z-zawābi'. The Treatise on Familiar Spirits and Demons by Abu Amir Ibn Shuhaid al-Ashja'i al-Andalusi*, introduction, translation and notes by James T. Monroe, Berkeley, CA: University of California Press, 1971.

84. Miguel Asin, *Islam and the Divine Comedy*, translated and abridged by Harold Sunderland, London: John Murray, 1926.

85. *Risāla at-tawābi' wa z-zawābi'*, p. 74.

86. The translations are by James Dickie and are included in his article, 'Ibn Šuhayd. A biographical and critical study', *Al-Andalus*, XXIX (1964), 242–310, at 290, 291. This fundamental study by James Dickie and his monograph, *El dīwān de Ibn Šuhaid al-Andalusi 382–426 H = 992–1035 C.*, Córdoba: Real Academia, 1975, together provide English and Spanish readers with a reliable and valuable source for the poet and his work.

87. Francesco Gabrieli, *Muhammad and the Conquests of Islam*, London: Weidenfeld and Nicolson, 1968, p. 112.

88. An alphabetical list, numbering thirty-eight possible Taifa states, with dates where known, sources and bibliography, is provided by David Wasserstein in *The Rise and Fall of the Party-Kings. Politics and Society in Islamic Spain, 1002–1086*, Princeton, NJ: Princeton University Press, 1985, pp. 83–98.

CHAPTER 4

The eleventh century – a time of change

The period of the independent kingdoms had begun before 1031, as early as 1009 according to Monès, in that a number of cities had already taken steps to determine their own destiny.[1] Notable amongst these was Seville, an effectively independent state since 1023 and a bulwark against the designs of those in Cordoba who wished to wrest power away from it. There had always been tension between the Syrian Umayyads who governed Cordoba and the Yemenis in Seville. Power was originally in the hands of Abū al-Qāsim b. 'Abbād, the *qāḍī* (d. 1042), and hence the Abbādid family dynasty, whose son and grandson were to make such an impact on Islam in al-Andalus. He appears to have been responsible for the stratagem of procuring the services of a doppel-ganger of the dead Caliph Hishām II (or rather of how he is presumed to have looked had he been alive) purportedly located in a dungeon in the small fortress town of Calatrava midway between Cordoba and Toledo. His purpose, if there is credence to the story, was to provide a figurehead acceptable to all Andalusis. He ordered that Hishām's name be mentioned in the *khuṭba* (the Friday address or sermon) in all mosques, whilst he relegated his own position to that of *ḥājib*. In so doing, he was conferring legitimacy upon his own position. He brought slaves of uncertain origin into the city with the express purpose initially of using them to repel attacks from Berbers, but this policy later enabled him to be aggressive towards his neighbours. When his son, known as al-Mu'tadid (he who invokes the protection (of God)) (r. 1042–69), succeeded his father the *qāḍī*, a period of unprecedented power and prestige was inaugurated for Seville. In the south-west of the Iberian Peninsula at that time, there were two major Hispano-Muslim states vying for supremacy. The Abbādids of Seville was one, the Aftāsids of Badajoz, the other. The latter had been established in 1022 by Ibn Aftās (r. 1022–45), a courtier from Cordoba with ancestors among the original Berber settlers of the eighth century long since acculturated to Islam, who had taken the name and the mantle of al-Mansūr and whose territory extended into present-day Portugal. He enlisted support from Berbers who had settled in the area and were distinct from those imported from North Africa in the previous century by al-Mansūr. After thirty years of conflict, the upper hand was finally gained by the Abbādids in 1051 in the person of al-Mu'tadid, who invaded the territory of Badajoz, laying waste to the crops and causing a famine among the rural population.

As occurs with Russian dolls, the smaller Taifa states taken over by Badajoz were absorbed by Seville when Badajoz itself was annexed in 1051, such that by the death of al-Mu'tadid in 1069, the latter state exercised control over vast swathes of the southern part of al-Andalus. The smaller cities that were subsumed in the maw of Seville included, to the south-west, Niebla, Mértola, Silves, Santa María del Algarve and Huelva; to the south-east, the prosperous city of Carmona on the route between Seville and Cordoba which minted its own currency, Ronda, Morón, Arcos and Algeciras. These last five were Berber states, formed by heads of tribes who had been such a powerful presence in al-Mansūr's armies and who had supported the claims for a Berber caliph in Cordoba during the *fitna*. This left one prominent Taifa state in control of Berbers: Granada, governed by Zīrids since 1012. Much has been made of the rivalry between the established Arab families and those of Berber descent, but by the eleventh century remote Berber roots, dating back to the eighth century, were by and large immaterial. What was of consequence was the recent influx of Berbers from North Africa who had flooded by invitation into al-Andalus in the second half of the tenth. These were not integrated into Arab society and, often because of their numbers and military strength, feared by the urban populations. When the Berbers played such a prominent role in the jockeying for power during the *fitna*, these strong feelings turned to loathing. In the sources, the phrase *ahl al-Andalus* (the people of al-Andalus) signified Andalusi in contradistinction to Berber Muslims. There is a reference in Ibn Idhārī to an earlier account noting the killing of anyone who had the appearance of a Berber after the battle of Guadiaro in 1010. Simply to call someone a Berber became a justification for murder.[2] The slaughter at this time of *fitna*, on this evidence, was underpinned by a racial element.

The Taifa state of Granada had been founded by Zāwī b. Zīrī in 1012, some eight years after he had entered al-Andalus in 1002. Hitherto, the prominent city in the area had been Elvira, known to have been an episcopal diocese (Iliberis) to which Recemundus was appointed in the 960s. According to the memoirs of the last king of Granada, a valuable primary source for the Taifa period, the inhabitants of Elvira, having written to Zāwī to petition his support and protection in return for the provision of property, were encouraged by the Berbers to relocate from the *vega* (plain) in order to make themselves less vulnerable to attack. They therefore abandoned their own city and adopted a site, some six miles distant according to al-Himyarī,[3] which 'an attacking enemy would be able neither to besiege nor to prevent anyone from leaving or entering on any mission required by the welfare of the inhabitants'.[4] The city of Granada, with its northern boundary entirely protected by the formidable Sierra Nevada, was ideal for their purpose. Andalusians and Berbers together built and fortified the city, which was not long in achieving prominence. It is noteworthy that those from Elvira should have seen the writing on the wall, as it were, and have recognised that they would have no future in the turbulent aftermath of the *fitna* unless they secured the patronage of a powerful ally. Later, Zāwī secured Granada's status with a victory over one of the claimants to the Caliphate outside the walls of the city in 1019, with his horsemen from the Sanhāja tribe, one of the principal federation of tribes in the Maghrib, controlling at that time most of the area from Tripoli to Tangier. Yet the sources record that this triumph was accomplished largely through the betrayal of his enemies by Khayrān, the Slav leader of Almería. Zāwī is subsequently said to have been aware of this act of treachery, and to have reasoned that his enemies would have emerged victorious from the engagement, had this not occurred. He decided to return to North Africa, perhaps because of the turn that political events had taken there. One of the features of this and other sources is that words are put into the mouths of protagonists. Given the reputation that Zāwī acquired, it does not seem impossible that he should have nursed sentiments of this kind, recorded less than two generations after the event. With the departure of one who may be described as one of the big players in the game, his place was taken as ruler of Granada by his nephew Habūs (r. 1019–38), who is given a positive character appraisal in the memoirs, even bearing in mind that they were written by the grandson of his successor Bādīs (r. 1038–73). He kept relations between Berbers and Andalusis on an even keel, maintained an active military presence and presided over a content pluralised community. One detail mentions that, under him, 'travel by road was safe', which is worthy of comment because travel in the sierras around Granada has been notoriously hazardous over the centuries, as they have been an habitual haven for highwaymen, certainly up until the nineteenth century. One may assume that one of the functions of the troops at his disposal was to police the roads to ensure safe passage for travellers and trade.

One of the notable acts of Habūs was to appoint the Jewish scholar, poet and scientist Abū Ibrāhīm Ismā'īl b. Yūsuf b. Naghrīla (known as Samuel ha-Nagid) (d. 1056) to a pre-eminent position in his administration, a role somewhat equivalent to that of British Chancellor of the Exchequer. This inaugurated a period of exceptional Jewish influence in the Granada of the Zīrids, as Samuel was to be succeeded by his son Yūsuf who enjoyed even greater ascendancy, and during their lifetimes Jewish culture enjoyed a period of unsurpassed creativity within an Arabic milieu. According to al-Himyarī, Granada was known as 'Gharnatāt al-Yahūd' (Granada, (city) of the Jews) because its first inhabitants had been Jews, but as he was writing three centuries later, it seems more likely that he or his source was responding to the durable reputation of the Jewish community established there in the first half of the eleventh century. There was a difference in the prestige commanded by father and son. Whereas Samuel appears to have been a paragon of the upright courtier, efficient and unassuming, his son Yūsuf, according to the author of the memoirs, as well as being overambitious and haughty, abused his position of power. According to Ibn Idhārī, he was responsible for poisoning the ruler's son, blaming his death on the latter's entourage of slaves, male and female, and going unpunished himself for the crime. Eventually, the Berbers, resentful of his extravagance and of the sway he had over the Zīrid ruler, incited by a poem of the *faqīh* Abū Ishāq al-Ilbīrī (from Elvira), which in effect constituted a vicious critique of both Yūsuf and the Jews in the city, who had become inordinately wealthy at the expense of the Muslims, attacked Yūsuf's residence and killed him, along with a large number of Jews. The number of those who perished in this pogrom of 1066 is given as 3,000, yet Jews continued to live in the city and province, though never again attaining such high-profile posts as to provoke the fanatic enmity of the populace. One sees here how a poem no doubt recited in public places occupied the role that street-corner oratory has had over the centuries.[5] A particular verse reflects the shrewdness of the *faqīh*: 'They have broken the pact that they had made with us; we cannot be blamed for punishing perjurers'.[6] This seems to be an overt reference to the *dhimma* entitling Jews and Christians to live at peace and unmolested in Islamic lands as long as Muhammad or Islam is not insulted in public. One might comment that the *faqīh* might have been stretching a point here, particularly as such crimes had to be brought before a judge, but as a weapon justifying mob violence, it was spectacularly effective.

What ambitions Samuel nurtured for the Jewish community in Granada can only be conjectured, but the impetus he gave to the efflorescence of Jewish culture led to the creation of a uniquely distinct Taifa state. A poet and learned man in both Hebrew and Arabic, and with the knowledge of many disciplines that characterised the office of the *kātib*, he sought to educate his own son along similar paths, and was the patron of Jewish scholars and poets, such as the renowned philosopher and poet Solomon b. Gabirol (c. 1021–60?), who settled in Granada having left the court of Saragossa in 1045. The transcendental feature of Yūsuf's period of power was the construction under his orders of a castle-cum-palace on the hill where the *madīna* (city of the Alhambra) is now located. The author of the memoirs wrote that Yūsuf had built *al-hisn al-hamrā* (the reddish-coloured fortress), no doubt to provide security for himself and his retinue, as his power base expanded and his political opponents conspired against him. Frederick Bargebuhr, relying in great measure on a poem in Hebrew by Ibn Gabirol in praise of Yūsuf, forcibly contended in the 1960s that there existed a Jewish fortress palace on the site of the Alhambra complex in the eleventh century.[7] In particular, Bargebuhr demonstrated that the 'Fount of Lions' stems from that time, although the surrounding courtyard comes from a later period. In Ibn Gabirol's poem, the basin is described as resting on lions which spout water out of their mouth, a replica, in fact, 'of Solomon's Temple fountain, with modifications in its zoological detail'.[8] It is interesting to note that both Solomon's oxen and the Alhambra lions had their hindquarters directed inwards, a pointer towards inspiration from the Old Testament, there being no equivalents in Islamic art at that time. If as Grabar has said 'there is now general agreement that the lions themselves are probably eleventh century', and even if the basin on which they rest is from the fourteenth century, then the importance of this initiative of Ibn Nagrīla becomes apparent. It is worth reiterating that his palace on the hill where the Alhambra stands was the residence of the Jewish chancellor. The Zīrids themselves had fortified the hill opposite, the Albaicín or Alcazaba (al-qasāba al-qadīma, the old fortress), so for a short while the two structures coexisted. In the succeeding centuries, notably the fourteenth under Muhammad V, the rulers of Granada created their own Alhambra precinct, maybe, as Grabar thought possible, seeking 'inspiration from the memory and remains of the palace erected in the eleventh century by the Jewish viziers'.[9]

Attention has been drawn to the period of Jewish hegemony in Granada in the eleventh century, because it may be regarded as one of the more remarkable features of the annals of al-Andalus. In the memoirs referred to above, Yūsuf, in the ten years between his father's and his own death, exercised such a level of control over the Zīrid ruler that he reduced the latter to something of a pawn in his often Machiavellian schemes. It seems that power as well as wealth was what he craved and since he was always shrewd enough to retain the ear of Bādīs, he was able to deflect the brickbats of his enemies. Whether or not his eventual assassination may be attributed to the fact that as a dhimmī, in this instance a Jew, he had authority over Muslims may never be determined with certainty. In retrospect, Yūsuf may be seen to have overreached himself, making his fall inevitable, but his legacy, certainly if the theories relating to his structures on the Alhambra site are valid, is lasting.[10]

One of Granada's neighbouring Taifa states was Almería, and the fluctuating relationship between the two, chronicled in the memoirs, indicates how volatile politics had become after the Caliphate of Cordoba had been declared vacant. It was originally a small port dependent on the neighbouring conurbation of Pechina (Bajjāna) four miles distant, until 'Abd ar-Rahmān III, realising its potential as a natural port, and at the time fearful of attacks by the Fātimids and the Norsemen, had its naval defences strengthened in the 950s. The inhabitants of Pechina moved down to the new city. The name Almería may derive from al-mariyya (watchtower), as the Caliph ordered many of these to be built along the eastern seaboard of al-Andalus. The city mosque, the mihrāb (prayer niche) of which survived and was restored in the twentieth century, had probably been constructed around the end of the tenth century. The city itself became a haven for those fleeing from Cordoba at the time of the fitna. Two prominent saqāliba, Khayrān (r. 1012–28) and his brother Zuhayr (r. 1028–38) reigned over Almería as wālīs.[11] They were responsible for the influx of fellow saqāliba before and after the demise of the Caliphate, and they improved the city's facilities and its security. Both had been prominent in the court of al-Mansūr, but, far from living in isolation, sought to extend their authority over surrounding territory. Soon, Almería assumed greater importance than Pechina, although the valley in which Pechina was located was famed for its orchards, the fruit going to Almería, which by the eleventh century was well on the way towards achieving prominence as a Taifa state. One should also mention its geographical location, with the Sierra de los Filabres in its hinterland, and the long barren coastal stretch reaching to the Cabo de Gata in the north. The construction of the redoubtable *alcazaba* (Khayrān's castle) on a knoll to the north testifies to the fact that not only the harbour but also the city itself needed to be protected. The quarter that housed the production of silk, known as the *alcaicería* (from Arabic *al-qaisāriyya*, covered marketplace or workshop), lay between the *alcazaba* and the shore with the major township to the east.[12] Almería came to have some 800 silk looms, more than any other in al-Andalus with the possible exception of Seville, producing silk of the highest quality for export to the East and elsewhere. The silk products comprised not only the much prized *tirāz*, which has already been mentioned, but also fabrics which bore names of cities in Persia where these special products had originated. The types of weave emanating from al-Andalus were of Persian inspiration but were so much a part of the thriving and prosperous industries that they came to be carefully regulated and monitored. During the Taifa period in the southern extent of al-Andalus, the states with the highest profile were the ports of Seville in the west and Almería in the east, with Granada dominating the hinterland.

When, in 1041, Almería came under the governorship of a Hispano-Arab family, the *Banū* Sumādih, and later in the person of al-Mu'tasim bi-llāh (the one protected by God) (r. 1052–91), whose great-grandfather was al-Mansūr, a new era was announced. *Saqāliba* leaders had made way for those to whom not only the Hispano-Arabic elite but also rank-and-file Muslims could relate, and one may imagine that tension abated thereby. Given the inevitable consequences of the fragmentation of power in al-Andalus, it is remarkable in retrospect that individual courts should have flourished to the extent that they evidently did. It was as if the political wrangling and competing for power was played out on a different level, yet one has to be reminded that al-Mu'tasim ruled for a period of nearly forty years, thereby providing stability of leadership for those over whom he held sway for over a generation. Crucial to the continuous prosperity of Almería were relations with neighbouring states, such as Valencia and, particularly, Granada, whose ruler Bādīs was ever ready to take advantage of any opportunity to extend his territory at the expense of his neighbours. It seems, from the records, that the town of Guadix, on the main route between Almería and Granada, but beyond the sierras above the former, and therefore closer to the latter, changed hands on several occasions in the years in which the reigns of al-Mu'tasim and Bādīs coincided. From its geographical location, and although possessed of a fortress, it could hardly be said to have had strategic value, but when, in 1066, it was seized by al-Mu'tasim, Bādīs had not only to undertake an inordinately costly campaign to recapture it, but also to invoke the support of the Taifa kingdom of Toledo. As a consequence of his successful intervention, Ibn Dhī l-Nūn of Toledo (r. 1044–75) was ceded the nearby town of Baza, very much an outpost of his territory. Two points emerge: first, alliances were readily made and as readily broken. The victor was the one who could choose the most expedient moment to act. The alliances did not entail friendship; rather they were akin to business deals, sealed to achieve a particular objective. Second, by the time that two-thirds of the eleventh century had elapsed, the three major Taifa states in al-Andalus were Granada, Toledo and Seville, although Valencia and Saragossa to the north and east were, as later events transpired, to retain their independence for longer.

Culture in the Taifa states

The apogee of the Taifa states was ephemeral, but the cultural legacy they bequeathed to posterity although largely unfamiliar to Western Europe, was significant. In the field of poetry, for example, the instance of the love of the poet Ibn Zaydūn (1003–71) for the society princess Wallāda is instructive on a number of levels. Born into what might be loosely called the Arab aristocracy in Cordoba, and a younger contemporary of Ibn Hazm, he became associated, in the late years of the turbulent 1020s when he had already acquired some fame as a poet, with the daughter of the deposed and assassinated Caliph al-Mustakfī (r. 1024–5), a descendant of 'Abd ar-Rahmān III. She is one of the 116 learned women of al-Andalus, identified by María Luisa Ávila, of whom about a quarter lived in the eleventh century.[13] Whether women considered themselves to be equal to men at that time, and whether their aspirations to emancipation were fulfilled, may never be determined, but Wallāda, a precocious poetic talent who presided over a salon where notable poets of the epoch assembled, enjoyed wide renown. Whether also her behaviour was 'marked by strong passion, extreme coarseness and materialistic realism', in Nykl's words, she was certainly a magnet attracting emerging literary talents and men of rank.[14] Ibn Zaydūn was infatuated with Wallāda and when a rival suitor in the person of a Cordoban *wazīr*, Ibn 'Abdūs, appeared on the scene, he wrote a long satirical epistle in verse purporting to come from Wallāda and sent it to Ibn 'Abdūs. It is worth noting that he would have written this on paper, which had become known in al-Andalus in the tenth century and was produced, in large quantities in paper mills powered by water, from flax some of which was imported from Egypt to meet demand. One may also note that the centre of paper-making was in Játiva where the industry was to thrive, even in the thirteenth century after the conquest of the region by the Aragonese.[15] So incensed was Ibn 'Abdūs that he trumped up charges against Ibn Zaydūn securing the latter's imprisonment during which confinement the latter continued to compose poetry, deriving inspiration from his persistent love for Wallāda. His affections had formerly been reciprocated but, as a result of his impetuosity and the verbal assault on Ibn 'Abdūs, Wallāda's attitude towards him cooled off. The conventional laments for the object of love from whom one is separated are dressed in terms of unusual intensity. Ibn Zaydūn fled from Cordoba after a year and a half in prison, ending up in Seville where in 1049 he became attached to the court of al-Mu'tadid. His celebrated *qasīda* (ode), in *nūn* (the *nūniyya*), so called because all the verses ended in the Arabic letter 'n', is a product of his disillusionment, and was sent to Wallāda without reply.[16] Whereas much of Andalusi verse is intricate, highly stylised and characterised by brilliant metaphors, this poem by Ibn Zaydūn betrays a depth of personal feeling, in the main absent elsewhere. He is not above sentiment or nostalgia, as, in a contemporary poem, he recalls happy days in the gardens of the palace of az-Zahrā'. The senses of sight, hearing and smell, all prompted by the delights of these gardens, lead Ibn Zaydūn to reflect on his adoration of Wallāda which, because it is one-way only, is tinged with remorse. The praise of gardens and flowers was such a feature of Andalusi poetry that it became a genre. Ibn Zaydūn, on the other hand, refrains from indulging in luxuriant descriptions and exotic metaphors. This stock idiom is embellished with an evidently emotional approach, evinced by the infusion of a more personal, self-centred involvement with his subject matter. There is poignancy in the way in which he expresses his desolation at being abandoned by Wallāda, who is far removed from the idealised beauty of the traditional Arabic ode. The *nūniyya* is a love poem, but Ibn Zaydūn's tendency to probe the nature of his feelings in verse is, as Pérès and others have pointed out, more akin to a Western and European characteristic than an Oriental one.

It needs to be pointed out that this is another of the contested issues arising from the study of al-Andalus. The poet and Arabist Emilio García Gómez, identifying the literary topoi in Ibn Zaydūn's poetry, argued thereby that his verse was imbued with Eastern traits. He was in effect an Arabic poet writing poetry after the classical Eastern fashion, but in al-Andalus, rather than an Andalusi poet exemplifying distinctive non-Classical features in his verse. The debate acquires added significance when the matter of the freedom enjoyed by women in al-Andalus compared to that in the rest of the Islamic world is discussed. Did the Andalusi woman of the eleventh century really feel equal to men, as Cantarino wrote?[17] One may deduce from Ibn Zaydūn's poetry and from elsewhere that Wallāda was mistress of her own universe, but she held a privileged position in society, and perhaps nobody dared question the liberty of movement and of mores that quite evidently governed her conduct. She may be the most glaring example, but many others of whom there are glimpses in the sources had a lifestyle unencumbered by the restrictions traditionally supposed to have been inflicted on women in an urban Islamic environment. Some were learned, and had the knowledge and culture of their male counterparts, their skill in writing not being confined to copying books. Yet the evidence as such that exists was by no means sufficient to convince Pierre Guichard whose extensive researches led him to conclude that the situation of women in the urban centres of al-Andalus did not differ much from the Orient, and that it is the height of exaggeration to claim that women were granted greater freedom in al-Andalus.[18] What is assumed to have been true for Islam in the East at the time is also assumed to have been true for the Islamic West, but the evidence is so sparse, complex and miscellaneous that it is hazardous to make assertions. For example, if the system of the harem and the seclusion of women was only introduced after the fall of the Umayyads in Damascus in the mid-eighth century,[19] and if the Umayyad dynasty prevailed in al-Andalus from 756 for the succeeding 250 years, then when, if at all, was the harem adopted? For the first three centuries of Islam, women were permitted to pray alongside men in mosques, and they did not have to be veiled. A slave who had borne children to her master as wife or concubine was liberated, along with her offspring, after his death. According to a *hadīth*, it was an injunction upon women as well as men to seek learning, and there is certainly evidence of this in al-Andalus, as has been demonstrated. A picture may be built up representing well-to-do women as enjoying the advantages of a liberated lifestyle, which Wallāda and others in an urban milieu did. There was no bar on female slaves acquiring literacy and achieving renown as poets. Was the latter activity restricted to close family circles? The picture may be misleading, but it is prudent to be reminded that the prevailing Mālikī law school permitted the incorporation of local customs and practices.[20] In other words, it is not inconceivable that indigenous elements should have had some influence on the formation of Islam in al-Andalus as it developed. Perhaps one should not venture beyond the one established instance of Wallāda as a free spirit calling the tune and not extrapolate beyond this. A final observation may be made at this point, namely that the Taifa state system crumbled because it was regarded by some to compromise some of the essential tenets of Islam. The Taifa courts were perceived as too free and easy-going which was essentially why, in the event, they were replaced by a system in which the rudiments of Islam were more strictly observed.

The second half of the eleventh century: the threshold of change

In the latter part of his life, from 1049, Ibn Zaydūn was to be found in the court of the 'Abbādids of Seville, first al-Mu'tadid (r. 1042–69) and then al-Mu'tamid (r. 1069–91). In the traditional manner of the court poet, he composed verses eulogising his patron, procuring for himself the office of *kātib*. Ibn Zaydūn witnessed the rapid extension of Seville's sphere of influence in the 1050s and 1060s, as a result of its policy of aggression, as it absorbed the smaller but not insignificant Taifa of Huelva, together with Silves and Niebla to the west, and Arcos, Morón, Ronda and Algeciras to the east. Ibn Zaydūn fulfilled his function with the regular production of verses that were considered highly, and survived the jealous machinations of rivals after al-Mu'tadid's death through the patronage of the new ruler al-Mu'tamid, a fellow poet and therefore kindred spirit. He even returned to Cordoba after it was captured by the 'Abbādids in 1070 following the death of its longstanding ruler Ibn Jahwar. The continual rivalry among what one might call the major Taifa states and the inevitable weakening of the political system in al-Andalus did not go unnoticed. As Ibn 'Idhārī wrote:

> whilst the frontier of al-Andalus went on getting weaker, and civil strife continued unabated among the *amīrs*, the enemy sought to dominate them all, when it got fed up with receiving annual payments, aimed to take the entire country out of the hands of the Muslims.[21]

This 'enemy' was Fernando I of Castile (r. 1035–65). The days of Muslim dominance of the Peninsula in the tenth century were long gone, and he recognised that the Caliphate of Cordoba had been torn apart, leaving a medley of smaller, less powerful states vulnerable to the military strength that he could muster. It was the age-old swing of the pendulum. When one state saw itself to be militarily superior to its neighbour, it stepped in to annex it. Irrespective of religion, at least until the final third of the eleventh century, it was a recurring paradigm in Peninsular politics that one state should expand its territory at its neighbour's expense when it felt powerful enough to do so. In 1057, Fernando invaded the Taifa state of Badajoz, capturing two cities, and in 1063, he took an army into the lands of the state of Seville, setting fire to villages without encountering military opposition. Within a short period of time, and in the same decade of the 1060s, Al-Mu'tadid, who had formerly committed filicide against one of his sons on the grounds of treason, attempted to make a deal with Fernando, the end product being a tacit recognition on his part of the superiority of the former. There was no alternative for al-Mu'tadid other than the payment of large sums annually in return for Fernando's guaranteed protection. One might note in passing that when Fernando died in 1065 and divided his vast kingdom amongst his three sons who immediately warred amongst themselves, Seville withheld these annual payments, known as *parias* (equal parts), until such time as the kingdoms of the north were able to enforce them again (in the 1080s). *Plus ça change . . .*

One gets the impression from various accounts that the Taifa state of Seville, with the wealth accrued from the annexation of other Taifas, together with its own natural resources, was not only an obvious target for Fernando I, but sufficiently opulent to absorb his repeatedly rapacious annual demands. Regarding the rural population, one may assume that their existence was settled and relatively undisturbed, apart for the conflagrations perpetrated by Fernando. If the invaders set fire to buildings, as the walls (*tapias*) were made from mud brick, or adobe (*at-tūb*), similar to cob walls, then only the wooden structures, such as wooden beams, roofs and pens for animals, would have succumbed. Crops that were burnt could be replaced within half a year, and it is difficult to imagine that any lasting hardship was caused. Such walls, which tended to be up to two feet thick, not only had the advantage of being made from local materials, but also provided interior warmth or coolness depending on the prevailing outside temperature. They were also durable, and vulnerable only to earthquakes. In the Treatise of Ibn ʿAbdūn which describes Seville at the beginning of the twelfth century, and which is an invaluable source for the life and practices of the time, weight-bearing walls had to be a minimum of two and half palms in width, equivalent to seven and a half inches.[22]

Under al-Muʿtamid, Seville prospered, and its citizens enjoyed a life of comparative ease for twenty-five years whilst their ruler pursued his expansionist policies. He succeeded in his quest to take control of Cordoba. This he did twice, once for a period of six months and the second time for twelve and a half years until it was captured by the Almoravids from North Africa in 1091. Also, in 1078, he took over command of the Taifa of Murcia, with its outlet into the Mediterranean at the port of Cartagena. At this stage, the territory of the Taifa state of Seville extended from the Atlantic Ocean, at the foot of present-day Portugal to the south of Badajoz and Mérida, northwards, bisecting the lands of the Taifas of Toledo in the centre and Valencia to the east, to the Mediterranean. Only Granada and Almería to the south prevented Seville from occupying the entire lower third of the Iberian Peninsula. This apparent territorial strength was of little avail to them, as their ephemeral existence was to be first threatened by enemies from the north and then shattered by supposed allies from North Africa.

Toledo acted as a form of buffer zone between the Christian kingdoms and the south, whereas Saragossa to the north-east was vulnerable to both its powerful neighbours, Castile and Aragón. The focus turned to Toledo during the crucial last troubled third of the century. The ancient Muslim family of Dhū Nūn, of remote Berber origin, held sway there and governed the Taifa state from 1036 to 1085. As Madrid was not yet established as a major city, Toledo, with its central geographical location and its legacy as a political capital in the Peninsula and headquarters of the Christian Church, very much occupied centre stage. The pivotal date is 1085, the year in which Toledo was occupied by Alfonso VI, king of Castile (r. 1072–1109), an event as significant in the history of the Iberian Peninsula as William of Normandy's invasion of the Islands of Britain in 1066 and victory at the battle of Hastings.[23] Almost at a stroke, the political map that had been more or less stable for three centuries was inexorably altered with a huge wedge being driven into al-Andalus, leaving only the south and the north-east intact. In order to account for such a transcendental change, it is necessary to move away temporarily from al-Andalus itself to focus on the religious reform that emanated from a revitalised papacy.

Under two successive popes, Alexander II (Pope 1061–73) and Gregory VII (Pope 1073–85), papal influence was exerted on the kingdoms of the Iberian Peninsula, notably Navarre and Castile, to a far greater extent than hitherto. When there was some doubt, for example, about the Hispanic liturgy (which has come to known as the Mozarabic liturgy), authorisation was sought for its use and achieved in a visit to Rome by three bishops in 1066.[24] In 1071, the dominant monastery of San Juan de la Peña in Aragón approved the substitution of the Hispanic with the Roman liturgy, on the express wishes of Alexander II who was disconcerted by the rumours of dissent and disunion within the realms of the Church in the Iberian Peninsula. The use of the new liturgy swept through Aragón and, by 1076, was also imposed in neighbouring Navarre. This conversion and other innovations in the Peninsula were orchestrated by the abbey of Cluny in East Central France, whose abbot, Hugh of Cluny (abbot 1049–1109), was to play a major role in the implantation of the reforms beyond the Pyrenees, not only this but also in the establishment of a commanding Cluniac presence. The power of the papacy was soon to have a stranglehold in the Christian kingdoms and to alter for at least three generations the perception of Islam within Christendom. This process whereby Christianity and Islam confronted one another as religious antagonists was to gain huge momentum from the Crusades in the eleventh century, and was to impact onto Andalusi/ Castilian and Andalusi/Aragonese relations. Although papal propaganda was persistent and effective, the change in attitudes took a long time to filter down beyond the highest level of society. Until the intervention of Cluny and the papal pressure on Christian monarchs, the politics of expediency governed the relations between al-Andalus and the other states in the Peninsula. One might suspect that there was an awareness of religious differences but, beyond this, no sentiments of animosity. Hostilities were engaged out of what might be called strictly military motives; these were often vigorous and brutal as was the norm in medieval warfare, but the latter was not, until the late-eleventh-century sea change in attitudes, complicated by factors of faith.

When Ferdinand died in 1065, he left his vast territories divided amongst his three sons, which inevitably led to a fierce dynastic conflict. Sancho inherited Castile but was assassinated outside the city gates of Zamora in October 1072. The kingdom of Castile then passed to his brother Alfonso who added it to that of León, which had been his legacy from Ferdinand; thenceforward he became Alfonso VI of Castile. The strained relations between the brothers had brought about grievous conflict, culminating in Alfonso's defeat and exile in the January of that year. He sought refuge in the Andalusi city of Toledo, where he stayed until he returned as sovereign of Castile after the violent death of his brother.

Although his time in Toledo has been strikingly described by Lévi-Provençal as a period of 'prison doré' (gilt imprisonment), he is more likely to have been treated more as an honoured guest of the then ruler al-Ma'mūn (r. 1043–75) than as a captive.[25] Al-Ma'mūn had presided over a period of prosperity in the city, extending his domains eastward to Valencia and, a few months before his death, to Cordoba, where he died. One may conjecture that, in granting asylum to Alfonso, al-Ma'mūn had an eye to the main chance. He would have recognised the potential political advantage of giving sanctuary to the enemy of the king of Castile, and would have relished the opportunity to impress his hard-pressed neighbour, someone with equal status to his own, with the scale of his achievements. However, one may also imagine the reverse to have been true: the future Castilian king, in a role akin perhaps to that of ambassador, observing how a successful Taifa state was governed, acquiring knowledge of its strengths and weaknesses, becoming acquainted with the leading figures in the city and cognisant of competing factions. Furthermore, he may have been able to assess Toledo's wealth, an essential feature of his strategy when preparing to capture the city and incorporate it into his own realm. One may also add to this the distinct probability that he became aware of Arabicised Christians living and worshipping in Toledo. Either from contact with them or with the court dignitaries, it is not inconceivable that he should have acquired some understanding of the Arabic language. They were to play an important function, acting as a kind of fifth column, when the takeover of the city took place in 1085.

The instance of a Christian monarch spending nine months or so in a Muslim court in the 1070s without any hint of religious differences being an obstacle to harmonious relations, has to be assessed in context. For the Pope, anxious, as has been seen, to expand the area of his jurisdiction, it must have been a worrying development and even perceived as 'fraternising with the enemy'. Alexander II does not appear to have been alert to what might be termed local diplomatic practices within the Iberian Peninsula, regarding the northern part at least as an errant flock that needed to be brought back securely within the fold. He was in the practice of granting indulgences to those who were prepared to fight against Muslims *qua* Muslims in the Iberian Peninsula, perhaps out of anger and revenge at the death of Ramiro I, the first king of Aragón (r. 1035–63) at the siege of the small township of Graus in 1063 which he was seeking to wrest from the Taifa state of Saragossa. There seems to be little justification for Runciman's claim that Ramiro's death 'stirred the imagination of Europe', but the eyes of Europe had started to focus beyond the Pyrenees, in part perhaps as a consequence of growing interest in the pilgrimage to Santiago de Compostela in Galicia in the north-west of the Peninsula. Major figures, such as William V, Duke of Aquitaine (969–1030), are said to have made the pilgrimage more than once, thereby getting to know the Leonese and Navarrese monarchs.[26] Partly out of self-interest, the gauntlet thrown down by Pope Alexander was taken up by Count Ebles of Roucy, who as Ramiro's brother-in-law might have been expected to have an axe to grind. The Count assembled a formidable army, but as far as is known no actual invasion materialised, understandable, perhaps, in view of the Pope's death, and some anxiety on the part of the recently crowned Aragonese king.[27]

As an earlier example of Alexander's initiative, one may mention the transpyrenean expedition of 1064 by Frankish knights which succeeded in capturing after a siege the frontier town of Barbastro, to the north-east of Saragossa and in the foothills of the mountains. This major assault on Islamic territory may have been sanctioned by Alexander in part to deflect hostile opinion away from his pontificate. The accolades that a full-scale campaign against Muslims could engender would cast him as a proponent of the Crusading ideal, but there are puzzling aspects to the expedition. Barbastro had certain strategic significance, but although it was described by al-Maqqarī as one of the strongest places in the Upper March, it is difficult to appreciate why it warranted so much attention. Arabic chroniclers such as Ibn Hayyān go into great detail about the strength and savagery of the assailants, stating that over 6,000 Muslims were massacred after the surrender, the women and children being taken in captivity.[28] According to al-Himyarī, 5,000 young women, distinguished by their beauty, were sent as a present to the Emperor of Constantinople.[29] The leader is said to have been a knight from Normandy, William of Montreuil, who fought on behalf of Alexander II and subsequently returned to Rome where he died. One might speculate, given the date of the Barbastro campaign why this warrior did not join forces with William of Normandy for the invasion of Britain and the promise of untold wealth and advancement there. However, the tales of the riches in Barbastro are astonishing, even allowing for the customary exaggeration of such accounts. These stories, particularly those relating to the opulence of the town which enjoyed a population of just over 6,000 in the late nineteenth century, seem out of all proportion to its significance. After all, Barbastro was in a frontier zone, with a garrisoned fortress, the living accommodation being outside. To believe that it was as large as it is claimed to have been, and as endowed with trappings of wealth as, say, Toledo is beyond the bounds of credibility. The reality may have been more prosaic. Alexander may have needed a gesture to be made for propaganda purposes; a massive army was assembled for the ostensible purpose of inflicting a defeat on Muslims. This may not fall into the category of a sledgehammer cracking a nut, but it was too large for what was required of it, and the target too insignificant. Arabic chroniclers may have embellished and exaggerated their accounts both to draw attention to the barbarity of the Frankish warriors and to focus on the plight of the outnumbered garrison. If the campaign was on such a major scale as has been made out, then the total folly of it may be recognised in the light of Barbastro's recapture by the

Taifa ruler of Saragossa with the assistance of the state of Seville the following year, 1065, with reciprocal atrocities.

In the 1070s, then, in the Iberian Peninsula, alliances were made and broken; *parias* were paid to one or other of the Christian kingdoms of the north by beleaguered Taifa states; and, at the highest level, Christian kings were still guests and not prisoners in Muslim courts. However, in the very character and career of Alfonso VI one may map the change. He may be said to have moved with the times, as by the time of his death in 1109, the changes in the religious attitudes between Muslim and Christian were an established feature of Peninsular life, due in part to the factors mentioned and in part to his marriage, in 1080, to Constance, the niece of Abbot Hugh of Cluny, which no doubt had an impact on the important pro-reform policies brought into effect in the 1080s. From then on, Muslims and Christians could not associate with each other as hitherto, cheek by jowl. This rupture of a state of affairs that had persisted for nearly four centuries came about not only through the intervention of the papacy and Cluny in the Iberian Peninsula. Christian intransigence was to be met by a hardening of Muslim attitudes in what may be considered as one of the most striking coincidences in the history of medieval Europe.

Just when the Crusading spirit came to prominence in the Christian West, so a resurgent Islam overwhelmed al-Andalus, such that both protagonists sought to impose their religion on the other. The Taifa states were taken over by the Almoravids (*al-murābitūn*, those who used a *ribāt*, a staging post for their horses and by extension a haven, refuge or retreat). These were a federation of tribes from the Maghrib, who built their capital at Marrakesh in present-day Morocco, and whose aspirations for expansion brought them to al-Andalus. They were also called *al-mulaththamūn* (wearers of the veil), derived from their practice of covering their faces with veils (*lithām*), which were black in their case, when riding on camels or on horseback in the desert. This was a measure brought on by necessity to keep the sand out of their nostrils. Al-Mu'tamid had initially invited them to shore up the oppressed Taifa states, which were saddled with paying crippling annual *parias* to the Christian monarchs, notably Alfonso VI. According to the memoirs of 'Abd Allāh, Mu'tamid asked the Almoravid *amīr* to prepare for *jihād*, a clear example of the word being used to describe warfare in defence of Islamic domains. The entry of the Almoravids into al-Andalus in 1086 under their leader, Yūsuf b. Tashufīn, met with startling success. All the power of Alfonso VI, fresh from his occupation of Toledo through negotiation the previous year, after the pressure of a protracted siege but without a battle, engaged the newcomers who were reinforced by the forces that the Taifa states could muster, at Zallāqa, a short distance from Badajoz. The Almoravids and their allies were victorious, an encounter that resulted in the relief of the immediate discontinuation of the payment of *parias*. The consequences were serious for Alfonso, in that as well as the loss of a large number of fighting men, he could make no progress with conquests to the west of Toledo. Thenceforward, his attention was directed to the east of the Peninsula where his forces were more successful in containing but not nullifying the Almoravid threat. For reasons that are not specified in the sources, Yūsuf returned to the Maghrib after Zallāqa, when it might have been expected that he would have taken advantage of Alfonso's disarray and marched toward Toledo with a view to its recapture. It is possible to speculate that he felt that he did not have the manpower and resources sufficient to retain Toledo, assuming that this city was a target. One might also indicate that he would have been far from confident of the total commitment of his Andalusi allies, who regarded him as a means to prevent further Christian incursions into their territory, but who were under no illusions about the weakness of their own position. In any event, he did not go back to al-Andalus until three years later, when he returned to assist the Andalusis in their attempt to storm the fortress of Aledo in the south-east of the Peninsula, in the present-day region of Murcia. It was adventurous of Alfonso to seek to maintain a stronghold that far south, which had held out against the periodic assaults by the Taifa rulers who were at loggerheads amongst themselves, for they each feared that action from another would be prejudicial to their own position, and therefore were unable to press home a united decisive attack. The Almoravids laid siege to Aledo in 1089 but withdrew after four months. Alfonso brought a substantial number of troops down to fortify and reprovision the afflicted fortress, but it was later overrun and taken by Almoravids in 1092.

It is clear from the sources that the Taifa states were seeking to find ways of taking advantage of the presence of the Almoravids in al-Andalus by discrediting their rivals for their own ends. It is equally evident that Yūsuf was aware of this, and in 1090 he annexed Granada from his fellow Berber, the Zīrid 'Abd Allāh, and, the following year, the great prize of Seville. The earlier role and later fate of al-Mu'tamid of Seville has received deserved attention, because he was a ruler of one of the most powerful Taifa states and also a poet. In the aftermath of Zallāqa, Al-Mu'tamid, now conscious of the formidable strength of the Almoravids, sought to appease Alfonso who had sent the Castilian nobleman Álvar Fáñez as support for the Zīrids of Granada, and to reclaim the *parias* which were paid three years in arrears. He, al-Mu'tamid, sent his daughter-in-law Sa'īda (Zaida, known as the *mora* Zaida) to Alfonso's court, together with the possession of certain strategic fortresses, including Alarcos, scene of a celebrated battle 100 years afterwards, Consuegra and Uclés, at the frontiers to the south and east of Toledo. She adopted Catholicism, and, with the name Isabella, married Alfonso possibly in late 1090, although it is said she was his mistress, and mother to a son by him, Sancho, who died at the battle of Uclés in 1108.[30] How she died is not known, but Alfonso took a fourth wife, Bertha, in 1100. Perhaps this diplomatic gesture was a last throw of the dice for al-Mu'tamid, who had seen Granada fall to the Almoravids in 1090, and who trusted in the age-old practice of dynastic interchanges, irrespective of religion. Alfonso, according to some sources, may have responded by dispatching Álvar Fáñez to assist him, recognising the menace to both Muslims and Christians in the Peninsula, but to no avail. Yūsuf b. Tashufīn may, in turn, have used al-Mu'tamid's attributed overture to Christians as a pretext for deposing him. Accordingly, he sent an army the following spring which accomplished his intentions, thus bringing to an end, to all intents and purposes, the period of the Taifa states. Al-Mu'tamid was sent, together with other members of his family, into exile at Aghmāt, near Marrakesh where he died in 1095, and where a modest shrine to his memory testifies to his last years there. His overthrow was hastened by the decrees of the *faqīh*s that the Taifa rulers had been levying unlawful and unpopular taxes which had been resented by Ibn Hazm, amongst others. The Almoravids observed the traditional practice of taxation according to the Māliki law school prevalent for so long in al-Andalus, but latterly neglected. Strict adherents to the Qur'ān and the *sunna*, and imbued with reformist zeal, they could therefore reason that they had legal authority and approval to impose conformity in Islam. It may be noted that this reversion to Islamic orthodoxy was occurring at the same time as in Europe, Christianity was being revitalised through the reforms championed by Cluny. The Crusading impulse of the north matched the revival of Islam in North Africa enforced by the effective Almoravid militia.

During his exile, al-Mu'tamid composed verses full of nostalgia and pathos, garnered from a number of different sources, that have touched romantic hearts and brought him posthumous fame. There was even a multinational gathering in Aghmāt in 1996 of poets from all over the Arab world in commemoration of the so-called poet king. His earlier poetry, when he presided over the brilliant and vibrant Sevillan court in happy, perhaps carefree days, conformed to patterns of Andalusi poetry, celebrating wine in the *khamriyya* genre and expressing love for the object of his desire in the familiar ornate language of the *ghazal* genre. However, the elegies that he composed when languishing in exile and in chains in Aghmāt have been described as 'unique in Arabic literature',[31] and some have been come to be well known in English and Spanish versions.[32] One may imagine him addressing his chains as follows: 'I say to my chains, don't you understand? I have surrendered to you. Why, then, have you no pity, no tenderness? You drank my blood. You ate my flesh. Don't crush my bones'.[33] Such expressions, however, may be considered understandable from someone who had been accustomed to a life of luxury, and who had, for a while at least, been 'a monarch of all he surveyed'. It is from the poems themselves that one receives a feeling for the former ruler's plight, as he looks around to the stars at night, to the moon and to flocks of partridges flying overhead, and reflects, in moving tones, on his predicament. They come across as the poignant rather than self-pitying utterances of someone trying to understand how joy can turn so precipitately to weeping, a prevailing theme.[34] After al-Mu'tamid's death in exile in 1095, al-Andalus may be seen as an enclave of North Africa, a province of an empire whose capital was in Marrakesh, although there remained a Taifa presence in the Levant and Saragossa.

El Cid

It has been remarked earlier that Alfonso VI, in the course of his lifetime, directed his focus towards Europe. He had spent nearly a year in the Muslim court of Toledo in 1072, but this would have remained a distant memory in later decades when the orientation of Castile and Aragón shifted decisively northwards. Rapprochement with al-Andalus was replaced, in a gradual process fostered by closer links with and the increasing attention of Christian Europe, by a perception of Muslims as an implacable foe. This concept was reinforced by the arrival, in al-Andalus, of the Almoravids. Not all Castilian courtiers, however, followed Alfonso's lead. Rodrigo Díaz, a Castilian nobleman from Vivar near Burgos (c. 1043–99), the subject of Spain's celebrated epic poem, compiled perhaps a century after his death, has acquired legendary status in history and been immortalised in poem, prose and film. At some time in his career, he was given the epithet 'El Cid', or 'Mío Cid', and has come to be universally known as such.[35] In a nutshell, he fought on behalf of Alfonso VI, went to Seville to collect *parias* and was exiled by him, twice; he served in the kingdom of the Taifa rulers of Saragossa for four years, during which he fought for Muslims against both Muslims and Christians; the latter part of his life was spent in the Levant, acquiring wealth from *parias* paid directly to him and entering Valencia as its ruler in 1094. He may be described, not disparagingly, as a mercenary, accompanied for the most part by a small contingent of loyal Castilians; he was undefeated in his battles and, in retrospect, may be seen as having held up the advances of the Almoravids in the east of the Peninsula. In twentieth-century history, in particular, he has been paraded as the hero of Castile, if not Spain, a patriot who effectively parried the Muslim threat throughout his lifetime, thanks mainly to the magnificent study by Menéndez Pidal.[36]

Yet issues are outstanding which need to be addressed. For example, a case could be made for considering El Cid to have been a Muslim hero. This argument is based on the name by which he has become known, of patently Arabic origin. Menéndez Pidal calls the word 'Cid' an honorific title, derived from the Arabic *çidi* (señor).[37] *Sayyid* in Arabic does indeed translate as 'lord' or 'chief', and with the ending *sayyidī* as 'my lord', etc, but the same word also signifies 'lion' or 'wolf'.[38] This link was explored by Epalza who, in an illuminating study, observed that *sīd* (lion) was an authentic military and warlike epithet, well known in the Arab world.[39] The point to make here is that *sayyid* meaning 'lord' is not an obvious epithet to describe someone's warlike capabilities, and is *prima facie* unlikely. It is far more probable that, in a Muslim environment ('*entre*

los moros),[40] he would have been called 'lion' in honour of his feats on the battlefield. One might make the relevant analogy with the English king, Richard
Coeur de Lion, the Lionheart (1157–99), who earned this title for his exploits
as a warrior. To take the parallel further, Richard would have been called
this by admiring French knights in his retinue, just as El Cid would have been
similarly designated by awestruck Muslims. Both were given a foreign acco-
lade that would remain with them when among their own people. It is worth
reiterating that the person celebrated in the twentieth century as the epitome
of a national hero who defended Christian Spain against Muslims is known by
his Arabic epithet. It is also instructive that, before El Cid occupied Valencia,
he was acclaimed by Taifa Muslims as the champion who was instrumental in
warding off the advances of the Almoravids in al-Andalus. Although, in near
contemporary Arabic texts, he is named in the transliterated form of the Latin
'Campiductor' (leader in the field of battle), which does cast notional doubt on
when he was called 'El' or 'Mío' Cid; although it has been suggested that 'we do
not indeed even know for certain whether it [his nickname] was used of him at
all during his lifetime', it does seem improbable if not impossible that it should
have been conferred upon him posthumously.[41] One should also allude to the
other instances of 'Mio Cid' in Latin sources. Menéndez Pidal called attention
to 'Mio Cid Petrus Roderici', also known as Pero Ruyz Miocid (*sic*), and there
are countless Citi (Citiz) but this is evidently a proper name.[42]

Rodrigo is first known to have operated within an Andalusi environment
in 1079–80 when he was dispatched to Seville to collect the *parias* on behalf of
Alfonso VI of Castile, whereupon al-Mu'tamid made use of his services in the
running dispute with neighbouring Granada. At the same time, Alfonso had
sent other Castilian noblemen to Granada on a similar mission. The two Taifa
states of Seville and Granada were in dispute over territory, and both rulers
made use of the presence of Castilian magnates to secure their relative positions. Rodrigo, no doubt drawing on the experience that he had had acting as
a lawyer in Alfonso's court after the assassination of Sancho II in 1072, wrote
to 'Abdallāh b. Buluggīn in Granada on al-Mu'tamid's behalf requesting him
to withdraw from the territory that he had seized, but this overture was to no
avail. Accordingly, he took 'his army', doubtless comprising the loyal cohort of
Castilians who had accompanied him throughout his journeyings, to Cabra,
which lay approximately midway between Cordoba and Granada, with the
intention of confronting the enemy from Granada who had occupied territory
belonging to the Taifa of Seville. What is intriguing about this episode, in which
El Cid emerged victorious, is that two sets of Castilian mercenaries who were
in conflict were both on the payroll of Taifa rulers.[43] The engagement at Cabra
thus throws light on the nature of Andalusi politics. A number of Castilian
magnates were intricately involved in the affairs of the Taifa states to the south,
acting in a diplomatic as well as military capacity, and were charged with the

responsibility of arranging the transmission of the *parias* to Alfonso's treasury. The two most powerful states in al-Andalus were being annually stripped of their assets, in the process of which their courts were penetrated by high-ranking Castilians who, certainly in the case of El Cid, fulfilled diplomatic, legal and military roles.

In exile from Alfonso's court in 1081, El Cid then went into the service of the adjoining Taifa state of Saragossa whose ruler, al-Muqtadir ('the potentate'), who had come to power in 1049 (d. 1082), 'received him with great honour, and treated him with much respect'. According to the *Historia Roderici*, his successor, al-Mu'tamin, 'relied on his counsel' which reflects once more that El Cid's prowess lay not solely on the battlefield. El Cid negotiated with leaders and overlords to the north-east, that is to say in present-day Aragón and Catalonia, the outcome of which was presumably unsuccessful, as he achieved resounding victories in a campaign against them in 1082, which brought him not only wealth and fame but also permanency in Saragossa. In 1084, El Cid was again victorious in a battle against the Aragonese, described as 'an overwhelming victory', which clearly indicates his ascendancy. As a consequence of the five years spent in the Taifa court of Saragossa, Rodrigo must have gained a command of Arabic and become well informed about the Islamic system of governance, reflecting Alfonso VI's experience in Toledo a decade earlier, but more so, one would imagine, given his longer period of residence. The lucrative system of *parias* whereby the ruler paid protection money to whatever Christian power to secure their own independence must have made an impact on El Cid. In the 1090s, having left Saragossa, he was in virtual control of the Levant, capturing towns and cities and exacting enormous quantities of *parias* from them, larger than those paid to Alfonso VI in previous decades. His crowning achievement, one might say, was the conquest of Valencia in 1094, although, paradoxically, he reduced the payments made by the Muslims to the statutory one-tenth, showing in passing his familiarity with Islamic fiscal practice. Once in possession of Valencia, he was ruling in the capacity of a Taifa striving to maintain his independence. His defeat of the Almoravids at nearby Cuarte in 1094 was the first setback that they had sustained in the Iberian Peninsula, but it was not a victory for Christianity, such as one might describe a feat by Crusaders. Muslim accounts of El Cid in Valencia relate how he acted in a juridical capacity when trying the *qāḍī* with the murder of the previous ruler. In a dramatic passage in Ibn Idhārī', El Cid is depicted as posing a question to the assembled crowd of Muslims and Franks (*ar-rūm*): 'What punishment in your law is there for someone who has killed the ruler?' They remained silent, so he replied: 'According to us, he should be punished by being burnt by fire'.[44] So it occurred. This may be seen as an example of justice being meted out dispassionately, in a similar fashion to the way those who transgressed against Islamic law were punished by *qāḍī*s in Cordoba in the ninth century.

It would seem, then, that Rodrigo Díaz, a Castilian nobleman, trained as a lawyer and diplomat and renowned as a warrior, operated with unparalleled success as a freelance mercenary within al-Andalus and on its borders, principally in the Levant. He moved within Christian and Muslim circles, fought for Muslim and Christian causes and, in the last years of his life, was monarch, in all but name, of all he surveyed. One may have sympathy, therefore, with Camón Aznar who argued that El Cid was an anachronism, a Castilian Christian who kept company with Muslims in an epoch, the 1080s and 1090s, when mutual tolerance and respect between the two faiths had been replaced by a much more hardened and uncompromising attitude.[45] Put another way, he lived fifty years too late. El Cid, to his Andalusi allies, was not primarily a Christian, but a military commander. After his military triumphs on their behalf, he was rewarded financially. In particular, the Andalusis would have appreciated his single-minded resolve to repel the Almoravid advance, such that his victory at Cuarte in 1094 could well have resulted in their naming him their *sīd*, their lion. In fact, though, he was merely delaying the inevitable, as the Almoravids did enter Valencia in 1102 after it had been evacuated on the orders of Alfonso VI who considered that it could not be defended. One may, lastly, observe that the Poem of El Cid, written a century or so after his death, reinforces the above view. The author of this epic poem calls all Muslims *moros*, both the friends and neighbours of El Cid in Saragossa and elsewhere, and the ethnically distinct fearsome Almoravids, although the latter are sometimes *moros de Marruecos* (from Morocco). This is a language free from religious invective, and suggests a grass-roots understanding of *moros* as friend or foe depending on the prevailing political situation and irrespective of race.

Notes

1.   Hussain Monès, 'Consideraciones sobre la época de los reyes de taifas', *Al-Andalus*, XXXI (1966), 305–28, at 321.
2.   This calls to mind the cautionary story in the Prologue of *Don Quixote*, part II, when a madman accustomed to dropping a slab of marble on any passing dog and watching it run away howling, did so one day on the *podenco* (perhaps a greyhound) belonging to a bonnet-seller. This person took great exception to the maltreatment of his hound, and beat up the madman, knocking him almost senseless, repeating the word 'greyhound'; 'you have done this to my greyhound; did you not see that it was a greyhound?' Some weeks passed before the madman ventured onto the streets again. When he did so, and came across a dog of whatever breed, he would examine it closely, call it a greyhound ('this one's a greyhound; watch out!') and resist the temptation to drop the marble slab on it. He never got up to his old tricks again.
3.   E. Lévi-Provençal, *La Péninsule ibérique au moyen-âge d'après le Kitāb ar-Rawd al-miʿtār fī habār al-aktār d'Ibn ʿAbd al-Munʿim al-Himyarī*, Leiden: E. J. Brill, 1938, p. 37.
4.   *The Tibyān. Memoirs of ʿAbd Allāh b. Buluggīn Last Zīrid Ruler of Granada*, translated by Amin T. Tibi, Leiden: E. J. Brill, 1986, p. 48.

5.   One is reminded of Antony's rabble-rousing speech in Shakespeare's *Julius Caesar*, which brought the people of Rome to a frenzied pitch, spurring them on to take revenge for Caesar's death.

6.   Henri Pérès, *La Poésie andalouse en árabe classique au XIe siècle. Ses aspects généraux, ses principaux thèmes et sa valeur documentaire*, Paris: Adrien-Maisonneuve, 1953 [1937], 2nd edition, p. 273 (originally published in 1937); Spanish translation by Mercedes García-Arenal with the title *Esplendor de al-Andalus*, Madrid: Libros Hiperión, 1983, p. 277. The whole episode is treated on pp. 265–73 (French), 270–8 (Spanish).

7.   Frederick P. Bargebuhr, *The Alhambra. A Cycle of Studies on the Eleventh Century in Moorish Spain*, Berlin: Walter de Gruyter, 1968. Bargebuhr's arguments are reiterated by Oleg Grabar in his classic study *The Alhambra*, London: Allen Lane, 1978, although the latter is inclined to the view that an imaginary palace is being described (p. 127); Raphael Loewe, *Ibn Gabirol*, London: Peter Halban Publishers, 1989, pp. 58–60 for the text of the poem.

8.   Bargebuhr, *The Alhambra*, p. 121.

9.   Grabar, *The Alhambra*, p. 204.

10. The life and demise of Yūsuf is analysed in detail by David Wasserstein, *The Rise and Fall of the Party-Kings. Politics and Society in Islamic Spain, 1002–1086*, Princeton, NJ: Princeton University Press, 1985, pp. 197–210.

11. One of the many facets of Hispano-Arabic studies has been the intense rivalry engendered over relatively minor issues, notably in the nineteenth century. In this instance, the Dutch Orientalist Reinhart Dozy had to defend his claim that the two rulers were brothers against the counter-arguments of his Spanish colleague, Pascual de Gayangos. The Arabic text of Ibn al-Khaṭīb cited by the former would seem to settle the matter: R. P. A. Dozy, *Recherches sur l'histoire politique et littéraire de l'Espagne pendant le Moyen Âge*, vol. I, Leiden: E. J. Brill, 1849, p. 37, n.1.

12. See Leopoldo Torres Balbás, 'Almería islámica: Crónica arqueológica de la España Musulmana, XLI', *Al-Andalus*, XXII (1957), 411–53; reproduced in *Obra Dispersa*, compiled by Manuel Casamar, Madrid: Instituto de España, 1983, vol. 6, pp. 217–63. The map, drawn by Manuel Ocaña Jiménez, representing Almería in the fourteenth century, but giving a good idea of the city in the eleventh, is to be found on pp. 236–7 of the latter.

13. Ma. Luisa Ávila, 'Las mujeres "sabias" en al-Andalus', in *La mujer en al-Andalus. Reflejos históricos de su actividad y categorías socials*, edited by Ma. J. Viguera, Madrid: Universidad Autónoma and Seville: Editoriales Andaluzas Unidas, 1989, pp. 139–84, at p. 177.

14. A. R. Nykl, *Hispano-Arabic Poetry and its Relations with the Old Provençal Troubadours*, Baltimore, MD. Printed by J. H. Furst, 1946, p. 107. See also *Casidas de amor profundo y místico. Ibn Zaydun, Ibn Arabi*, translated by Vicente Cantarino, Mexico City: Editorial Porrúa, 1977, especially pp. 22–31.

15. See Thomas F. Glick, *Islamic and Christian Spain in the Early Middle Ages*, Princeton, NJ: Princeton University Press, 1979, p. 242.

16. See James T. Monroe in *Hispano-Arabic Poetry. A Student Anthology*, Berkeley, CA: University of California Press, 1974, pp. 178–87, including facing text in Arabic. See also Nykl, *Hispano-Arabic Poetry*, pp. 115–17.

17. Cantarino, *Casidas de amor profundo y místico*, p. 22.

18. Pierre Guichard, *Al-Andalus. Estructura antropólogica de una sociedad islámica en Occidente*, Barcelona: Barral, 1976, p. 178. My paraphrase.

19. Reuben Levy, *The Social Structure of Islam*, Cambridge: Cambridge University Press, 1962, p. 127.

20. *Sūra* 4, v. 34 of the Qur'an: 'Men are overseers of women because God has granted some of them bounty in preference to others. Righteous women are obedient [to God], guarding

the invisible (taken as a euphemism for "guarding the husband's rights"), because God has guarded [them]. Admonish those women whose rebelliousness (desertion) you fear, shun them (leave them alone) in [their] resting-places and hit them'. The latter injunction has attracted much commentary. Such chastisement 'was discouraged in practice', and if administered 'must be very slight'. *The Qur'ān*, translated into English by Alan Jones, Oxford: Gibb Memorial Trust, 2007, p. 92; comments in parentheses and within quotation marks from *The Holy Qur-án*, containing the Arabic text with English translation and commentary by Maulvi Muhammad Ali, Woking: The Islamic Review Office, 1917, pp. 211–12.

21. Ibn Idhārī al-Marrākushī, *Al-bayān al-Mughrib*, translated by Felipe Maíllo Salgado, *La caída del Califato de Córdoba y los Reyes de Taifas*, Salamanca: Universidad, 1993, p. 199; my adaptation.
22. Emilio García Gómez and E. Lévi-Provençal, *Sevilla a comienzos del siglo XII. El tratado de Ibn 'Abdūn*, Seville: El Ayuntamiento, 1981, p. 112. The first edition was published in 1948.
23. It has become customary to call Alfonso VI King of León-Castilla, as does Bernard F. Reilly, *The Contest of Christian and Muslim Spain 1031–1157*, Cambridge, MA and Oxford: Blackwell, p. 76, and elsewhere. Yet this seems unwieldy and unnecessary, as incongruous as if the British monarch were called the King/Queen of Wales-England. The kingdoms Alfonso possessed were subsumed under the one title, King of Castile, after 1072. Indeed, the title that Alfonso himself preferred, from 1077 onwards, was *imperator totius Hispaniae* (Emperor of all Spain), or equivalent.
24. Archdale A. King, *Liturgies of the Primatial Sees*, London: Longmans, Green, 1957, pp. 501–2 for a detailed discussion.
25. Wasserstein, *Rise and Fall of the Party-Kings*, p. 253.
26. Americo Castro, *The Spaniards. An Introduction to their History*, translated by Willard F. King and Selma Margaretten, Berkeley, CA: University of California Press, 1971, p. 424.
27. For its wide-ranging coverage and its almost addictive readability, see Derek W. Lomax, *The Reconquest of Spain*, London: Longman, 1978, pp. 55–63. His dating of the Count's expedition to 1073 is not now generally accepted. Lomax mentions the prevalence at this time of marital alliances between French counts and daughters of monarchs in the Christian kingdoms of the Iberian Peninsula, and vice versa (p. 56).
28. Ahmed ibn Mohammed al-Makkari, *The History of the Mohammedan Dynasties in Spain*, translated by Pascual de Gayangos, 2 vols, London: RoutledgeCurzon, 2002, vol. II, pp. 266–7.
29. Lévi-Provençal, *La Péninsule ibérique au moyen-âge*, Arabic text, p. 40.
30. Lomax, *Reconquest of Spain*, p.72.
31. Nykl, *Hispano-Arabic Poetry*, p. 150.
32. Dulcie Lawrence Smith, *The Poems of Mu'tamid, King of Seville*, London: John Murray, 1913. Wisdom of the East Series; Nykl, *Hispano-Arabic Poetry*, pp. 134–54, at pp. 147–52; María Jesús Rubiera Mata, *Al-Mu'tamid Ibn 'Abbād, Poesías. Antología bilingüe*, Madrid: Instituto Hispano-Árabe de Cultura, 1987. Many poems have been included in anthologies.
33. Cola Franzen, *Poems of Arab Andalusia*, San Francisco, CA: City Light Books, 1989, p. 90; Nykl, *Hispano-Arabic Poetry*, p. 152, for the first two phrases opts for: 'My chains: do you not know that I am Muslim', recognising that the root *salama* can also convey the sense of surrender or submission. Whether al-Mu'tamid intended this play on words, as Nykl suggests (p. 216), can never be known, but a reference to his belief at this time of great hardship seems eminently feasible.
34. The poetry of al-Mu'tamid has merited the full-length study of Raymond P. Scheindlin, *Form and Structure in the Poetry of Al-Mu'tamid Ibn 'Abbād*, Leiden: E. J. Brill, 1974; see also

the acutely argued analysis of one poem by Julie Scott Meisami, 'Unsquaring the circle: rereading a poem by Al-Mu'tamid Ibn 'Abbād', *Arabica*, 35 (1988), 293–310.

35.   Two excellent biographies of his life are Stephen Clissold's eminently readable *In Search of the Cid*, London: Hodder and Stoughton, 1965, and Richard Fletcher's *The Quest for the Cid*, London: Hutchinson, 1989, an absorbing and eclectic narrative.

36.   Ramón Menéndez Pidal, *La España del Cid*, 2 vols, 5th edition, Madrid: Espasa-Calpe, 1956, reissued in 1969. The first edition was published in 1929 by Editorial Plutarco in Madrid. A 'compressed version' was translated into English by Harold Sunderland, with the title *The Cid and His Spain*, London: John Murray, 1934; this was attractively reprinted in London, but without the maps, by Frank Cass in 1971.

37.   Ramón Menéndez Pidal, *Cantar de Mio Cid. Texto, gramática y vocabulario*, 3 vols, Madrid: Bailly-Baillière, 1908–11, vol. II, p. 574. Later editions include the 4th edition, published by Espasa-Calpe (3 vols) in 1964.

38.   J. G. Hava, *Al-Faraid. Arabic-English Dictionary*, Beirut: Catholic Press, 1964, p. 343.

39.   Mikel de Epalza, 'El Cid = El León: ¿Epiteto árabe del Campeador?', *Hispanic Review*, XLV (1977), 67–75.

40.   Menéndez Pidal, *Cantar*, vol. II, p. 574.

41.   Richard A. Fletcher and Simon Barton, eds, *The World of El Cid: Chronicles of the Reconquest*, Manchester: Manchester University Press, 2001, p. 3; this possibility was first raised by H. Butler Clarke, *The Cid Campeador and the Waning of the Crescent in the West*, London: Putnam, 1897, pp. 29–30.

42.   Menéndez Pidal, *Cantar*, vol. II, pp. 574–7.

43.   For some thought-provoking opinions on this episode and its aftermath, see Fletcher, *The Quest for the Cid*, pp.129–32.

44.   Charles Melville and Ahmad Ubaydli, *Christians and Moors in Spain, Volume III, Arabic Sources*, Warminster: Aris & Phillips, 1992, pp. 102–3, facing text and translation, the latter adapted.

45.   José Camón Aznar, 'El Cid, personaje mozárabe', *Revista de Estudios Políticos*, XVII (1947), 109–41.

CHAPTER 5

Al-Andalus under the rule of the Berber dynasties

A rather strange phenomenon occurred with the submission of al-Andalus to the Almoravids, a flashback, albeit a shortlived one, to a previous era. Over a period of time the Andalusi aristocrats reasserted themselves in the principal cities, and there was a renaissance of court culture. Yūsuf died in 1107 having overseen a period of remarkable expansion brought about by astute strategy and skilful diplomacy. The impetus he provided was maintained for several years under his successor. By 1114, the Almoravid empire enjoyed its maximum extent, comprising the whole of al-Andalus from Lisbon to Saragossa, captured in 1109, all of present-day Morocco and western Algeria. It included the Western Sahara as far south as Senegal, and thus controlled the lucrative trade routes from central Africa. In 1108, the town of Uclés, between Valencia and Madrid, was taken by the Almoravids, during which engagement Alfonso's son Sancho was killed. This victory laid the way open to gain the prize of Toledo, which had been an objective of Yūsuf. This city, however, although besieged in 1109, did not again form part of al-Andalus. The strength of the Almoravids lay in their militia. Once this was disbanded, and the former commanders were put in charge of the main cities, the structure began to crumble. As the twelfth century unfurled, so the once formidable Almoravids became more ineffectual. By mid-century, the Almoravids, overthrown in North Africa where they had been replaced by the Almohads (al-muwahhidūn, the seekers after unity), were no longer guardians of orthodox Islamic practice. They had become as wedded to opulence and easy living as those whom their predecessors had ousted two generations previously.

Much detailed information about the municipal organisation in Seville at the turn of the eleventh century, as well as about the economy and society of the city, is provided by Ibn 'Abdūn who died in 1137 and who was therefore writing about the contemporary situation. His work is, in essence, a short treatise on *hisba* (correct behaviour), particularly in matters relating to markets and public morals, and provides valuable insights into the workings of an Andalusi city. The fact that an officer (*muhtasib*) existed to regulate such aspects as weights and measures is evidence that malpractice existed and needed to be curbed. On the evidence of Ibn 'Abdūn, Seville survived the transfer of authority from the 'Abbādids to the Almoravids without trauma. Some of the dos and don'ts have a modern ring to them. In a section that reminds the reader that Seville was a thriving port, the boatmen on the quay must not allow anyone to take illicit merchandise, including wine, on board; if they do so, they are subject to severe punishment. Moreover, the port area must remain the property of the state; no part of it should be built on, and no part of it should be in private hands. All the operations and transactions within it, the export business, the influx of foreigners and the shipyard should be under the jurisdiction of the *qāḍī*.[1] As to prisons, these should be segregated, the women being supervised by a well-respected elderly man. Male prisons should be in the charge of a sole jailer, who should never strike a prisoner, and should permit the visit of an *imām* to conduct prayers. It would appear from this that only Muslim offenders were to be incarcerated.[2] Regarding interfaith relations, there are a number of comments, from which various inferences may be drawn. A Muslim must not massage a Jew or Christian, neither can he look after their horses or pack animals, subject to nothing more serious than a reprimand. Some members of the *dhimma*, it follows, were sufficiently well-to-do to own horses and to run mule trains. There are harsh words about priests and their behaviour, but curiously there is a specific injunction prohibiting Muslim women from entering churches. It may only be speculated in what circumstances they would do so; the text implies immoral purposes, but other interpretations are possible. Jews and Christians should have a mark on their clothing so that they could be recognised as such. There is a suggestion of a religious stigma in this reference. They are not allowed to be dressed in the same attire as 'honourable people', so that a Muslim, on seeing them, should avoid greeting them with *salām 'alaykum* (peace be upon you).[3] They are to be despised and avoided. As this seems to be an isolated reference, this may not have represented the actual status quo at the start of the twelfth century. In another section, boatmen are forbidden from giving passage to any citizen, one presumes Muslim, who is taking containers to buy wine from Christians. In a note, the translator suggests that this indicates that there existed 'an important Mozarab community' in Triana, the district of Seville that lay on the other side of the Guadalquivir, where one could encounter the principal Christian areas of the city. The text would not per se appear to support such a suggestion, though, and more to the point, it does indicate that Muslims went to Christians for their wine, that it was made by the latter and consumed by the former. Other passages mention a ban on making wine goblets, and the existence of wine sellers, again presumably Muslims, acting clandestinely and illegally.

The society that Ibn 'Abdūn's treatise reveals seems to be one in which authority was intrusive, and in which everyone had to be forever looking over their shoulder for fear of committing an infringement of the law. Furthermore, those from the country, peasants or farmers seemed to have been considered if not second-class citizens, then certainly open to correction if they ventured into the city. It is assumed by the author that men with long hair came from the country. They have to have it cut and be shaved, or else suffer corporal punishment, because having long hair is the mark of a criminal or delinquent. There are so many restrictions listed that if they were all complied with, any freedom to live one's life would have been virtually non-existent. This being the case, the treatise may not reflect the reality of life in Seville, rather the existence of regulations governing how one should behave. It is instructive that many of the chapters start with the words 'one should' or 'one should not', implying that that the injunction that follows may not actually be in place. How is one to interpret, for example, the prohibition on the game of chess on the grounds that it distracts the players from the fulfilment of their religious duties, when it was known from other sources that chess was widely played in al-Andalus? The ban on children playing fisticuffs is equally baffling. The reason given that such activity gives rise to brawls and commotion is hardly convincing. Nonetheless, glimpses of current practice are afforded. The sale of scientific books to Christians or Jews should be made illegal unless such works deal with their religion. The interesting reason given is that they will then be translated and their authorship attributed to Christians or Jews, or even, somewhat bizarrely, to their bishops, when in reality the works were written by Muslims. That this was not the case can be shown by the activity of translators of Arabic works, principally in Toledo, in the twelfth and thirteenth centuries. In the same paragraph, but at a slightly different angle, Jewish and Christian doctors should not be allowed to heal Muslims, the rationale being that if they have no sympathy towards Muslims, why should they be entrusted to save their lives?[4] There is no cause for doubting that such doctors observed what then passed as the Hippocratic oath. In sum, one has to say that the prescriptive nature of the treatise seems to be at odds with the easy-going lifestyle over which the Almoravid governors presided in the first half of the twelfth century.

Amongst the literary figures who were prominent in the Almoravid period, one should mention the nature poet Ibn Khafāja (1058–1139). He had lived his youth through the period of the Taifa states but had rejected their invitations to join their courts, preferring to remain on his estate at Alcira on the river Júcar between Valencia and the then prominent city of Játiva. It lay in a fertile area, noted for its fruit trees, according to al-Himyarī, who quotes a poem by Ibn Khafāja himself in praise of the natural beauty of the region.[5] Ibn Khafāja gained a reputation as a poet in his lifetime and earned the soubriquet al-jannān (the gardener), on account of the prolific descriptions of flowers and gardens in his poetry, which were emulated by later poets. His poems are in the traditional qasīda form and are rich in exotic metaphors, yet they also contain sentiments that often seem deep and sincere. Flowers and natural phenomena are personified, a feature to be found in Eastern poetry, but his Eastern counterparts did not have the lush and fertile land watered by the river Júcar from which to draw inspiration. Whether or not emotional content of a rare quality and some specific references are sufficient to justify claiming that Ibn Khafāja's poems are 'permeated by a thoroughly Andalusian sensibilité', as Nykl does, is open to question.[6]

One is struck by the creativity in the imagery and the intellectual dexterity of many of the poems, although translations of his poetry cannot fully reveal 'the originality of both syntax and vocabulary'.[7] In his embellishment of images and sheer inventiveness, Ibn Khafāja is a precursor of of the seventeenth-century poet Luis de Góngora, with whom he has been compared.

Perhaps the poet who stands out in the Almoravid era is Ibn Quzmān, who died in Cordoba in 1160 and who lived to see the advent of the new rulers from North Africa, the Almohads. He broke the mould by composing verse in a strophic form known as the *zajal*, using the spoken language of the people of Cordoba and contravening the accepted practice of composition in classical Arabic, although he also wrote in the *qasīda* form. Interpretations of the origin of the metrical patterns he employed have been notably divergent. Some metres may reflect the influence of pre-existing Romance forms, although in the wake of the prudent conclusions of T. J. Gorton, it is generally now thought that Ibn Quzmān's versification conforms to the classical Arabic system, albeit with some puzzling irregularities.[8] What is striking about his *dīwān* is its raciness. The sentiments are often coarse and explicit, set within a 'wine, women and song' framework. The appeal of his poetry, which was greatly imitated, but for which he claimed a technical virtuosity second to none, lay not only in the sheer unrestrained exuberance of his verse, but in his depiction of an unsophisticated proletarian society. Bacchic themes were not uncommon but he enlivened his descriptions with the apparent incorporation of the word 'vino' (wine), one of a number of Romance words woven into his poetry, indicating his familiarity with the diglossic nature of the spoken idiom of Cordoba.[9] The transliteration of Romance words into Arabic script is an extremely problematic area, frequently because of difficulties in deciphering the original manuscript, and the many possible such words in Ibn Quzmān's text have been open to debate.[10] When Ibn Quzmān's *dīwān* was initially studied, it was heralded for its noted similarities with the lyrics of the Provençal troubadours, in both form and content. Nykl suggests that the similarities of verse structure and the use of a refrain, together with many thematic common features, point 'rather to an imitation than to an independent invention'.[11] If a plausible link between the two is forthcoming, then al-Andalus through the poetry of Ibn Quzmān would have had a formative impact on the earliest known lyric poetry of Europe. As none such has materialised, then this can only be speculation. Leaving aside the heady emotions that such thoughts may engender, one can point to the real and radical influence of Islamic scholarship in al-Andalus in other spheres on what has been described as the twelfth-century renaissance in Europe.

Before embarking on this, it is important to consider the changes that occurred in al-Andalus in the twelfth century in interfaith relationships. An instructive example is provided in the sources for the expedition made by Alfonso I of Aragón (r. 1104–34) into al-Andalus in 1125–6. The Almoravids, it is known, overthrew the Taifa states with the approval of the Māliki *faqīh*s but, after the death of their first two leaders, their hold on al-Andalus weakened, partly in the aftermath of the loss of Saragossa to Alfonso in 1118. It was an era in which the kings of Castile and Aragón were pressing the Andalusi states; on one such occasion, non-Muslims of Granada and its environs, *muʿāhidūn* (those who lived under the protection of a pact or treaty), petitioned Alfonso to set them at liberty promising that they would mount an internal rebellion when he reached Granada. In the event, Alfonso's troops surrounded Granada in January 1126, but an epidemic forced them to withdraw and although they returned there in March, he decided to make the journey back to Aragón, accompanied by as many as 2,000 members of the indigenous community who were relocated as immigrants in various Aragonese locations. As far as Alfonso was concerned, the mission had failed in that they had not succeeded in capturing their prime objective, for which he blamed those who had invited him because their promised rebellion came to nothing. Perhaps also he appreciated the impracticality of maintaining a garrison in Granada.

The episode raises a number of intriguing issues. It has been understood as being an example of the persecution by Muslims, here the Almoravids of Christians who, in desperation, sought the aid of their co-religionaries. Whilst it is recorded by a contemporary source, the historian as-Sayrafī, that the Almoravid leader had ordered the destruction of a prominent church in Granada in 1099, this occurred some twenty years before the abortive uprising. Between 1102 and 1108, Almoravid forces had invaded Catalonian territory and, according to the testimony of Ibn al-Kardabūs, razed churches to the ground and demolished belfries. The bells were removed and subsequently converted into lamps to be hung in the main mosque in Valencia. Nonetheless, there is little to indicate that the general hostility of the Almoravids towards the outward representations of Christianity within and outside al-Andalus transmuted into persecution of individual Christian communities. It seems more probable that an enterprising member of the indigenous community, Ibn al-Qallās, who is not identified specifically as a *nasārī*, should seek to capitalise on the political malaise of the 1120s. As a man of consequence within his community, and the implication is that this comprised mainly farmers and villagers, he could call upon substantial numbers sufficient to engineer a coup with outside help. Alfonso, it seems, required certain guarantees; there was a lengthy exchange of letters, the Arab sources mentioning a letter from Ibn al-Qallās with a list of 12,000 auxiliaries who would be drafted in. One might note that there is no complaint on the part of the petitioner of any religious persecution which one might have been led to expect had there been any. In contrast, the religious fervour of Alfonso's troops is recounted with relish by the Arab historian. Alfonso, wary of embarking on such a potentially hazardous expedition, was tempted to 'seize the moment', but in the event was thwarted by an opposition that was stronger than anticipated and by the failure of his 'fifth column' to materialise in sufficient numbers.

The Norman monk and historian Ordericus Vitalis gave a brief exposé of the whole enterprise in 1141, relying, it would seem, on the first-hand accounts of veterans of the expedition, who may have passed through the Benedictine monastery of St Évroult in Normandy where he resided. Although the information is not unambiguous, it would seem to suggest that some of those who went into exile with Alfonso were baptised as Christians in al-Andalus but were unable to practise out of ignorance of the doctrines of the Church. The implication is that priests were not allowed to instruct them but this is not explicitly stated. The word that Ordericus uses for these Christians is *muceravii*, a rather mangled Latin form of the word *must'arab* (Arabicised). Once in the territory of Aragón, they were given lands to inhabit and cultivate and granted generous privileges, including exemption from tax on merchandise, which enabled them to thrive as Arab-speaking co-religionaries. Alfonso issued a *fuero* (charter) in the town of Alfaro on the river Ebro north-west of Saragossa in 1126 in which he specifically mentions *totos christianos mozarabis* whom he had 'brought out of Saracen control with God's help and led into Christian lands'.[12] As in the case of the settlers from al-Andalus in Leonese territories two centuries earlier, one may suspect that the refugees from Granadan lands became overt in their practice of Christianity in their new environment, no doubt in part to merit and justify the privileges granted to them. As for those left behind, the *nasārā mu'āhidūn*, they were deemed to have forfeited the protection afforded by the pact, and deported *en masse* to cities such as Meknes, Fez and Salé in present-day Morocco, in October 1126. This measure would have been taken in reprisal for the treacherous behaviour of their fellow *mu'āhidūn*, perhaps regarded by the authorities as co-conspirators. It is interesting to note that for this community in exile, Bishop Michael caused a copy of the Gospels to be made in Arabic in 1137, which testifies to their adherence to Christianity. Some of those exiled may have been from the city and near environs of Granada, where under the Zīrids in the eleventh century they had lived peaceably and unmolested under the terms accorded to Christians and Jews under Islam.

Alfonso I of Aragón and Alfonso VII of Castile (r. 1127–51) subjected the frontiers of al-Andalus to unrelenting harassment during their reigns. The path was not always a smooth one for them. Lérida, for instance, was not conquered until 1149, and Almoravid forces from there assisted troops from Cordoba in the recapture of the nearby strategic township of Fraga in 1134, inflicting a severe defeat on the besieging army of Alfonso I in which a number of nobles and bishops perished. The Upper and Middle Marches with their bases at Saragossa and Toledo, however, whilst no longer in Muslim hands, continued to be repositories of Arabic and Islamic culture. The Aljafería palace in Saragossa built under the Taifa rulers in the previous century remained a symbol of Islamic splendour and was to be the paradigm for the *mudéjar* style of architecture that emerged in Aragón after the conquests. Those responsible for such structures, notably churches, were known as *mudéjares*, which was long thought to derive from the Arabic *mudajjān* (permitted to remain), referring to those Muslims who were allowed to retain their religion in Christian states. There are a number of alternative etymons, including *mudhdhakhar*, with the sense of someone kept away or preserved, or from the root *dahara* (to be defeated or to succumb). The style of these churches was characterised by the intricacy of its external brickwork and its tiling patterns, and is a testimony to the heritage of Islam in Christian territories in the thirteenth and fourteenth centuries.

Toledo, though, after its capture by Alfonso VI in 1085, had a more remarkable contribution to make. Whereas what may be termed *mudejarismo* was confined to Iberia, the labour of the so-called 'translators of Toledo' in the twelfth century was to have repercussions far beyond the Pyrenees, and may be said to have been instrumental in the evolution of learning in Europe. This was an extremely confused time. What had been part of al-Andalus for around 400 years was now Christian territory. Gradually the new values were imposed, but the way of life and culture that evolved under Islamic rule persisted. Cities such as Toledo and Saragossa which had hitherto been renowned as centres of Muslim civilisation may have had new masters after their capture, but they remained ineluctably stamped with an Islamic imprint. They were *inter alia* repositories for learning, and named Christian scholars from within the Iberian Peninsula and from other parts of Europe, including England, came to Toledo specifically in order to acquire mathematical, astronomical, astrological and sundry scientific knowledge hitherto unavailable to them. Much of the subject matter was Greek in origin and had been translated into Arabic in the Islamic East, sometimes with added commentaries, before being brought by scholars to al-Andalus. When Raymond de Salvetat, a Benedictine monk from Gascony, was Archbishop of Toledo (1126–52), he encouraged the Arabic-speaking inhabitants of the city, the Mozarabs, to assist in the serious activity of translation. His motive would have been to pave the way for scholars to disseminate the substance of Arabic texts in centres of learning beyond the Iberian Peninsula. Such texts would have been brought to Toledo either from Cordoba, the focal point for Islamic culture in al-Andalus in the tenth century, or Seville – the city had taken over this mantle in the eleventh – or indeed from the former library of the Banū Hūd, the Taifa rulers of Saragossa.

Modern and contemporary scholars have been at pains to unravel both the complexities of the process of translation and the identities and activities of individual translators. Settling on solutions with which all can concur continues to be problematic. The following are two classic viewpoints. Regarding the methodology, 'translations were frequently made from Arabic into Castilian (Romance), and the work completed by a further translation by those who knew Castilian and Latin'. The whole operation 'was beset with difficulties and took much labour and time, and the Latin version, if it emerged at all, did so often after long delay'.[13] In respect of the role and mission of the translators, Marie-Thérèse d'Alverny's statement aptly summarises a possible and plausible scenario: 'Men born in Spain, who spoke Arabic and the Romance vernacular, [and who] sometimes knew Latin if they were clerics, and many scholars coming from far-away countries tried to extract the treasures of science from the books of the Saracens'.[14] A significant example of the former, one familiar with both Arabic and Latin, was Johannes Hispalensis (John of Seville), who had translated medical and other material before coming to Toledo where he worked later in his life between 1135 and 1142, undertaking translations of astronomical and astrological texts, which may be said to have been his priority at that time.[15] He became a kind of elder statesman for translators, which may be ascertained by the fact that some translations were dedicated to him.[16] With the exception of Hugh of Santalla, a priest in Tarazona in Aragón who had acquired a knowledge of Arabic and who dedicated his translations, many of which related to aspects of divination, to his patron Bishop Michael of that city, most of the translators from abroad had to rely on local intermediaries.

Hermann of Carinthia, the southernmost state in present-day Austria, at that time a duchy, and the English-born Robert of Ketton, a small village near Stamford in Lincolnshire, who was archdeacon of Pamplona and later canon in Tudela, were responsible for the translation of Muslim works at the behest of Peter the Venerable, abbot of Cluny (1092–1156, abbot from 1122). Peter had visited Spain in 1142, at the request of Alfonso VII of Castile and persuaded translators, two of whom were Hermann and Robert, to divert their attention, temporarily at least, from scientific to religious texts. To the latter is attributed the first rendering of the Qur'ān into Latin.[17] This has been called more of a paraphrase, but it provided Western scholars with the opportunity to study and interpret Islam, albeit critically, from a scholarly perspective.[18] Hermann's translations of works by the ninth-century Eastern Islamic scholar, philosopher and astrologer Abū Ma'shar, who was familiar with Aristotle's works on natural sciences, came to be known in Western European Christian circles. The latter's astrological writings were prominent in arguments among Eastern scholars concerning the compatibility of astrology with Islamic doctrine, and in Europe were later central to debates on its admissibility or otherwise in Christian theology. One may also note that some of these translators composed works in their own right. Domingo González (also known as Gundisalvo or Gundisallinus) (died c. 1181), for example, a colleague of Juan Hispalense and fellow translator, was responsible for propagating the ideas of the Eastern philosopher al-Fārābī (died 950), who argued for the compatibility of Greek philosophy within Islam through his own work which augmented the latter's classification of the sciences.

The outstanding name in the field of translating in the twelfth century is undoubtedly that of Gerard of Cremona in Northern Italy (1114–87), a scholar who, disillusioned with the comparatively paltry extent of knowledge available to him, went to Toledo at some time in the mid-century where he is attributed with upwards of seventy translations.[19] His output was prolific and covered a wide range including, from the Arabic, Ptolemy's immensely influential astronomical treatise, the *Almagest*. He translated into Latin, amongst numerous other works, the fundamental treatise on algebra by the ninth-century Eastern Islamic scholar al-Khwārizmī, thus acquainting Western scholars with this branch of mathematics, and the encyclopedic work on medicine the *Qānūn fi't-tibb* by Ibn Sīnā (Avicenna), which, after a fifteenth-century revision, was to become the standard book of reference for the subject. He used as his aid a Mozarab, Ghālib (Galippus), although later in his career he translated directly from the Arabic. His fields of expertise covered philosophy, mathematics, astronomy, medicine (embracing surgery and optics), astrology, alchemy and divination, and his overall contribution to the breadth of knowledge now made accessible to Western scholars was to have far-reaching consequences in succeeding centuries.[20] The purpose of this excursus into the burgeoning activity of translation, which was to extend into the thirteenth century, has been to draw attention to the debt that these seemingly indefatigable translators had to al-Andalus, the repository for this precious storehouse of primary material. As many have pointed out, they were the vital intermediaries in the transmission of Greek knowledge via Arabic to a renascent Europe.

The Almohads

The *muwahhidūn* (those who herald the oneness of God), held sway in al-Andalus for around eighty years. Their founder, Ibn Tūmart (d. 1130), a Berber whose support came from the Masmūda clan in the south of Maghrib, studied under the *qāḍī* in Cordoba before making his epoch-changing sojourn in the Islamic East where he became acquainted with leading jurists and scholars including – probably, although it is not certain that they met – the great figure of al-Ghazālī (1058–1111), whose ideas, which were condemned in al-Andalus as heretical, were so influential in Islamic thought.[21] Around 1121, Ibn Tūmart was recognised by his followers as the infallible *imām*, the *mahdī*, literally one who is rightly guided but, according to Islamic tradition, a person with special, often charismatic, qualities divinely sent to complete the work of Muhammad, banishing evil and bringing justice to the world. His was a God-sent mission with the objective of reviving Islam which, in the political context in which he lived, meant the overthrow of the Almoravids; he had met their leader in Marrakesh in 1120, who apparently did not appreciate the threat that he was later to pose. Ibn Tūmart subsequently installed himself in Tīn Mallal, in a fertile region to the south-west of Marrakesh where he established his system of government in which differing tribal groups all had a role, launching a programme of 'ideological warfare' against the Almoravids.[22] One method he employed for uniting and edifying his followers was to set out his beliefs in Berber, thus facilitating their understanding of his creed, although he was also eloquent in Arabic. His measures included the denunciation of their corrupt practices, the prohibition of music, wine and dancing, an emphasis on piety and the disapproval of excess. He advocated the reinstatement of the Qur'ān, the traditions (*hadīth*) and the *sunna* as the governing principles of Islamic law. In essence, his was a reform movement in reaction to what he perceived to be the immorality of the Almoravids, seen for example in their deployment of non-Muslim mercenaries whose stipend was exacted through extra levies on Muslims, and their lax adherence to the fundamental and uncompromising tenets of Islam. The prime mover in Almohad expansion was 'Abd al-Mu'min who presided over the movement as Caliph from 1133 until his death in 1163, during which period the invasion of al-Andalus occurred. He inaugurated a dynasty and together with his successors assigned themselves an Arabic lineage to provide outward legitimisation for their government, although Berber tribes in North Africa provided consistent background strength.[23]

Almoravid authority in al-Andalus disintegrated in the 1140s, with the incessant raids by Alfonso VII on frontier cities, which notably secured the Tagus valley for the Castilians. In the west, Alfonso I, who was recognised as 'King of the Portuguese' by Alfonso VII in 1143, besieged and captured Lisbon in 1147, with the assistance of an English fleet carrying crusaders to the Middle East.[24] In the same year, Alfonso VII, at the head of a large army of Christian allies, penetrated al-Andalus as far as the prosperous trading port of Almería, which he captured whilst ships from Genoa and Pisa sealed off the maritime passages. Al-Himyarī, quoting Idrīsī, lamented the fall of this highly prized city to the Christians who, he wrote, 'disfigured its beauty spots, took its inhabitants off into captivity and destroyed its buildings'.[25] The fortune of the Almohads waxed as that of the Almoravids waned. Also in 1147, 'Abd al-Mu'min had taken over control in the Maghrib, seizing Fez, Meknes and the capital Marrakesh from the Almoravids, slaughtering many of the inhabitants and eliminating all outward signs of their regime. Almohad forces had already invaded al-Andalus in 1145, occupying Cádiz, gateway for trade to the northern kingdoms, the following year, and towns and cities in that area and due north as far as Badajoz. In January 1147, Seville, together with its imposing *alcazaba*, capitulated after a violent struggle in which leading Almoravids perished.[26] In the following decade, in which Almoravid power fragmented in al-Andalus, and upward of twenty-five cities governed themselves autonomously in the absence of a central authority, the Almohads made their presence felt in the Peninsula. With the decisive repossession of Almería in 1157 which passed into Muslim hands after a siege from land and sea, they took control over the south and west of al-Andalus. A substantial area in the Eastern Levant of al-Andalus, incorporating the cities of Murcia, Denia and Valencia, was taken over by Ibn Mardanīsh, a Muslim from a leading *muwallad* family but known in Christian chronicles as 'el rey Lobo' (the Wolf King) or Lope, under whom it not only survived but flourished as an anachronistic Taifa kingdom until his death in 1172.[27] In effect, he obstructed the Almohad cause for twenty-five years, thus postponing their inexorable advance throughout al-Andalus. In a detail recorded by some historians, he 'used Christian dress and arms' and spoke Spanish, presumably Castilian, but his career is one that bespeaks that of a powerful Taifa ruler akin to those who had been so dominant in the previous century.[28] He made alliances with Christians, notably with Ramón Berenguer IV, Count of Barcelona (Count 1131–62), on his northern border, and was from time to time in league with other Muslim leaders in their quest to staunch the Almohad tide. He was also aggressive towards the invaders and occupied various Almohad outposts, including that of Carmona with its redoubtable fortress in 1159. It is clear from the sources, though, that when he and his allies inflicted a defeat on Almohad forces in al-Andalus, this only provoked a response from the Caliph in Marrakesh who would dispatch troops to regain what was lost. He was, finally, overpowered by an army led by 'Abd al-Mu'min's successor as Caliph, outside his own city of Murcia in 1165. When he died, his heirs submitted to the Almohads, thus bringing this epoch to a close; the new rulers from the Maghrib were destined to command al-Andalus into the thirteenth century.

Perhaps surprisingly, in view of the fact that the Almohad movement has habitually been associated with austerity, the twelfth century was an age in which culture and literature, in particular philosophy, flourished. The first influential figure, chronologically, Ibn Tufayl (c. 1110–85), may have been a disciple of the philosopher poet Ibn Bajja, known as Avempace, the Latinised form of his name, who was in Granada and Seville in the 1130s, and who died in Fez in 1139. Born in Guadix, he was trained as a *kātib* in Granada, and became personal physician to Abū Ya'qūb Yūsuf (r. 1163–84), who re-established the Almohad capital in al-Andalus in Seville and was a munificent patron. Ibn Tufayl is principally known for a remarkable work, *Hayy ibn Yaqzān* (literally 'Alive, the Son of Awake', translated into Spanish as *El filósofo autodidacto* ('The Self-taught Philosopher'). It is the tale of a child who appears on an island, either washed ashore in a box or the product of spontaneous generation. He was suckled and looked after by a roe deer which had lost its fawn, and when it died he dissected its body, searching for the source of its life and death. He became aware of his superiority over the creatures around him and, by perception and reflection over a period of many years, acquired a knowledge of the natural world and of sciences such as astronomy. Through intelligence, he strives for union with the sublime, but 'what Hayy witnessed at this lofty plane' cannot, and here Ibn Tufayl as author intervenes, be related in words.[29] That is to say, man can reach a state of understanding the Divine, but cannot ever achieve divine union. In the respect that he is touching on humankind's spiritual potential, Ibn Tufayl is reflecting Sūfī beliefs. Somebody comes from a neighbouring island who had become as enlightened as the state of knowledge available to him allowed. He taught Hayy speech and together they left for the second island, where Hayy found his teaching misunderstood and rejected. Disillusioned, the two returned to Hayy's island, where Hayy pursued his quest for ecstasy and his colleague sought to emulate him. Much interest has been focused on the initial phase of the book and its seeming similarity to Defoe's *Robinson Crusoe*, but parallels have also been noted with *El criticón*, an allegorical novel by Baltasar Gracián (1601–58) completed in the decade before his death, in which the protagonist has an analogous upbringing. Sir Paul Rycaut, the translator of this work into English in 1681, wrote in the prologue that 'the design of both is almost the same, being only to show how far the spiritual and immortal soul of man, is able in its natural capacity, and by its own reflex acts to consider its proper being, and the existence of something above it'.[30]

In essence, the message of the book is that philosophy and revealed religion can be reconciled. Put in contemporary twelfth-century terms, philosophy is not incompatible with Islam, although Islam is not specifically mentioned. The truth may be arrived at both through the intuitive forces of reason and through traditional learning. The irony of *Hayy ibn Yaqzān* is that while both protagonists desire to promote the welfare of the people, the latter find theories unpalatable and are content to live in the 'comfort zone' of the religion that has been handed down to them. In effect, the people were incapable of understanding any higher form of religion. It is true that the work has been the subject of multiple inter- pretations, in particular the intriguing question as to where the climax lies, but it is fundamentally an illustrative story which the author composed in response to a request to reveal 'the secrets of Oriental philosophy'. This request 'set off a stream of ideas', but what resulted was not a collection of aphorisms.[31] Rather, it is a fluent and coherent account of how one person, unaided, can attain entire knowledge, related in an agreeable and accessible manner. Its originality lies in the innovative treatment of current concepts within the outer story-book frame- work. The work appealed to both Muslims and Christians: in the seventeenth century, Quakers were drawn to a readable narrative in which it is described how a man can experience the Divine without relying on intermediaries. The Scot George Keith (1639–1716), first a Quaker and then in later life an Anglican, rendered a Latin version into English in 1674 for what might be termed evident propaganda purposes. *Hayy ibn Yaqzān* also struck chords with Anglicans such as George Ashwell, whose translation from the Latin, published in 1684, was likewise motivated by the desire to demonstrate how 'human Reason, improved by diligent Observation and Experience, may arrive at the knowledge of natural things, and from thence to the discovery of the supernaturals'.[32] It has remained an influential work.

Between 1153 and 1157, although the date is uncertain, Ibn Tufayl introduced Ibn Rushd (born in Cordoba in 1126, died in Marrakesh in 1198, known by his Latin name of Averroes) to the future Almohad Caliph Abū Ya'qūb Yūsuf, who was so impressed by the latter's learning that he asked him to write explanatory commentaries on Aristotle's works. On Ibn Tufayl's retirement, Ibn Rushd, who in Cordoba had studied law and 'the works of the ancients', by which are understood Greek sciences, became in 1182 the Caliph's physician. He was a *qāḍī* both in Seville and in Cordoba, yet it was neither as a physician nor as a legal scholar that he achieved his later fame, although he composed works on both subjects. Indeed, his medical encyclopedia dealt with a wide range of disciplines and, incidentally, showed that 'he understood the functioning of the retina of the eye'.[33] The intellectual climate remained favourable for the pursuit of philosophy until the death of Abū Ya'qūb Yūsuf as a result of a wound received whilst besieging Santarem in present-day Portugal in 1185, and for much of the reign of his successor. Philosophy was outlawed in the mid-1190s, and practitioners persecuted. Ibn Rushd was banished from Cordoba and was only reunited with the Almohad court in Marrakesh in the last year of his life, when the decrees condemning philosophy were lifted. Fundamentally, his mission was to show that the contradictions between revealed religion and philosophy were apparent rather than real, and that the two were capable of being reconciled. In his defence of philosophy, he composed a skilfully argued legal response to al-Ghazālī's denunciation of philosophy. The latter had written *tahāfut al-falāsifa* ('The Incoherence of the Philosophers'), to which Ibn Rushd's bold and measured refutation was *tahāfut al-tahāfut* ('The Incoherence of the Incoherence'), which clearly demarcated the differences between the two schools of thought.[34] His commentaries on Aristotle were translated into Latin by Michael Scot (c. 1175–c. 1235), a scholar in his own right who is known to have been in Toledo in 1217, thus being responsible for the introduction to the Western European world of learning what became known as Averroism, embodying the idea of the harmony of religion and reason. 'The translations of Michael Scot familiarized the Latin world of the first half of the thirteenth century not merely with ancient Greek science, but also with recent writing and thought in Arabic'.[35] The translations of other works by Ibn Rushd may be attributed to Michael Scot, such that the latter may be regarded as one of the significant conduits by means of which Western scholars became acquainted with the Islamic stratum of culture which flourished under the Almohads in al-Andalus. The extent of the debt of Thomas Aquinas (1225–74), for example, to the original doctrines of Ibn Rushd, and the nature of the influence of the latter on the former, has been the subject of many studies with divergent views and opinions, but 'the profound resemblances between medieval Islam and medieval Christendom' cannot be denied.[36]

A slightly younger contemporary of Ibn Rushd was Mūsā b. Maymūn, known as Moses Maimonides (1135–1204). He was born into a distinguished

Jewish family in Cordoba, and was trained, as was the custom, in medicine, law and theology. Although his formation as a scholar was in the Muslim West, both al-Andalus and the Maghrib, he spent the latter part of his life in present-day Egypt, where he wrote his most celebrated work, in Arabic, *Dalālat al-hā'irīn'*, ('The Guide for the Perplexed'). In this, he showed how the Law of Moses could be reconciled with contemporary belief, which shows some knowledge of the works of Ibn Rushd, amongst other Islamic scholars, and some affinity toward the ideas expressed by Ibn Tufayl in *Hayy ibn Yaqzān*.[37] Parallels between the works of Ibn Maymūn and Ibn Rushd have been drawn, and they both attracted the suspicion of their peers. Some effusive remarks linking the two have been expressed by M. R. Menocal, who points out that they were both considered as Andalusis, rather than as Muslim and Jew, and both suffered exile. Furthermore, both 'would be avidly appreciated and appreciatively read, used, and translated by Frederick II [r. 1220–50] for the benefit of others and for the enlightenment of the rest of Europe'.[38] One should also note that Ibn Maymūn contributed to medical knowledge as Ibn Rushd had done, his *Medical Principles*, based on Galen and with added criticisms of the latter's work, covering such subjects as anatomy, fevers, surgery and drugs. As Winter has pointed out, there are 'valuable instances of direct observation' including 'a clinical description of belladonna poisoning'.[39]

The matter of the intolerance of the Almohads towards those who did not share their belief in *tawhīd* (oneness), would seem to be at odds with their patronage of thinkers such as Ibn Tufayl and Ibn Rushd. Ibn Tūmart had upheld the *dhimmī* status of Christians and Jews, and was keen to ensure that they continued to pay the additional tax. This does not run counter to his policy of pressing for conversion of non-Muslims, or to the campaigns undertaken by later Almohad caliphs in the Iberian Peninsula to counter the aggression of the Christian states. These expeditions often had catastrophic consequences for the indigenous rural communities whose properties and crops could be destroyed if they happened to be in the 'conflict zone', leading to deprivation and starvation. Arabic accounts, such as that of Ibn Khaldūn, provide an almost exclusively political record of events with the names of all those involved. It is not surprising that attention is paid to the victory achieved by Ya'qūb al-Mansūr (r. 1184–99) near the frontier castle of Alarcos, beyond the sierras to the south of Toledo, in 1195. The Muslim army was composed both of Berbers who had come from North Africa with the Caliph, and troops that reunited with him from cities in al-Andalus, comprising both Berbers and Arabs. It appears as though superior strategy and battlecraft, notably in the deployment of his cavalry, were the determining factors. Ibn Khaldūn gives the number killed in the engagement as 30,000 Christians and 5,000 Muslims. It was not, however, the decisive encounter that such an emphatic success would appear to indicate. Although the Almohads later consolidated their presence in the area, recapturing Benavente and

Calatrava, they did not proceed to take Toledo, which now lay exposed to the north, and the opportunity to reclaim one of the previous jewels in the crown of al-Andalus was foregone. The Castilians under Alfonso VIII (r. 1158–1214) were clearly caught off guard by the defeat, as is revealed by a detail furnished by Huici Miranda following an Arabic source. The Christians had been so sure of their triumph in advance that they had in their retinue many Jewish traders laden with money with which to buy future prisoners together with booty, with a view to profitable resale.[40]

Clearly stung by this rebuff, Alfonso spent years negotiating with fellow Christian states, forging alliances in the Peninsula with, amongst others, the Kings of León, Aragón and Navarre. His cause was aided by Pope Innocent III (Pope 1198–1216), then preoccupied with affairs in England where King John was excommunicated for rejecting the papal candidate for the see of Canterbury. Innocent had ten years previously sanctioned the Fourth Crusade, and now called on knights throughout Europe to join in a crusade against the Muslims in the Iberian Peninsula, promising them, and those who provided them financial backing, full forgiveness of sins and a share in eternal salvation. The Christians were furthermore bolstered by the Archbishop of Toledo and chronicler Rodrigo Jiménez de Rada (Archbishop 1209–47), whose immense energy was a factor in the assembly of so many knights to fight the Christian cause. Alfonso's opponent on this occasion was an-Nāsir, the son of his conqueror in 1195. This latter turned out to be no match for Alfonso's superior forces. The available sources make it possible for interpreters of these events to view the confrontation at Las Navas de Tolosa in July 1212 – known in Arabic accounts as *ul-ʿiqāb* (high places) – as a religious one. Certainly, Rodrigo's own account makes abundantly clear that Alfonso's forces prevailed as Christians, notably in the singing *elevatis vocibus* (with loud voices) of the *Te Deum laudamus, te Dominum confitetur*.[41] However, it is not transparent that an-Nāsir was opposing a Crusade with a *jihād*. Ibn Khaldūn refers to the Caliph's anxiety when in 1210 in Morocco, he learnt of the loss of many fortresses in the Valencia area. He is said to have asked for support from an ally to recommence *jihād*, but this was denied. In the circumstances of this plea, one may consider that *jihād* in this situation would have been for defensive purposes, to protect the terrain, property and well-being of Muslims against foreign incursions. Notwithstanding, he invaded the Peninsula in 1211, achieving initial successes and residing in Seville. The primary objective was to regain Salvatierra, a fortress situated in the approaches to Calatrava where the religious military Order of the Knights of that name had been established in 1164 to protect the southern frontiers of Castile. This particular military order, in essence a brotherhood, emerged from volunteers who, in the 1140s, had striven to secure the town against the Almohads. According to al-Himyarī, an-Nāsir used a form of siege engine known as a mangonel in the siege. These machines erected *in situ* were designed to break down defences by bombarding walls with rocks hurled from catapults, and were used across Europe at that time. The besieged knights seem to have been unfamiliar with them as, when a ceasefire was agreed, a delegation went to Alfonso in Toledo to report on their plight with fragments of the missiles that had been projected. Alfonso authorised the evacuation of Salvatierra which further spurred him on to assemble a force that would break the strength of the Almohads. The value of Salvatierra for both sides lay in its strategic position, a heavily fortified outpost where a garrison could command the main route from Toledo to Bailén where it forked to Jaén and Granada due south and to Cordoba and Seville to the west. If Salvatierra could be held, then Baeza and Andújar which were next in line for attack, were secure.

The reasons given in some Arabic sources for the defeat of the Almohads at Las Navas de Tolosa, on the plains or, more strictly, flat and low, sometimes marshy, land between mountains (*navas*) leading up to the Sierra Morena just east of the crucial communication route mentioned above, and some forty miles north of Jaén, read more like excuses. Al-Himyarī recounts that the regular soldiers were reluctant to fight as they had not been paid and had just been given a few paltry instalments. They were also discontented because the Muslim commander at Calatrava who had surrendered to the Christians had been put to death by an-Nāsir. Furthermore, al-Himyarī also refers to treachery on the part of the Christians who had publicly declared a truce whilst, one assumes, clandestinely although he does not say as much, deploying their troops into favourable positions from which they routed the Muslims. Such claims are often made by the defeated party, but it is more likely that Alfonso's victory was achieved through more measured aggression and tactical knowhow on his side, and overconfidence vested in the superiority of numbers (possibly 100,000 as opposed to 60,000) together with dissension in the ranks on the Muslim side. Most accounts concur with the detail that whereas Alfonso, together with the Archbishop, were active in attack, an-Nāsir was inactive, remaining in his tent surrounded by the Caliphal guard. Maybe this accounts for the tradition that the Christians took possession of the magnificently woven battle standard of the Almohads when they penetrated an-Nāsir's inner sanctum. It is inscribed with Qur'ānic verses and now, having been repaired and restored, it resides in the Monastery of Las Huelgas, Burgos.[42] It is interesting to note that the Arabic name for this banner is al-ʿuqāb (literally 'the eagle', but also the word used to designate the banner of the Prophet Muhammad). This transliteration is the preferred name in recent times for Las Navas de Tolosa rather than al-ʿiqāb, perhaps because of the Arabic name for the nearby castle, hisn al-ʿuqāb (the castle of the eagle), or maybe on account of the enormous symbolical significance attached to the banner.[43]

The outcome at Las Navas has been celebrated as the decisive victory for the Christians and lamented as a great catastrophe for the Muslims in al-Andalus, but these are retrospective judgments. Territorially, the underbelly of al-Andalus was exposed to the northern army. However, the king of Aragón withdrew with his forces and the larger proportion of the spoils of battle; the Castilians and Navarrese pursued the enemy southwards, occupying the prosperous town of Baeza which had been evacuated, and captured Úbeda seven miles distant, both places situated on the direct route westwards to Cordoba. The citizens of Úbeda were either slaughtered or led away as captives, and the provisions with which the town was liberally endowed shared amongst the Christian forces; the ramparts were destroyed.[44] Christian troops even got as far as Seville where they suffered an unanticipated setback. This defeat, coupled with fact that the army was apparently stricken with an unspecified illness, obliged them to return north, thus providing al-Andalus with a respite. In an astonishing reversal of fortunes, within twenty years the Almohad-based power in al-Andalus had effectively been broken. In the third decade of the thirteenth century, a member of the Banī Hūd family, a descendant of the Taifa rulers of Saragossa in the previous century, originally based in Murcia, was recognised by the citizens of Seville as their leader. When the Almohad governor returned to North Africa, Ibn Hūd took advantage of his absence and, bolstered by popular support, ousted the Almohads from al-Andalus.[45] Furthermore, the frontier with the northern kingdoms changed irrevocably. Whereas in the twelfth century, the Muslims sought tenaciously to recapture Toledo, the key to controlling the status quo in the centre of the Peninsula, and thereby protecting the precious route due south to the principal cities of al-Andalus, in the thirteenth their priority was to keep hold of these cities in their very heartland. According to a distinguished French historian of the Almohad movement, the collapse on the battlefield of Las Navas was 'a sign that one of the essential springs of the Almohad machinery was broken'.[46]

Subsequent to the debacle at Las Navas, the Almohads came under pressure from the dissident Berber tribe, the Marīnids in North Africa, and with the continuing harassment of their borders in al-Andalus, their empire quite quickly disintegrated. In the late 1220s, they forfeited control of the major cities to Andalusi Muslims. Fernando III of Castile (r. 1217–52) provided what was to all intents and purposes the *coup de grâce* by engineering the capture of Cordoba in 1236 and of the great prize of Seville in 1248. Thus, from 1250 onwards, al-Andalus was confined to the south-east corner of the Iberian Peninsula, with about 200 miles of coastline and the inland capital of Granada.

Before considering the final phase of the independent Muslim state in the Peninsula, one has to consider the legacy of the Almohads. Attention has already been paid to their patronage of philosophers, but to what extent can Le Tourneau's claim that 'the Almohad empire bore very high the torch of Muslim civilization' be justified?[47] As Seville was the capital city of the Almohads, it is natural to look there for signs of their presence. In order to cater for the burgeoning size of the population, a enormous new mosque was built between 1172 and 1182 on the site of which a massive Gothic cathedral was constructed in the fifteenth century. For evidence of Almohad architecture, one has to look to the minaret completed in 1198, transformed into a belfry, and known since the 1560s as the Giralda, from the weather vane in the form of a human figure placed at its summit at that time. The central parts of the tower, once 230 feet high and similar in design to extant minarets in North Africa from the same period, show the decorative intricacy of the brickwork, with patterns in the form of arches.[48] As a monument, it must have served as the external symbol of Almohad invincibility, three years after the crushing victory over the Christians at Alarcos. Perhaps the severe damage done to the city barely two years later in February/March 1200, when the Guadalquivir flooded and rose to unprecedented levels, served as a sober reminder of human vulnerability.[49] Even after the defeat at Las Navas, Seville retained its dignity and authority as the capital of al-Andalus. The twelve-sided *torre del oro*, so called because of the *azulejos* (glazed gilt tiles) that once embellished its exterior, was built in 1220 or 1221 at the orders of the then governor of the city. It was a sturdy fortification standing at the limit of the city walls that were extended to the edge of the Guadalquivir and guarded the entrance to the harbour. It is said that a heavy iron chain linked it to a similar but not so grand structure on the other side of the river, and that this chain was raised at times when the city was under threat.

As far as fine art is concerned, the love story of Bayād and Riyād, surviving in a manuscript on paper assigned to Seville in the Almohad epoch, probably the beginning of the thirteenth century though possibly as late as 1240, is noteworthy for its miniatures. Although Qur'āns from this same period with beautiful calligraphy are extant, this manuscript affords a remarkable insight into a secular world, comparable in this respect to Ibn Hazm's *Tawq al-hamāma* of the eleventh century. The execution of the fourteen miniatures not only evinces exquisite artistry, but also provides glimpses of contemporary architectural styles, costume, including headgear, and hairstyles.[50] One prominent image shows a *noria* (water-wheel), indispensable for irrigation in al-Andalus. Primitive ones, drawn by mules in harness, survived in Andalucía into the twentieth century; the one in the illustration seems more sophisticated, and is drawn in all its detail. It was probably a form of hydraulic wheel 'moved by the force of water alone, which lifted water from large rivers or canals'.[51] As it is beside the water, one may assume that it falls into this category. One might point out that the images may not necessarily reflect the reality of the day, as the chessboard in the miniature where Bayād is apparently engaged in a game is the wrong way round,[52] an error that one does not see in the illustrations to Alfonso X's *Libro de Ajedrez* later in the century. Nonetheless, the existence of such a manuscript is a testimony to the refinement of culture in Almohad Seville at a time when one might have anticipated that the hatches would have been battened down. As well as the battle banner referred to above, several sumptuous woven silks dating to the beginning of the thirteenth century also confirm the taste for quality luxury products. In this instance also, one infers the presence of skilled artisans and craftsmen unaffected by political crises.

In his Epistle on the Superiority of al-Andalus, ash-Shaqundī (d. 1231) devotes a section to individual cities.[53] Pride of place is accorded to Seville, as Shaqundī casts light on aspects of life hitherto unrecorded. He mentions the propensity of the people for drinking wine, once suppressed by the governors, presumably when they were imbued with the initial zeal of the Almohad movement in al-Andalus, but now, in the first decades of the thirteenth century, tolerated, provided that drunkenness did not lead to unruly behaviour. At a time when the rulers were preoccupied with political and military affairs, such an issue as wine drinking, particularly when outlawing it might provoke unrest amongst the people, would have been low on the list of priorities. Many musical instruments, including the ʿūd (lute), the rabāb (rebec) and various kinds of flutes, were played in Seville and the surrounding area, leading one to speculate that ceremonies and celebrations amongst the rural communities were accompanied by music.

Similarly, as has been properly acknowledged, varieties of fruit, introduced from the Islamic East, contributed to the prosperity of the region, thanks not only to the fertile lands around the Guadalquivir but also to the irrigation techniques such as the noria and the qanāt. The latter, described as a horizontal well, was a system of Persian origin for carrying water underground, an 'irrigation-linked rural landscape feature'.[54] Oranges, lemons and apricots were amongst the species of fruit brought in by the Muslims which depended on a proper-functioning irrigation system for the abundance of their crops. Shaqundī mentions two types of fig that flourished on the lower slopes of the Sierra Morena beyond the northern banks of the Guadalquivir, one of which may have been the prickly pear now rampant in Andalucía.[55] He is so lavish in his praise of life as to court disbelief, as when he claims that in the palatial precincts built respectively by 'Abd ar-Rahmān III and al-Mansūr in Cordoba one could walk for ten miles under an uninterrupted sequence of street lights.[56] One may deduce from Shaqundī's description of Almería that the local community profited from the mineral resources of the region, notably agates, which in turn suggests that the affluence of a region did not depend solely on agricultural produce. Many people would furthermore have been involved in the lucrative silk trade.

Some light is thrown onto rural daily life by an Almohad cookery book of extraordinary interest, undated but estimated to have been compiled in the 1220s.[57] The text comprises over 500 recipes which enable the reader to visualise the culinary tastes of the time, the remedial properties or side effects of certain dishes, as well as the availability of ingredients. There may be some strange dishes to the modern taste, such as a two-pigeon omelette with eight eggs, but there is certainly refinement in the use of herbs and spices which include cinnamon of two types (one from China), coriander, clove, lavender, cumin, saffron and basil, the latter three all being made known to Western Europe via the Iberian Peninsula. There is even a recipe for lamb with truffles which are normally associated with the more northern areas of Europe.[58] Because of the range and nature of the produce, one may assume that a substantial section of the rural community was engaged in its cultivation and preparation for consumption. Some of the crops such as olives had been harvested since the Roman era, but many were introduced into al-Andalus from the East and the techniques and knowhow of their production communicated to the indigenous population. One encounters dishes prepared in the palace kitchen in Marrakesh, a beef or mutton dish cooked in vinegar and coloured by saffron consumed at wedding feasts in Cordoba and Seville, dishes for both the main course and dessert, amongst the latter a type of *quesada* or cheese concoction known as 'the seven bellies', and a kind of toasted roll made in Niebla, a small town once a Taifa state to the west of Seville. One notes the preponderance of eggs in recipes for both meats and sweets; these together with detailed instructions as how to prepare fried chicken and *coq au vin* – but made with *nabīd* (date wine) – amongst other chicken dishes suggest that poultry farming was practised and profitable. Quite clearly, though, the palate of the well-to-do was not the only one that was being catered for, as is testified by the recipe for a type of sausage confected 'after the manner of the people of the market'.[59] Occasionally, one finds references to medicinal preparations such as the complex potion made from meat juice spiced with onion, coriander and endive administered on 'the day of the fever'. In all, it may be said that this Almohad cookery book in which those places that are mentioned suggest a familiarity with towns in North Africa and in the western part of al-Andalus, Cordoba and Seville but not Granada, provides evidence of plenty rather than of hardship. The sheer range of produce mentioned in the recipes is indicative of a relatively affluent society, one seemingly untroubled by the political upheavals which, as has frequently been shown to have been the case, would have mostly affected the upper echelons of the state. This book was probably compiled at a time when the Almohad empire was on the brink of collapse in al-Andalus, and so reflects habits and mores that were soon to be superseded by a different set of values. The culinary properties of the ingredients listed, however, were perpetuated and have been reflected in Andalusian cuisine since then.

Notes

1.   Emilio García Gómez and E. Lévi-Provençal, *Sevilla a comienzos del siglo XII. El tratado de Ibn 'Abdūn*, Seville: El Ayuntamiento, 1981, pp. 101–3. This was García Gómez's adaptation, first published in 1948, of Lévi-Provençal's French version brought out in Paris in 1947. For the market, see Pedro Chalmeta, *El Zoco Medieval: Contribución al estudio de la historia del mercado*, Madrid: Fundación Ibn Tufayl, 2010.

2. García Gómez and E. Lévi-Provençal, *Sevilla a comienzos del siglo XII*, pp. 76–7.

3. Ibid., p. 157.

4. Ibid., p. 173.

5. E. Lévi-Provençal, *La Péninsule Ibérique au moyen-âge d'après le Kitāb ar-Rawd al-mi'tār fī habār al-aktār d'Ibn 'Abd al-Mun'im al-Himyarī*, Leiden: E. J. Brill, 1938, Arabic text pp. 102–4, translation pp. 126–7.

6. A. R. Nykl, *Hispano-Arabic Poetry and its Relations with the Old Provençal Troubadours*, Baltimore, MD. Printed by J. H. Furst, 1946, p. 228.

7. Quoted from Salma Khadra Jayyusi in her meticulous and perceptive essay 'The Rise of Ibn Khafāja' in *The Legacy of Muslim Spain*, edited by Salma Khadra Jayyusi, Leiden: E. J. Brill, 1992, pp. 379–95, including related bibliography, at p. 381. See also the useful analyses of several poems by Frederick P. Bargebuhr, *The Alhambra. A Cycle of Studies on the Eleventh Century in Moorish Spain*, Berlin: Walter de Gruyter, 1968, pp. 249–56.

8. T. J. Gorton, 'The metre of Ibn Quzmān: a "classical" approach', *Journal of Arabic Literature*, VI (1975), 1–29; '*Zajal* and *Muwaššah*: the continuing metrical debate', *Journal of Arabic Literature*, IX (1978), 33–40.

9. James T. Monroe, *Hispano-Arabic Poetry. A Student Anthology*, Berkeley, CA: University of California Press, 1974, p. 261.

10. A list of Romance words and phrases is supplied by Emilio García Gómez in *El mejor Ben Quzmán en 40 zéjeles*, Madrid: Alianza editorial, 1981, pp. 226–8. An alternative reading, one of many, of one of the clusters is to be found in this author's 'The interpretation of Romance words in Arabic texts: Theory and practice', *La Corónica*, XIII, 2 (1985), 243–52.

11. Nykl, *Hispano-Arabic Poetry*, p. 271.

12. The document is reproduced by J. M. Lacarra in his 'Documentos para el estudio de la reconquista y repoblación del valle del Ebro' (Primera Serie), no. 51 in *Estudios de Edad Media de la Corona de Aragón*, vol. II, Saragossa, 1946, pp. 513–14; my translation.

13. H. J. J. Winter, *Eastern Science. An Outline of its Scope and Contribution*, London: John Murray, 1952, p. 88. This work of 114 pp. is a reliable and intelligible guide to its subject.

14. Marie-Thérèse d'Alverny, 'Translations and translators', in *Renaissance and Renewal in the Twelfth Century*, edited by Robert I. Burns and Giles Constable, Oxford: Clarendon Press, 1985, pp. 421–62, at p. 440.

15. For insights into the identity of this figure, see Maureen Robinson, 'The history and myths surrounding Johannes Hispalensis', *Bulletin of Hispanic Studies*, 80 (2003), 443–70.

16. He was characterised as the most important intellectual of the first half of the twelfth century by Juan Vernet, *La cultura hispanoárabe en Oriente y Occidente*, Barcelona: Editorial Ariel, 1978, p. 115.

17. For Hermann, see Charles Burnett, 'Hermann of Carinthia', in *A History of Twelfth-Century Western Philosophy*, edited by Peter Dronke, Cambridge: Cambridge University Press, 1988, pp. 386–404; also the same author's 'A group of Arabic-Latin translators working in Northern Spain in the mid-12th century', *Journal of the Royal Asiatic Society*, 109, 1 (1977), 62–108; and his accessible overview, 'The translating activity in Medieval Spain', in *The Legacy of Muslim Spain*, edited by Salma Khadra Jayyusi, pp. 1036–58.

18. Cf. Norman Daniel, *The Arabs and Mediaeval Europe*, London: Longman, Librairie du Liban, 1975, 2nd edtion 1979, especially pp. 267–302, who calls it 'frequently unintelligible as well as inaccurate' (p. 274), thus explaining, perhaps, some of the misconceptions of Islam that circulated later.

19. W. Montgomery Watt, *The Influence of Islam on Medieval Europe*, Edinburgh: Edinburgh University Press, 1972, puts the number at 'about a hundred', but later scholars may have

assigned a translation to him 'when in doubt', pp. 60–1. Cf. also d'Alverny, 'Translations and translators', 452–4.

20. D'Alverny, 'Translations and translators', 453.

21. Madeleine Fletcher concludes after a cogent argument that 'the notion that Ibn Tūmart might have seen the famous scholar seems possible and even probable': 'Ibn Tūmart's teachers: the relationship with al-Ghazālī', Al-Qantara, XVIII (1997), 305–30, at 329.

22. This term is used by H. T. Norris, The Berbers in Arabic Literature, London: Longman, 1982, p. 171. Chapter 8 (pp. 157–84) comprises a most accessible and succinct account of Ibn Tūmart and the earlier phases of the Almohad achievement.

23. Maribel Fierro, 'Alfonso X "The Wise": The last Almohad Caliph?', Medieval Encounters, 15 (2009), 175–98, at p. 185, also published in The Almohad Revolution, Farnham: Ashgate, 2012, Variorum Collected Studies Series, Chapter XIV. I am grateful to the author for making this important study accessible.

24. Derek W. Lomax, The Reconquest of Spain, London: Longman, 1978, p. 92.

25. Lévi-Provençal, La Péninsule Ibérique au moyen-âge, p. 223.

26. Jacinto Bosch Vilá, La Sevilla Islámica 712–1248, Seville: Universidad, 1984, p. 146; Jean-Pierre Molénat, 'Sur le rôle des almohades dans la fin du christianisme locale au Maghreb et en al-Andalus', Al-Qantara, XVIII (1997), 389–413, at pp. 394–5, where convincing reasons are provided for the preference of this date.

27. The superficial resemblance that his name bears to Martínez, although seemingly accepted by Thomas F. Glick, Islamic and Christian Spain in the Early Middle Ages, Princeton, NJ: Princeton University Press, 1979, p. 188, is not generally thought to provide a solution to the origin of his name.

28. Lomax, The Reconquest of Spain, p. 90.

29. The book has been translated into many languages, including Latin, English (both in the seventeenth century), Dutch, German, French and Spanish. The quotation is taken from Hayy Ibn Yaqzān by Ibn Tufayl, translated from the twelfth-century Arabic by Lenn Evan Goodman, New York: Twayne, 1972, p. 15.

30. Paul Rycaut, The Critick, Written Originally in Spanish by Lorenzo Gracian one of the Best Wits in Spain, London: n.p., 1681, Prologue. The links with Robinson Crusoe were explored in the pioneering work by Antonio Pastor, The Idea of Robinson Crusoe, Watford: The Gongora Press, 1930, especially part III.

31. Hayy Ibn Yaqzān, translated by Goodman, p. 95.

32. Philip Dixon, 'Ashwell, George (1612–1694)', Oxford Dictionary of National Biography, Oxford: Oxford University Press, 2004.

33. Winter, Eastern Science, p. 77.

34. The word tahāfut has also been rendered as 'inconsistency' and as 'rebuttal'. See Alice E. Lasater, Spain to England. A Comparative Study of Arabic, European, and English Literature of the Middle Ages, Jackson, MS: University of Mississippi, 1974, p. 22.

35. Lynn Thorndike, Michael Scot, London: Thomas Nelson & Sons, 1965, p. 24. Scot was also associated with astrology and alchemy, chapters X and XI; see also E. J. Holmyard, Alchemy, Harmondsworth: Penguin Books, 1968 [1957], pp. 216–18; Dorothee Metlitzki, The Matter of Araby in Medieval England, New Haven, CT and London: Yale University Press, 1977, pp. 41–6.

36. Gustave E. Von Grunebaum, Medieval Islam. A Study in Cultural Orientation, Chicago, IL: University of Chicago Press, 2nd edition, 8th impression, 1971, p. 343. The first edition was published in 1946, the second in 1953.

37. See Lenn Goodman, ''Ibn Tufayl', in The Literature of Al-Andalus, edited by María Rosa Menocal et al., Cambridge: Cambridge University Press, 2000, pp. 318–30, at p. 324.

38. María Rosa Menocal, *The Arabic Role in Medieval Literary History*, Philadelphia, PA: University of Pennsylvania Press, 1990, Chapter 6, especially pp. 148–9.

39. Winter, *Eastern Science*, p. 77.

40. Ambrosio Huici Miranda, *Historia política del imperio Almohade*, 2 vols, Granada: Universidad de Granada, 2000, vol. I, p. 365. This is a facsimile reprint with a new 140 pp. 'estudio preliminar' by Emilio Molina López and Vicente Carlos Navarro Oltra of the first edition (1956–7) of this thorough and well-regarded history.

41. Rodrigo Jiménez de Rada (Archbishop of Toledo, 1209–47), *De rebus Hispaniae*, pp. 182–7, at p. 187.

42. It has also been claimed that this banner was one of the trophies acquired by the campaigning King Fernando III several decades afterwards. See, for example, with image, Jerrilynn D. Dodds, *Al-Andalus. Las artes islámicas en España*, Madrid: Ediciones El Viso, 1992, p. 326.

43. For example, Mercedes García-Arenal, *Messianism and Puritanical Reform. Mahdīs of the Muslim West*, Leiden: E. J. Brill, 2006, p. 206, where the author refers to 'the battle of Las Navas de Tolosa (al-'Uqāb)'. I owe the information concerning the debate surrounding the Arabic name of Las Navas to the kindness of Professor L. P. Harvey (private communication).

44. E. Lévi-Provençal, *La Péninsule Ibérique au moyen-âge*, Arabic text, p. 16.

45. Ibn Khaldūn, *The Muqaddimah. An Introduction to History*, translated from the Arabic by Franz Rosenthal; abridged and edited by N. J. Dawood, London: Routledge and Kegan Paul, 1978 [first edition in this form 1967], p. 236.

46. Roger Le Tourneau, *The Almohad Movement in North Africa in the Twelfth and Thirteenth Centuries*, Princeton, NJ: Princeton University Press, 1969, p. 85.

47. Ibid., p. 88.

48. Amongst the many studies of Almohad architecture, see Henri Terrasse, *Islam d'Espagne. Une rencontre de l'Orient et de l'Occident*, Paris: Librairie Plon, 1958, pp. 149–54; Leopoldo Torres Balbás, *Artes Almoravide y Almohade*, Madrid: Instituto de Estudios Africanos, 1955, Marianne Barrucand and Achim Bednorz, *Moorish Architecture in al-Andalus*, Cologne: Rolf Taschen, 1992, especially pp. 153–73, the latter a succinct, reliable commentary with stunning illustrations. Also, *Al-Andalus. Las artes islámicas en España*, op., cit. pp. 77-81, 86-95.

49. E. Lévi-Provençal, *La Péninsule Ibérique au moyen-âge*, Arabic text, p. 27.

50. See Dodds, *Al-Andalus. Las artes*, pp. 306–13, with two of the illustrations reproduced in colour (pp. 312–13). The text has been translated, studied and analysed by Cynthia Robinson, *Medieval Andalusian Courtly Culture in the Mediterranean. Hadīth Bayād wa Riyād*, London and New York: Routledge, 2010, especially pp. 70–112.

51. Thomas F. Glick has contributed a major monograph on irrigation techniques: *Irrigation and Society in Medieval Valencia*, Cambridge, MA: Harvard University Press, 1970. See also Glick, *Islamic and Christian Spain*, pp. 74–6, 235–8.

52. Robinson, *Medieval Andalusian Courtly Culture*, p. 64.

53. Al-Šaqundī, *Elogio del Islam Español (risāla fī fadl al-andalus)*, translated into Spanish by Emilio García Gómez, Madrid: Estanislao Maestre, 1934. The section on the cities occupies pp. 95–116. The epistle was written to refute the claims of another writer that the Maghrib was superior to al-Andalus. His work was known to and quoted by al-Maqqarī; extracts in English by Pascual de Gayangos, *The History of the Mohammedan Dynasties in Spain*, 2 vols, London: RoutledgeCurzon, 2002, for example in vol. I, pp. 52–3.

54. Keith Sutton, '*Qanats* in al-Andalus: The continued presence of Moorish irrigation technology in the Campo de Tabernas, Almeria, Spain', *The Maghreb Review*, 26, 1 (2001), 69–78. I owe this reference to the kindness of Dr M. Ben Madani.

55. Gayangos, *The History of the Mohammedan Dynasties in Spain*, pp. 364–5. This claim is, however, dismissed by García Gómez as being 'cosa poco probable' (p. 97).

56. Al-Šaqundī, *Elogio del Islam español (risāla fī fadl al-Andalus)*, translated by Emilio García Gómez, Madrid: Estanislao Maestre, 1934, p. 105.

57. Translated by Ambrosio Huici Miranda, *Traducción española de un manuscrito anónimo del siglo XIII sobre la cocina hispano-magribí*, Madrid: Editorial Maestre, 1960, p. 43 from a unique seventeenth-century manuscript.

58. Comparisons may be made with modern cookery books, such as *Moorish Recipes*, collected and compiled by John, Fourth Marquis of Bute, K. T., Edinburgh: Oliver and Boyd, n.d. (but between 1947 and 1956), in which the Moroccan dishes show an abundant use of herbs and spices; see also Rupert Croft-Cooke, *Exotic Food*, London: George Allen and Unwin, 1969, for example the recipe for 'Chicken in Honey' at p. 92.

59. Huici Miranda, *Cocina hispano-magribí*, p. 155. The title of the recipe is 'Isfiriyā a la manera de la gente del zoco'. The first word, the author explains, is the Moroccan name for a kind of mutton.

CHAPTER 6

The thirteenth and fourteenth centuries

After 1228, al-Andalus reverted to a period when individual Muslim potentates jockeyed for control of what amounted to a political void. Out of the squabbling and intrigues, one chieftain emerged who was to carve out a kingdom for himself and establish a dynasty that would see an independent Muslim state continuing in the Iberian Peninsula for a further 250 years. This seemed to be a most unlikely scenario in the wake of the capture of Seville in 1248, as a consequence of decades of relentless and ruthless campaigning by the kings of Castile and Aragón. From a historical perspective, when in 1236 Cordoba was taken by Fernando III, who had united his own realm with that of León in 1230, the imminent triumph of the Christian kingdoms seemed assured, even more so when Seville, called by Lomax 'the greatest city in Western Europe' changed hands after a siege in 1248.[1] Knights from the military orders occupied Cordoba and were rewarded for their role in the conquests by the grants of vast tracts of land. Their discipline and order were invaluable at a time when settlers from other parts of the Peninsula went south. The Great Mosque was immediately dedicated as a cathedral, a clear symbol to the population that Christianity would be replacing Islam. Fernando allowed the inhabitants of Seville a short period of time to collect their possessions together before they evacuated the city, leaving it empty for three days before the resettlement began. They were escorted to the safety zone of the frontier protected by an armed detachment. Perhaps on account of his humane treatment of the defeated, he was attributed with *siyāsa* ('adroit or smart conduct of affairs'),[2] and it is not without interest that the same source states that when he died, he was buried in the *qibla* of the Great Mosque, by that time, four years later, fully functional as a cathedral.[3] In the East, Valencia was conquered by James (Jaume) I (r. 1213–76) of Aragón after a two-year siege in September 1238. He entrusted the security of the city to several hundred knights from provenances as far afield as Narbonne and even England, but Muslims were permitted to stay and continue their way of life in the city or in the conquered areas. Many, perhaps 50,000, left with their belongings and were escorted to the resort of Cullera. It was surely only a matter of time before the cities in the south-east corner of al-Andalus would follow the example of their counterparts in the west. Yet this was not to happen.

The chieftain who obstructed this outcome was Muhammad b. Nasr, known as al-Ahmār, ('the Red'), who established himself first in Arjona and then in neighbouring Jaén in the early 1230s, and schemed to expand his authority westwards, exercising brief control over Cordoba and Seville in 1233, but being rejected by the citizenry of both cities because of the austerity of his rule, further details of which are undisclosed. He was the founder of the Nasrid kingdom of Granada under the title of Muhammad I (r. 1237–73).[4] It seems as though he intuitively knew from an early age when to make and when to break alliances. For example, according to a Christian source, he entered in league with the powerful King Fernando III in the final stages of the latter's siege of Cordoba, being instrumental in the surrender of the city without further damage to its buildings and properties. He became the ruler of Granada in 1237, and his authority was, within a short period of years, acknowledged in the two key ports to of Almería and Málaga. Fernando had his eyes set on Granada, but first had to negotiate a way past the city of Jaén protected by an enormous fortress. Al-Ahmār tried to lift the siege in 1244 but his attempt to supply the city with victuals failed and, with a pragmatism that characterised his political decisions, he signed a twenty-year peace treaty with Fernando, and abandoned the inhabitants of Jaén many of whom fled to the coast and thence to exile in North Africa. During these two decades, al-Ahmār consolidated his position, and showed himself to be more than adept at diplomatic manoeuvring. During the protracted siege of Seville in 1248, he put a detachment of his own troops at the disposal of Fernando who used them to maintain pressure on the city.[5] He was, in effect, keeping the Castilian king 'sweet' whilst pursuing his own policies, notably initiating contacts with Muslims in different parts of the Islamic world. He sent a delegation to the newly established Hafsid dynasty in present-day Tunisia, ever mindful of the need of future support and resources should his own position be threatened. Furthermore, in 1264, an agreement was reached with the Marīnids who had replaced the Almohads in the Maghrib and, as a consequence, warriors were dispatched to the Peninsula to counter the Castilian menace. In the same year, it seems as though al-Ahmār fostered revolt among the Mudejars, Muslims now residing in lands under Christian control, perhaps through an ambition to unite the whole of the southern part of the Peninsula within his domain.

One may assign the survival of the Nasrid state in the thirteenth century to a number of factors. Certainly, al-Ahmār's diplomacy was crucial. He was able to keep both the Castilian and Aragonese kings at bay by judicious treaties, expedient concessions of fortresses and measured aggression. In 1266, he renounced all rights to the regions of Murcia – he had occupied the city of Murcia since 1264 – and Jerez in a peace treaty signed with Fernando's successor, Alfonso X (r. 1252–84) in return for the latter's withdrawal of support for rebels within his state. Second, it suited the Christian kings that dissident Muslims in newly conquered territory should find a nearby haven thus reducing the potential for sedition. Many came to the city of Granada forming a community of immigrants in the Albaicín, the quarter on the hill opposite the Alhambra around which a defensive wall was built. Third, the secure geographical location of the city, protected in the north by the Sierra Nevada, rendered a surprise attack improbable. Many of the townships between the capital and the frontier were fortified. Coupled with this inland defensive wall, there were some 200 miles of coastline stretching from Algeciras through Málaga and Almería to beyond Mojácar in the east. Thus, al-Ahmār's kingdom enjoyed direct access to North Africa through its seaports, facilitating not only trade but also troop movements as occasion demanded. It occupied approximately a sixth of the extent of al-Andalus at the height of its powers in the tenth century, the last bulwark of independent Islamic presence in the Peninsula. Fourth, a vigorous trade with both Christian and Muslim states at least until the fifteenth century conferred an economic self-sufficiency onto the region. A fifth factor was the emergence of the Marīnids who supplanted the Almohads in the middle of the thirteenth century, capturing Marrakesh in 1269; these Berbers were ever willing and ready to cross over to al-Andalus in support of their beleaguered co-religionists. A pattern was to unfold over the following two centuries wherein the Nasrids called upon the Marīnids to come to their aid when the incursions of the Christians were threatening, and conversely appealed to the Christians when the Marīnids sought to extend their foothold in al-Andalus as their predecessors had done. It was the politics of expedience.

The accession of Alfonso X (1221–84) to the throne of Castile in 1252 heralded a new epoch in the Iberian Peninsula. In so far as his policies impinged on the Nasrids of al-Andalus, it was evident that he was intent on picking up where his father Fernando had left off. He had taken part in the siege of Seville (1247–8), and reclaimed cities that had severed their dependence on Seville after his father's death.[6] Aside from his ambitions in Europe including his pretensions to be declared Holy Roman Emperor, he was determined to extend his territory beyond Iberian shores to the south. In 1260, he organised a raid on the North African coast, with the possible objective of establishing a base there for trade from Cádiz. The enterprise came to nought, but it did cement the hostility of the Marīnids, as for instance when they invaded from the south-west destroying lands around Seville and even as far as Cordoba, without any response from Alfonso. From the political angle, Alfonso accomplished neither the conquest of the Nasrid state of Granada, nor the expansion of the empire that he inherited into North Africa. Yet he spent long periods of his life living in Seville, where he employed Muslim craftsmen to repair and extend the Alcázar in the *mudéjar* style. The one point to make in this regard is that Alfonso, far from wishing to eradicate Muslim civilisation, sought to perpetuate it in what was now Christian territory. Furthermore, known to history as Alfonso El Sabio (the Learned), he promoted the translation of scientific works from Arabic into Castilian from the outset of his reign, and was the first Christian monarch to appreciate the wealth of knowledge available in Arabic sources.[7] It is noteworthy that he ordered the translations to be made into the vernacular language of Castilian rather than into Latin, thus fostering an understanding among his subjects of disciplines hitherto unknown except by the very few. Alfonso was not some remote patron, but an active participant who oversaw much of the work done to his bidding, and he may have had a hand in some of the productions himself. The locations for this activity were Toledo, where there was a repository of manuscripts and where translations had been made for over a century, and Seville. One may highlight the fact that, in the three decades after the death of Fernando III, a monarch who had been responsible for such a decisive shift of power in the Peninsula, his son Alfonso X was actively encouraging the dissemination of the culture of the vanquished. Islamic culture was the one that dominated at that time. If the Christians were pre-eminent militarily, the Muslims were superior in learning. That certain knowledge was only accessible through Muslim sources in the Peninsula was no obstacle to its acquisition. Islam was near to being extinguished in the Iberian Peninsula in the mid-thirteenth century, yet paradoxically this was an age when it exerted its maximum influence. Just as was the case in the kingdom of León in the tenth century, Islamic and Arabic influences permeated Christian society, although the circumstances were not quite the same. Now in the thirteenth century, there were thousands of Muslims left high and dry in the conquests, who inhabited Castilian and Aragonese territories. It was an Islamic culture that Alfonso inherited as a result of his father's conquests, and which he was quick to tap into and exploit for the benefit of himself and of his realm.

The transmission of Arabic learning to Western Europe, in which Alfonso had an integral role, was his lasting legacy. If one examines Alfonso's itinerary, one may discern that he had a spell of three months in Toledo in 1254, and spent the whole year there in 1259. For the next ten years he resided in Seville before returning to Toledo in the summer of 1269, followed by a three-month visit in 1273, and a lengthy stay of nine months in 1278–9.[8] Some of the translations and indeed other works, both legal and historical, have been ascribed to Alfonso, but his role in their composition may have been limited to selection of work, appointment of translator and oversight of illustrations where present. He was like the artist in the studio, providing an outline of the intended project, and then allowing experts in specific fields to undertake and complete the task in Toledo, adding touches such as the prologue himself. He commissioned translations of astronomical and astrological works including what became known as the Alfonsine tables which were 'tables of the movements of the planets', based on those of al-Zarqālī, the Cordoban astronomer (d.1100), but 'corrected and extended from fresh observations' made in Toledo.[9] Originally composed in Castilian, there was a Latin version before the end of the thirteenth century, and the tables were not only known in England in the following century, and adapted to the latitude of Oxford but were also used in Europe up to the sixteenth century.[10] Also significant was a compilation of some fifteen astronomical works mainly dealing with instruments, all translated from or based on Arabic originals, known as *Los libros del saber de astronomía* ('The Books of Astronomical Knowledge'), which was illustrated with copious diagrams. Closely allied to astronomy is astrology, the study of the influences of the celestial on the terrestrial sphere, and a science to be pursued and understood. One of the two most powerful men in the Iberian Peninsula at that time, the other being James I of Aragón, Alfonso commanded a knowledge of astrology sufficient to order the translation of several well-known Arabic works on the subject, not into Latin but into Castilian so that their contents would be accessible to more than the erudite minority. For example, the *Libro de las cruzes*, dating to 1259 when Alfonso, as noted above, was in Toledo, and recognised as the first astrological work in Castilian, was translated from the Arabic, and contained data that could be of use to him as monarch. Moreover, another such work, the *Lapidario* (lapidary), judging from the exquisite multicoloured illustrations within the text, was given pride of place in the royal workshop. According to its prologue, this treatise on precious stones was translated from the original Chaldean, or Aramaic, thence to Arabic and finally Castilian. Alfonso himself had obtained the manuscript in Toledo in 1243 when he was twenty-two, from a Jewish merchant or scholar. No details are given as to the latter's profession, but the text does say that he had the manuscript hidden and was reluctant that others should make use of it, both pieces of information which would suggest that he was aware of its contents and had a measure of learning. In the treatise, which is arranged according to the signs of the zodiac, each one of some 300 stones is described. Their degree within the star sign is given, and the particular star which has power over it. The properties and utilities of each are given at length and also their geographical location. A curious example is what might be described as the anaesthetic stone, in the eighth degree of Taurus, which is found in Egypt and which, when ground up with liquid added, is placed on the part of the body where the surgeon is going to operate, rendering it numb. This clearly indicates if not current surgical practice then a tested medical procedure. Another example, of a stone which when attached to the thigh of a pregnant woman affords an easy and risk-free birth, suggests local practice and belief. Alfonso's lapidary was valued as a compendium of knowledge about astrology, alchemy, mineralogy, folklore, superstition, medicine including surgery, ophthalmology and gynaecology, among many other disciplines.[11]

Alfonso founded what might be termed a school of Arabic and Latin in Seville in the 1250s, a foundation that was to receive the official seal of Pope Alexander IV (Pope 1254–61) in 1260. During the decade of the 1260s, which Alfonso X spent in Seville, now a centre for scholars from within the Peninsula and elsewhere, the key may be found to sections of Dante's *Divina Commedia*. A far-reaching polemic was sparked off by Miguel Asín Palacios when in 1919 he published a work in which he controversially argued that Dante was cognisant of Islamic accounts for the description of his spiritual journey: 'in Moslem sources there were to be found prototypes of features in the Divine Comedy'.[12] Asín, in a thoroughly documented study, drew attention to numerous parallels between Dante's work and putative Islamic antecedents as, for example, the fact that both Muhammad and Dante had the service of guides for their journeys, Gabriel and Virgil respectively. Notable amongst the possible models was the legend of Muhammad's nocturnal ascent to heaven, known as the *mi'rāj* (meaning ladder and ascent), preserved in *hadīth*, and which would have been approved in Māliki circles in al-Andalus. Alfonso had commissioned his physician and scholar, Abraham of Toledo, to translate the narration of Muhammad's night journey into Castilian, a manuscript that has not come to light. Following this, in 1264 one of the circle of Italians then in Seville, Bonaventura de Siena, notary and scribe as he describes himself in his prologue, a collaborator of Alfonso, rendered this version into French and Latin, but it was not until 1949 that these two texts were published.[13] The manuscript of the French translation has a delightful illustration at the foot of the first folio, of a person dressed in a purple tunic, presumably Muhammad, looking round as he climbs up the rungs of a ladder. An analysis of these texts enabled Muñoz Sendino to conclude that the *mi'rāj* provided Dante with a world of inspiration.[14]

The most likely way in which Dante could have acquired an awareness of this particular text, always bearing in mind that the account of Muhammad's nocturnal journey was not by any means the sole Islamic work of which he may have had knowledge and which could have provided him with inspiration, was through Brunetto Latini (c.1220–94), like Dante (c.1265–1321) from Florence. Latini was sent on a political mission by the elders of Florence to Alfonso X, and spent several months in the summer of 1260 at the King's court at Seville and later, perhaps, at Cordoba. He may well have got to know the translators as well as their works, and have acquired manuscripts which he took back to Tuscany whither he returned after an enforced exile in 1267. Latini became Dante's teacher and mentor perhaps in the mid-1280s and no doubt communicated to him what he had learnt at Alfonso's court and from correspondence with Alfonso.[15] It is possible that he came into contact with Bonaventura de Siena when the latter was in Seville engaged in the translation of the *mi'rāj* from Castilian into French and Latin, but too little is known of the life of the latter for there to be any certitude about this. It may therefore be concluded that Islamic influences not only made their presence felt in northern Europe but also, more pervasively, and therefore perhaps more subtly, in the work of a poet of the stature of Dante.[16] Alfonso was the catalyst in the thirteenth century, but he himself was mesmerised by the immense world of learning that contact with al-Andalus had made accessible for him. In a period when the only independent Islamic state in the Iberian Peninsula was confined to its south-east corner, and

when its political future on the European stage looked precarious, the intellectual and cultural legacy of al-Andalus was at its most vigorous.

Alfonso's preoccupation with Arab culture was shared, if less so, by his
counterpart, James I of Aragón whose *Libre de la saviesa* (Book of Wisdom), drew
in part on material translated into Catalan from a Hebrew version of a ninth-
century Arabic original. However, the dominant figure in Catalan thought and
letters in the this period was the indomitable Ramón Llull (c. 1232–1316) who
travelled throughout the Mediterranean and Europe, and learnt Arabic for the
purpose of converting Muslims to Christianity. Although he travelled three
times to North Africa as well as to the Middle East for missionary purposes,
he was conscious of the many Muslims on his own home island of Mallorca.
Consequently, towards the end of his life, in 1299, he returned there with the
express intent of persuading Muslims to convert to Christianity, his weapon
always being the word rather than the sword.[17] The situation of the *mudéjar* communities, of which those in Mallorca was one, was one of changing fortunes as
the centuries succeeded. In the thirteenth century, however, the regal legislation
makes their status within both Castile and Aragón quite clear. In his legal code,
the *Siete Partidas* (Seven Divisions), drawn up in Castilian, Alfonso X formulated
unambiguous guidelines for Muslims, and also for Jews, living under Christian
law. Whether or not the *mudéjares* were 'an anomaly to Christian lawyers and
administrators', provision was made for their peaceful coexistence with their
neighbours. They could live their lives according to the precepts of their own
statutes, could rest assured that their property could not be seized from them
and did not have to wear any discriminatory insignia. This latter prescription
ran counter to a decree in the Fourth Lateran Council of 1215 which specifically
stipulated that Muslims and Jews should wear distinctive garments. Although
Alfonso's law code may have the appearance of being a recipe for what has
become known as *convivencia* ('living together'), it has to be kept in mind that, as
Harvey wrote, 'the *partidas* were not a code actually in force; rather, they were
an ideal compilation of laws Alfonso would have liked to see in existence'.[18]
It is nonetheless generally accepted that the official injunctions on Christians
to allow *mudéjares* to live at peace among them were complied with. One must
also remember that Muslims were encouraged to cross the border to Nasrid
Granada, but this was a truly hazardous undertaking in the last third of the
thirteenth century when the southernmost part of the Peninsula was in a state
of tumultuous conflict.

James I, likewise, granted charters to *mudéjares* in the Valencian region, one of
which, in a rural area, specified that they could live as Muslims, worship in their
mosques, instruct their sons in the reading of the Qur'ān and be governed by
their own *qādī*, subject to paying an eighth of all their produce, except fruit and
vegetables, in tax.[19] One may say that, just as Christians had been permitted to
practise their faith in Islam conditional on the payment of a special tax in the

early centuries of al-Andalus, so now the boot was on the other foot. Muslims in Christian territory could continue to be regulated by the *sunna*. One could interpret this as a Peninsular phenomenon, but attention should also be drawn to the factor of ethnicity. The religion of a person could not be determined unequivocally by physical features. One's clothing might betray one's trade, and that trade may be known to be run by persons of a particular religion, but appearance alone was not a sufficiently determining factor. Certainly, the features of individuals may differ from community to community, but within a particular demographic region, one's religion was judged by other than ethnic factors.[20]

In the Nasrid state, as has been intimated, during the final two decades of the thirteenth century, what one might call 'the survival business' depended on the ruler having sufficiently reliable intelligence reports to form and to break alliances, which often happened with bewildering alacrity, when the moments to do so were at their most propitious. For example, at the time when the Marīnids made their fourth major expedition into the Peninsula in 1285, Sancho IV, Alfonso's successor, was an ally of the Nasrid ruler, Muhammad II (1273–1302), so that the two could jointly defeat a powerful rebellious rival Muslim faction, the Banū Ashqilūla (Escayola), which had taken control of Málaga.[21] What transpired was that the Marīnids, who were invited by the rebels to bring them succour and to assist them in their struggle for survival, raided Sancho's territory to the east of Granada, to such destructive effect that the latter had to petition for peace. Muhammad was meanwhile disengaged from this and remained in his own realm. In an Arabic text, written about forty years afterwards, Sancho's meeting with the Marīnid *amīr* in the latter's camp outside the city of Jerez, is described in all its barely credible detail: how Sancho participated in a form of what might have been jousting with his warriors as a spectacle for the *amīr*; how he also gave an impassioned speech acknowledging the latter's mastery of his 'whole country' and 'subjects'; and how the treaty was concluded with the *amīr* requiring Sancho to send him 'Muslim books and copies of the Qur'ān'. This Sancho did to the tune of 'thirteen loads of books' which were subsequently sent back to Fez.[22] One might observe that it stands to reason that the North African *amīr* was aware of the cultural heritage present in what was formerly al-Andalus. His purpose in reclaiming the Arabic books, on such subjects as the *hadīth* and law, was to ensure that scholars and students in his own state could reap profit from them. There may also be a suggestion that such material should not be harboured within a Christian state, whether or not it was being employed for the benefit of Muslims therein. A further point that may be raised is how Sancho or his representatives acquired these thirteen cargoes (*hamla*) of books. Were they requisitioned from private collections? Were they removed from the repository of books in the college of Arabic and Latin set up by his father in Seville? Did they adversely affect the profession of translating Arabic works into Castilian that he had put in place?

A further instance of expedient alliance-making occurred in 1290 when Muhammad II secretly agreed with Sancho that the latter should attack the Marīnids in Tarifa and then hand the town over to the Nasrids, receiving in return four frontier fortresses.[23] Sancho accomplished this with the offshore assistance of the Aragonese but the Castilians retained the port and took possession of the promised castles, so reneging on the previous covenant. Thus Muhammad had further recourse to the Marīnids, and so the criss-crossing of alliances proceeded as if within a labyrinth from which there was no exit. The castles and fortresses mainly in the northern frontier zone separating the Nasrid kingdom from that of Castile came to be what amounted to essential bargaining chips in the negotiations that established a pattern in Peninsular politics.[24] Towns such as Baeza twenty miles to the north of Jaén but on the other side of the Guadalquivir, which had been conquered by Fernando III in 1226 and garrisoned by knights of the Order of Calatrava, was used as a base camp for 5,000 horses when the Marīnids surged towards Talavera in 1283. Unsuccessful in his quest, the Marīnid *amīr* retreated to Baeza, looted it and returned to Fez via Algeciras with an incalculable number of captives, wealth and cattle.[25]

Frontier life was precarious, and there was always the risk of sudden displacement, but the indigenous population stayed put unless they were forcefully removed, encouraged to persevere no doubt because of the dependable and perennial productivity of the land. Jódar, on the southern plains of the Guadalquivir which was a centre for olive-oil production, was more in the firing line and, along with Quesada, an important city according to al-Maqqarī, and Cazorla, was subject to the vicissitudes of frontier existence. The towns of Cabra and Lucena en route to Seville were similarly vulnerable. The area to the north-east was protected by the formidable fortress towns of Guadix and Baza governing the route from that direction into Granada, Guadix (*wadī Āsh*, after its Roman name Acci) in particular having been in the past a favoured location for the Almohads for one of whom a botanical garden was especially created at the beginning of the thirteenth century. Being so strategically situated, it not unnaturally had daunting fortifications surrounded by stone ramparts to protect the inhabitants.[26] Baza, also noted as a fertile area, was a centre for olive groves and was known for its silk products. In times of peace, both these places prospered and commerce flourished. The land to the east of Granada was peppered with fortified small towns and villages, a testimony to the extent to which the early Nasrids invested in defence. One should mention that Loja commanded the *vega*, or plain, which was the only realistic route for a direct assault on Granada and therefore had a vital role to play in so far as the defences of that city were concerned. Archidona and Antequera, both nearer to Seville on the direct route, were heavily fortified and probably had small detachments of troops billeted there on an indefinite basis. Archidona, directly to the north of Málaga and separated from it by the Sierra de Cártama, was the centre of a province where governors and officials were stationed, and was responsible for the administration of many towns and villages. The coastal defences comprised some sixty sturdy, brick-built *atalayas* (watchtowers), some of which had been constructed in the tenth century and located at regular intervals. They served as look-outs and were linked to castles such as those at Almuñécar and Salobreña when marine assaults were imminent. It was important also to provide protection for seaports such as Almería whose trade with the northern Mediterranean harbours and with the Middle East was essential to the economy of the Nasrid state.

It should be observed that the single-minded focus of the early Nasrid rulers on fortifications along the frontiers both north and south, with fortressed towns as well especially to the west of Granada where it was most vulnerable to attack, is evidence of what might be called perimeter building. That is to say, the emphasis was on defence and not offence, although sorties were made that resulted in the often temporary possession of a border castle. What was of primary importance was the preservation of the interior of what remained of al-Andalus. These were measures that were taken to secure the survival of the state. Nowhere and at no time was the region invulnerable to attack, but this military framework coupled with the other factors previously mentioned, not to mention the buoyant trade in the fourteenth century, went a long way toward ensuring the longevity of the state. It is apparent from various sources that Castilians and Aragonese had their eyes on Granada, if not the city specifically, then the territory under the sway of its rulers. Notwithstanding, expeditions from the north, even joint ones, were unlikely to succeed in achieving their objective because of potential reinforcements from the Marīnids at crucial moments, and because the Nasrids were blessed with a sound internal economy. Treaties provided breathing spaces and could alter the political spectrum drastically. Above all, despite hostilities being maintained at a greater or lesser level throughout the fourteenth century, diplomatic and commercial interchanges persisted, paving the way for a mutual acculturation between Castile and Granada.

The fourteenth century

During the twenty-nine-year reign of Muhammad II, al-Andalus had achieved a relationship with his northern and southern neighbours akin to a somewhat uncomfortable *ménage à trois*. Stability was obtained at the cost of constant wheeling and dealing and the acceptance of porous borders as a fact of life. The treaty drawn up with the Castilians in 1310, for example, included a term to the effect that Fernando IV (r. 1295–1312) should appoint an officer to legislate in disputes in the border zones, thus in a way acknowledging the status quo. Under Muhammad II's three immediate successors, Muhammad III (r. 1302–09), the latter's brother Nasr (r. 1309–14) and Muhammad IV (r. 1325–33), a kind of unwritten frontier code was observed between al-Andalus, Castile and Aragón.

An example of this is perceived in the life of Don Juan Manuel (1282–1349?), nephew of Alfonso X and grandson of Fernando III who was sent to the Murcian frontier with Muslims when he was only twelve years old although he was not actually a witness to any confrontation. Some thirty years later, he was appointed governor of the self-same province of Murcia where he later died. A man of letters, with a large literary output, Don Juan Manuel was also a peace-loving statesman, obsessed in his writings with how a man, in particular a states-man, should behave in order to retain his honour and reputation. Consequently, he ascribed to Muslim knights, with many of whom he would have had dealings on the border with the Nasrid state of Granada, the same lofty code of chivalric conduct to which he himself adhered. The book of his with the widest dissemina-tion, *El Conde Lucanor* ('The Tales of Count Lucanor'), completed in the decade prior to this death, consists of fifty-one stories of varied subject matter, each with a moral. They are told by an elder statesman to his protégé, the young count, and address problems of concern to an aspirant nobleman. Some of the stories are folkloric in origin, but others concern named contemporaries and historical figures such as Saladin (Salāh ad-Dīn, 1137–93), the *soldán de Babilonia* (Sultan of Babylon), fierce and indomitable opponent of the Crusaders, depicted as a man of honour, in fact the epitome of the chivalric knight in two memorable tales. In the 140 or so years since Saladin's lifetime, his reputation as a noble with the same highest moral principles as a Christian knight had permeated through to the border country in the Iberian Peninsula.[27] For an example of how a noble-man should face up to and solve the multifarious problems confronting him, the Christian Don Juan Manuel turned to the Muslim Salāh ad Dīn. Chivalric ideals were not obstructed by religious factors. A man was worth what a man was worth, irrespective of the creed which he espoused. If the channel for the transmission of such stories were Crusader chronicles, which is to say that they came via the northern coastline of the Mediterranean, then another small group of tales clearly originated from within al-Andalus.

There are three that have actual Arabic words as what might be termed the punchlines. Two are specifically set in al-Andalus, one in the tenth and the other in the eleventh century. The former relates to al-Hakam II and the latter to al-Mu'tamid, who satisfies his wife Rumayqīya's whim by ordering that a palace court be covered with a fragrant form of clay formed out of rosewater, cinnamon, cloves and other spices so that she and her companions could tread in it with bare feet, just as she had seen a woman knee-deep in mud making *adobes* (bricks) on the river's edge. When she complained to her husband that he never did anything to please her, he remarked, '*wa lā nahār at-tīn*' ('and not on the day of the clay'). Later versions of this story were recorded by al-Maqqarī in the seventeenth century naming his sources, known to have been reliable, and it is quite conceivable that Don Juan Manuel was familiar with one of the earli-est of these. It is indeed feasible to postulate that he knew a written account of the episode, and that his source therefore was a written and not an oral one.[28] It follows that Don Juan Manuel, in his role as frontier statesman, could speak and understand Arabic, a skill perhaps acquired to facilitate his negotiations with Nasr in 1313/14 which resulted in a treaty of friendship, although there is mention of him sending a *moro* as an intermediary. Nasr referred to this alliance in a letter to James II of Aragón (r. 1291–1327) ten days before he was deposed in February 1314 and forced to take refuge in nearby Guadix, so it was evidently a final desperate attempt to cling on to power with the help of support from the Aragonese. Don Juan Manuel, who had his own small private contingent of Castilian knights to preserve his independence just as El Cid had had his own loyal band 150 years earlier, in these years led a tightrope existence between Castilian and Aragonese, requesting the assistance of the Nasrid ruler in 1326 and subsequent years, for example as a reprisal for his treatment by the Castilian Alfonso XI (r. 1312–50).

The south-west enclave of the Nasrid state was an ongoing bone of contention, notably the towns of Tarifa, just beyond the border zone, Algeciras and the rock of Gibraltar, the latter two on facing sides of a wide bay which provided a natural harbour for traffic going to and fro across the straits. Tarifa, well fortified with walls and an *alcázar*, had been captured by the Castilians in 1292 and was ever in the sights of the Nasrids who sought, unsuccessfully, to regain it by treaty as early as 1303. For the Marīnids, also, it was of critical importance, as a base for expeditions within the Peninsula; they later besieged it prior to their shattering defeat at the battle of Salado in 1340 by the combined forces of the Castilians and Portuguese. Algeciras, after many fluctuations in its fortunes, was finally captured from the Marīnids by Alfonso following a protracted two-year siege in 1344. It was retaken by the Nasrids in 1369, only to have its defences dismantled and town demilitarised several years later at the command of Muhammad V, thus, in Harvey's words, moving 'the question of the straits away from the center of international concern'.[29] On the eastern side of the bay, Gibraltar, with its imposing defensive capability, was gained by the Castilians in 1309, but in 1333, it was regained by the Marīnids, who immediately set about reconstructing its buildings and fortifications, causing a thick wall to be built at the foot of the rock. Al-Maqqarī provided this detail and added that it 'surrounded [the rock] on all sides as the halo surrounds the crescent moon'.[30] Despite Alfonso XI's attempt to repossess it, it remained thenceforth in the control of the Nasrids for a further hundred years. The global traveller Ibn Battūta, who saw Gibraltar in the early summer of 1350, shortly after Alfonso had perished from the Black Death during the siege, was impressed by what he saw. He called it the 'Mountain of Victory', and observes that he would like to have been one of those serving there until the end of his life. His chronicler added that Gibraltar was the stronghold of Islam and 'a choking obstruction in the throats of the worshippers of idols'.[31] One might mention that the port of

Almería to the east, so essential for trade, also had a magnetic attraction for the Christians who had occupied the town for ten years in the twelfth century. Now, 160 years later, their descendants tried again. A combined force of Aragonese and Castilians besieged the city in 1309–10 but the inhabitants were well provisioned and, with the help of troops sent by the Nasrid ruler, were able to withstand the blockade.

As far as the Nasrid state during the first three decades of the fourteenth century was concerned, it had survived a precarious period by dint of the politics of expediency and the timely assistance of the Marīnids. It was an alliance between Muhammad IV (r. 1325–33) and the Marīnids that is said to have provoked his assassination. The situation was to change dramatically with the accession of Yūsuf I (r. 1333–54), whose reign inaugurated an unprecedented period of efflorescence for the Nasrids. On the political front, an immediate truce with Castile upon his assumption of power may have been ratified largely as a matter of convenance, but the pacts signed with the Aragonese kings in 1334 and 1336 ushered in a chapter of stability in the relations between these two kingdoms and, *inter alia*, allowed the Muslims in Aragón the liberty to pass freely over into Muslim lands.[32] The defeat of Nasrid troops, which included soldiers drafted from distant frontier posts allied to the Marīnids at the battle of the river Salado in 1340, had more disastrous consequences for the latter who never launched a further major assault on the Peninsula, but Tarifa, which was the Marīnid target, was beyond the frontiers of the Nasrid state and therefore did not technically constitute a loss of territory. Two years later, between 1342 and 1344, Yūsuf was actively engaged in the defence of Algeciras which, although a disputed area, lay within his borders. This was yet a further episode in the perennial struggle to control access to the straits and, on this occasion ended with the loss of that city, a negotiated peace and a ten-year suspension of hostilities with Castile. After Alfonso XI's death, Yūsuf reaffirmed the peace treaty with Pedro I (r. 1350–69). The principal war zone during Yūsuf's reign was around the Straits of Gibraltar, although the frontier fortress town of Alcalá la Real on the route between Granada and Cordoba was besieged and captured by the Castilians in 1342. This allows one to reflect that the reality of life in the amorphous swathe of border territory was a relatively tranquil one, sufficient certainly to enable crops to be harvested, olives to be gathered and flocks to be tended unmolested.

Throughout Yūsuf's reign and that of his successor Muhammad V (1354–9 and 1362–91), despite constant feuding and periods of significant political unrest, Granada flourished. The city, soon after al-Ahmār's establishment there in the thirteenth century, was able to thrive, not only thanks to its natural defences which rendered it virtually impregnable except from the direction of the *vega* as mentioned, but also because of its economic prosperity and culture. Ibn al-Khatīb (1313–74), historian and poet, knowledgeable in many disciplines

including philosophy and medicine, was a *wazīr* (minister), as some of his ancestors had been, and diplomat who wrote extensively about Granada and the
Nasrids, and whose works are a major source of information. On the medical
front, he wrote a disquisition on the plague that raged in Granada in 1348–9
which accounted for the death of an unspecified number of its citizens. He
attributed its spread to contagion, and advocated total isolation as the only really
effective preventative measure, citing the example of the prisoners in the Arsenal
at Seville about whom he must have learnt, who survived 'even though the city
itself was hard hit'. His account has been described as 'a coherent, internally
consistent description of the transmission of disease by human contact'.[33] Those
living in rural areas away from the coast and the cities were least affected. The
verses that Ibn Khatīb composed as a youth in honour of Yūsuf soon became so
widely known that he was rewarded with a post at court. He later became Yūsuf's
chosen adviser on appointees to administrative positions, which enabled him to
amass a considerable personal fortune in what might be termed gratuities.

It is from Ibn al-Khatīb that we learn that the city was encircled by orchards
and royal estates which were lavishly appointed, and that beyond there were
100 gardens (*jannas* or *jannāt*), some named after their owners. Everywhere there
were vines, apple trees and irrigated land that produced a range of cereal crops
and vegetables, such that they engendered much wealth.[34] During his period 'in
post', he was employed by both Yūsuf and his successor to compose letters to the
ruler in Fez, the contents of which reveal the close ties between the two states.
After Yūsuf's sudden demise in 1354 at the hands of a deranged assassin whilst
breaking his fast in the mosque, his sixteen-year-old eldest son took his place as
ruler as Muhammad V. In 1359, he was replaced in a coup, aptly described by
Harvey as a palace revolution, that saw two rival kinsmen briefly occupy the
throne, leading to the king's exile to Fez where the Marīnid ruler who himself
had spent some time in asylum in Granada was an ally.[35] Muhammad V was
restored to power in 1362 when the second of the two who had temporarily
replaced him was murdered at the hands of Pedro I of Castile, then in Seville.
Ibn al-Khatīb had been imprisoned and only after some difficulty was able to
take refuge in Morocco as his monarch had done. He returned to his lofty position at court at the restoration of Muhammad V, after being summoned by the
Marīnid ruler to take charge of the safe transit to Granada of Muhammad's
womenfolk and children. He was well received, and enjoyed an Indian summer
of ten years in high office during which time he read out decrees on behalf of the
monarch in the Great Mosque. Then, perhaps inevitably given the unpredict-
ability of a courtier's existence at that time, fickle fate intervened once more,
and Ibn al-Khatīb fell out of favour in 1372, being obliged to return to Morocco
where, after a change of ruler, he was imprisoned and put to death.

It was during the reigns of Yūsuf and Muhammad that what is known as the
Alhambra was metamorphosed into one of the most iconic structures of Western

Europe. Its appearance nowadays bears little relation to the buildings that so amazed visitors during its heyday in the fourteenth and fifteenth centuries. An unnamed Egyptian traveller of 1337, for example, commented on the mosque, its silver lamps, the decorated plasterwork of the *mihrāb*, the ivory and ebony inlay of the pulpit. The whole area fell into such desuetude that at the beginning of the nineteenth century, it was just an agglomeration of ruins, almost entirely bereft of its former grandeur. At a time of opulence and prosperity in the fourteenth century, the buildings that had been put in place 300 years earlier were transformed to meet the needs of the rulers, so the Alhambra provided a threefold function of state rooms, living quarters and fortress. The name is the Arabic adjective *al-hamrā'*, meaning reddish or ruddy, probably on account of the colour of the stone on which it was built, and may have been attached to one of three nouns, thus: *al-qal'a* or *al-hisn*, both in the sense of fortress or citadel, or *al-madīna*, town or city. The distinguished fine art historian Oleg Grabar opted for the first of the above, thus 'the red fort', 'probably because of the red clay of the surrounding terrain', whereas Ibn al-Khatīb called it *al-madīna al-hamrā'* which would seem to be the preferred derivation, as this pertained to the entire precinct rather than to one building or one set of buildings.[36] James Dickie considers Granada at this time to have been two cities, this one which he calls royal, and 'a bourgeois city', the Madīna Gharnāta, 'lying beneath it on the plain and extending over the surrounding hills'.[37] Ibn al-Khatīb also had an alternative and quite feasible explanation for the denomination of *hamrā'*, so called, he argued, because the lights of myriad torches at night shining on the walls produced a deep red or ochre colour. The main dwellings and palace rooms were all located at the edge of the precipice whereas the fortified tower commanded the approach across the valley. The entrance from the direction of the town was through the *bāb ash-shar'ia* (strictly the Gate of Law, although known as the Gate of Justice), dated from an inscription to 1348. It may have been the place where justice was administered or executed, or it may have had a mainly ceremonial function, but it is interesting to note that it was only one of two architectural elements 'with an apparently specific religious connotation', the other being the mosque that has now disappeared.[38] Further up towards the interior on the same slope and currently standing on its own is the Puerta del Vino, possibly a translation of *bāb al-khamra* (the Wine Gate), the generally accepted explanation being that it dates from the sixteenth century when wine was deposited there to avoid taxation. An inscription reveals that it was constructed or remodelled with a new façade during the reign of Muhammad V, and its purpose is feasibly interpreted as having been to provide 'a decorative opening in the wall dividing civilian and military areas'.[39]

As well as a multitude of dwellings with specific functions, there were once six palaces on the plateau all organised around a rectangular courtyard where noble families had their households, but alterations and restoration on a massive scale have had the effect of obliterating the original layout.[40] The palace nearest to the *alcazaba*, though separated from it by an open space, is the Comares Palace (*dār qumārish*), possibly so called after the fortressed town of Comares near Málaga.[41] It was used as living quarters and for ceremonial purposes, and its patio, known since the nineteenth century as the Patio de los Arrayanes (Court of the Myrtles) dates to the time of Yūsuf I. In the tower is to be found the Sala de los Embajadores (the Room of the Ambassadors), the largest in the precinct, used as a reception room where the ruler formally welcomed visitors. Between the Patio and the throne room was the antechamber known as the Sala de la Barca, possibly from the Arabic *baraka* (blessing or benediction), whose ceiling was destroyed in a fire in 1890, probably used as a living room or quarters. The poems in the two alcoves to the right and left of this chamber have been identified as being by Ibn al-Khaṭīb, a rarity because the rest of his poems were erased when he fell from grace. A jug of water 'almost certainly for physical as well as for spiritual refreshment',[42] stood in niches on either side. Ibn al-Khaṭīb referred to it as resembling 'a man at prayer when he is praying fervently in the *qibla* of the *miḥrāb*', providing a striking visual image of a man with his hands together at prayer in the sacred place in the direction of Mecca.[43]

The Palace of the Lions, which is now artificially connected to the Comares Palace, was originally entirely separate from it, there being no access between the two.[44] Construction may have begun in Muhammad V's reign to meet his less formal requirements and it is surmised that the monarch used this for leisure and relaxation. Because of the economic prosperity of the state, Muhammad was able to lavish every expense on its construction. For example, the summer season chamber of the Hall of the Two Sisters, dating to 1362, is renowned for its spectacular honeycombed ceiling known as the *muqarnas*, the nearest equivalent in English being a cornice, or ornamental moulding, both words having their possible mutual origin in the Latin word *coronis*.[45] This form of decoration, which was also used in the arches of the colonnade, had been a feature of some Islamic buildings since the eleventh century, but in the dome of the Hall of the Two Sisters it reached its apogee, incorporating the use of 5,000 prisms. Just as occurs in the stained-glass windows of some Christian churches, the Cathedral of León for example, the visual effect of the *muqarnas* alters according to the time of day. In essence, it was a technique for embellishing a vaulted space in the same way that the squinch was used to cover the rigid angles of a corner, as in the Umayyad palace of al-Ukhaydir in Iraq, and elsewhere. The orders of Muhammad V to his architects and builders were surely to design and construct a sublime hall excelling all others in splendour, an enduring affirmation of his supremacy.

Many of the rooms are adorned with the poetry of Ibn Zamraq (1333–c. 1393), court poet and later chief minister superseding Ibn Khatīb when the latter fell from favour. Although Ibn Zamraq was instrumental in Ibn al-Khaṭīb's downfall, the latter had earlier described him as the standard bearer (al-fāris) of poetry, then of prose, a source of gentleness.[46] His verses, which are inscribed and preserved for immortality in the Courtyard of the Myrtles, the Hall of the Two Sisters and elsewhere, constitute a paean of praise to the beauty of the building as well as to his patron Muhammad V. His ode around the walls of the Hall of the Two Sisters describing the palace is an example of the 'use of poetry to embellish architecture'.[47] The sense of sight is wholly satisfied, and one may note the plethora of celestial references that interlace with the decoration of the interior. 'The stars would have a place in the cupola such is the sparkling effect of its ornamentation and even the moon draws near to share in its radiance'.[48] This hyperbolic language, redolent of the poetry of the Caliphate in its heyday, serves to enhance the visible impression of opulence. This poetry was far from simply being confined to remote inaccessible inscriptions; the verses would have been recited or possibly sung in front of the ruler. Apparently on one occasion, in 1366, Muhammad V advised his poets to use less exaggeration in praise of him personally, aware that such turns of phrase were more appropriately associated with the Prophet Muhammad.[49] The original tiling (azulejos) in the Hall of the Two Sisters which remains intact demonstrates an extraordinary sophistication in geometric design.[50] This was noted in the nineteenth century by Owen Jones, who observed that

> their [the Muslims'] fondness for geometrical forms is evidenced by the great use they made of mosaics, in which their imagination had full play. However complicated the patterns may appear, they are all very simple when the principle of setting them out is once understood. They all arise from the intersection of equidistant lines round fixed centres.[51]

Other chambers leading off the Courtyard of the Lions display features equally worthy of note, but the purpose here has been to indicate something of the scope of the achievement of Muhammad V. A century after it seemed as though al-Andalus would succumb to the might of the combined Christian kingdoms of the north of the Peninsula, he revitalised Islam, not only protecting the Nasrid state from external interference, but also, in his attention to the Madīna al-hamrā', sending out a message that his Islamic state was prosperous and second to none in its magnificence.

The population of the Nasrid state in the fourteenth century is estimated at between 4 and 5 million and that of the city of Granada at 200,000. In the matter of ethnicity, credence may be given to Ibn al-Khaṭīb who listed the names of many Arab tribes as being a 'good testimony' of the authentic Arab lineage of many of the inhabitants. He may, though, be considered to have been parti pris in that he was one of the principal representatives of Muhammad's court and anxious to assert its Arab and Islamic pedigree. Whilst what Ibn al-Khaṭīb wrote may well apply to the city of Granada itself, it cannot be said to have been true of the bulk of the population who, although now Muslims in name and customs, would have been descendants of indigenous stock. One may perhaps see a similar dichotomy between urban and rural as the one that had been apparent since the start of Islamic hegemony in the Peninsula. As one might suppose, the majority of the information regarding the mores and lifestyle of the inhabitants of the Nasrid state of Granada refers to city dwellers. For example, the contemporary North African polymath Ibn Khaldūn (1333–82) opined that

> the vanquished always want to imitate the victor in his distinctive characteristics, his dress, his occupation, and all his other conditions and customs . . . At this time, this is the case in Spain [al-Andalus]. The Spaniards [Nasrid Muslims] are found to assimilate themselves to the Galician [Christian] nations in their dress, their emblems, and most of their customs and conditions. This goes so far that they even draw pictures on the walls and have them in buildings and houses. The intelligent observer will draw from this the conclusion that it is a sign of being dominated by others.[52]

There is no indication as to how these influences came to make themselves felt. In any event, one has difficulty in seeing this having any application to rural areas. Likewise, there are the curiously suggestive references assembled by Al-Abbādī quoting both Ibn Zamraq and Ibn al-Khatīb that there were bull-fights in Granada in the fourteenth century.[53] Whether or not one can concur with Ribera that there was music and singing on every street corner of every town, both Ibn Khaldūn and Ibn al-Khatīb record that singing and instrumental music were features of Andalusi life in the fourteenth century.[54]

If the ecclesiastical authorities tacitly accepted festivities with music and, according to some sources, wine, then perhaps one is entitled to look for equal latitude in the matter of religion. Such evidence as can be garnered does not point to any substantial indigenous Christian activity, but rather to a minimal presence, as one might expect following the expulsion and exodus in the time of the Almohads. Those of whom there is record were in the main in the Nasrid state for reasons of profession or trade. Muhammad V had a much valued Christian bodyguard, billeted in the Alhambra precinct, and Christian merchants plied their trade in the city. Pedro IV of Aragón sent a letter to Catalans in Granada asking them to influence Muhammad V in respect of some concessions that he was soliciting. There were also war prisoners and slaves, and an oblique reference to Christians, possibly from one or other of the latter groups having been involved in the massive building works in the Alhambra.[55] Still less is known of the Jewish communities. From isolated references, one learns of Jewish doctors and merchants, and of protection accorded by Muhammad V to a community of 300 families who were caught in the bitter dynastic dispute between his ally Pedro I of Castile (r. 1350–69) and Henry of Trastamara (r. as Henry II 1369–79), and to whom he gave refuge. Later, in 1391, many members of Jewish communities sought asylum in the Nasrid state of Granada when the pogrom erupted in Seville and spread throughout the non-Muslim territories in the Peninsula.[56] Religious antagonism appears, then, to have been absent from Muhammad V's court, and relations among the adherents of Islam, Christianity and Judaism pragmatic if not cordial. *Convivencia* is a word normally applied to a Castilian or Aragonese context, where it described an attitude of tolerance and mutual respect between the three creeds originally in the thirteenth century. In the Nasrid state during the following century, it is not applicable because there were no Christian communities as such. As in the eleventh century, alliances could be made and as easily broken between rulers, be they Muslim or Christian, irrespective of differences in religion. The fourteenth century was one in which the Christian kingdoms came to terms with the *de facto* existence of an independent neighbouring Islamic state, a vigorous, economically self-sufficient trading partner. Indeed, Pedro I was not only a friend with Muhammad V, but also a fervent admirer of the latter's architectural achievements. When Pedro chose to extend the Alcázar in Seville, his workmen, possibly from Granada, created rooms that were strongly redolent of a Nasrid palace, even to the detail of including Arabic inscriptions. In truth, it has been remarked that this is 'proof of the extent to which Peter considered Islamic style appropriate to manifest royal dignity and power'.[57]

Notes

1. Derek W. Lomax, *The Reconquest of Spain*, London: Longman, 1978, p. 150.
2. The definition is taken from R. Dozy, *Supplément aux dictionnaires arabes*, 2 vols, Beyrouth: Librairie du Liban, 1968 [1881], vol. I, p. 701, my translation.
3. E. Lévi-Provençal, *La Péninsule Ibérique au moyen-âge d'après le Kitāb ar-Rawd al-mi'tār fī habār al-aktār d'Ibn 'Abd al-Mun'im al-Himyarī*, Leiden: E. J. Brill, 1938, Arabic text pp. 21–2.
4. Two important works on the Nasrids among very many studies of individual aspects are Rachel Arié, *L'Espagne musulmane au temps des Nasrides (1232–1492)*, Paris: Éditions Boccard, 1973, and Cristobal Torres Delgado, *El antiguo reino nazarí de Granada (1232–1340)*, Granada: Ediciones Anel, 1974. This latter work has a double-sided fold-out coloured map, and 122 remarkable photographs, some in colour, of buildings, the remains of buildings and geographical locations, enabling the reader to get a real feel for the Nasrid kingdom in the thirteenth and fourteenth centuries.
5. Julio González, *Las conquistas de Fernando III en Andalucía*, Madrid: Consejo Superior de Investigaciones Científicas, Instituto de Jerónimo Zurita, 1946, pp. 106–21, with an informative map of the siege, opposite p. 114. The author does not, however, mention the role of the Nasrids in the siege.
6. The political aspects of Alfonso's reign are well covered by Joseph O'Callaghan, *A History of Medieval Spain*, Ithaca, NY and London: Cornell University Press, 1975, pp. 358–81.
7. *Sabio* translates as wise or learned. 'Learned' would seem to be preferable as it more closely corresponds to what is known of his life and character. O'Callaghan, *History of Medieval Spain*, forbears from making a decision, calling him 'the Wise or the Learned' (p. 359) but on this point one cannot sit on the hedge. Alfonso X was the learned king.

8. Following the partial itinerary given by José A. Sánchez Pérez, in his *Nota preliminar* to Alfonso el Sabio, *Libro de las cruzes*, edited by Lloyd A. Kasten and Lawrence B. Kiddle, Madrid: Consejo Superior de Investigaciones Científicas, 1961, at p. viii.

9. The quotations are from E. S. Procter, 'The scientific works of the court of Alfonso X of Castille: the King and his collaborators', *Modern Language Review*, XL (1945), 12–29, at 13. This author estimates that there was 'a group of some fifteen persons, including Jewish physicians, Castillian [*sic*] ecclesiastics, and Italians employed in the royal chancery, who were engaged in the work of translating, revising, compiling, and editing under the king's direction' (p. 27).

10. Juan Vernet, *La cultura hispanoárabe en Oriente y Occidente*, Barcelona: Editorial Ariel, 1978, p. 189.

11. An excellent text in modern Spanish, but without the illustrations, was provided by María Brey Mariño in Alfonso X, Rey de Castilla, *Lapidario*, Madrid: Editorial Castalia, Odres Nuevos, 1968. A chromolithographic facsimile, *Lapidario del Rey D. Alfonso X, Códice Original*, was published in Madrid: Imprenta de la Iberia, in 1881, with an appendix where the text is reproduced in modern typographic characters (76 pp.) by José Fernández Montaña.

12. Miguel Asín Palacios, *La escatología musulmana en la 'Divina Comedia'*, Madrid: Estanislao Maestre, 1919; a third edition was published in 1961, where the text is followed by *Historia y crítica de una polémica*. The first edition was translated and abridged by Harold Sunderland with the title *Islam and the Divine Comedy*, London: John Murray, 1926. The quotation is from the English version, p. xiv.

13. The work used here is *La escala de Mahoma, traducción del árabe al castellano, latín y francés, ordenada por Alfonso X el Sabio*, edited by José Muñoz Sendino, Madrid: Ministerio de Asuntos Exteriores, 1949.

14. The first folio is reproduced in Muñoz Sendino, *La escala de Mahoma*, opposite p. 251; for Muñoz Sendino's conclusion, see pp. 246–7.

15. For Brunetto Latini and his contact with Alfonso X, see Julia Bolton Holloway, 'The road through Roncesvalles: Alfonsine formation of Brunetto Latini and Dante – diplomacy and literature', in *Emperor of Culture. Alfonso the Learned of Castile and His Thirteenth-Century Renaissance*, edited by Robert I. Burns, S.J., Philadelphia, PA: University of Pennsylvania Press, 1990, pp. 109–23, 239–47, particularly pp. 122–3.

16. For a balanced appraisal of the controversy, see Philip F. Kennedy, 'The Muslim sources of Dante?', in *The Arab Influence in Medieval Europe*, edited by Dionisius A. Agius and Richard Hitchcock, Reading: Ithaca Press, 1994, pp. 63–82.

17. A brief and accessible life of Lull was provided by E. Allison Peers, *Fool of Love. The Life of Ramon Lull*, London: S. C. M. Press, 1946.

18. L. P. Harvey, *Islamic Spain 1250 to 1500*, Chicago, IL and London: University of Chicago Press, 1990. The quotations in the text are from pp. 63 and 67. This thorough and detailed study is of great value for an understanding of the period.

19. Ibid., p. 125.

20. This being the case, it would be difficult to accept such claims as 'Medieval Spaniards . . . tended to see cultural differences primarily in religious terms', Thomas F. Glick and Oriol Pi-Sunyer, 'Acculturation as an explanatory concept in Spanish history', *Comparative Studies in Literature and History*, II (1969), 136–54, at 149.

21. Otherwise known as the Banū Escallola: María Jesús Rubiera Mata, in *Andalucía Islámica*, Granada: Universidad, 1983, vols 2 and 3, pp. 85–94.

22. From the *Rawd al-qirtās*, whose probable author was Ibn Abī Zarʻ. Quotation taken from an extract translated with facing Arabic text in Charles Melville and Ahmad Ubaydli,

Christians and Moors in Spain. Volume III: Arabic Sources, Warminster: Aris & Phillips, 1992, pp. 160–5, at pp. 162–3.

23. Harvey, *Islamic Spain*, p. 160; Chapter 10 comprises a full account of the reign of Muhammad II.

24. Over 100 of these are identified on one side of the instructive map that accompanies Torres Delgado's book.

25. Ibn Abī Zar', *Rawd al-qirṭās*, translated with notes by Ambrosio Huici Miranda, 2 vols, Valencia: Anúbar, 1964, vol. II, pp. 638–9.

26. Lévi-Provençal, *La Péninsule Ibérique au moyen-âge*, p. 233.

27. For the later 'evolution of the Saladin myth', see Carole Hillenbrand, *The Crusades. Islamic Perspectives*, Edinburgh: Edinburgh University Press, 1999, pp. 592–600.

28. This is not to say that he definitely had a reading command; the Arabic text may have been read out to him. The issues are discussed in the author's 'Don Juan Manuel's knowledge of Arabic', *Modern Language Review*, 80 (1985), 594–603.

29. Harvey, *Islamic Spain*, p. 217.

30. Ahmed ibn Mohammed al-Makkari, *The History of the Mohammedan Dynasties in Spain*, translated by Pascual de Gayangos, 2 vols, London: RoutledgeCurzon, 2002, vol. II, p. 355.

31. H. A. R. Gibb, *The Travels of Ibn Battūta A. D. 1325–1354*. Translated with revisions and notes from the Arabic text. Edited by C. Defrémery and B. R. Sanguinetti, The translation was completed by C. F. Beckingham, London: Hakluyt Society, 1994, vol. IV, pp. 934–5; Ross E. Dunn, *The Adventures of Ibn Battuta. A Muslim traveller of the 14th century*, London and Sydney: Croom Helm, 1986, pp. 281–2.

32. Rachel Arié, *L'Espagne musulmane au temps des Nasrides (1232–1492)*, Paris: Éditions Boccard, 1973, p. 102.

33. William B. Ober, M. D. and Nabil Alloush, M. D., 'The plague at Granada, 1348–1349: Ibn al-Khatib and ideas of contagion', *Bulletin of the New York Academy of Medicine*, 58 (4) (1982), 418–24, at 422.

34. Leopoldo Torres Balbás, *Ciudades hispanomusulmanas*, 2 vols, [Madrid]: Instituto Hispano-Árabe de Cultura, n.d. [1972], p. 156.

35. Harvey, *Islamic Spain*, p. 209.

36. Oleg Grabar, *The Alhambra*, London: Allen Lane, 1978, p. 25. This major study may be read in conjunction with James Dickie (Yaqub Zaki), 'The Alhambra: Some reflections prompted by a recent study by Oleg Grabar', in *Festschrift for Ihsān 'Abbās on his sixtieth birthday*, edited by Wadād al-Qāḍī, Beirut: American University of Beirut, 1981, pp. 127–49. See also Michael Jacobs, *Alhambra*, London: Frances Lincoln Limited, 2000, with dazzling photographs and incisive text; Marianne Barrucand and Achim Bednorz in *Moorish Architecture*, Cologne: Rolf Taschen, 1992, use the term 'palace city', pp. 183–211. This last volume has a useful glossary of architectural terms, pp. 228–30.

37. James Dickie, 'Granada: A case study of Arab urbanism in Muslim Spain', in *The Legacy of Muslim Spain*, edited by Salma Khadra Jayyusi, Leiden: E. J. Brill, 1992, pp. 88–111, at p. 88.

38. Grabar, *The Alhambra*, pp. 132–3.

39. Dickie, 'The Alhambra', p. 129.

40. 'Noble' is preferred to 'royal', as it is less restrictive and more representative of the inhabitants. Jerrilynn Dodds, 'The arts of al-Andalus', in *The Legacy of Muslim Spain*, edited by Jayyusi, pp. 599–620, claims that there were 'as many as seven palaces' (p. 616), without going into the detail that Dickie does in identifying six, 'The Alhambra', pp.128–31.

41. Jacobs, *Alhambra*, p. 90, mentions that Francisco Bermúdez de Pedraza derived the name from 'the African town of Qumaris, from which, he claimed, the principal craftsmen

employed by Yusuf I came'. Bermúdez (1585–1655), a native of Granada and a historian, relied on the work of the noted scholar of Islamic Spain and chronicler of the Moriscos, Luis del Mármol Carvajal (1520–1600), a much respected source.

42. Dickie, 'The Alhambra', p. 138.
43. María J. Rubiera Mata, 'De nuevo sobre los poemas epígrafos de la Alhambra', *Al-Andalus*, XLI (1977), 207–11, at 211.
44. As Dickie has pointed out, it was the former director of the Alhambra, Jesús Bermúdez, who 'grasped' that the Court of the Myrtles and the Court of the Lions 'are not two court-yards of the same palace but two different palaces constituting discrete entities not linked to each other in any way whatever', 'The Alhambra', p. 132. The lyrical description of these two palaces and their adjoining chambers with their inscriptions in Richard Ford's *Hand-Book for Travellers to Spain*, first published in 1845 and many times republished, is worth reading.
45. The history and application of the *muqarnas* is excellently discussed by Grabar, *The Alhambra*, pp. 175–82.
46. Ibn al-Jaṭīb, *Historia de los reyes de la Alhambra*, translated by José Ma. Casciaro Ramírez, Granada: Universidad de Granada, 1998, p. 148.
47. Dickie, 'The Alhambra', p. 141.
48. Ibid., p. 141.
49. Ahmad Mujtār al-Abbādī, *El reino de Granada en la época de Muhammad V*, Madrid: Instituto de Estudios Islámicos, 1973, p. 159.
50. Jerrilynn D. Dodds, *Al-Andalus. Las artes islámicas en España*, Madrid: Ediciones El Viso, 1992, p. 144.
51. Owen Jones, *The Grammar of Ornament*, London: Day and Son, 1856, p. 74. Jones, an archi-tect, had studied the interior of the Alhambra on site in 1834 with Jules Goury. When the latter died of cholera, he returned in 1837, later to produce his magnificent work, *Plans, Elevations, Sections, and Details of the Alhambra*, London: Vizitelly Brothers, 1843, 1846, which enterprise left him bankrupt. For a detailed analysis of the patterns, see also Issam El-Said & Ayşe Parman, *Geometric Concepts in Islamic Art*, London: World of Islam Festival Publishing Company Ltd., 1976.
52. Ibn Khaldūn, *The Muqaddimah. An Introduction to History*, translated from the Arabic by Franz Rosenthal; abridged and edited by N. J. Dawood, London: Routledge and Kegan Paul, 1978 [first edition in this form 1967], p. 116.
53. Al-Abbādī, *El reino de Granada*, p. 150.
54. Julián Ribera, *La música de las Cantigas. Estudio de su origen y naturaleza*, Madrid: Tipografía de la Revista de Archivos, 1922, p. 61.
55. Al-Abbādī, *El reino de Granada*, pp. 160–2.
56. For a brief informed appraisal, see Joseph O'Callaghan, *A History of Medieval Spain*, Ithaca, NY and London: Cornell University Press, 1975, pp. 536–8.
57. Jerrilynn D. Dodds, 'Mudejar tradition and the synagogues of medieval Spain: Cultural identity and cultural hegemony', in *Convivencia. Jews, Muslims, and Christians in Medieval Spain*, edited by Vivian B. Mann, Thomas F. Glick and Jerrilynn D. Dodds, New York: George Brazilier, 1992, p. 126.

Plate 1 The bay at Almuñécar where Abd ar-Rahmān I landed in 755 AD.

Plate 2 The interior of the Mosque in Cordoba. Nineteenth-century chromolithograph showing the *miḥrāb*, the variety of arches and the different shades of marble.

Plate 3a The ivory pyxis made for al-Mughīra in 968, in the Musée du Louvre.

Plate 3b San Miguel de Escalada before restoration. Early twentieth-century photograph.

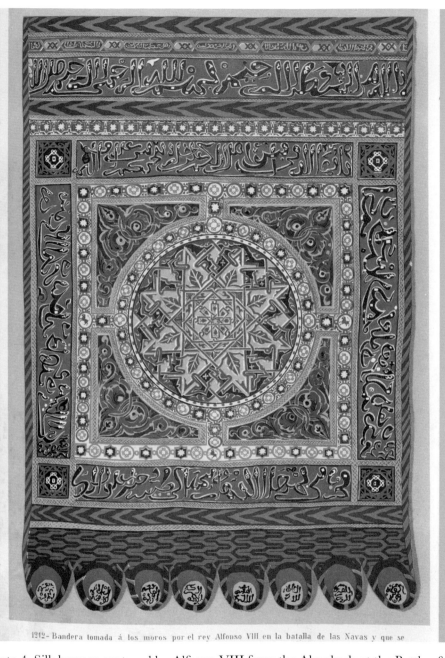

1212- Bandera tomada á los moros por el rey Alfonso VIII en la batalla de las Navas y que se

Plate 4 Silk banner captured by Alfonso VIII from the Almohads at the Battle of Las Navas de Tolosa. Nineteenth-century chromolithograph. Restored and in the Monastery of Santa María la Real de Huelgas, Burgos.

Plate 5 The Giralda at Seville.

Plate 6 The Alhambra, Granada, northern façade of the Patio de Comares.

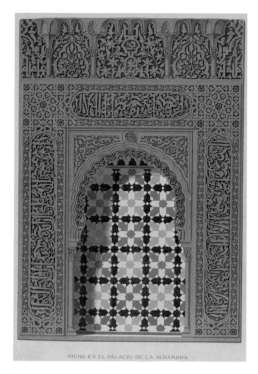

NICHO EN EL PALACIO DE LA ALHAMBRA

Plate 7a Nineteenth-century chromolithograph of niche in the Alhambra showing elaborate tiling and calligraphy.

ARMAS PERTENECIENTES Á BOABDIL, ÚLTIMO REY MORO DE GRANADA

Plate 7b Collage showing fifteenth-century Nasrid armour. The upper of the two swords and the dagger are said to have been taken from Boabdil in 1483 and to have remained in the possession of the same Spanish family until the beginning of the twentieth century. The sword is in the Museo del Ejército, Madrid; the dagger in the Real Armería, Palacio Real, Madrid.

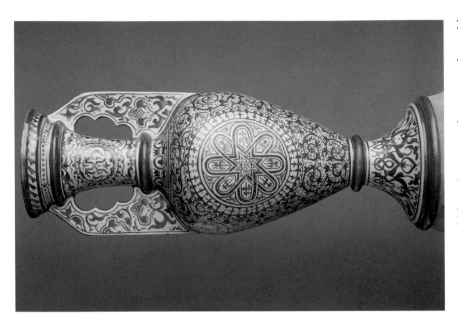

Plates 8a and 8b Two Hispano-Moresque vases, probably nineteenth century, in the style of fifteenth-century lustreware but with a darker terracotta colour, brighter blue, lacking translucence.

CHAPTER 7

The fifteenth century – the final phase of Muslim rule in al-Andalus

The transformation of the buoyant Nasrid state of the fourteenth century to a corrupt and ineffective one within 100 years may be considered on various levels. It is customary to point to a downturn in the economy as a reason for the decline of Nasrid Granada in the fifteenth century, yet the evidence is far from conclusive. In the matter of figs, for example, one of the mainstays of the economy, these went on being exported to Castile and European states including Britain throughout the century. As Seville was the principal southern peninsular port, there probably existed a steady trade in a number of products such as olive oil and spices from Granada westwards. Where a difference was noted was in the silk trade. This had been a commercial milch cow, with Granadan silks being prized in both the north and east, but in the fifteenth century 'Andalusi silk no longer enjoyed the prestige and economic dominance, either in Europe or in the Mediterranean, that it had once commanded'.[1] This was in part due to the fact that silk was now being produced in other parts of the Iberian Peninsula and in Sicily, with an increased market in the fifteenth century, and partly because there was no longer a demand for Granadan silks. In the Muslim East, for example, merchants could obtain their silks from the Silk Road from China.[2] The rise in demand for Castilian wool was also a factor. Within the Nasrid state itself, Málaga and Almería were the two main ports, with the former assuming greater prominence, but trade with Barcelona, which had been booming, slackened. The Genoese continued to use Málaga, as is testified by the fact that they had established a special walled compound for their citizens within the city although no further details are forthcoming.[3] Increasing frontier raids coupled with the destruction of olive groves and mulberry trees essential for the life of the silkworm also adversely affected the economy of the region. Similarly detrimental to the economy would have been the tribute of 20,000 gold doblas paid by the Nasrids to the Castilians annually from 1430, although it is not known how long this lasted.[4] Certainly a policy of squeezing the Nasrid economy could only serve to further undermine its constitution.

Ever more frequent instances of internecine conflict in the fifteenth century undermined the stability of the political structure of the Nasrid state. A family that achieved prominence and later notoriety was the Banū Sarrāj, known in Spanish as the Abencerrajes, from Guadix, who were able to secure the throne for Sa'd (r. 1453–64), for example. They were at the forefront of intrigue, and when on the orders of Sa'd, who for reasons that are unclear 'turned so violently against his erstwhile backers',[5] many of their leaders were assassinated en bloc in 1462, their renown in history was assured. Those that survived fled to Málaga. A member of the family was the protagonist of a short novel of the sixteenth century and shown to possess the same chivalric ideals as his Christian adversary, and the Abencerrajes later captured the imagination of many European writers particularly in the Romantic era.[6] That the final conquest was so long delayed has been attributed to disunity among the Castilian and Aragonese routinely at loggerheads throughout the century. This was certainly a factor, but it did not prevent individual forays into Nasrid territory. Although the inland frontier became more permeable, it was the seizure of Gibraltar described as 'the greatest bulwark of Islam in al-Andalus' in 1464, during the reign of Enrique IV of Castile (1454–74) that constituted a hammer blow.[7] Enrique had penetrated as far as Málaga in 1456, venturing across the sierra toward Granada when internal feuding within his own kingdom forced him to return north. The capture of Gibraltar at the hands of individual Castilian noblemen not acting in concert has memorably been described by Harvey as 'black farce, for the garrison appears to have been more anxious to give in than were the besiegers to accept surrender'.[8] 'Abd al-Basīt alludes to the dissension among the Muslims of al-Andalus: they were distracted 'from defending Muslim strongholds by the disorders in their ranks'. As he was a contemporary writing in Tlemcen in present-day Algeria, and therefore *au fait* with events in the Peninsula, his account may be seen as a verification of the perception of a Nasrid state riven by discord. From the same author, we learn that there were also truces with the Castilians which afforded some respite for the rural population.

It was becoming apparent that rural communities were suffering as a consequence of what was in effect the scorched earth policy of the Castilians. Their lands were constantly being ravaged and their livelihood affected. In addition, the days had long gone when assistance of any kind was at hand from the Maghrib. The fact that a mission was sent to Cairo to elicit support in 1487 is an indication of the total absence of salvation from traditional allies across the straits. The region had in the past benefited from the innovations in terms of crops and the means to till and harvest them that had been introduced from overseas. By this time, those working the land would have adopted Arabic names and probably have spoken Arabic, except perhaps in the remoter sierras. Yet their allegiance to the rulers in Granada would have been sorely tested as the century progressed. There is no indication that the common tie of Islam united them nor that Islam as a religion was in any way relevant to their survival. If they harboured resentment, it was against those at the head of a stuttering regime in Granada who, as they saw it, were responsible for the deterioration in their standard of living, modest as it may well have been.

The anomaly of an independent state in the south-east corner of the Iberian

Peninsula was rectified by an external turn of events. Much has been written about who was the motivating force when in 1469 Isabella (1451–1504), the heir to the Castilian throne, married Fernando (1452–1516), the heir to the Aragonese kingdom, but the outcome was that both partners succeeded to their respective realms. Isabella inherited Castile when her father died in 1474 but was immediately plunged into a war of succession, and in 1479, Fernando succeeded to the Aragonese throne on Juan II's death. Thenceforward they reigned together as monarchs of Castile and Aragón from 1479 to 1504, thus definitively uniting the two most powerful states in the Peninsula. With this union, no amount of diplomatic subterfuge on the part of the Nasrids could deflect them from their ultimate objective. In the 1470s, the preoccupation of the Catholic kings was to secure the throne of Castile for Isabella, so a succession of truces, in 1475, 1476 and 1478, meant that there was no concerted putsch against Granada until the following decade. A number of border skirmishes, the result of individual initiatives in the 1470s, paved the way for a full-scale attack in the early spring of 1482 on the small clifftop town of Alhama midway between Málaga and Granada on the direct route. It lay south of the broad sweep of land governing the entrance into Granada itself and was perhaps chosen for the vital stores of provisions that it held for the city. It was a bold venture full of danger for the Castilians so there had to have been a strategic purpose. The attack on Alhama may have been conceived as an essential preliminary stage to the occupation of Loja which did command access to the Vega, in other words, as Harvey suggests, with the intention of maintaining a permanent base in the town.[9] The spirited rescue mission which led to a protracted siege of the Castilian victors led by the ruler of Granada himself, although initially full of promise, was ultimately of no avail. There was, however, success for the Nasrids in the defence of Loja where Fernando himself, fruitlessly on this occasion, sought to overwhelm the city but was forced to retreat to Cordoba.

The relentless pressure exerted by the Castilians in the decade of the 1480s, coupled with serious rifts among the leadership of the Nasrids, ensured that the eventual outcome was not in doubt. Nevertheless, it was by no means a rollercoaster of a ride, as individual towns were well fortified, and it seems that the Muslims were able to contain if not repel the invading forces on occasions. In 1482, Muhammad XII, known to history and legend as Boabdil (Abū 'Abd Allāh), with the aid of the Abencerrajes had assumed control over a divided state. He even needed to lead an assault against the Alhambra in order to claim it from a rival faction, but he himself was captured by Castilians when he sought to repossess Lucena. He was released later by Fernando, perhaps at the instigation of Isabella, more a politically expedient than a magnanimous gesture in the light of later dealings between the three monarchs. The campaigns year on year led by Fernando gradually chipped away at Nasrid territory, with Muhammad being distracted by internal conspiracies. Ronda surrendered in

1485 despite the presence of African reinforcements when the besieging forces bombarded the walls with cannonballs and cut off the water supply,[10] and the crucial seaport of Málaga in 1487, after a crippling siege and, according to the chronicles, brave defiance on the part of the inhabitants, thus triggering the surrender of nearby small townships.[11] It is inferred that Muhammad's failure to intervene in this three-month siege suggests the existence of a secret pact between him and the Catholic kings. One of the chroniclers further mentions that Muhammad ordered that a relief detachment led by his rival en route for Málaga be intercepted and defeated, thus greatly pleasing Fernando and Isabella and earning unspecified rewards.[12] The terms that were agreed after the surrender of the major cities of Almería and Guadix, one on the coast, the other inland, in December 1489 read more like deals between elite equals. Well-to-do and influential Muslims signed up to vassalage but on favourable conditions, including tax exemption. Citizens of rank and file had their houses repossessed and had to move out of the city with what they could take with them. According to an Arabic source, all the inhabitants accepted *mudéjar* status, similar to their co-religionaries in other parts of Aragón and Castile. This runs counter to the statement by one historian, following a contemporary chronicler, that most *malagueños* 'became and remained slaves', being distributed amongst Christian nobles and churchmen, 100 of them even being dispatched to Pope Innocent VIII (Pope 1484–92).[13] If the population of the city was around 25,000 at this time, then the enslavement of around a tenth of the population may be possible to accept, although there is a discrepancy with the treatment of the vanquished at Granada two years later. After Almería's defeat, the concession of a free passage lasting a year was granted to those who wished to pass across to North Africa either with their belongings or with the proceeds from their sale. Whether this was a popular option at that time is not recorded, but it would have been a last resort. In a telling detail, the same source records that al-Zaghal, the *amīr* who had conceded defeat in Guadix, a bitter and intransigent adversary of his nephew Muhammad XII, was granted the equivalent of seigneury over territory in the Alpujarras, a mountainous region stretching between the Sierra Nevada and the coastline. However, within a few months he sold these 'villages and districts to the ruler of Castile' with a view to taking revenge on Muhammad, wishing to 'cut Granada off, so as to destroy it in the way that the rest of the country had been destroyed'. He subsequently moved with his suite across to North Africa.[14]

It was a war of attrition with only one final result. From 1490, the city of Granada was isolated, although Muhammad did endeavour to forge a supply line to the coast and was successful in periodic forays. Crucially, though, the Castilians now occupied the *vega*, with Fernando commanding the siege, thus controlling food supplies to the city, with the inevitable onset of famine for its inhabitants. In 1491, at Isabella's instance, a whole new town was constructed by the besiegers and given the name Santa Fe, preparatory to the takeover of Granada. The royal monarchs set up their headquarters there. When the divergent accounts of contemporary chroniclers, historians and eyewitnesses are evaluated, they affirm the existence of two agreements. First, Muhammad met with Fernando in August in secret and agreed to hand over the city. This may be interpreted as having been a means to safeguard his people from further hardship, made clandestinely because of the opposition from hardline factions within the city. Other possibilities are that it was a final act of betrayal, as he had been in league with the Catholic kings for a number of years, or that it was a simple instance of political realism as the writing by this time was on the wall.[15] The second was a lengthier public document setting out the terms of surrender of the fortified city, known as the Capitulations, signed on 25 November 1491, and in Prescott's terms 'ratified by respective monarchs'.[16] In effect, then, the end of the Nasrid kingdom occurred in 1491 although the Catholic kings did not make their official entry into Granada until 2 January 1492, by which date all had been signed and sealed.[17]

The conditions, which are known in both Castilian and Arabic versions although they do not wholly coincide, were favourable to the vanquished. Both documents were drawn up and signed by Hernando de Zafra (c. 1444–1508), the kings' secretary and a pivotal figure in the administration. According to al-Maqqarī, there were sixty-seven clauses in the Capitulations. Among these were the following stipulations: that great and small should be granted 'safety of person'; that Muslims could remain in their own properties both in the city and outside it; that the laws of Islam should continue to apply to them and that 'no-one should judge them except by these laws'; that mosques should be preserved and that the muezzin could continue to be proclaimed; daily prayers should not be prohibited; that Muslims should carry on having jurisdiction over Muslims, which is to say that that the Muslim community would be governed by Muslims; that Muslims should not have to wear any distinctive clothing; that there should not be any forced deportation, although those who wished to leave should not be prevented from doing so.[18] These and similar decrees legislated for the continuation of Islam in Granada. One could argue that the inhabitants of the city were being accorded a status similar to that of *mudéjares* in other of parts of Castile and Aragón. These tolerant conditions seem to be at odds with the severe measures against the Jewish communities. By the 1490s, there were two main categories, the *conversos*, those who had converted to Christianity, and those who continued, though under restrictive circumstances, to practise Judaism. In July 1492, a decree was issued to the effect that the latter be expelled, thus provoking a continent-wide diaspora. This would seem to indicate that religion was not a factor in the advantageous terms that were granted to the Muslims of Granada. In 1491, when the Capitulations were drawn up, they were an enemy that had been vanquished and and which did not pose a religious threat.

Fernando may have reasoned that the offer of safe-conduct passage to North Africa would encourage an exodus, but it seems more probable that he wished to restore the region to its former prosperity. Much devastation had been caused during the war leading up to the conquest of Granada. The rural population in particular had had their livelihood reduced to tatters, yet they were the people who had the expertise to make the land productive. Fernando therefore took pragmatic measures to ensure that those who had this special knowledge were not impeded from putting it into practice. It was essential that what had been the Nasrid state should pull its weight economically; the way to kick-start the economy was to utilise the inhabitants and not to drive them away. The war had been inordinately costly, even though it had, in part, been funded by the Bulls of Crusade conceded by Popes Sixtus IV (Pope 1471–84) and Innocent VIII to the Catholic kings. One of 1482 recognised that the resources at the disposal of the Catholic kings were 'not sufficient to recover the kingdom of Granada', and it was therefore necessary to 'exhort all men' from both within Spain and abroad to assist the monarchs 'with their wealth and persons according to their various abilities'.[19] There were regular renewals of the Bull of Crusade, the final one being on 1 October 1491, but even allowing for the large sums amassed and the efforts made by the Popes to retain one-third of the revenues, the expenses of the war of Granada left the coffers if not empty then requiring urgent and practical measures for their recovery. When the victory was ultimately secured, Fernando wrote to Pope Innocent that 'in your time and with your help, one has achieved the result which past Pontiffs, your predecessors, so wished and provided assistance for, to the praise of our Lord God and to the exaltation of your Apostolic See'.[20] He was recognising papal support and putting his enormous feat in the context of a triumph for Christianity over 'the enemies of our Holy Faith'. This diplomatic language was de rigueur, but in Granada itself what was required were swift solutions such that the practicalities of the situation 'on the ground' demanded.

It seems as though the Catholic kings were wary of the populace in Granada once they had occupied the Alhambra and appointed as governor the Conde de Tendilla (1440–1515), an elder statesman, known admirer of Islamic culture and employer of Muslims on his vast estates in the region. Al-Maqqarī records that Fernando ordered the strengthening of its fortifications, and went back and forth from his base at Santa Fe daily 'fearing, no doubt, some treachery on the part of the inhabitants',[21] providing another reason why the terms of the treaty should have been conciliatory. Muhammad XII had been granted a substantial sum of money together with the ownership of lands in the Alpujarras centred on the small township of Laujar de Andarax from which the Castilian troops had been withdrawn.[22] The circumstances of his departure the following year for North Africa and death in exile in Fez are uncertain, but he played no further role in Granadan politics. Within the city, there was political continuity with named Muslims including four *faqih*s, three *kātib*s and two *qādī*s forming part of the first *ayuntamiento* (town council). There was an initial ingress of some Castilian settlers, but one must also bear in mind that the Capitulations did not legislate for an integrated community. Within a year, Muslims were anxious about their status and, as the decade progressed, grew increasingly aware that their situation was becoming more hazardous. An inkling of this tension was apparent to Hieronymus Münzer (1447?–1508), a German scholar who travelled extensively through the Iberian Peninsula in 1494–5 and who provides a meticulous record of Granada from a Christian perspective.[23] He mentions that the Albaicín was separated from the Alhambra, which he calls a city by a wall, and contained 14,000 houses (in the city as a whole there were 100,000), and describes a Friday gathering at the Great Mosque of 2,000 or 3,000 men.[24] At the entrance to the Mosque were many beggars, Muslims who had been held captive by the Christians and were now free. On the whole, though, Münzer gives a detailed account of a prosperous Muslim city gradually being reformed by Fernando. A tenth of the revenue from the entire kingdom went into the building of churches in the city, whilst at the same time the practice of Islam continued unmolested.

Zafra was not the chief magistrate in Granada, but was what one might call its chief administrator, and he favoured a policy of conversion. In particular, he saw the Muslim elite as a threat, and may have been instrumental in the settlement of Muhammad XII with whom he had often had personal dealings, together with his retinue, on lands in the Alpujarras. In surviving documents, one can see that he encouraged Muslims to sell all their belongings and go into voluntary exile.[25] Possibly around 8,000 left in 1493, but Zafra also expressed anxiety at the number remaining. On the other hand, Hernando de Talavera (1428–1507), formerly Bishop of Ávila in Castile, confessor to the catholic kings and appointed first Archbishop of Granada, was sympathetic and sought to promote conversion through persuasion rather than by coercion. This was perhaps the case because he himself may have had Jewish ancestry, but certainly his stance vis-à-vis the population of Muslims in the former Nasrid state left, as it were, high and dry after their defeat at the hands of the Catholic kings, was more that of the dove than the hawk. He learnt Arabic himself, had a number of clerics trained in the language and ordered an Arabic grammar to be composed as an aid to peaceful proselytisation. Letters from the Catholic kings to Talavera in 1495 reveal that he was the person who wielded authority over Muslims and was *au fait* with their concerns. In one, for example, dated 11 March 1495, the kings address Talavera's concern at the number of Muslims coming down from the Alpujarras into the city of Granada, stating that he, Talavera, should tell the governor of the region to put a halt to this migration. Income from the *mudéjares* in Granada continued to be a preoccupation and, in 1496, the Catholic kings wrote to the Archbishop complaining that many Muslims, male and female, had passed across to North Africa without paying the requisite dues, both on their persons and on their possessions. There was no longer a free passage, and ships' captains had to ensure that the requisite taxes had been paid.[26] They entrusted the Archbishop with the task of appointing an overseer to put a stop to these unlawful departures. Nevertheless, whilst Tendilla remained governor in the Alhambra and Talavera Archbishop, the status quo could be maintained.

The influx of Christian immigrants into Granada, both the city and the region, in greater and greater numbers had an inevitable consequence. In 1498, Granada was divided into two halves: the Albaicín became a Muslim quarter, and the city proper the reserve of the new settlers. In the same year, some orders were made more restrictive. Muslim bath-houses could no longer be used, and Christian women were forbidden from availing themselves of the services of Muslim midwives, midwifery long having been a preserve of the latter. There is an argument that by 1498, the Muslims in the city were by and large rank and file, ordinary people with crafts and professions, the nobility by this time having all departed, leaving respected citizens, sheikhs, in charge of their well-being. They were still subservient and disinclined, it seems, to exacerbate the existing state of affairs. They were aware that the Catholic kings were introducing measures to encourage conversion to Christianity by inducements such as allowing those who did convert the right to receive their share of any inheritance under Islamic law. Their resistance continued to be passive and they were resigned to living under the restrictions imposed upon them.

However, the intervention of the Franciscan Archbishop of Toledo and Isabella's confessor, Francisco Jiménez de Cisneros (1436–1517) in Granada in the autumn of 1499 had far-reaching and irrevocable consequences, and effectively marked the end of the existence of Muslims in Granada. One might say that when he entered the fray, the cauldron was simmering; he caused it to boil over. His drive for the conversion of non-Christians was unremitting and emanated from a deep personal conviction. It is instructive to note that in 1497, he had visited El Cid's tomb in Burgos and, in a symbolic act, kissed his bones. Evidently he believed that El Cid represented the Christian spirit of crusade against the Muslims, even though the reality of the situation in the eleventh century had been somewhat different. He instigated a policy of offering greater incentives, but when this did not result in conversions at the pace he wanted, he started to unravel the terms of the Capitulations, in effect dismantling the treaty. All mosques were to be consecrated as churches, with bells replacing the muezzin. He then implemented the strategy of forced conversion through aspersion, the scattering of holy water over assembled crowds. The touchpaper had been lit and when an official *alguacil* dispatched to the Albaicín was overpowered and killed, leading to rioting and houses being burnt, Cisneros had the excuse he required for ridding Granada of all Muslims. This revolt was quelled thanks to the mediation of both Talavera, still trusted by the Muslim community, and Tendilla, who left his family (wife and sons) in the Albaicín as a gesture of his faith in their goodwill. The latter then negotiated the surrender of the rebels' weapons, and secured an amnesty for those who had fled from the city.[27]

Talavera had not been replaced as Archbishop of Granada, and was described by Cisneros in a letter, written from Granada by the latter and dated 4 January 1500, to his fellow clerics in Toledo as 'a saintly person' who 'shares our firm belief' that 'no-one who is not a Christian should [be permitted to] stay in the city'. On the 16th of the same month, Cisneros was able to write that 'there is now no-one in the city or round about, *al derredor*, who was not Christian; 50,000 souls [out of a population of 200,000] have been converted; all the mosques are now churches where masses are sung'.[28] In the first six months of 1500, there was unrest in the Alpujarras with some fortresses being captured by Muslims, presumably aware of what had occurred in Granada. There were local uprisings in Almería and Ronda, and when these were finally quashed, the Catholic kings issued a royal decree on 12 February 1502 to the effect that all *mudéjares* in the kingdom, that is to say not only in what was formerly the Nasrid state of Granada but also elsewhere, should be baptised or expelled. Henceforward, there were officially no Muslims in Spain, only Moriscos, the word given to those who converted from Islam. Given the choice, most *mudéjares* chose to convert, as they and their forebears before them had lived in the Peninsula for hundreds of years. However, conversion through aspersion, whereby holy water was sprinkled over the assembled crowd by a priest from a balcony in a village or township, would scarcely have been a significant event. One suspects that many people, particularly in the more remote areas, unimpressed by this external show of Christianity, continued to practise Islam. As the century progressed, the Holy Inquisition sought to ensure that conversion to Christianity brought with it a sincere and genuine change of religious allegiance. The Catholic kings, by repealing the Capitulations, had in effect created a community of crypto-Muslims who were to be a thorn in the side of their successors Charles V and Philip II. A decree was eventually issued ordering the expulsion of all Moriscos in 1609.

Politically, then, 'Islamic Spain' ceased to exist in February 1502, but Cisneros was not content with this victory. At about the same time – the date is uncertain – he ordered the *alfaquíes* to amass all Qur'āns, Arabic manuscripts and books for them then to be burnt in a public conflagration.[29] Cisneros sought to eradicate Islamic culture, although he did make an exception of 300 or so medical works which were to be delivered to the new library of the University of Alcalá which he himself had founded. According to Gómez de Castro, the sixteenth-century biographer of Cisneros, the intention was to 'totally rid their souls [those of the Muslim inhabitants of Granada] of all errors of the Muslim sect'.[30] Some medical works were spared because of the Muslims' expertise in this discipline and their affinity for it. When around 5,000 volumes had been piled up, bystanders were astonished at the quality of the volumes to be destroyed and asked to be given some as gifts. No one was granted anything, and the books were consumed by the fire. One might understand the motive behind Cisneros' insistence on the utter destruction of the religious and cultural heritage of Islam. He wanted to remove any potential obstacle in the way of former Muslims becoming true Christians, to eliminate all props, as it were. It was a desperate act calculated to be prejudicial to Islam, but it was also an act of Christian pragmatism, demonstrating publicly that the old order was to be definitively replaced by the new.

Notes

1. Olivia Remie Constable, *Trade and Traders in Muslim Spain. The Commercial Realignment of the Iberian Peninsula, 900–1500*, Cambridge: Cambridge University Press, 1994, p. 223. See in particular Chapter 8, pp. 209–39, where the author has assembled much relevant and useful data.
2. Ibid., p. 225.
3. F. Guillén Robles, *Málaga Musulmana*, Málaga: Enrique Montes Oliver, 1957 [1880], p. 338. See also *The Unconquered Knight. A Chronicle of the Deeds of Don Pero Niño by his Standard-Bearer, Gutierre Diaz de Gamez (1431–1449)*, translated and selected by Joan Evans, London: George Routledge & Sons, 1928, p. 56, where reference is made to Pero Niño's men who, in 1404, were 'entertained in the house of the Genoese'.
4. Jaime Vicens Vives, 'The economies of Catalonia and Castile', in *Spain in the Fifteenth Century 1369–1516*, edited by Roger Highfield and translated by Frances M. López-Morillas, London: Macmillan, 1972, pp. 31–57, at p. 48.
5. L. P. Harvey, *Islamic Spain 1250 to 1500*, Chicago, IL and London: University of Chicago Press, 1990, pp. 264–5.
6. Antonio Villegas, *El Abencerraje*, A collaboration of Francisco López Estrada and John Esten Keller, Chapel Hill, NC: University of North Carolina Press, 1964, with Spanish text and facing English translation.
7. 'Abd al-Basīt (1440–1514), in *Christians and Moors in Spain*, edited by Melville and Ubaydli, pp. 172–3. The translators give their reasons for preferring the date of 1464 to that of 1462, given by Arié and Harvey.
8. Harvey, *Islamic Spain*, p. 262.
9. A detailed and gripping account of this episode with shrewd analysis is provided by Harvey, *Islamic Spain*, pp. 269–74. See, in particular, p. 272.
10. Rachel Arié, *L'Espagne musulmane au temps des Nasrides (1232–1492)*, Paris: Éditions Boccard, 1973, p. 165.
11. See also Manuel Acién Almansa, *Ronda y su serranía en tiempo de los Reyes Católicos*, 3 vols, Málaga: Universidad de Málaga, 1979, vol. I, pp. 146–50.
12. Harvey, *Islamic Spain*, p. 298.
13. Peggy K. Liss, *Isabel the Queen. Life and Times*, New York and Oxford: Oxford University Press, 1992, p. 219.
14. The *Nubdha al 'asr*, 'Fragment of the epoch', in Harvey, *Islamic Spain*, pp. 304–5; Arié, *L'Espagne musulmane*, p. 175.
15. Arié, *L'Espagne musulmane*, p. 177.
16. William H. Prescott, *History of the Reign of Ferdinand and Isabella, the Catholic Monarchs of Spain*, 3 vols, London: Richard Bentley, 1838, vol. II, pp. 174–81.

17. See Ma. del Carmen Pescador del Hoyo, 'Cómo fué de verdad la toma de Granada, a la luz de un documento inédito', *Al-Andalus*, XX (1955), 283–344, with many interesting details; the present author's 'The conquest of Granada in nineteenth-century English and American historiography', in *Medieval Spain. Culture, Conflict and Coexistence. Studies in Honour of Angus MacKay*, edited by Roger Collins and Anthony Goodman, Basingstoke: Palgrave Macmillan, 2002, pp. 242–65, where a comparison of ten accounts show that then as now, there was no consensus on details such as the date of the formal entry into the city. Despite some romantic overwriting, particularly by Washington Irving (1829), the accounts show a concern for scrupulous accuracy.

18. Ahmed ibn Mohammed al-Makkari, *The History of the Mohammedan Dynasties in Spain*, translated by Pascual de Gayangos, 2 vols, London: RoutledgeCurzon, 2002, vol. II, pp. 388–9. A translation of the Castilian version, with some of the clauses summarised, is provided by Harvey, *Islamic Spain*, pp. 314–21.

19. José Goñí Gaztambide, 'The Holy See and the reconquest of the kingdom of Granada (1479–1492)', in *Spain in the Fifteenth Century 1369–1516. Essays and Extracts by Historians of Spain*, edited by Roger Highfield, London: Macmillan, 1972, pp. 354–79, at pp. 357–8.

20. 'En vuestros días y con vuestra ayuda se aya alcançado el fruto que los Pontífiçes passados, vuestros anteçessores tanto dessearon y ayudaron a loor de Dios, Nuestro Señor, y enxalçamiento de vuestra Sancta See Apostólica'. Text in Miguel Ángel Ladero Quesada, *La Guerra de Granada (1482–1491)*, Granada: Diputación. Los Libros de la Estrella, 2001, p. 125, my version.

21. Al-Maqqarī, *History of the Mohammedan Dynasties*, vol. II, p. 389.

22. For a discussion of the circumstances of the 'arrangements' for Muslim noblemen, see Miguel Ángel Ladero Quesada, *Castilla y la conquista del reino de Granada*, Valladolid: Universidad, 1967, pp. 96–7; 2nd edition of the 1988 reprint, Granada: Diputación Provincial de Granada, 1993.

23. Jerónimo Münzer, *Viaje por España y Portugal (1494–1495)*, Madrid: Ediciones Polifemo, 1991, pp. 89–113.

24. Ibid., p. 135.

25. Julio Caro Baroja, *Los moriscos del reino de Granada. (Ensayo de historia social)*, Madrid: Instituto de Estudios Políticos, 1957, p. 9.

26. Miguel Ángel Ladero Quesada, *Los mudéjares de Castilla en tiempos de Isabel I*, Valladolid: Instituto 'Isabel la Católica', 1969, pp. 211–12.

27. Ibid., p. 72; Andrew C. Hess, *The Forgotten Frontier. A History of the Sixteenth-Century Ibero-African Frontier*, Chicago, IL and London: University of Chicago Press, 1978, pp. 134–6, who provides a brief, incisive account of these events; Harvey, *Islamic Spain*, pp. 329–35.

28. Ladero Quesada, *Los mudéjares*, pp. 235–6: 'una santa persona'; 'que creamos firmemente que ninguno no ha de quedar que no sea christiano' (p. 235); 'no queda ya ninguno en esta cibdad que no sea christiano . . . de manera que son ya convertidas mas de cincuenta mill animas'; 'todas las mezquitas son yglesias y se dice en ellas misa' (p. 236), author's renderings into English.

29. See, for a thorough account, Daniel Eisenberg, 'Cisneros y la quema de los manuscritos granadinos', *Journal of Hispanic Philology*, 16 (1992), 107–24.

30. Alvar Gómez de Castro, *De las hazañas de Francisco Jiménez de Cisneros*, edited and translated by José Oroz Reta, Madrid: Fundación Universitaria Española, 1984, a translation of the Latin text published in 1569; the phrase adapted into English is 'extirpar radicalmente de sus almas todo el error mahometano', p. 99.

Conclusion

In the conclusion to his *History of Islamic Spain*, W. Montgomery Watt asked a number of perceptive questions. As some of them are linked in a sequence, I quote the appropriate passage:

> Yet should our appreciation of a beautiful object be affected by our lack of appreciation of the culture from which it springs? May it not, on the contrary, be the case that appreciation of a beautiful object is able to provide a key to the appreciation of the alien culture? May it not even be that the beautiful object is the measure and validation of the culture? Because of lovely buildings like the Great Mosque of Cordova and the Alhambra in Granada must not the culture of Islamic Spain be a great culture?

These questions no doubt arose when Watt reflected on the book that he had just finished writing and they merit careful consideration. The final question posed above is one that has stuck in my mind since first reading the book in 1965. It does not seem possible to me to provide an unambiguous answer to it. Buildings can be the benchmark of a culture, but the Alhambra as it stands today has been altered over the centuries and restored so extensively that it would seem imprudent to make claims of the culture from which it emerged based on its present state. Furthermore, even if one takes into account contemporary evidence of the splendour of the Alhambra, it is not representative of al-Andalus over the eight centuries of its existence. Whilst it is legitimate to venture an evaluation of a culture on the evidence of its monuments, one does so at the risk of neglecting to take into account other criteria.

The thoughts that preoccupied me when I finished writing this book were of a different nature. For example, how could one explain the fact that al-Andalus, as an Islamic state in the West, existed in the Iberian Peninsula for nearly 800 years? Perhaps this is not so surprising. Christians had no 'divine' right of possession over the territory. Furthermore, the Muslims were not an occupying power in Christian territory; they were a permanent presence in the continent of Europe. Their state was one which was governed by a different raft of beliefs, but this circumstance did not necessarily obstruct relations with other powers. The fact is simply that the Iberian Peninsula was conquered in 711 by Muslim forces because they were a stronger military force. Al-Andalus eventually became an Islamic state because the ties of the conquerors were with the East, and it acquired its distinctiveness from importations of a whole gamut of features from the East. As the Western outpost of an empire, it survived independently through having help at hand from North Africa when occasion demanded, and through economic self-sufficiency. It left its mark on the indigenous culture and way of life in a similar way that the British Empire did in India in the nineteenth century, but it passed, as all empires in history have passed. What concerned Watt was the nature of the legacy of al-Andalus, or more specifically Andalusi culture. In a telling phrase, he refers to an 'alien culture'. It will be apparent from what I have written that, as far as al-Andalus is concerned, there was no such alien culture. In retrospect, one may observe objectively that, by a number of yardsticks, the level of civilisation, for want of a better word, as manifested in al-Andalus was superior to that found elsewhere in the Iberian Peninsula and, in some periods, in the rest of Western Europe. The reason for this is just that this civilisation had a particular spurt at a particular time that saw it surge ahead in the West. This indicates that it was more advanced but it was not alien. Neither I believe was it 'different'. If the phrases 'Spain is different' and 'Africa begins at the Pyrenees', the latter reputedly of early-nineteenth-century French origin, allude to the presence of Muslims in the Peninsula, then they are neither accurate, apposite nor true.

    To state what occurred in as unadorned a fashion as is possible, the land mass known as the Iberian Peninsula was invaded by a powerful army. This action led to conquest and settlement, just as happened in the Norman invasion of Britain in 1066. Those in control were only able to exercise their authority whilst they had sufficient forces to support them. At the times when they were weak, other states in the Iberian Peninsula made incursions into their territory and became stronger. In the later centuries, both the northern powers and the southern state, al-Andalus, availed themselves of external support. When these northern powers were at last united, as transpired in the fifteenth century, they prevailed because of their superior military strength. This basic premise becomes less simplistic when one takes into consideration certain additional facets. In the first place, one has to reckon with the role of religion, specifically Christianity. The land invaded had officially been a Catholic state since 587 although Christianity was introduced far earlier, in the first century AD. The history of the Iberian Peninsula in the Middle Ages has traditionally been presented as that of two opposing creeds, yet the sources do not support this interpretation. When there were major thrusts from the north southwards or vice versa, it was when politi-cal or military weaknesses were perceived by either side. Such incursions were not motivated by religious interests, except at the time of the Crusades, as I have argued. There was no inherent hostility existing between al-Andalus and other powers in the Iberian Peninsula because of differing religious beliefs, at least for the first three and a half centuries after 711.

    Second, with regard to ethnicity, the advent of the Visigoths in the fifth century and of the limited number of Arabs who settled between the eighth and eleventh centuries had minimal impact. The Arabs were, however, the conduit for a civilisation and culture hitherto unknown in Western Europe. The lifestyle of vast sectors of the Iberian Peninsula which had been implanted during the Roman Empire underwent a radical transformation in al-Andalus over the centuries. The impact of Islamic culture, itself having absorbed Greek and Latin knowledge in the East, was far-reaching, thus providing the trigger for the European Renaissance. In the immediate aftermath of the remarkable conquests by the Castilians and Aragonese in the first half of the thirteenth century, not only were many aspects of the way of life of the vanquished imitated by the conquerors, but the achievements of the Muslims in the spheres of scholarship and architecture were enthusiastically embraced.

It seems to me then that it may be more pertinent to evaluate al-Andalus in terms of its impact on those who invaded it and eventually secured its submission, rather than by focusing on reconstructed ruins. The Alhambra might reflect the greatness of a bygone era, in the same way that Leptis Magna encapsulates the glory of Rome on the Libyan coastline, but the process of what might be called inadvertent yet predictable acculturation must carry far greater weight. When there ceased to be an independent Islamic state in the Iberian Peninsula, pressure was exerted by the Catholic Christian authorities on those who had formerly lived within al-Andalus to conform, but that was because of the changing political and religious climate at the end of the fifteenth century. If these people, the Moriscos, were perceived to be 'alien', it was not because they were not Spaniards. Rather, it was because, at that moment in time, the nation's past and present could not be reconciled. It would be a truism to say, however, that the legacy of al-Andalus, like the legacy of Rome, could ever be eradicated.

Bibliography

Arabic texts

['Abd Allāh, Zīrid ruler of Granada], *The Tibyān. Memoirs of 'Abd Allāh b. Buluggīn Last Zīrid Ruler of Granada*, Translated from the Emended Arabic Text and Provided with Introduction, Notes and Comments by Amin T. Tibi, Leiden: E. J. Brill, 1986

[Abū al-Fidā'] [Joseph-Toussaint Reinaud,] *Géographie d'Aboulféda*, translated from the Arabic by 'M. Reinaud', Paris: n.p., 1848

Ad-Dabbī, *Bughyat al-multamis fī tārīkh rijāl ahl-al-Andalus*, ed. Francisco Codera, Leiden: Brill, 1889 (Biblioteca Arabico-Hispana, vol. III)

[Akhbār Majmū'a] Emilio Lafuente Alcántara, *Ajbar Machmuâ (Colección de tradiciones) Crónica anónima del siglo XI, dada á luz por primera vez*, Madrid: Ediciones Atlas, 1984. Facsimile of the 1867 edition

[al-Himyarī] E. Lévi-Provençal, *La Péninsule ibérique au moyen-âge d'après le Kitāb ar-Rawd al-mi'tār fī habār al-aktār d'Ibn 'Abd al-Mun'im al-Himyarī*, Leiden: E. J. Brill, 1938

[al-Khushānī] Julián Ribera, *Historia de los jueces de Córdoba por Aljoxaní*, Arabic text and Spanish translation, Madrid. E. Maestre, 1914

[al-Maqqarī] Ahmed ibn Mohammed al-Makkari, *The History of the Mohammedan Dynasties in Spain*, translated by Pascual de Gayangos, 2 vols, London: RoutledgeCurzon, 2002. First published by the Royal Asiatic Society, 1840, 1843

[al-Maqqarī] *Analectes sur l'Histoire et la Littérature des Arabes d'Espagne par al-Makkari*, edited by R. Dozy, G. Dugat, L. Krehl and W. Wright, 2 vols, Amsterdam: Oriental Press, 1967, a facsimile of the Leiden edition of 1855–61

[al-Mu'tamid] María Jesús Rubiera Mata, *Al-Mu'tamid Ibn 'Abbād, Poesías. Antología bilingüe*, Madrid: Instituto Hispano-Árabe de Cultura, 1987

[al-Šaqundī], *Elogio del Islam español (risāla fī fadl al-Andalus)*, translated by Emilio García Gómez, Madrid: Estanislao Maestre, 1934

[ar-Rāzī] Don Pascual de Gayangos, *Memoria sobe la autenticidad de la Crónica denominada del Moro Rasis*, Madrid: La Real Academia de la Historia, 1850. This is a translation of Ahmad ar-Rāzī (887–?961) *Tarīkh mulūk al-Andalus*

['Īsā b. Ahmad al-Rāzī] *Anales palatinos del califa Al-Hakam II, por 'Īsā b. Ahmad al-Rāzī (360–364 H. = 971–975 J. C.)*, translated by Emilio García Gómez, Madrid: Sociedad de Estudios y Publicaciones, 1967

['Arīb b. Sa'īd] Antonio Arjona Castro, *'El libro de la generación del feto, el tratamiento de las mujeres embarazadas y de los recien nacidos' de 'Arīb Ibn Saʿīd (Tratado de Obstetricia y Pediatría hispano árabe del siglo X)*, Cordoba: Diputación Provincial, 1983

['Arīb b. Saʿīd] Juan Castilla Brazales, *La Crónica de 'Arīb sobre al-Andalus*, Granada: Impredisur, 1992

[Calendar of Cordoba] Guglielmo Libri, *Histoire des sciences mathématiques en Italie*, 4 vols, Paris: Renouard, 1838–41, volume I, pp. 469ff

[Calendar of Cordoba] Charles Pellat, *Le Calendrier de Cordoue publié par R. Dozy*, new edition with annotated French translation, Leiden: E. J. Brill, 1961

[*Crónica anónima*] *Una crónica anónima de 'Abd al-Rahmān al-Nāsir*, translation with introduction and notes by E. Lévi-Provençal and Emilio García Gómez, Madrid, Granada: Editorial Maestre, 1950

[Ibn 'Abdūn] Emilio García Gómez, E. Lévi-Provençal, *Sevilla a comienzos del siglo XII. El tratado de Ibn 'Abdūn*, Seville: El Ayuntamiento, 1981. The first edition was published in 1948

Ibn Abī Zar', *Rawd al-qirtās*, translated with notes by Ambrosio Huici Miranda, Valencia: Anúbar, 2 vols, 1964. Textos Medievales, 12–13

[Ibn Bannā'] H. P. J. Renaud, *Le Calendrier d'Ibn Bannā' de Marrakech (1256–1321 J. C.)*, Paris: Larose, 1948

[Ibn Battūta] H. A. R. Gibb, *The Travels of Ibn Battūta A. D. 1325–1354*. Translated with revisions and notes from the Arabic text. Edited by C. Defrémery and B. R. Sanguinetti, vol. IV. The translation was completed by C. F. Beckingham, London: Hakluyt Society, 1994

[Ibn Hayyān] *Al-Muqtabis: fī akhbār balad al-Andalus*, edited by Abd ar-Rahmān 'Alī Hajjī, Beirut: Dār al-Thaqāfah, 1965

Ibn Hayyān de Córdoba, *Crónica del califa 'Abdarrahmān III, an-Nāsir entre los años 912 y 942 (al-Muqtabis V)*, translation with notes by Ma. Jesús Viguera y Federico Corriente, Saragossa: Anúbar, 1981

Ibn Hayyān, *Al Muqtabis*, II-1, translated as *Crónicas de los emires Alhakam I, y 'Abdarrahmān II entre los años 796 y 847*, by Mahmūd 'Alī Makkī y Federico Corriente, Saragossa: La Aljafería, 2001

[Ibn Hazm] *El collar de la paloma. Tratado sobre el amor y los amantes de Ibn Hazm de Córdoba*, translated from the Arabic by Emilio García Gómez, Madrid: Sociedad de Estudios y Publicaciones, 2nd edition, 1967. The first editon of this version was published in 1952

[Ibn Idhārī al-Marrākushī, *Al-bayān al-Mughrib*] Felipe Maíllo Salgado, *La caída del Califato de Córdoba y los Reyes de Taifas*, Salamanca: Universidad, 1993

Ibn al-Kardabūs, *Historia de al-Andalus (Kitāb al-Iktifā')*, edited by Felipe Maíllo Salgado, Madrid: Akal, 1986

[Ibn al-Khatīb] Ibn al-Jatīb, *Historia de los reyes de la Alhambra*, translated by José Ma. Casciaro Ramírez, Granada: Universidad de Granada, 1998

Ibn Hawqal, *Configuración del mundo*, translated with notes by María José Romani Suay, Valencia: Anúbar, 1971, p. 53. Textos Medievales, 26

Ibn Khaldūn, *The Muqaddimah. An Introduction to History*, Translated from the Arabic by

Franz Rosenthal. Abridged and edited by N. J. Dawood, London: Routledge and Kegan Paul, 1978 (first edition in this form 1967)

[Ibn al-Qūtīya] David James, *Early Islamic Spain. The History of Ibn al-Qūtīya*, with translation, notes and comments, London: Routledge, 2009

[Ibn Shuhayd] *Risāla at-tawābi' wa z-zawābi'. The Treatise on Familiar Spirits and Demons by Abu Amir Ibn Shuhaid al-Ashja'i al-Andalusi*, introduction, translation and notes by James T. Monroe, Berkeley, CA: University of California Press, 1971

[Ibn Shuhayd] *El dīwān de Ibn Šuhaid al-Andalusi 382–426 H = 992–1035 C.* Edited and translated by James Dickie, Cordoba: Real Academia, 1975

[Ibn Tufayl] *Hayy Ibn Yaqzān by Ibn Tufayl*, translated from the twelfth-century Arabic by Lenn Evan Goodman, New York: Twayne, 1972

[Ibn Zaydūn] *Casidas de amor profundo y místico. Ibn Zaydun, Ibn Arabi*, translated by Vicente Cantarino, Mexico City: Editorial Porrúa, 1977

Melville, Charles and Ahmad Ubaydli, *Christians and Moors in Spain*, vol. III, Arabic sources, Warminster: Aris & Phillips, 1992

The Holy Qur-án, containing the Arabic text with English translation and commentary by Maulvi Muhammad Ali, Woking: The Islamic Review Office, 1917

The Qur'ān, translated into English by Alan Jones, [Oxford]: Gibb Memorial Trust, 2007

Velashq [Velasco] al-Qurtubī, Ishāq b., Arabic translation of the Gospels in the Archives of the Cathedral of León, MS 35

Other sources

Alfonso el Sabio, *Libro de las cruzes*, edición de Lloyd A. Kasten y Lawrence B. Kiddle, Madrid: Consejo Superior de Investigaciones Científicas, 1961

Alfonso X, Rey de Castilla, *Lapidario*, Madrid: Editorial Castalia, 'Odres Nuevos', 1968. Text in modern Spanish by María Brey Mariño

[Alfonso X el Sabio] *Lapidario del Rey D. Alfonso X, Códice Original*, Madrid: Imprenta de la Iberia, 1881. Text is reproduced in modern typographic characters by José Fernández Montaña

[*El Abencerraje*] Antonio Villegas' *El Abencerraje*, a collaboration of Francisco López Estrada and John Esten Keller, Chapel Hill, NC: University of North Carolina Press, 1964, with Spanish text and facing English translation

[Eulogius] *Obras completas de San Eulogio*, bilingual edition, Spanish translation by R. P. Agustín S. Ruiz, Cordoba: Real Academia de Córdoba, 1959

Fletcher, Richard A. and Simon Barton, eds, *The World of El Cid: Chronicles of the Reconquest*, Manchester: Manchester University Press, 2001

Gil, Ioannes, *Corpus Scriptorum Muzarabicorum*, 2 vols, Madrid: Consejo Superior de Investigaciones Científicas, 1973

[Jiménez de Rada, Rodrigo], Rodericus Ximenius de Rada, *De rebus Hispaniae*, in *Opera*, Valencia: Anúbar, 1968, Textos Medievales, 22. Facsimile of 1973 edition, with indices added by Ma. Desamparados Cabanes Pecourt

Lacarra, J. M., 'Documentos para el estudio de la reconquista y repoblación del valle del Ebro', (Primera Serie), no. 51 in *Estudios de Edad Media de la Corona d Aragón*, vol. II, Saragossa, 1946

[Muñoz Sendino, José] *La escala de Mahoma, traducción del árabe al castellano, latín y francés, ordenada por Alfonso X el Sabio*, edited by José Muñoz Sendino, Madrid: Ministerio de Asuntos Exteriores, 1949

Münzer, Jerónimo, *Viaje por España y Portugal (1494–1495)*, Madrid: Ediciones Polifemo, 1991

Paz y Meliá, A. 'Embajada del Emperador de Alemania al Califa de Córdoba, Abderrahman III', *Boletín de la Academia de Ciencias, Bellas Letras y Nobles Artes de Córdoba*, 1931. First published in 1872

[Pero Niño] *The Unconquered Knight. A Chronicle of the Deeds of Don Pero Niño by his Standard-Bearer, Gutierre Diaz de Gamez (1431–1449)*, translated and selected by Joan Evans, London: George Routledge & Sons, 1928

[*The Chronicle of 754*] in Kenneth Baxter Wolf, *Conquerors and Chroniclers of Early Medieval Spain*, translated with notes and introduction, Liverpool: Liverpool University Press, 1990.

Works in English

Abu-Haidar, J. A., *Hispano-Arabic Literature and the Early Provençal Lyrics*, Richmond: Curzon Press, 2001

Alder, Catherine, 'Arabic versions of the psalter in use in Muslim Spain', unpublished PhD dissertation, University of St Andrews, 1953

Asin, Miguel, *Islam and the Divine Comedy*, translated and abridged by Harold Sunderland, London: John Murray, 1926

Bargebuhr, Frederick P., *The Alhambra. A Cycle of Studies on the Eleventh Century in Moorish Spain*, Berlin: Walter de Gruyter, 1968

Barrucand, Marianne and Achim Bednorz, *Moorish Architecture in al-Andalus*, Cologne: Rolf Taschen, 1992

Beckwith, John, *Caskets from Cordoba*, London: HMSO, 1960

Blair, Sheila S., 'What the inscriptions tell us: Text and message on the ivories from al-Andalus', *The Journal of the David Collection*, edited by Kjeld von Folsach and Joachim Meyer, Copenhagen, 2005, vol. 2, part I, pp. 75–95

Bulliet, Richard W., *Conversion to Islam in the Medieval Period. An Essay in Quantitative History*, Cambridge, MA: Harvard University Press, 1979

Burnett, Charles, 'A group of Arabic-Latin translators working in northern Spain in the mid-12th century', *Journal of the Royal Asiatic Society* (1977), 62–108

Burnett, Charles, 'Hermann of Carinthia', in *A History of Twelfth-Century Western Philosophy*, edited by Peter Dronke, Cambridge: Cambridge University Press, 1988, pp. 386–404

Burnett, Charles, 'The translating activity in Medieval Spain', in *The Legacy of*

Muslim Spain, edited by Salma Khadra Jayyusi, Leiden: E. J. Brill, 1992, pp. 1036–58

[Bute, Marquis of] *Moorish Recipes*, collected and compiled by John, Fourth Marquis of Bute, K. T., Edinburgh: Oliver and Boyd, n.d., but between 1947 and 1956

Castro, Americo, *The Spaniards. An Introduction to their History*, translated by Willard F. King and Selma Margaretten, Berkeley, CA: University of California Press, 1971

Cavadini, John C., *The Last Christology of the West. Adoptionism in Spain and Gaul, 785–82*, Philadelphia, PA: University of Pennsylvania Press, 1993

Clarke, H. Butler, *The Cid Campeador and the Waning of the Crescent in the West*, London: Putnam, 1897

Clissold, Stephen, *In Search of the Cid*, London: Hodder and Stoughton, 1965

Collins, Roger, *The Arab Conquest of Spain 710-797*, Oxford: Basil Blackwell, 1989

Constable, Olivia Remie, *Trade and Traders in Muslim Spain. The Commercial Realignment of the Iberian Peninsula, 900–1500*, Cambridge: Cambridge University Press, 1994

Constable, Olivia Remie, *Medieval Iberia. Readings from Christian, Muslim, and Jewish Sources*, Philadelphia, PA: University of Pennsylvania Press, 1997

Coope, Jessica A., *The Martyrs of Córdoba. Community and Family Conflict in an Age of Mass Conversion*, Lincoln, NE and London: University of Nebraska Press, 1995

Croft-Cooke, Rupert, *Exotic Food*, London: George Allen & Unwin, 1969

Curchin, Leonard A., *Roman Spain. Conquest and Assimilation*, London: Routledge, 1991

d'Alverny, Marie-Thérèse, 'Translations and translators', in *Renaissance and Renewal in the Twelfth Century*, edited by Robert I. Burns and Giles Constable, Oxford: Clarendon Press, 1985, pp. 421–62

Daniel, Norman, *The Arabs and Mediaeval Europe*, London: Longman, Librairie du Liban, 1975, 2nd edition 1979

Dickie, James, 'Ibn Šuhayd. A biographical and critical study', *Al-Andalus*, XXIX (1964), 242–310

Dickie, James (Yaqub Zaki), 'The Alhambra: Some reflections prompted by a recent study by Oleg Grabar', in *Festschrift for Ihsān 'Abbās on his sixtieth birthday*, edited by Wadād al-Qādī, Beirut: American University of Beirut, 1981, pp. 127–49

Dickie, James, 'Granada: A case study of Arab urbanism in Muslim Spain', in *The Legacy of Muslim Spain*, edited by Salma Khadra Jayyusi, Leiden: E. J. Brill, 1992, pp. 88–111

Dixon, Philip, 'Ashwell, George (1612–1694)', *Oxford Dictionary of National Biography*, Oxford: Oxford University Press, 2004

Dodds, Jerrilynn D., 'Mudejar tradition and the synagogues of medieval Spain: Cultural identity and cultural hegemony', in *Convivencia. Jews, Muslims, and Christians in Medieval Spain*, edited by Vivian B. Mann, Thomas F. Glick and Jerrilynn D. Dodds, New York: George Brazilier, 1992

Dunlop, D. M., 'Hafs b. Albar – the last of the Goths?' *Journal of the Royal Asiatic Society*, 1953, 137–51

Dunlop, D. M., 'Sobre Hafs ibn Albar al-Qūṭī al-Qurtubī', *Al-Andalus*, XX (1955), 211–13

Dunn, Ross E., *The Adventures of Ibn Battuta. A Muslim Traveller of the 14th Century*, London and Sydney: Croom Helm, 1986

El-Hajji, Abdurrahman Ali, *Andalusian Diplomatic Relations with Western Europe during the Umayyad Period (A.H. 138–366/A.D. 755–976)*, Beirut: Dar al-Irshad, 1970

El-Said, Issam and Ayşe Parman, *Geometric Concepts in Islamic Art*, London: World of Islam Festival Publishing Company Ltd, 1976

Fierro, María Isabel, 'Heresy in al-Andalus', in *The Legacy of Muslim Spain*, edited by Salma Khadra Jayyusi, Leiden: E. J. Brill, 1992, pp. 895–908

Fierro, Maribel, 'Alfonso X "The Wise": The last Almohad caliph?', *Medieval Encounters*, 15 (2009), 175–98

Fierro, Maribel, *The Almohad Revolution*, Farnham: Ashgate, 2012, Variorum Collected Studies Series

Fierro, Maribel and Julio Samsó, eds, *The Formation of al-Andalus. Part 2: Language, Religion, Culture and the Sciences*, Aldershot: Variorum, 1998

Fletcher, Madeleine, 'Ibn Tūmart's teachers: the relationship with al-Ghazālī', *Al-Qantara*, XVIII (1997), 305–30

Fletcher, Richard, *The Quest for the Cid*, London: Hutchinson, 1989

Folsach, Kjeld von and Joachim Meyer, 'The ivories of Muslim Spain', *The Journal of the David Collection*, Copenhagen, 2005, vols 2.1 and 2.2

Forcada, Miquel, 'Books of *anwā*' in al-Andalus', in *The Formation of Al-Andalus, Part 2: Language, Religion, Culture and the Sciences*, edited by Maribel Fierro and Julio Samsó, Aldershot: Ashgate, 1998, pp. 305–28

Franzen, Cola, *Poems of Arab Andalusia*, San Francisco, CA: City Light Books, 1989

Gabrieli, Francesco, *Muhammad and the Conquests of Islam*, London: Weidenfeld and Nicolson, 1968

García-Arenal, Mercedes, *Messianism and Puritanical Reform. Mahdīs of the Muslim West*, Leiden: E. J. Brill, 2006

Glick, Thomas F., *Irrigation and Society in Medieval Valencia*, Cambridge, MA: Harvard University Press, 1970

Glick, Thomas F., *Islamic and Christian Spain in the Early Middle Ages. Comparative Perspectives on Social and Cultural Formation*, Princeton, NJ: Princeton University Press, 1979

Glick, Thomas F. and Oriol Pi-Sunyer, 'Acculturation as an explanatory concept in Spanish history', in *Comparative Studies in Literature and History*, II (1969), 136–54

Goñí Gaztambide, José, 'The Holy See and the reconquest of the kingdom of Granada (1479–1492)', in *Spain in the Fifteenth Century 1369–1516. Essays and Extracts by Historians of Spain*, edited by Roger Highfield, , translated by Frances M. López-Morillas, London: Macmillan, 1972, pp. 354–79

Gorton, T. J., 'The metre of Ibn Quzmān: a 'classical' approach', *Journal of Arabic Literature*, VI (1975), 1–29

Gorton, T. J., '*Zajal* and *Muwaššah*: the continuing metrical debate', *Journal of Arabic Literature*, IX (1978), 33–40

Grabar, Oleg, *The Alhambra*, London: Allen Lane, 1978

Harvey, L. P., *Islamic Spain 1250 to 1500*, Chicago, IL and London: University of Chicago Press, 1990

Hess, Andrew C., *The Forgotten Frontier. A History of the Sixteenth-Century Ibero-African Frontier*, Chicago, IL and London: University of Chicago Press, 1978

Hillenbrand, Carole, *The Crusades. Islamic Perspectives*, Edinburgh: Edinburgh University Press, 1999

Hitchcock, Richard, 'The interpretation of Romance words in Arabic texts: Theory and practice', *La Corónica*, XIII, 2 (1985), 243–52

Hitchcock, Richard, 'Don Juan Manuel's knowledge of Arabic', *Modern Language Review*, 80 (1985), 594–603

Hitchcock, Richard, 'Arabic medicine: The Andalusí context', in *The Human Embryo: Aristotle and the Arabic and European Traditions*, edited by G. R. Dunstan, Exeter: Exeter University Press, 1990, pp. 70–8

Hitchcock, Richard, 'The conquest of Granada in nineteenth-century English and American historiography', in *Medieval Spain. Culture, Conflict and Coexistence. Studies in Honour of Angus MacKay*, Basingstoke: Palgrave Macmillan, 2002, pp. 242–65

Hitchcock, Richard, *Mozarabs in Medieval and Early Modern Spain. Identities and Influences*, Aldershot: Ashgate, 2008

Holloway, Julia Bolton, 'The road through Roncesvalles: Alfonsine formation of Brunetto Latini and Dante – diplomacy and literature', in *Emperor of Culture. Alfonso the Learned of Castile and his Thirteenth-Century Renaissance*, edied by Robert I. Burns, S. J., Philadelphia, PA: University of Pennsylvania Press, 1990, pp. 109–23 and 239–47

Holmyard, E. J., *Alchemy*, Harmondsworth: Penguin Books, 1968 [1957]

Howell, Alfred M., 'Some notes on early treaties between Muslims and the Visigothic rulers of al-Andalus', in *Actas del I Congreso de historia de Andalucía*, Cordoba: Monte de Piedad y Caja de Ahorros, vol. I, pp. 3–14

Imamuddin, S. M., *Some Aspects of the Socio Economic and Cultural History of Muslim Spain 711–1492, A. D.*, Leiden: E. J. Brill, 1965

Jacobs, Michael, *Alhambra*, London: Frances Lincoln Limited, 2000

Jayyusi, Salma Khadra, ed., *The Legacy of Muslim Spain*, Leiden: E. J. Brill, 1992

Jayyusi, Salma Khadra, 'The rise of Ibn Khafāja' in Salma Khadra Jayyusi, ed., *The Legacy of Muslim Spain*, Leiden: E. J. Brill, pp. 379–95

Jones, Owen, *The Grammar of Ornament*, London: Day and Son, 1856

Jones, Owen and Jules Goury, *Plans, Elevations, Sections, and Details of the Alhambra*, London: Vizitelly Brothers, 1843, 1846

Kassis, Hanna, 'The Mozarabs', in *The Literature of Al-Andalus*, edited by María Rosa Menocal, Raymond P. Scheindlin and Michael Sells, Cambridge: Cambridge University Press, 2000, pp. 420–34

Kennedy, Philip F., 'The Muslim sources of Dante?', in *The Arab Influence in Medieval Europe*, edited by Dionisius A. Agius and Richard Hitchcock, Reading: Ithaca Press, 1994, pp. 63–82

King, Archdale A., *Liturgies of the Primatial Sees*, London: Longmans, Green, 1957

Lasater, Alice E., *Spain to England. A Comparative Study of Arabic, European, and English Literature of the Middle Ages*, Jackson, MS: University of Mississippi, 1974

Lattin, Harriet Pratt, *The Letters of Gerbert with his Papal Privileges as Sylvester II*, New York: Columbia University Press, 1961

Le Tourneau, Roger, *The Almohad Movement in North Africa in the Twelfth and Thirteenth Centuries*, Princeton, NJ: Princeton University Press, 1969

Levy, Reuben, *The Social Structure of Islam*, Cambridge: Cambridge University Press, 1962

Liss, Peggy K., *Isabel the Queen. Life and Times*, New York and Oxford: Oxford University Press, 1992

Livermore, H. V., *The Origins of Spain and Portugal*, London: George Allen & Unwin, 1971

Loewe, Raphael, *Ibn Gabirol*, London: Peter Halban Publishers, 1989

Lomax, Derek W., *The Reconquest of Spain*, London: Longman, 1978

Makki, Mahmoud, 'The political history of al-Andalus (92/711–897/1492)', in *The Legacy of Muslim Spain*, edited by Selma Khadra Jayyusi, Leiden: E. J. Brill, 1992, pp. 3–87

McCormick, Michael, Paul Edward Dutton and Paul A. Mayewski, 'Volcanoes and the Climate Forcing of Carolingian Europe, A.D. 750–950', *Speculum* 82 (2007), 865–95

Meisami, Julie Scott, 'Unsquaring the circle: Rereading a poem by Al-Mu'tamid Ibn 'Abbād', *Arabica*, 35 (1988), 293–310

Menéndez Pidal, Ramón, *The Cid and His Spain*, translated by Harold Sutherland, London: John Murray, 1934, reprinted without the maps by Frank Cass, 1974

Menocal, María Rosa, *The Arabic Role in Medieval Literary History*, Philadelphia, PA: University of Pennsylvania Press, 1990

Menocal, María Rosa, Raymond P. Scheindlin and Michael Sells, eds, *The Literature of Al-Andalus*, Cambridge: Cambridge University Press, 2000

Metlitzki, Dorothee, *The Matter of Araby in Medieval England*, New Haven, CT and London: Yale University Press, 1977

Miles, George C., *The Coinage of the Umayyads of Spain*, 2 vols, New York: The American Numismatic Society, 1950

Monroe, James T., *Islam and the Arabs in Spanish Scholarship (Sixteenth Century to the Present)*, Leiden: E. J. Brill, 1970

Monroe, James T., *Hispano-Arabic Poetry. A Student Anthology*, Berkeley, CA: University of California Press, 1974

Norris, H. T., *The Berbers in Arabic Literature*, London: Longman, 1982

Nykl, A. R., *Hispano-Arabic Poetry and its Relations with the Old Provençal Troubadours*, Baltimore, MD: Printed by J. H. Furst, 1946

Ober, William B., M.D., and Nabil Alloush, M.D., 'The plague at Granada, 1348–1349: Ibn al-Khatib and ideas of contagion', *Bulletin of the New York Academy of Medicine*, 58 (4) (1982), 418–24

O'Callaghan, Joseph, *A History of Medieval Spain*, Ithaca, NY and London: Cornell University Press, 1975

Pastor, Antonio, *The Idea of Robinson Crusoe*, Watford: The Gongora Press, 1930

Peers, E. Allison, *Fool of Love. The Life of Ramon Lull*, London: S. C. M. Press, 1946

Pérez de Urbel, Justo, *A Saint under Muslim Rule*, Milwaukee, WI: The Bruce Publishing Company, 1937

Prado-Vilar, Francisco, 'Enclosed in Ivory: The miseducation of al-Mughira', in *The Journal of the David Collection*, edited by Kjeld von Folsach and Joachim Meyer, Copenhagen, 2005, vol. 2, part 1, pp. 139–63

Prescott, William H., *History of the Reign of Ferdinand and Isabella, the Catholic Monarchs of Spain*, 3 vols, London: Richard Bentley, 1838

Procter, E. S., 'The scientific works of the court of Alfonso X of Castille: the King and his collaborators', *Modern Language Review*, XL (1945), 12–29

Reilly, Bernard F., *The Contest of Christian and Muslim Spain 1031–1157*, Cambridge, MA and Oxford: Blackwell

Riaño, Juan, *The Industrial Arts of Spain*, London: Chapman and Hall, 1879

Rivoira, G. T., *Muslim Architecture. Its Origins and Development*, translated from the Italian by G. McN. Rushforth, Oxford: Humphrey Milford, 1918 [1914]

Robinson, Cynthia, *Medieval Andalusian Courtly Culture in the Mediterranean. Hadīth Bayād wa Riyād*, London and New York: Routledge, 2010

Robinson, Maureen, 'The history and myths surrounding Johannes Hispalensis', *Bulletin of Hispanic Studies*, 80 (2003), 443–70

Rycaut, Paul, *The Critick, Written Originally in Spanish by Lorenzo Gracian, one of the Best Wits in Spain*, London: n.p., 1681

Schacht, Joseph, *An Introduction to Islamic Law*, Oxford: Clarendon Press, 1964 (reprinted 1982)

Schaff, Philip, *History of the Christian Church*, A P & A [reprint], [no date,?1970s]. 8 vols in 3. Originally published 1858-1890

Scheindlin, Raymond P., *Form and Structure in the Poetry of Al-Mu'tamid Ibn 'Abbād*, Leiden: E. J. Brill, 1974

Serjeant, R. B., *Islamic Textiles. Material for a History up to the Mongol Conquest*, Beirut: Librairie du Liban, 1972

Shaban, M. A., *Islamic History A. D. 600–750 (A. H. 132). A New Interpretation*, Cambridge: Cambridge University Press, 1971

Singer, Charles, *A Short History of Scientific Ideas to 1900*, Oxford: Clarendon Press, 1959

Smith, Dulcie Lawrence, *The Poems of Mu'tamid, King of Seville*, London: John Murray, 1913. Wisdom of the East Series

Sutton, Keith, 'Qanats in Al-Andalus: The continued presence of Moorish irrigation technology in the Campo de Tabernas, Almería, Spain', *The Maghreb Review*, 26 (1) (2001), 69–78

Taha, A. D., *The Muslim Conquest and Settlement of North Africa and Spain*, London: Routledge, 1989

Thompson, E. A., *The Goths in Spain*, Oxford: Clarendon Press, 1969

Thorndike, Lynn, *Michael Scot*, London: Thomas Nelson & Sons, 1965

Tolan, John V., *Saracens. Islam in the Medieval European Imagination*, New York: Columbia University Press, 2002

Vernet, Juan and María Asunción Catalá, 'The mathematical works of Maslama of Madrid', in *The Formation of Al-Andalus, Part 2: Language, Religion, Culture and the Sciences*, edited by Maribel Fierro and Julio Samsó, Aldershot: Variorum, 1998, pp. 359–79

Vives, Jaime Vicens, 'The economies of Catalonia and Castile', in *Spain in the Fifteenth Century 1369–1516. Essays and Extracts by Historians of Spain*, edited by Roger Highfield, translated by Frances M. López-Morillas, London: Macmillan, 1972

Von Grunebaum, Gustave E., *Medieval Islam. A Study in Cultural Orientation*, Chicago, IL: University of Chicago Press, 2nd edition, 1971

Wasserstein, David, *The Rise and Fall of the Party-Kings. Politics and Society in Islamic Spain, 1002–1086*, Princeton, NJ: Princeton University Press, 1985

Wasserstein, David, 'The library of al-Hakam II al-Mustansir and the culture of Islamic Spain', *Manuscripts of the Middle East*, 5 (1990–1), 99–105

Watt, W. Montgomery, *Islamic Philosophy and Theology*, Edinburgh: Edinburgh University Press, 1962

Watt, W. Montgomery, *The Influence of Islam on Medieval Europe*, Edinburgh: Edinburgh University Press, 1972

West, Louis C., *Imperial Roman Spain. The Objects of Trade*, Oxford: Basil Blackwell, 1929

Winter, H. J. J., *Eastern Science. An Outline of its Scope and Contribution*, London: John Murray, 1952

Zwartjes, Otto, *Love-Songs from al-Andalus. History, Structure & Meaning of the Kharja*, Leiden: E. J. Brill, 1997

Works in Spanish and French

Abadal y Vinyals, Ramón de, *La batalla del adopcionismo en la desintegración de la Iglesia visigótica*, Barcelona: Real Academia de Buenas Letras, 1949

al-Abbādī, Ahmad Mujtār, *El reino de Granada en la época de Muhammad V*, Madrid: Instituto de Estudios Islámicos, 1973

Acién Almansa, Manuel, *Ronda y su serranía en tiempo de los Reyes Católicos*, Málaga: Universidad de Málaga, 1979

Acién Almansa, Manuel, *Entre el feudalism y el Islam. 'Umar b. Hafsūn en los historiadores, en las fuentes y en la historia*, Jaén: Universidad, Colección Martínez de Mazas, 1994

Arnaldez, Roger, *Grammaire et théologie chez Ibn Hazm de Cordoue. Essai sur la structure et les conditions de la pensée musulmane*, Paris: Librairie Philosophique J. Vrin, 1956

Arié, Rachel, *L'Espagne musulmane au temps des Nasrides (1232–1492)*, Paris: Éditions Boccard, 1973

Asín Palacios, Miguel, *La escatología musulmana en la 'Divina Comedia'*, Madrid: Estanislao Maestre, 1919

Asín Palacios, Miguel, *Abenhazam de Córdoba y su crítica de las ideas religiosas*, 5 vols, Madrid: Revista de Archivos, Bibliotecas y Museos, 1927–32; reissued Madrid: Ediciones Turner, 1984

Ávila, Ma. Luisa, 'Las mujeres "sabias" en al-Andalus', in *La mujer en al-Andalus. Reflejos históricos de su actividad y categorías sociales*, edited by Ma. J. Viguera, Madrid: Universidad Autónoma, and Seville: Editoriales Andaluzas Unidas, 1989

Borrás Gualis, Gonzalo M., *El Islam de Córdoba al Mudéjar*, Madrid: Silex, 1997

Bosch Vilá, Jacinto, *La Sevilla Islámica 712–1248*, Seville: Universidad, 1984

Camón Aznar, José, 'El Cid, personaje mozárabe', *Revista de Estudios Políticos*, XVII (1947), 109–41

Caro Baroja, Julio, *Los moriscos del reino de Granada. (Ensayo de historia social)*, Madrid: Instituto de Estudios Políticos, 1957

Chalmeta, Pedro, *Invasión e Islamización. La sumisión de Hispania y la formación de al-Andalus*, Madrid: Editorial Mapre, 1994

Chalmeta, Pedro, *El Zoco Medieval: Contribución al estudio de la historia del mercado*, Madrid: Fundación Ibn Tufayl, 2010

Devoto, Daniel, *Introducción al estudio de don Juan Manuel y en particular El Conde Lucanor*, Madrid: Editorial Castalia, 1972

Dodds, Jerrilynn D., *Al-Andalus. Las artes islámicas en España*, Madrid: Ediciones El Viso, 1992

Dozy, R. P. A., *Recherches sur l'histoire politique et littéraire de l'Espagne pendant le Moyen Âge*, vol. I, Leiden: E. J. Brill, 1849

Dozy, R., *Supplément aux dictionnaires arabes*, 2 vols, Beyrouth: Librairie du Liban, 1968 [1881]

Daniel Eisenberg, 'Cisneros y la quema de los manuscritos granadinos', *Journal of Hispanic Philology*, 16 (1992), 107–24

Epalza, Mikel de, 'El Cid = El León: ¿Epiteto árabe del Campeador?', *Hispanic Review*, XLV (1977), 67–75

Ferrandis, José, *Marfiles árabes de Occidente*, 2 vols, Madrid: Estanislao Maestre, 1935, 1940

Fierro, María Isabel, *La heterodoxia en al-Andalus durante el período Omeya*, Madrid: Instituto Hispano-Árabe de Cultura, 1987

Fontaine, Jacques, *L'Art Mozarabe. L'Art Préroman Hispanique II*, Paris: Zodiaque, 1977, Collection "la nuit des temps", vol. 47

García-Arenal, Mercedes, *Esplendor de al-Andalus: la poesía and aluza en árabe clásico, s. XI*, Madrid: Libros Hiperión, 1983. Translation of Henri Péres, *op. cit.*

García Gómez, Emilio, *El mejor Ben Quzmán en 40 zéjeles*, Madrid: Alianza Editorial, 1981

Gómez de Castro, Alvar, *De las hazañas de Francisco Jiménez de Cisneros*, edited and translated by José Oroz Reta, Madrid: Fundación Universitaria Española, 1984

Gómez-Moreno, Manuel, *Iglesias mozárabes. Arte español de los siglos IX a XI*, 2 vols, Madrid: Centro de Estudios Históricos, 1919; reprinted in one volume, Granada: Universidad, 1975

González, Julio, *Las conquistas de Fernando III en Andalucía*, Madrid: Consejo Superior de Investigaciones Científicas, Instituto de Jerónimo Zurita, 1946

Guichard, P., 'Les arabes ont bien envahi l'Espagne: les structures sociales de l'Espagne musulmane', *Revue Annales, Économie, Sociétés, Civilisations*, XXIX (1974), 1483–1513

Guichard, Pierre, *Al-Andalus. Estructura antropólogica de una sociedad islámica en Occidente*, Barcelona: Barral, 1976

Guillén Robles, F., *Málaga Musulmana*, Málaga: Enrique Montes Oliver, 1957 [1880]

Huici Miranda, Ambrosio, *Traducción española de un manuscrito anónimo del siglo XIII sobre la cocina hispano-magribí*, Madrid: Editorial Maestre, 1960

Huici Miranda, Ambrosio, *Historia política del imperio Almohade*, 2 vols, Granada: Universidad de Granada, 2000, vol. I. This is a facsimile reprint with a new 140-page 'estudio preliminar' by Emilio Molina López and Vicente Carlos Navarro Oltra, of the first edition of 1956–7

Ladero Quesada, Miguel Ángel, *Castilla y la conquista del reino de Granada*, Valladolid: Universidad, 1967, 2nd edition of the 1988 reprint, Granada: Diputación Provincial de Granada, 1993

Ladero Quesada, Miguel Ángel, *Los mudéjares de Castilla en tiempos de Isabel I*, Valladolid: Instituto 'Isabel la Católica', 1969

Ladero Quesada, Miguel Ángel, *La Guerra de Granada (1482–1491)*, Granada: Diputación Los Libros de la Estrella, 4, 2001

Lapiedra Gutiérrez, Eva, *Cómo los musulmanes llamaban a los cristianos hispánicos*, Valencia: Instituto de Cultura 'Juan Gil-Albert', 1997

Manzanares de Cirre, Manuela, *Arabistas españoles del siglo XIX*, Madrid: Instituto Hispano-Árabe de Cultura, 1972

Manzano Moreno, Eduardo, *La frontera de al-Andalus en época de los Omayas*, Madrid: Consejo Superior de Investigaciones Científicas, 1991

Marín, Manuela, 'En los márgenes de la ley: el consumo de alcohol en al-Ándalus', in *Identidades marginales*, edited by Cristina de la Puente, Madrid: Consejo Superior de Investigaciones Científicas, 2003, pp. 271–328

Mármol Carvajal, Luis del, *Historia del rebelión y castigo de los moriscos del reino de Granada*, Madrid: Imprenta de Sancha, 2nd edition, 1798. First edition published in 1600

Menéndez Pidal, R., *Cantar de Mio Cid. Texto, gramática y vocabulario*, 3 vols, Madrid: Bailly-Baillière, 1908–11.

Menéndez Pidal, Ramón, 'Repoblación y tradición en la cuenca del Duero', in *Enciclopedia Lingüística Hispánica*, edited by M. Alvar et al., vol. I, Madrid, 1960

Menéndez Pidal, Ramón, *Orígenes del español. Estado lingüístico de la península ibérica hasta el siglo XI*, Madrid: Espasa-Calpe, 5th edition, 1964

Menéndez Pidal, Ramón, *La España del Cid*, 2 vols, Madrid: Espasa-Calpe, 5th edition, 1956, reissued in 1969.

Meyerhof, Max, 'Esquisse d'histoire de la pharmacologie et botanique chez les Musulmans d'Espagne', *Al-Andalus* III (1935), 1–41

Millás Vallicrosa, J. M., *Estudios sobre la historia de la ciencia española*, Barcelona: Consejo Superior de Investigaciones Científicas, Instituto 'Luis Vives' de Filosofia, 1949

Molénat, Jean-Pierre, 'Sur le rôle des almohades dans la fin du christianisme locale au Maghreb et en al-Andalus', *Al-Qantara*, XVIII (1997), 389–413

Monès, Hussain, 'Consideraciones sobre la época de los reyes de taifas', *Al-Andalus*, XXXI (1966), 305–28

Olagüe, Ignacio, *Les Arabes n'ont jamais envahi l'Espagne*, Paris: Flammarion, 1969

Pavón Maldonado, Basilio, *Memoria de la excavación de la mezquita de Medinat al-Zahra*, Madrid: Ministerio de Educación Nacional, 1966

Pérès, Henri, *La Poésie andalouse en arabe classique au XIe siècle. Ses aspects généraux, ses principaux thèmes et sa valeur documentaire*, Paris: Adrien-Maisonneuve, 2nd edition, 1953 [1937]

Pescador del Hoyo, Ma. Del Carmen, 'Cómo fué de verdad la toma de Granada, a la luz de un documento inédito', *Al-Andalus*, XX (1955), 283–344

Puertas Tricas, Rafael, *Iglesia hispánicas (siglos IV al VIII). Testimonios literarios*, Madrid: Patronato Nacional de Museos, 1975

Ribera, Julián, *La música de las Cantigas. Estudio de su origen y naturaleza*, Madrid: Tipografia de la Revista de Archivos, 1922

Rivera, Juan Francisco, *Elipando de Toledo. Nueva aportación a los estudios mozárabes*, Toledo: Editorial Católica Toledana, 1940

Rubiera Mata, María Jesús, *Andalucía Islámica*, Granada: Universidad, vols 2 and 3, 1983, pp. 85–94

Rubiera Mata, María J., 'De nuevo sobre los poemas epígrafos de la Alhambra', *Al-Andalus*, XLI (1977), 207–11

Sánchez-Albornoz, Claudio, *Una ciudad de la España cristiana hace mil años*, Madrid: Ediciones Rialp, 1966 [1926]

Simonet, Francisco Javier, *Historia de los mozárabes de España deducida de los mejores y más auténticos testimonios de los autores christianos [sic] y árabes*, Amsterdam: Oriental Press, 1967 [1903]

Tailhan, J., 'Les Bibliothèques espagnoles du Nord Ouest', in *Nouveaux mélanges d'archéologie, d'histoire et de littérature sur le Moyen Âge*, edited by Charles Cahier, Paris: Firmin Didot, vol. IV, 1877, 297–346

Terrasse, Henri, *Islam d'Espagne. Une rencontre de l'Orient et de l'Occident*, Paris: Librairie Plon, 1958

Torres Balbás, Leopoldo, *Artes Almoravide y Almohade*, Madrid: Instituto de Estudios Africanos, 1955

Torres Balbás, Leopoldo, *Ciudades hispanomusulmanas*, 2 vols, [Madrid]: Instituto Hispano-Árabe de Cultura, n.d. [1972]

Torres Balbás, Leopoldo, 'Almería islámica: Crónica arqueológica de la España Musulmana, XLI', *Al-Andalus*, XXII (1957), 411–53; reproduced in *Obra Dispersa*, compiled by Manuel Casamar, 8 vols, Madrid: Instituto de España, 1983, vol. 6, pp. 217–63

Torres Delgado, Cristobal, *El antiguo reino nazarí de Granada (1232–1340)*, Granada: Ediciones Anel, 1974

Urvoy, M.-T., *Le Psautier de Hafs le Goth*, Toulouse: Presses Universitaires du Mirail, 1994

Vallvé, Joaquín, *Nuevas ideas sobre la conquista de España. Toponimia y Onomástica*, Madrid: Real Academia de la Historia, 1989

Vernet, Juan, *La cultura hispanoárabe en Oriente y Occidente*, Barcelona: Editorial Ariel, 1978

Supplement to bibliography

The books and other works listed in the bibliography are those mentioned in the chapter endnotes. It seems appropriate to add, for the benefit of the English reader, those works written in English which have not been specifically mentioned, but which have been consulted and will be found to be useful and interesting for those who wish to pursue certain aspects further.

General

Bovill, E. W., *The Golden Trade of the Moors*, London: Oxford University Press, 1958

Barton, Simon and Peter Linehan, eds, *Cross, Crescent and Conversion. Studies on Medieval Spain and Christendom in Memory of Richard Fletcher*, Leiden: E. J. Brill, 2008

Chejne, Anwar G., *Muslim Spain. Its History and Culture*, Minneapolis, MN: University of Minnesota Press, 1974

Collins, Roger, *Early Medieval Spain. Unity in Diversity, 400–1000*, London: Macmillan, 1983, 2nd edition 1995

Collins, Roger, *Spain: An Oxford Archaeological Guide*, Oxford: Oxford University Press, 1998

Fletcher, Richard, *Moorish Spain*, London: Weidenfeld & Nicolson, 1992

Gerli, E. Michael, ed., *Medieval Iberia: An Encyclopedia*, London: Routledge, 2003

Kennedy, Hugh, *Muslim Spain and Portugal. A Political History of al-Andalus*, London and New York: Longman, 1996. A comprehensive account of the political history of the period

MacKay, A., *Spain in the Middle Ages. From Frontier to Empire, 1000–1500*, London: Macmillan, 1977

Reilly, Bernard F., *The Medieval Spains*, Cambridge: Cambridge University Press, 1993

Van Kleffens, E. N., *Hispanic Law until the End of the Middle Ages*, Edinburgh: Edinburgh University Press, 1968

Watt, W. Montgomery, *A History of Islamic Spain*, Edinburgh: Edinburgh University Press, 1965, paperback edition 1977

Islamic

Abun-Nasr, Jamil M., *A History of the Maghrib in the Islamic Period*, Cambridge: Cambridge University Press, 1987, especially Chapters 2 and 3

Ashtor, E., *A Social and Economic History of the Near East in the Middle Ages*, London: Collins, 1976

Bulliet, Richard W., *Conversion to Islam in the Medieval Period. An Essay in Quantitative History*, Cambridge, MA: Harvard University Press, 1979

Crone, Patricia, *Slaves on Horses: The Evolution of the Islamic Polity*, Cambridge: Cambridge University Press, 1980

Dunlop, D. M., *Arab Civilization to A. D. 1500*, London: Longman and Beirut: Librairie du Liban, 1971, reprinted 1975

Hitti, Philip K., *The Near East in History. A 5000 Year Story*, Princeton, NJ: D. Van Nostrand Company, Inc., 1961

Holt, P. M., Ann K. S. Lambton and Bernard Lewis, eds, *The Cambridge History of Islam. Volume 2: The Further Islamic Lands, Islamic Society and Civilization*, Cambridge: Cambridge University Press, 1970

Lewis, Archibald, ed., *The Islamic World and the West 622–1492 A.D.*, New York: John Wiley & Sons, 1970

Saunders, J. J., *A History of Medieval Islam*, London: Routledge and Kegan Paul, 1965

Schacht, Joseph and C. E. Bosworth, eds, *The Legacy of Islam*, Oxford: Clarendon Press, 2nd edition, 1974

Southern, R. W., *Western Views of Islam in the Middle Ages*, Cambridge, MA: Harvard University Press, 1962

History to 1031 AD

Christys, Ann, *Christians in al-Andalus (711–1000)*, Richmond: Curzon Press, 2002

Colbert, Edward P., *The Martyrs of Córdoba (850–859): A Study of the Sources*, Washington, DC: The Catholic University of America, 1962

Keay, S., *Roman Spain*, London: British Museum Publications Ltd., 1988

Reinaud, J.-T., *Muslim Colonies in France, Northern Italy and Switzerland*, Lahore: Sh. Muhammad Ashraf, 1964 [1955]. Translation by Haroon Khan Sherwani of the original French edition of 1836

Safran, Janina M., *The Second Umayyad Caliphate. The Articulation of Caliphal Legitimacy in al-Andalus*, Cambridge, MA: Harvard University Press, 2000

Shatzmiller, Maya, *The Berbers and the Islamic State. The Marīnid Experience in Pre-Protectorate Morocco*, Princeton, NJ: Marcus Wiener, 1999

Wasserstein, David, *The Caliphate in the West. An Islamic Political Institution in the Iberian Peninsula*, Oxford: Clarendon Press, 1993

Wolf, Kenneth Baxter, *Christian Martyrs in Muslim Spain*, Cambridge: Cambridge University Press, 1988

History 1000–1500 AD

Burns, Robert I., *Muslims, Christians, and Jews in the Crusader Kingdom of Valencia*. Cambridge: Cambridge University Press, 1984

Handler, Andrew, *The Zirids of Granada*, Coral Gables: University of Miami Press, 1974

Pick, Lucy K., *Conflict and Coexistence. Archbishop Rodrigo and the Muslims and Jews of Medieval Spain*, Ann Arbor, MI: University of Michigan Press, 2004

Procter, Evelyn S., *Alfonso X of Castile, Patron of Literature and Learning*, Oxford: Clarendon Press, 1951

Scales, P. C., *The Fall of the Caliphate of Cordoba: Berbers and Andalusis in Conflict*, Leiden: E. J. Brill, 1994

Literature and science

Agius, Dionisius A. and Richard Hitchcock, eds, *The Arab Influence in Medieval Europe. Folia Scholastica Mediterranea*, Reading: Ithaca Press, 1994. Seven chapters, including one by Kennedy mentioned in the main bibliography. Subjects include trade, metalwork and music

Arberry, A. J. *Moorish Poetry. A Translation of The Pennants, an Anthology Compiled in 1243 by the Andalusian Ibn Sa 'id*, Cambridge: Cambridge University Press, 1953, reprinted by RoutledgeCurzon, 2001, 2006

Dunlop, D. M., *Arabic Science and the West*, Karachi: Pakistan Historical Society, 1958

Farmer, Henry George, *A History of Arabian Music to the XIIIth Century*, London: Luzac & Company, 1973 [1929], especially Chapter V

Giffen, Lois Anita, *Theory of Profane Love among the Arabs: The Development of the Genre*, London: University of London Press Ltd, 1972. First published New York: New York University Press, 1971

Hamori, Andras, *On the Art of Medieval Arabic Literature*, Princeton, NJ: Princeton University Press, 1975 [1974]

Hourani, George F., *Averroes: On the Harmony of Religion and Philosophy*, London: Luzac, 1976 [1961], E. J. W. Gibb Memorial Series, New Series XXI

Kunitzsch, Paul, *The Arabs and the Stars. Texts and Traditions on the Fixed Stars and their Influence in Medieval Europe*, Northampton: Variorum, 1989. Collection of studies, including several on the astrolabe

López-Baralt, Luce, *Islam in Spanish Literature from the Middle Ages to the Present*, translated by Andrew Hurley, Leiden: E. J. Brill, San Juan: Editorial de la Universidad de Puerto Rico, 1992

Nicholson, Reynold A., *A Literary History of the Arabs*, Cambridge: Cambridge University Press, 1966. First Cambridge edition, 1930; first published 1907

Samsó, Julio, *Islamic Astronomy and Medieval Spain*, Aldershot: Variorum, 1994

[Ibn Tufayl] *The History of Hayy Ibn Yaqzan*, translated from the Arabic by Simon Ockley. Revised, with an introduction, by A. S. Fulton, London: Chapman and Hall, 1929

Tolan, John V., *Sons of Ishmael. Muslims through European Eyes in the Middle Ages*, Gainesville, FL: University of Florida, 2008, Chapter 6 on Saladin

Index

abacus, 89
Al-Abbādī, M., 178
Abbādids of Seville, 113, 121, 137
'Abbās b. Firnās, polymath & inventor, 52–4
'Abbāsids, 40–1, 43, 46, 67, 84, 92
'Abd Allāh, *amīr*, 62–3
'Abd Allāh b. Buluggīn, 97, 127
'Abd al-'Azīz, son of Mūsā, 21–2, 26–7, 30
'Abd al-'Azīz b. Marwān, governor of Egypt, 14
'Abd al-Basīt, 184
'Abd al-Malik al-Muzaffar, 99–100, 104
'Abd al-Malik b. Qatan, *wālī*, 32–5
'Abd al-Mu'min, 146–7
'Abd ar-Rahmān I, 36, 40–5, 48
'Abd ar-Rahmān II, 53–7, 60
'Abd ar-Rahmān III, 66–9, 71–7, 79–84, 87, 102, 117, 119, 155
'Abd ar-Rahmān V, 103
'Abd ar-Rahmān Sanchūl, 199
Abencerrajes *see* Banū Sarrāj
Abraham of Toledo, physician and translator, 166
Abū 'Alī al-Qālī, 86
Abū Ibrāhīm Ismā'īl b. Yusuf b. Naghrila *see* Samuel ha-Nagid
Abū Ishāq al-Ilbīrī, *faqīh*, 116
Abū Ma'shar, 144
Abū Ya'qūb Yūsuf, 147, 149
aceifas, 72, 96
adab, 75
ad-Dabbī, 22
adoptionism, 46–7
Aftāsids of Badajoz, 113
Aghmāt, near Marrakesh, 129
ahl adh-dhimma, 11, 23, 31, 58, 60, 105, 116, 137, 150
ahl al-Andalus, 114
ahl al-kitāb, 11, 49, 58, 69
Ahmad ar-Rāzī, 82
Aïla *see* Egilona
'ajam, 'ajamī, 58, 69
Akhbār Majmū'a, 21, 33–4, 36, 40–1, 66

al-Ahmār, 161–3, 173
Alarcos, 128, 150, 154
al-Awzā'ī, 48
Albaicín, 117, 162, 189–90
Albelda, monastery of, 89
Alcalá la Real, 173
alchemy, 87
Alcuin, 47
Aledo, siege of, 128
Alexander II, Pope, 124–6
Alexander IV, Pope, 165
al-Fārābī, 144
Alfaro, 142
Alfonsine tables, 164–5
Alfonso, abbot, 70–1
Alfonso I of Asturias, 37, 68
Alfonso I, of Aragón, 140–2, 146
Alfonso II of Asturias, 50, 92
Alfonso III of León, 61, 68–9
Alfonso V of León, 70
Alfonso VI of Castile, 123–5, 128–32, 143
Alfonso VII of Castile, 142, 144, 146
Alfonso VIII of Castile, 151–2
Alfonso X of Castile, 154, 162–8, 171
   legal code, 167
Alfonso XI of Castile, 172–3
Algeciras, 2, 18, 122, 163, 172–3
al-Ghāfiqī, 32
al-Ghazāl, poet, 53–4
al-Ghazālī, 145, 149
al-Hakam I, 48–54
   library, 91–2, 97
al-Hakam II, 84–5, 87, 90–1, 93–6, 171
Alhama, 185
Alhambra, 116–17, 162, 174–8, 194, 196
   'Fount of Lions', 116
   Palace of the Lions, 176–7
   Puerta del Vino, 175
Alhándega, battle of, 69, 73
al-Himyarī, 25–6, 114–15, 126, 139, 146, 151–2
al-hisn al-hamrā see Alhambra
al-Hurr, *wālī*, 30

al-Khushanī, 45, 52, 60
al-Khwārizmī, 89, 145
al-Mahdī, 'Abbāsid Caliph, 42
al-Ma'mūn, ruler of Toledo, 125
al-Mansūr, 86, 95–9, 101, 103–4, 113,
    117–18, 155
al-Maqqarī, 17, 21, 26, 30, 34, 40, 43, 50–2,
    54, 60, 63, 73, 82–3, 87–8, 91, 93, 96,
    126, 169, 171–2, 187–8
Almería, 71, 83, 103, 115, 117–18, 123, 146,
    155, 162–3, 170, 173, 183, 186, 191
Almohads, 137, 145–7, 149–5, 162, 178
    architecture, 154
    battle standard, 152
Almoravids, 123, 127–30, 132–3, 137, 140–2,
    145–6
al-Mughīra, 94
al-mulaththamūn see Almoravids
al-Mundhir, 62
Almuñécar, 40, 170
al-Muqtadir, 132
al-murābitūn see Almoravids
al-Mu'tadid, 113–14, 120–2
al-Mu'tamid, 121–3, 127–9, 131, 171
    poetry, 129
al-Mu'tamin, 132
al-Mu'tasim, 118
al-muwahhidūn see Almohads
Alpujarras, 186, 188–9, 191
al-Ukhaydir, Umayyad, palace, 176
al-Zaghal, 186
Álvar Fáñez, 128–9
al-Zarqālī, 164
amīr al-mu'minīn, 83
'Anbasa, wālī, 31
an-Nāsir, Almohad leader, 151–2
Andújar, 152
Antequera, 169
Aquinas, Thomas, 149
Arabic language, 9, 82, 86, 104, 106, 125,
    140, 143, 189
Arabic poetry, 81–2
Aragón, 124–5, 130, 132, 141, 151, 153, 161,
    164, 170, 172–3, 184–7, 196
Archidona, 169
Arjona, 161
Arberry, A. J., 103
'Arīb b. Sa'īd, 66–7, 76–7
arrabal, insurrection, 49
ar-Rāzī, 27, 30, 45
ar-rūm, rūmī, 58, 132
ash-Shaqundī, 155
Ashwell, George, 148
Asín Palacios, Miguel, 103, 105, 165–6

as-Sayrafī, 141
as-Sumayl, 36, 40–1
as-sūq, 72
Astorga, 35, 37, 69
astrolabe, 90
astrology, 55, 144, 164–5
astronomy, 77, 164–5
Asturias, 47–8, 60, 68–9
atalayas, 57, 170
Ávila, M. L., 119

Badajoz, 63, 113, 122, 128
Bādīs, 115, 117–18
Baeza, 71, 153, 169
Bailén, 152
baladiyyūn, 28
Balj b. Bishr, 34–6
Banū Ashqilūla (Escayola), 168
Banū Hūd, 143, 153
Banū Sarrāj, 183–5
Banū Sumādih, 118
Banū 'Udhrā, 104
Barbastro, 126
Barbate, river, 19, 37
Barcelona, 56, 61, 79, 88–9, 96, 183
Bargebuhr, F., 116
Basques, 2, 42–3, 48, 50, 61, 69
Bayād and Riyād, 154
Baza, 169
Benavente, 150
Berbers, 18–19, 27–8, 33–7, 49, 51, 73, 84,
    96, 100–2, 106, 113–16, 123, 146, 163
Berenguer, Ramón, count of Barcelona, 147
Boabdil (Abū 'Abd Allāh) see Muhammad XII
Bobastro, 23, 62–3
Bonaventura de Siena, 166
books, 91–2, 97–8, 139, 168
Borell, Ramón, Count of Barcelona, 88
Bulliet, Richard, 75
Burgos, 68, 190

Cabra, 131
Cádiz, 2, 37, 57, 146, 163
Cairo, 184
Calatañazor, 98–9
Calatrava, 113, 151–2
    Military Order, 169
Calendar of Cordoba, 77–8, 83
Caliphal titles, 67
Camón Aznar, J., 133
Cantarino, V., 120
Capitulations, 187, 189–91
Carmona, 147
Cartagena, 20, 52, 123

Castile, 61, 68, 102, 124, 130–1, 141, 146, 161, 163–4, 169–70, 172–3, 183–7, 196
  counts of, 96
Catalonia, 47, 89, 100, 132, 141
Catholic kings, 186–90
Cazorla, 169
Ceuta, 2, 16, 18, 34, 83
Chalmeta, Pedro, 7
Charlemagne, 41–3, 46–7
Charles Martel, 32
Christians, 31–2, 138–9, 141–2
Chronicles, 61
Chronicle of 754, 31–3
Cluny, abbey, 124, 127, 129
coins, 46, 67, 72
Collins, 7
Constantine VII, Byzantine emperor, 75
Constantinople, 53, 126
Consuegra, 128
convivencia, 167, 179
cookery, cuisine, 55, 155–6
Cordoba, 3, 21, 27, 30, 32–3, 36, 40–1, 43, 45–6, 48–50, 52, 54–6, 58–9, 60–4, 66–7, 71, 73–6, 78–80, 82–93, 96–107, 113–14, 117, 119, 122, 131–2, 140, 142–3, 145, 149, 152–3, 155–6, 161–3, 166, 173, 185
  embassies to, 87–88
  Great Mosque, 43–4, 48, 56, 70, 74, 90, 98
  mihrāb, 98
Covadonga, battle of, 31
Crusades, 124, 129, 132, 146, 151, 188, 194
Cuarte, 132–3
Cullera, 161
Curtius, 56

Damascus, 8, 11, 25–8, 30–2, 43
Dante, 105, 165–6
d'Alverny, M. T., 144
Denia, 52, 147
Dioscorides, 75–6
Duero, river, 29, 37, 50, 61, 68–70
dhimmīs see *ahl adh-dhimma*
Dhū Nūnids, 66, 119, 123
Don Juan Manuel, 171–2

earthquake, 63, 123
Ebles of Roucy, Count, 126
Ebro, river, 25, 29, 50, 68, 142
Écija, 21
eclipse of the sun, 74
Egica, 23
Egilona, 26

El Cid, Rodrigo Díaz, 130–3, 172, 190
  title, 130–1
El Conde Lucanor, 171
El criticón, 148
Elipandus, 46–7
Elvira, 36, 40, 80, 114
  Council of, 5
Enrique IV of Castile, 184
Epalza, M. de, 130
Escalada, San Miguel de, 70–1
Esla, river, 68, 70
Eulogius, 57–9

famine, 29, 36–8, 40, 51, 62–3, 186
faqīh, fuqahā', 48, 66, 97, 99, 116, 141, 189, 191
Fātimids, 57, 67, 83, 117
Felix, bishop of Urgel, 47
Fernando I of Castile, 122–4
Fernando III of Castile, 153, 161–4, 169, 171
Fernando IV of Castile, 170
Fernando II of Aragón, 185–9; *see also* Catholic kings
Fez, 168–9, 174, 188
Fierro, M. I., 86
fitna, 61, 73, 99, 102, 105, 114, 117
Florence, 166
Fourth Lateran Council, 167
Fraga, 142
Franks, 50, 56, 58, 83, 132

Gabrieli, F., 107
Galicia, 4, 35, 47, 58, 98
García Gómez, E., 120
Gayangos, Pascual de, 51, 85
Gerard of Cremona, translator, 144–5
Gerbert of Aurillac, Pope Sylvester II, 89–91
Ghālib, 85, 92
Ghālib (Galippus), 145
Gibraltar, 18, 172–3, 184
Giralda, Seville, 154
Glick, Thomas, 68, 72
Gómez de Castro, A., 191
Góngora, Luis de, 140
González, Domingo, translator, 144
Gospels in Arabic, 81, 142
Grabar, O., 117, 175
Gracián, Baltasar, 148
Granada, 1, 107, 114–19, 123, 128, 131, 141–2, 152, 156, 162, 168–71, 173–9, 183–91
  population, 177
Graus, siege of, 125
Gregory VII, Pope, 124
Guadalete, river, 19

Guadalquivir, river, 1, 3, 26, 29, 40, 48, 57,
    138, 154–5, 169
    flooded, 67
Guadiana, river, 4
Guadix, 118, 147, 169, 183, 186
Guichard, P., 121
Guitart, 88

Habūs, 115
Hafs al-Qūtī, 81
Hafsid dynasty, 162
hājib, 95, 97, 100, 113
Harvey, L. P., 172, 174, 184–5
Hasdai b. Shaprūt, 75, 79, 81, 87
Hatto, Bishop of Vich, 89
Henry II of Castile, 178
heresy *see zandaqa*
Hermann of Carinthia, translator, 144
hisba, 137
Hishām I, 48
Hishām II, 95, 100–1, 113
Hispania, 1–2
Hispano-Romans, 29, 51
Historia Roderici, 132
horseshoe arch, 44
Huelva, Taifa state, 122
Hugh, abbot of Cluny, 124, 127
Hugh of Santalla, translator, 144
Huici Miranda, A., 151

Iberia, Iberian Peninsula, 1, 195–6
Ibn ʿAbd ar-Rabbih, 64
Ibn ʿAbdūn, 123, 137
Ibn ʿAbdūs, *wazīr*, 119
Ibn Abī ʿĀmir *see* al-Mansūr
Ibn al-Athīr, 29
Ibn al-Bannāʾ, 78
Ibn al-Kardabūs, 19, 141
Ibn al-Khatīb, 173–8
Ibn al-Qallās, 141
Ibn al-Qūtīya, 20, 49
Ibn ash-Shamir, astrologer, 55
Ibn Bajja, Avempace, 147
Ibn Battūta, 172
Ibn Hajjāj, 62
Ibn Hawqal, 27, 29, 71
Ibn Hayyān, 50–3, 66–7, 73–4, 82, 87–8,
    92–3, 96, 126
Ibn Hazm, Abū Muhammad ʿAlī, 102–6, 119,
    129
    Tawq al-hamāma, 103, 154
Ibn ʿIdhārī, 62–3, 99–100, 114–15, 122, 132
Ibn Jahwar, Abū al-Hazm, 106, 122
Ibn Juljul, 75–6

Ibn Khafāja, 139–40
Ibn Khaldūn, 55, 150–1, 178
Ibn Khallikān, 73
Ibn Mardanīsh, 146
Ibn Quzmān, 140
Ibn Rushd, Averroes, 149–50
Ibn Sāʿid, also known as Sāʿd al-Andalusī,
    85
Ibn Shuhayd, Abū ʿĀmir Ahmad b., 105–6
Ibn Tufayl, 147–50
Ibn Tūmart, 145, 150
Ibn Zamraq, 176–8
Ibn Zaydūn, 119–21
Idrīsī, 146
Ifrīqiyya, 14, 36, 40–1
Innocent III, Pope, 151
Innocent VIII, Pope, 186, 188
ʿĪsā b. Ahmad ar-Rāzī, 82, 88, 92
Isabella I, of Castile, 185–6, 190; *see also*
    Catholic kings
Ishāq, surgeon, 76
Ishāq b. Velashq al-Qurtubī, 81
Isidore of Seville, 6
ivories (pyxides), 93–5

Jaén, 152, 162, 169
James I of Aragón, 161, 165, 167
James II of Aragón, 172
Játiva, 119, 139
Jerez, 162, 168
Jewish communities, 6, 22–4, 31, 49, 59,
    115–16, 138–9, 178–9, 187
    pogrom of 1066, 116
    traders, 151
Jiménez de Cisneros, Francisco, 190–2
Jimémez de Rada, archbishop Rodrigo, 98,
    151
jihād, 10, 96, 127, 151
jizya, 11, 22
Jódar, 169
Johannes Hispalensis *see* John of Seville
John, bishop of Cordoba, 79
John of Seville, 144
John of Gorze, abbot, 79–80
Jones, Owen, 177
Julian, 16–19, 24
junds, 36
Justa and Rufina, saints, 26

Kāhina, 12
kātib, 52, 189
Keith, George, 148
kitāb al-anwāʾ, 77
Khayrān, 103, 117–18

lapidary, 165
Las Navas de Tolosa, battle, 151–4
Latini, Brunetto, 166
Laujar de Andarax, 188
Leo III, Pope, 46–7
León, 59, 68, 71–2, 78, 87, 96, 151, 161, 164
    Cathedral, 176
leprosy, 29
Leptis Magna, 196
Lérida, 142
Le Tourneau, R., 153
Lévi-Provençal, 87, 98, 125
Liébana, Beatus of, 46
Lisbon, 137, 146
Llull, Ramón, 167
Loja, 169, 185
Lomax, D. W., 61, 69–70, 98–9, 161
Lucena, 169, 185
Lupitus (Llobet), 89

Madīna az-Zahīra, 102
Madīna az-Zahrā', 73–5, 79–80, 88, 93, 101–2
Madrid, 86, 123, 137
majūs see Norsemen
Makki, M. A., 95
Málaga, 40, 62, 71, 162–3, 168, 183–6
Māliki law school, 45, 48, 60, 86, 97, 104, 121, 129, 141, 166
malaria, 29
Mallorca, 167
Marches, 43, 63, 66, 68
    Lower March, 42, 50
    Middle March, 50, 101, 142
    Upper March, 42, 50, 126, 142
Marīnids, 153, 162–3, 168–70, 172–3
Marrakesh, 145–7, 149, 156
martyrs of Cordoba, 57
Maslama b. Ahmad al-Majrītī, 86–7
Massif des Maures, 50, 79
mawlā, malāwī, 9, 11, 15, 19, 28–9, 49, 83–4
Maysara, Berber leader, 33–4
Mecca, 44–5
Medinaceli, 98, 101
medicine, 76–7, 139, 174, 191
Menéndez Pidal, Ramón, 68, 130
Menocal, M. R., 150
Mérida, 3–4, 25, 37, 45, 50, 68–9
    aqueduct, 44
Michael, Bishop, 142
mi'rāj, Muhammad's night journey, 166
Mirón Bonfill, 89
Mojácar, 163

Monès, H., 113
Morales, Ambrosio de, 59
Moriscos, 191, 196
Morocco, 142, 151, 174
moros, 133
Moussais la Bataille, 3
Mozarabs, 59, 138, 142–3, 145
    architecture, 70
    liturgy, 124
    Mozarabism, 71
mu'āhid, mu'āhidūn, 58, 142
Mu'āwiya b. Sālih, qādī, 45
Mudejars, mudéjares, 143, 162, 167, 186, 191
    style of architecture, 143, 163
Muhammad I, 57, 60–1
Muhammad V, 117
Muhammad b. Bashīr, qādī, 52
Muhammad b. Nasr, Muhammad I of Granada see al-Ahmār
Muhammad II, Nasrid ruler, 168–70
Muhammad III, Nasrid ruler, 170
Muhammad IV, Nasrid ruler, 170, 173
Muhammad V, Nasrid ruler, 172–9
Muhammad XII, ruler of Granada, 185–6, 188–9
mulūk at-tawā'if see Taifa kings
Muñoz Sendino, J., 166
Münzer, Hieronymus, 189
Murcia, 36, 123, 147, 153, 162, 171
Musa b. Maymūn, Moses Maimonides, 149–150
Mūsā b. Nusayr, 8, 12, 14–18, 20, 22, 24–8, 36
music, 54, 90, 155
musta'rib see Mozarab
muwallad, 25, 60, 62, 63
muwashshahāt, 81–2

nasārā, 49, 58, 142
Nasr, Nasrid ruler, 170, 172
naval defences, 83
Navarre, 68, 124, 151
Nicholas, monk, 75–6
Niebla, 156
noria, 154–5
Norsemen, 56–7, 85
Nuwayrī, 61
Nykl, A. R., 119, 139–40

Olagüe, 8
olive oil, 3, 169
Ordericus Vitalis, 142
Ordoño I, 60
Ordoño II, 68

Ordoño IV, 87
Otto I, 79–80, 88
Otto II, 90
Oxford, 164

Pamplona, 42–3, 61
paper, 52, 119
parias, 130–2
Paul Alvar, 57
Pechina (*Bajjāna*), 117
Pedro I of Castile, 173–4, 178–9
Pedro IV of Aragón, 178
Pelayo, 31
Pérès, H., 120
Peter the Venerable, abbot of Cluny, 144
Pisuerga, river, 68
Poema de Fernán González, 72
Portugal, 123, 172
Prescott, H., 187
Provençal troubadours, 140
Ptolemy, 86, 145
Pyrenees, 1, 30, 32–3, 42, 48, 50, 56, 124,
    195

qāḍī, quḍāt, 45, 48, 52–3, 58, 60, 72, 85, 113,
    132, 138, 145, 149, 167, 189
qanāt, 155
Qairawān, 8, 12, 18, 20, 24, 31, 33–4
Qays, 35–6
Quesada, 169
Qur'ān, 9–10, 46–7, 54, 94, 97, 99, 104, 129,
    146, 154, 167, 191

Rabīʿ b. Zayd al-Usquf, 77–81, 114
Ramiro I of Aragón, 125
Ramiro II of León, 69
Ramiro III of León, 96
Recemundus *see* Rabʿī b. Zayd al-Usquf
Rheims, 89, 91
Ribera, J., 178
Richard I, Coeur de Lion, 131
Richer, 90
Río Tinto mines, 30
Ripoll, Santa María de, 89
Robert of Ketton, translator, 144
Robinson Crusoe, 148
Roderic, 17–21, 24, 26
Rodrigo Díaz *see* El Cid
Roman Empire, 4–5
Roman liturgy, 124
Ronda, 52, 122, 185, 191
Runciman, S., 125
Rusāfa, palace of, 43
Rycaut, Sir Paul, 148

Saʿd, ruler of Granada, 183–4
Sahagún, monastery, 71, 78
Saladin, Salāh ad-Dīn, 171
Salado, battle, 172–3
Salamanca, 69
Salobreña, 170
Salvatierra, 151–2
Salvetat, Raymond de, Archbishop of Toledo,
    143
Samuel ha-Nagid, 115, 117
Sánchez-Albornoz, Claudio, 68, 72
Sancho II of Castile, 124, 131
Sancho 'The Fat', 87
Sancho, son of Alfonso VI, 137
Sancho IV of Castile, 168–9
Sancho García, Count of Castile,
    100–1
Sanhāja, tribe, 115
Santa Fe, 187–8
Santa María de Melque, 23
Santarem, 149
Santiago de Compostela, 96, 98
    pilgrimage, 125
saqāliba, 83–4, 101–2, 118
Saragossa, 4, 25–6, 36, 41–2, 50, 63, 68,
    101, 116, 119, 125–7, 130, 132–3, 137,
    141–3, 152–3
    Aljafería palace, 142
Scot, Michael, 90, 149
sereno, 48
Seville, 21, 26, 30–3, 36–7, 45, 57, 62, 71,
    83, 107, 113–14, 118–23, 127–8, 130–1,
    137–9, 143, 146–7, 149, 151–6, 161–6,
    168–9, 174, 179, 183
    Alcázar, 163, 179
    torre del oro, 154
Shaban, M. A., 84
shāmiyyūn, 35
Sierra Morena, 152, 155
Sierra Nevada, 114, 163
Siete Partidas, 167
silk products, 169, 183; *see also tirāz*
Silves, 122
Simancas, battle of, 87; *see also* Alhándega
Simonet, F. J., 81
Sixtus IV, Pope, 188
Slavs *see saqāliba*
Solomon b. Gabirol, 116
sūdān, 18
Sūfi beliefs, 148
Sulaymān, Caliph, 27
Sulaymān al-Mustaʿīn bi-llāh, 100–3
sunna, 129, 167
Syrians, 34–6, 113

Tagus, river, 24–5, 29, 35, 57, 85, 146
Taha, A. D., 28
Taifa kings (states), 114, 118, 121, 123, 125, 126, 128–31, 141, 143, 147, 153
Talavera, 169
Talavera, Hernando de, Archbishop of Granada, 189–91
Tālūt, *qāḍī*, 49
Tangier, 15–17, 34, 37, 83, 115
tapias, 123
Tarazona, 144
Tarīf b. Zurʿa, 15–16
Tarifa, 15, 37, 169, 172–3
Tāriq b. Ziyād, 8, 14–21, 24–5, 31
Tarragona, 4
Tendilla, Conde de, 188, 190
Terrasse, Henri, 44, 74
thaghr, thughūr see Marches
Theodomirus, 17–18, 21–2
Theophilos, Byzantine emperor, 56
tirāz, 71, 78, 118
Toda, Queen of Navarre, 87
Toledo, 24–5, 36, 41, 46–7, 50, 60, 63, 66, 68, 113, 119, 123–6, 128, 130, 137, 142–5, 149–53, 164–5, 191
    Council of, 6, 22
    translators, 143–4, 165
    translations, 139, 163–5, 168
Tormes, river, 69
Torres Balbás, 84
Tortosa, 50, 79, 83
travel, 79, 114–15
treaties, 21–2, 170, 187
Tudmīr *see* Theodomirus

Úbeda, 153
Uclés, 128, 137
ʿUmar b. Hafsūn, 61–3, 66–7
ʿUqba b. Nāfiʿ, 12

Valencia, 118–19, 125, 130, 132–3, 137, 139, 147, 151, 167
Valladolid, 68
Vandals, 5, 19
Vikings *see* Norsemen
Visigoths, 5–6, 20–2, 24–6, 61, 195

Walīd, Caliph, 20, 24
Wallāda, 119–21
Wasserstein, D., 91–2
Watt, W. M., 104, 194–5
weather, 92, 99–100
William, Duke of Normandy, 123, 126
William of Montreuil, 126
William V, Duke of Aquitaine, 125
wine, 54, 76, 99, 129, 138, 140, 155–6
Winter, H. J. J., 150
Witiza, sons of, 20–1
Wolf, K. B., 61
women in al-Andalus, 119–21, 138

Yaman, 35–6, 113
Yaʿqūb al-Mansūr, 150
Yūsuf, son of Samuel ha-Nagīd, 115–17
Yūsuf I, ruler of Granada, 173–4
Yūsuf al-Fihrī, *wālī*, 36, 40–1
Yūsuf b. Tashufīn, 127–9, 137

Zafra, Hernando de, 187, 189
Zāhirī law school, 104
Zaida, wife of Alfonso VI, 128
zajal, 140
zakāt, 97
Zallāqa, battle of, 127–8
Zamora, 68–9, 124
zandaqa, 86, 98
Zāwī b. Zīrī, 114–16
Zīrids, 114–16, 128, 142
Ziryāb, 54–5, 71
Zuhayr, 117